The Betrayal of Liberal Economics

Amos Witztum

The Betrayal of Liberal Economics

Volume I: How Economics Betrayed Us

Amos Witztum
Centre for Philosophy of Natural and Social Sciences
London School of Economics and Political Sciences
London, UK

ISBN 978-3-030-10667-6   ISBN 978-3-030-10668-3   (eBook)
https://doi.org/10.1007/978-3-030-10668-3

Library of Congress Control Number: 2019934108

This Palgrave Macmillan imprint is published by the registered company Springer Nature Switzerland AG.
The registered company address is: Gewerbestrasse 11, 6330 Cham, Switzerland

To the three pillars of my life:
My wife, Daphna
My son, Alon
My daughter, Tamar.

Acknowledgements

It has not been easy to rise against such a powerful and dominant discipline like economics. It is extremely difficult to argue against something which, at least on the face of it, has the affluent appearances of success. I needed a lot of support, which I was lucky to receive. This book had been four years in the making and it would not have reached fruition without those who gave me the support that such a project requires. First of all, I must express my deepest gratitude to Professor Pascal Bridel, from the Centre Walras-Pareto at the University of Lausanne, who has been a dear friend to me over many years and has always showed appreciation and support to my line of research. With this book, Pascal was kind enough to offer me his companionship from the very beginning of the project. With infinite patience and diligence, he carefully read each chapter, gave me valuable comments and engaged with me in arguments and discussions. It is difficult to overstate the isolation within which those who wish to argue against the mainstream operate. Pascal was a lifeline to me. Not only has he lent me his mind, his heart was there too.

I have also benefitted a great deal from the generosity of the Department of Economics at the Hebrew University of Jerusalem. Though very much a prominent mainstream department, it has nevertheless invited me, as a visiting professor, to regularly teach two courses that were entirely based on my own research and helped me organise my thoughts in the process of writing this book. It is rare in this day and age to find mainstream economics departments that are willing to embrace genuinely critical thinking. I am therefore particularly grateful to Professor Saul Lach, who in his capacity of head of department opened the door to such an adventure. More so, I am grateful to my friend Professor Joseph Zeira, who was not only instrumental in facilitating the engagement with the department but has been a wonderful friend and supporter over many years and throughout the writing of this book. I am also in debt to the numerous and wonderful students who came to my courses and showed incredible interest and enthusiasm that flowed like chilled and clear water in the parched landscape of academic dissent.

The late Professor Tony Atkinson was another source of inspiration and strength. In spite of his illness, he showed great interest in my work and I benefited a great deal from the numerous discussions which I had had with him in the years leading to his untimely death. Tony's enthusiasm for this project—emanating from the depth of his decency and commitment to justice—was an inspiration and an important fuel that helped drive my own stamina.

Throughout these years in the academic wilderness, I was lucky to be supported by the friendship of Professor David De-Meza. Although himself part of the establishment and, thus, the object of my slings and arrows, and although he tried heroically to defend the indefensible (even though he was the one in the fortified castle), he never failed to be there for me and to give encouragements in hours of need. As is the case with such large undertaking, one can never escape the cyclical nature of hope. David, like the topic of insurance which he loves so much, helped smoothen the experience.

And now I come to the essence of things. There are three people in this world who hold the edges of my soul supporting the canopy of my being. They are my wife Daphna, my son Alon and my daughter Tamar. I could say that their love has given me the inspiration and the strength to endure the treacherous winding road that is the creative process in a very harsh environment, and it did. I could say that it was my love for them that has filled my purpose and has fed the engine that drove me all the way to here, and it has. But the truth is that there are no words to describe what these three people mean to me.

Contents

Prologue: Introduction and Summary

There is something foreboding about the title of a book which contains the word *Betrayal*, but I would like to say from the outset that this is not about anything sinister, nor is it about intrigues or conspiracy. It is, in fact, far more serious than that. It is a lamentation on the state of our thinking about economics and society and a sense of loss due to the fact that we have reached this point because we have abandoned something which was richer, more relevant and far more promising.

In this respect, this book is a critique, mainly of modern economic thinking, but it has implications for broader issues in the domain of social organisation. It is, of course, not the first time that modern economics is being criticised, but the reason why there may be a need for a fresh approach is the fact that it has shown a remarkable resilience.[1] In spite of years of various forms of intellectual opposition, very little of substance has changed in what may be considered its intellectual agenda (or, in

---

[1] The resilience of economics' paradigmatic core is far more astonishing when one considers how vast the literature is in opposition to it. This, of course, is not the place to review all this, although it may be worthwhile pointing at the difference between my approach and that taken by most other critiques. In a nutshell, while others criticised economics because of its failings either to predict or to explain, we propose to examine the internal logic of the subject and suggest that what appears as failing is nothing but the footprint of a fallacious paradigm. In other words, it is the promise of economics that we would like to examine rather than its ability to deliver it in practice. Naturally, if the promise is false, so will be its delivery but there is a fundamental difference between a failing which is a problem of execution and a failing of purpose.

other words, its paradigmatic core).[2] This core, which is more about principles of economic and social **organisation** than it is about **predictions**, has also become increasingly more influential in the way it formed and informed political and ideological debates and, in this way, this doctrine exerts immeasurable power over the lives of so many of us. There are, perhaps, no better expressions to the power behind economics' paradigmatic core than the rapid spread of market economies in the world (both developed and developing): the spread of it into increasing areas of human lives (including education, research and culture), the rise in free trade agreements (culminating in the World Trade Organization) and, finally, the unstoppable spread of globalisation.[3]

It is true that the recent financial crisis and its aftermath have led to a rising opposition to globalisation, but there are two key elements in this opposition which put modern economics beyond the reach of these protestations. The first is the fact that much of the anger has been directed at

---

[2] Among the more prominent modern opposition, I would like to mention Keynes and the post-Keynesians. The former, as will be discussed later, was mainly concerned with what I would like to call 'correction' or policy issues, but some aspects of the latter—harking back to Keynes's earlier years—are also committed to a more fundamental disagreement about the general role of market analysis. There are also the Sraffian or neo-Ricardian, who are mainly focused on offering alternative—more classical—explanations to distribution variables and the return to capital in particular. As you will see as you read along, I have some sympathy to their supposition that classical economics offers a better analytical framework than modern economics. There is, of course, Polanyi (1944), with whose direction I also sympathise, although not necessarily with his analysis. As will be explored later in the book, I do not consider institutional or behavioural economics a real opposition to the modern paradigm. As you will see, the line we take is fundamentally different as it is focused neither on corrections or policy nor on the explanatory aspects of the theory. Instead, it is more focused on the organisational implications of the theory and the social significance of economic analysis. In this respect, it is worthwhile citing Marglin (2010), who confronts economics at this fundamental level by arguing that the markets replace and corrupt communities. Our line of reasoning, however, develops at somewhat different directions.

[3] The term 'globalisation' is on many occasions used to describe the internationalisation of economic activities. Throughout this book, however, we shall make a distinction between the idea of free trade in which we refer to the international trade in goods and services only and the idea of globalisation in which we refer to the free movement of means of production (capital and labour). To some extent, one can refer to the former as an expression of globalisation during the Bretton-Woods era (which ended in the 1970s) and was mainly manifested in the various forms of tariffs agreements (General Agreement on Tariffs and Trade [GATT]) and the latter as the post Bretton-Woods period. There is a clear distinction between globalisation that includes the free mobility of factors and the one which only refers to free trade in goods and services. In the former case, the economic sovereignty of individual states will inevitably be restricted—both in terms of monetary policy (sometimes referred to as the monetary policy trilemma) and the ability to raise taxes (fiscal policy)—but not necessarily so in the latter.

the role of large corporations (and the corrupt behaviour of those with power) in the global system. However, there is nothing in economics' paradigmatic core which suggests that large corporations—or powerful agents—should play a role in any economic system. In fact, most economists would be in agreement with all attempts to curb large corporations, the powers of which undermine the essence of competitive decentralisation. Therefore, these kinds of attacks are not really attacks on the principles of economic thinking but rather an attack on the execution of it, which allows forces to act in a way that subverts the promise embedded in the paradigmatic core.

Secondly, the language of the debate is mostly about the way out of the crisis rather than a fundamental review of economic arrangements within countries and across them. In many respects, it is a return to the old debate between Keynesians and new classical economics. In simple terms, it is a debate about whether the system can recover from shocks by itself or it needs help in the form of increased government spending to be stimulated. The reason why this criticism does not touch the core of economic thinking is already present in Keynes's own writings. While in the end, Keynes identified only two areas where markets may chronically fail (financial markets and the labour market), he does acknowledge that in a world of full employment, competitive markets can be relied upon to successfully co-ordinate economic activities. The reasons why investment must be socialised (to use Keynes's own language) and governments pursue fiscal policies are mainly designed to help markets reach their equilibrium or point of full employment, rather than to propose alternative principles for economic organisation.[4] Put differently, this is basically a

---

[4] Keynes famously agreed, in his *General Theory (GT)*, that once we are in full employment, the classical school 'comes to its own' (GT, p. 378). To be fair to Keynes, however, the story of understanding his contribution has been quite complex and the debate about him has been stretching across two extremes (Backhouse 2006 provides a good summary of the history of this debate). At the one end Keynes seemed to have argued the complete abolition of equilibrium analysis, in which case he would have offered a structural alternative to modern economics. Townshend (1937), Shackle (1967) and Robinson (1974) picked up on Keynes's own response to the debate in the *Quarterly Journal of Economics (QJE)* to claim that the contribution of the GT was to introduce time and expectations into the market mechanism of *all* goods. Coupled with Keynes's insistence on the irreducibility of uncertainty by probability—and thus, a form of bounded rationality—this meant the introduction of a non-equilibrium approach to economic analysis. Leijonhufvud (1968) agreed that the contribution of the GT was about market failure but not just because of time and

policy debate rather than a structural one. Moreover, the Keynesian controversies are mainly about those who are left outside the competitive system (the involuntarily unemployed), or the victims of markets' failures; it is not about the fate of those who are in the system and where markets seem to work. Yes, a lip service is being paid to the fate of these people through other debates about redistribution of wealth and income[5]

---

expectations. It was a failure because of the absence of an 'auctioneer' and, thus, the GT is not merely about non-equilibrium but rather about disequilibrium economics. Together with time and expectations, this would be extended into an analysis of inter-temporal disequilibrium. In turn, a whole literature of disequilibrium macroeconomics developed (Solow and Stiglitz 1968; Barro and Grossman 1971; Benassy 1986), but from the point of view of the methodological debate, as captured by Leijonhufvud, this was not really a proper modelling of disequilibrium. These models were simply Walrasian models with rationing and, as such, they did not, in his view, capture the spirit of the GT or offered a serious challenge to the idea of markets. (A more localised and focused attempt at interpreting Keynes was concentrated upon in Chap. 2 (and 19) of the GT or the possibility of non-clearing labour market. However, here too, the focus of attention has been primarily methodological. Hoover (1995) provides a summary of this line of investigation). At the other extreme, the one which became more dominant, there were the less 'revolutionary' interpretations like Clower (1965), Patinkin (1965) and more recently Laidler (1999), where methodology was not at the heart of the discussion. For them, the main contribution of the GT was the role of money in exchange. Due to the fact that people exchange goods with money and labour with money, the presence of unemployment may trigger a co-ordination of decision failure. The seeds of these confusions about Keynes's contribution, in my view, rest in the ambiguities in Keynes's position on the 'classical' (should be read, neoclassical or modern) school. Skidelsky (1992) writes, 'the validity of Keynes's "general theory" rests on his assertion that the classical theory … is, as he put it in his lectures, "nonsense". If [the classical theory] were true, the classical "special case" would in fact, be the "general theory", and Keynes's aggregate analysis … empty and redundant' (p. 512). He then goes on to say that in the post-war period, Keynes's theory was indeed perceived as a special case of classical economics. But what exactly is meant by 'classical economics'? Davidson (2007) asserts, 'Classical economic theory … provided the rationale for the laissez-faire or "no government intervention in the market place" philosophy that dominated discussions of how to cure the unemployment problem and promote prosperity' (p. 22). In fact, there are two aspects of classical economics to which Keynes is referring to. Firstly, it is the market clearing mechanism and, secondly, the perfunctory role which the theory ascribes to money. However, his analysis does not go beyond the role of money in plugging the gap in the labour market. In the end, in spite of Keynes's expressed motivation to contest the universality of what he calls the 'classical' conception of the labour market's mechanism, according to the GT he has not really parted way with that school. For one, he famously agreed that once we are in full employment the classical school 'comes to its own' (GT, p. 378). But more importantly, in spite of the failing of the labour market (and the unnecessary high demand for liquid assets), he clearly believed that the classical model allocates all the **employed** resources well (this point is clearly stated in Chap. 24 of the GT and will be discussed further later). But perhaps more than anything, the fact that Keynes's contribution remained only policy oriented rather than structural can be seen in the way it was absorbed in modern macroeconomics, where the distinction between new classical economics and Keynesian economics was reduced to a long-run, short-run distinction.

[5] See, for instance, Piketty (2014) and Atkinson (2015).

but, as will be shown, these are not really criticisms of economics' paradigmatic core as they are attempts to make **corrections** which will allow the competitive system to become compatible with social values.[6] As I will show in Chap. 2, there is nothing about this which is in any way a demand for a fundamental change in the way in which we think about economic organisation. We still perceive markets—or competitive decentralisation—as the best way to organise economic activities but as there are obstacles on the way to the Promised Land, society should interfere to make amends. Among other things, this book is more a critique of this fundamental way of thinking than it is about specific policies, corrections or means to alleviate temporary malaises which may be attributed to **market failures**. Instead, we would like to focus our attention on what we call **failures of the markets**. Namely, we are not interested in what happens when markets fail in the sense that they are unable to perform as we would expect them to do (which is the way in which the term 'market failure' is normally used); but we are interested in that which we should expect markets to achieve when they do work well. We would like to argue in this book that the problems which societies face are more acute when markets actually work well than they are when there is something which impedes their operation.

*   *   *

---

[6] In modern times, the idea of 'correction' (rather than replacement) starts already with Pigou's *The Economics of Welfare* (1920), where the need to correct arose from the apparent inefficiency of the competitive outcome in the presence of externalities (before Coase). Namely, the completely decentralised competitive system could not have reached an equilibrium which is Pareto-efficient without government intervention. This, inevitably, gave rise to a great debate about the measure of individual welfare and the subsequent discussion of how to judge outcomes. Once this has been achieved, the next type of correction is the one associated with redistribution and is aimed at reaching the socially desirable outcome without undermining the rule of markets as the key co-ordinators of human interactions. Indeed, in Pigou's own writing this did not represent a lack of confidence in the neoclassical message. Instead, it was, as it were, a mere correction which is necessary when we move from the 'light'—or the abstract science—into the 'fruit': its application. In other words, the key point in his argument was not the inefficiency of the actual outcome but rather the ability to correct it. To this end, it became imperative to be able to judge deviations from the efficient outcomes and the effects of measures taken to correct them. Hence, the practical focus of welfare economics became the measurement of wellbeing but this was all within the agenda of approaching the ideal: the benefits of the competitive outcome.

It may be useful to begin our examination by clarifying some elements in the title of this book. We need to explore what is meant by *liberal economics* as well as what we mean by *Betrayal*. Most modern economists may be surprised by the use of the term *liberal economics*. For them, modern economics is just **economics**. It is a science. They would like to think that it is a bit like physics, where we study how particles behave and how opposing forces lead to an equilibrium which produces the world of matter in front of us. Of course, we can mould this world and, through interference, change the shape of things, but the laws governing the behaviour of particles and the way in which forces are balanced are still the same.[7] Therefore, the association of the word 'liberal' with the science of economics seems quite unsettling. After all, economics, as a science, should be ethically neutral and, therefore, compatible with all possible forms of social/political/ethical considerations, concepts which are more naturally embedded in notions like liberalism.

Notwithstanding the debate about the scientific nature of economics and whether it is indeed universal and ethically neutral—which is, of course, partly the subject of our examination—I use the term 'liberal' to help us locate modern economics in the broader context of the ways in which humanity has been thinking about this subject over centuries. As our study will span beyond mainstream contemporary thinking about economics, we have to acknowledge that throughout most of the history of human thought the study of economics seemed to have been significantly less detached from political/social/ethical considerations and, therefore, the kind of detachment we observe today may, in fact, be no more than wishful thinking.

To some extent, the difference in the disposition, within economic thinking, towards broader social considerations is well reflected in the difference in the meaning of the term *Political Economy* in classical and

---

[7] Conveniently, economists prefer to look only at classical mechanics while completely ignoring other aspects of physics, like thermodynamics, which is a one-directional development that also influences the way in which particles interact. Needless to say, I do not for a moment suggest that there is any merit in such a position but I fear that the intellectual behaviour of many economists—such as it is—reflects this kind of belief in the nature and powers of the science of economics. Moreover, I do not wish to engage in any discussion about whether economics is or is not a science. The reference to physics is not a claim about the scientific nature of the subject as it is about its similarity with natural sciences. In general, I prefer the word 'discipline' to science but I feel that such semantics is a waste of time.

modern economics. During the classical period (in the eighteenth and nineteenth centuries), there was no other name for the dealing with economics than political economy. It was so because economics was always considered as something which is embedded—and, therefore, influenced—by a social, ethical and, hence, political context. With the development of neoclassical economics—perceived by many as an extension, or maturing, of one particular line of examination within classical political economy—there was quickly a shift towards economics as a discipline which can be treated separately and independently from all other social or ethical considerations. Subsequently, with the apparent success of economics as an academic discipline (mainly due to excessive formalism and the commercialisation of academia), it began to infiltrate other social disciplines including sociology and politics and, thus, gave birth to the new political economy in which economics' conceptual framework is used to analyse social and political issues. In other words, economics has shifted from being **in** context to becoming **the** context.

Given that classical economics, or the real political economy, conceived economic interactions as part of the more general social context, the way it developed was not independent of these other considerations. Therefore, there was a need to distinguish between the ways in which sociality affected economic analysis. The term *liberal economics* is used here to identify a broad line of reasoning where everything is channelled through the individual (basically, a form of methodological individualism). This predominantly individualistic—but not necessarily a-social—approach goes all the way from the French physiocrats and their laissez-faire, through Adam Smith, David Ricardo to John Stuart Mill, who also happened to be one of liberalism's greatest champions. This line is distinguished in both method and substance, from other classical economists who opted for a more explicit socially based analysis and who can be identified by scholars like Louis Blanc, Saint-Simon and culminating in Marx and his followers. In other words, classical economics has always been embedded in social and ethical analysis but there were different ways in which such connections have been manifested. We call liberal, that stream of thought which seems to be entirely focused on the individual and his or her private and social needs, and we call socialist, that stream where economic analysis was driven by social concepts or developments.

But by calling modern economics, liberal economics, we are actually doing more than just identifying the subject matter of our investigation, which is, of course, modern economics itself. We are, in some sense, defying its expressed purpose which is to advocate a presumed natural order as a universal and ethically neutral form of economic organisation and, thus, exposing some of its failings. By calling it liberal economics, we are suggesting that whether explicitly or implicitly even the brave attempt to make economics neutral cannot really hide the fact that it is a clear expression of a very particular position on things social and ethical. In this way, we are suggesting the removal of the pretence that competitive decentralisation is a form of economic organisation which is either universal or consistent with all possible conceptions of society, of culture and of political organisation everywhere in the world. Instead, we would like to expose modern economics for what it really is: a narrowly defined individualistic theory with a false conception of the natural and where sociality is purely functional and ethics, subservient to its functionality. As such, it is a conception of society and the economy which sits well with some approaches to social theory and ethics but not with others, and, hence, it cannot be universal or neutral. It certainly sits well with more recent expressions of liberal thinking as manifested in the idea of *civic society*. Such a society—being fundamentally functional—is merely a structure, the purpose of which is to keep the peace, facilitate prosperity (whatever this means[8]) and protect the individual from others and this very same structure. Everything else, in civic society, including sociality, is based on voluntary interactions. However, and this is where the betrayal will come in, it does not sit well at all with the tradition from which it claims to have sprung: *liberal classical economics.*

If you read the title again, you will see that there is a certain ambiguity in it. *The betrayal of liberal economics* can mean either that liberal economics has betrayed us or that we have betrayed it. In this book, we shall argue that both forms of betrayals have, sadly, taken place. On the one hand, modern economics has failed us in its promise, and what is even more worrying is that many who have recognised it have failed to act on

---

[8] Normally interpreted as material wellbeing but, as such, is in no way a neutral objective and therefore not an obvious element of a universally functional society.

it. On the other hand, we failed economics by allowing it to twist the idea of liberal economics—as it was originally conceived in classical economics—in such a way that modern economics (and, to some extent, modern liberalism) based its promise on false conceptions of human sociality and, subsequently, on a wrong conception of methodological individualism which inevitably led to the wrong idea of natural order and wrong conclusions about the appropriate form of economic (and social) organisation.

The one thing which modern economics shares with more traditional approaches to liberal economics is the focus on the individual as the basic element of the social and economic system. And in this respect, there may be something to be said about potential universality. However, the way one conceives the individual may not always be the same, and even if the conception is the same, the manifestation of the notion may differ across societies and cultures. What is specifically implied by modern economics is that individuals—who are always rational in the sense that they seek the best means to an end—have interests which make the social or economic organisation useful to them. It is clearly a functional approach to society which is more Hobbesian in nature than it is Lockean. In the former, individuals *escape* into a social contract because they seek security and must escape the natural state of permanent violence; in the latter, they are *drawn* into the social arrangement to allow something in them to be fulfilled which cannot be fulfilled outside society.[9] While there is an element of functionality in both approaches, there is nevertheless a meaningful distinction between them. The former is mercenary, and the latter is purposeful. It is not difficult to imagine that the social or economic organisation emanating (both in practise and as an ideal) from one form

---

[9] Locke's position on the social contract is rather complex. There is no doubt that in his case, people are drawn to society but the reasons for this are not as straightforward as it may appear. He mentions the precariousness of the natural state, but Locke also cites the fact that people 'want and love society' as a reason why they enter the social contract. More importantly, in Locke, reason and theology are never far from each other. To some extent, the natural state corresponds to the *covenant of works*, which means the laws of nature and of actions as prescribed by the scriptures. The social bond is more akin to the *covenant of faith*, which is the more spiritual aspect of life. Not obeying the first covenant may make someone unrighteous (and this may cost him his life) but faith can compensate for it (see his *The Reasonableness of Christianity 22*) and give spiritual immortality. So, both in religion and in society, people part with some of their sovereignty for something better. As reason itself is divine and as it is the cause of the social contract, society must also entail a higher form of living than the natural state.

of sociality would be different from another. Moreover, if the social drive is altogether intrinsic, social and economic arrangements would certainly be different in these scenarios. Indeed, we can see this already in the case of Hobbes and Locke. In the mercenary society, individuals forgo most of their rights in favour of an authoritarian ruler, while in the case where individuals are drawn into society their rights (whatever they are) must be protected.

∗   ∗   ∗

So, what is the promise that modern economics hides in its paradigmatic core and in what way has it betrayed us? It is certainly not the ideas of demand and supply, though modern economics has a lot to say about it (and most of it not very new). One must bear in mind that the basic notions of demand and supply and how they affect prices have been known for centuries. One can already find them discussed in Aristotle and St Thomas of Aquinas; they were certainly well understood by classical economists of both liberal and socialist persuasions. It is true that modern economics has introduced a high level of sophistication which allows for more subtle and complex (though not necessarily empirically true) analysis of demand and supply but the essence of the idea has not changed much over the centuries. Nor has the idea of markets as such (or competitive decentralised decision-making) been the great revelation of modern economics. It is not a secret that the market phenomenon is a natural phenomenon in the sense that across cultures and throughout time there have always been markets in the forms of bazaars or markets in town squares. But the fact that markets may be a natural phenomenon does not mean that it is something that should be praised, promoted or idealised.[10] Indeed, the difference between the entire history of human thought about economics and modern economics is that until now markets were seen as a natural phenomenon which may, sometime, be good for society but often not good at all. In modern economics, on the other hand, markets have become an ***ideal***. While much of the work of contemporary economists is dealing with the details of how markets operate, the overarching

---

[10] There are many natural phenomena which humanity has struggled to contain rather than abet.

message of modern economics is organisational: the pursuit of competitive decentralisation is the ideal form of economic organisation.

If we take a cursory look at the evolution of economic thinking, we will find repeatedly that while scholars show a remarkable understanding of the way in which markets operate, the focus of their attention was not the mechanism itself but how it serves a broader, social, purpose. Thus, we can find in Aristotle recognition that demand and supply determine prices, but also a definition of what may be seen as a just price.[11] However, market prices may or may not conform to the just price. When they do, the economy performs in a manner consistent with the broader social/ethical context; when they do not, markets cannot be deemed as working in line with social objectives and need to be corrected.[12] Clearly, the reason why an ethical concept becomes the reference point for his economic investigation is because economic interactions are part of the institutions that create the 'good society' which, according to Aristotle, is the purpose of social organisation. Hence, economics analysis is not focused on how markets work but rather, given that they exist, on whether and under what conditions will markets comply with some exogenous benchmark which is socially or ethically determined.[13] These ideas were carried through into the Middle Ages through the doctrines of St Thomas of Aquinas, who was a follower of Aristotle. In post-Enlightenment Europe, in Adam Smith, who is also (wrongly) considered to be the founding father of modern economics,[14] the commentary about the working of markets is far from complimentary. It is true that Smith saw competitive markets as a much

---

[11] Aristotle does not use this terminology but he does refer to an exchange which is consistent with justice. It was St Thomas of Aquinas, heavily influenced by Aristotle, who develops the notion of a just price.

[12] The discussion of prices is conducted in the context of what Aristotle calls corrective justice.

[13] Although not explicit, Aristotle provides some hints regarding the cases where market prices are more likely to deviate from their just values. According to him, people can satisfy their need either through home production or through exchange. But he also identifies demand which originates from want (rather than need) and which he deems to be immoral. It is thus implied that when demand and supply are comprised of those who seek merely to satisfy their needs, exchange will lead to the just price. But when demand and supply are comprised also of those who seek things to satisfy their wants, market prices are likely to deviate and thus reflect the immorality which he associates with such (excessive) behaviour.

[14] The desire to connect to classical economics is both a reflection of the inadequacy of the modern conceptual framework and the lack of scholarship among modern economists.

better way to organise society in comparison with Mercantilism, but this does not mean that he considered the natural phenomenon of the markets as something which is inherently socially beneficial.[15] Like Aristotle and St Thomas, he too has two competing concepts of price. One is the market price as is understood from the fluctuating interactions between demand and supply, and the other a notion of the natural price which was, in many respects, a benchmark for whether markets work in a manner which is socially beneficial.[16] Smith was quite clear that while market prices may tend to gravitate towards the natural rates, they can nevertheless deviate from them for centuries (to use his own words).

Marx, too, should be understood as following the same line of reasoning even though he was clearly influenced by Ricardo, who, unlike Smith, sought in natural prices (or absolute values) only the long-run technological conditions which govern the fluctuation of market prices. For Marx, as for Smith, there were values (or prices) which reflected social circumstances rather than just technological ones. Nevertheless, the difference between them is that unlike Smith, whose analysis is based on the individual agent, Marx derived the social benchmark for market interac-

---

[15] There is a certain ambiguity in what one may mean by the natural phenomenon of the market. We normally refer to it in the form of competitive markets (a bit like a bazaar) in the sense that people can enter or leave at will and there is no one who exerts any power over the other. It is, of course, true that the natural form of the market could be one in which agents are trying to acquire power over the others but this is not what is generally meant by laissez-faire. It is the outcome of people of equal power engaging in economic interactions. It assumes, of course, that it is natural for people to interact with others on the basis of equality. We do not think that this is true—and it is part of the problem—but we will not expand on these matters here. Instead, when we talk about the natural phenomenon of the markets, we talk about the natural outcome of equally sovereign individuals which interact for economic purposes.

[16] There is some disagreement about the meaning of the natural rate in Adam Smith. From the perspective of modern economics, many think that it is simply what they call, the long-run equilibrium price. However, Smith was not a modern economist and such an interpretation does not seem right for anyone who properly investigates his complete writings. It is true that some of these views have been tainted by Ricardo's interpretation of 'natural price' as some kind of an absolute value which is the real value of goods and to which prices will always gravitate. But while Smith too saw in natural price a focal point for prices, the construction of that value is not technologically based but, rather, socially inspired. I will defend this interpretation in greater details in Chap. 8. At this stage, I would say only that the natural price, in Smith, was the one where all those who participate in the production process consume a socially constructed subsistence and the entire surplus is being invested which, in Smith, means an increase in wages. This, as will be explained later on, is an ethical requirement for markets not to violate the true sense of morality (the conscience) of those who are in the system.

tions from more metaphysical concepts based on what he considered to be the **essence** of commodities.[17] As he declared labour to be the essence of commodities, he shows how in the presence of money-driven market interactions, the surplus created by workers (the amount of work they put in above that which they need for their own subsistence) is expropriated by capitalists. Hence, labour values should not be understood as an attempt to explain market prices; Marx was fully aware of the dynamics which determines them.[18] Instead, labour values should be understood as a reference point, like the Aristotelian just price or the Smithian natural rate. In Marx's case, whenever there are profits—an expropriation of surplus values—market prices will not be the same as labour values.[19] More generally put, for all these scholars, when prices deviated from their reference point, the natural phenomenon of markets was socially harmful. When prices conform to the benchmark, the natural phenomenon of markets is beneficial. The main question, of course, is whether market prices have indeed a tendency to converge to, and actually reach, their benchmark values. If such a process exists, it would make sense to argue that the natural phenomenon of the market is socially desirable.

---

[17] There are, of course, serious methodological differences between them as Smith seems to be more of an empiricist, while Marx was clearly a rationalist. The former based his analysis on experience and observations, while the latter, who felt that we cannot trust our senses, believes in a priori knowledge. The strange thing is—and we will not have the space to examine this here—that there are rationalistic elements in Smith's thinking and the real founding father of modern economics (Leon Walras) was, like Marx, a rationalist.

[18] Though the attempts to use labour values as an explanation of market prices have been quite considerable and are captured by the literature on the problem of transformation, their somewhat misguided nature can be understood from the fact that Marx himself did not bother about the problem of transformation until the third volume of *Das Kapital*, which, to a great extent, was influenced by others and represents a much less coherent contribution to his writings than the first two volumes. Nevertheless, one must acknowledge that Marx was, to an extent, following Ricardo, for whom the idea of the absolute value was an attempt to explore the underlying technological causes of market prices. In this respect, the problem of transformation is very important. But still, one cannot ignore the fact that for Marx a C-C exchange (a commodity-commodity—barter—exchange) will, like in Aristotle, lead to an exchange reflecting labour values. It is when we face an M-C-M exchange that the expropriation takes place and money prices will inevitably deviate from labour values.

[19] We reiterate that Marx was really using labour values to expose the fact that prices entail, in terms of labour values, exploitation (in profits); in other words, he was using labour values to unmask market prices. The way we present this idea here is somewhat different but still true to the spirit of his writing and in conjunction with the problem of transformation which he has himself acknowledged in the third volume of *Das Kapital*.

Naturally, the question here is not whether Marx, Smith or even Aristotle were right or wrong in the way they constructed their social/ ethical benchmark or whether we find their proposed contents of it appealing. It is about the fact that until very recently many scholars did not think that their role is to refine their understanding of how markets operate.[20] Instead, they considered their role as passing judgement on the natural phenomenon called markets by comparing their consequences to a certain yardstick. It is therefore interesting to note that one of the founders of modern economics seemed to have followed a similar line of reasoning but the interpretation of his work has led to a complete change in the way people think about economics without a very good reason. I am referring here to Leon Walras.

Walras was a rationalist and, like Marx, he too was searching for the essence of things (and in particular, economic goods). But unlike Marx, he thought that utility (what Marx would have called value in use) is the essence of things. He then asked whether market prices will indeed yield outcomes which reflect these relative utilities and to answer this question he examined the logical limit of the natural phenomenon of the market by looking at a world with perfect (or complete) competition. His model of general equilibrium—which lies at the heart of the modern paradigmatic core[21]—suggests that when competition is complete (or perfect), the phenomenon of markets will lead to pricing of goods which reflects their essence. Goods will exchange according to the relative utility of the units exchanged (what we call marginal utilities) and all rational plans will coincide. This means that all individuals will achieve that which they had reason to expect. In modern days, this has also been associated with *efficiency* and the *general solution of the economic problem* which society faces.

---

[20] Even Ricardo, who could have been seen as pursuing this end, the overall purpose of his study was nevertheless to explore a fundamental social issue: the distribution of income.

[21] There are those, like Colander (2000), who claim that modern economics has nothing to do with neoclassical economics. I fear that I completely disagree. As will be demonstrated in Chap. 2, economics' textbooks are thoroughly neoclassical. The fact that economists are not researching general equilibrium does not mean that they are not using concepts and criteria which are derived from it. Conducting a partial equilibrium analysis does not mean that there is no general equilibrium behind it.

But by saying that there exists a price where all goods exchange according to their socially constructed values,[22] one does not tell us much about whether the reality of markets will indeed lead to such prices. As we saw in the previous cases, the fact that there is a just price in Aristotle, a natural price in Smith and labour value prices in Marx was only part of the economists' exercise. The real question was whether or not market prices deviate or converge to these social benchmarks. In the case of Marx, prices will always deviate from their true labour value as long as there is profit in the system (i.e. a positive return on capital); for Smith, this depended on the behaviour of those who possess the surplus, which means that they are likely to deviate for a long time and, therefore, markets will not conform to the social criterion. So what about Walras? He was, of course, acutely aware of the fact that while there exists a vector of prices such that all markets are in equilibrium and all goods are exchanged at their real relative value (value in use or marginal utility), it is not entirely clear how actual market dynamics will produce these prices. In other words, while it was clear that there exists a price vector that is consistent with the socially constructed benchmark, it is not clear whether the process of price formation, which takes place within the natural phenomenon of the markets, will form these ideal prices. In this respect, Walrasian general equilibrium prices are the equivalents of Smith's natural prices, Marx's labour values and Aristotle's just price.

To address the question of whether there exists a process which would lead to the formation of Walrasian general equilibrium prices, Walras suggested the mechanism of Tatonnement (or groping). He thought that he had proven that such a mechanism will indeed lead to the formation of those equilibrium prices but the mechanism is so remote from anything real (i.e. any market process), as well as fundamentally wrong (as was demonstrated later on), that the meaning of the general equilibrium prices became unclear.[23] In many respects, it was less clear than Marx's

---

[22] The fact that labour or utility is the intrinsic value of goods is not an observation as it is a social construct.

[23] Though our discussion is in general terms, which can include a variety of processes, it is all part of the more general problem captured in the discussions about stability of general equilibrium. Franklin Fisher wrote: 'The search for stability at great level of generality is probably a hopeless one. This does not justify economists dealing only with equilibrium models and assuming the problem

labour values. We knew what we had to do to produce them (abolish profits) but we had no idea whatsoever what to do to obtain Walrasian prices. Equally, we know what needs to happen for Smith's natural rate to be obtained even though we have little control over it (the behaviour of those who possess the surplus). In the case of Walras, there was no mechanism which connected what actually happens in markets and the social benchmark of his analysis. This led to a fallacious belief that if we only made sure that all markets were perfectly competitive as they are in Walras's abstract framework, then surely Walrasian equilibrium prices will emerge. Alternatively, they attribute the properties of Walrasian prices to the actual competitive prices even though we know with certainty that they are not the same.

The contribution of Walrasian general equilibrium to the paradigmatic core of modern economics is crucial. It provided it with the fundamental organisational principle in the sense that competitive decentralisation is a form of economic organisation which produces outcomes that are consistent with the social benchmark *whatever are the social values* from which it has been derived. The fact that utility (or value in use) is the essence of economic goods is sufficiently universal and the only difference which may appear across societies and cultures is the specifics of those values. As Robbins (1935, pp. 25–26) claimed, the only difference between a community of sybarites and a community of ascetics is that the prices of wine and ecclesiastical artefacts are going to be different, reflecting the difference in the value (utility) which members of society lay on these types of goods. This means that in every society the price of goods will always reflect—in a perfectly competitive environment—the subjective values of things to members of that society. This, of course, is associated with the

---

away. It is central to the theory of value' (Fisher 2011, p. 43). Some would argue that there is a difference between stability and price formation and may cite the idea of temporary equilibrium—conceived by Marshall and expanded by Hicks—as the place to look for an answer but here too the outcome was not helpful. Hicks himself recanted his theory on two grounds which reflect this kind of disappointment: firstly, because he thought it wrong to discard a slow process of equilibrium (which is indeed what we refer to as price formation mechanism), and secondly, because he felt that it was far too removed from the world it was supposed to conceive. More generally, he realised, correctly in our view, that there is nothing between this story and Walras: 'Where I now feel that I went wrong was in my attempt to represent the markets of that week as being in equilibrium, even in 'general equilibrium' in the sense of my static theory' (Hicks 1977, VI).

fact that all individuals are rational in the sense that they choose the best means to an end and they have, therefore, all solved their economic problem which is how to reconcile the fact that they desire things which are scarce. Moreover, as the meaning of Walrasian equilibrium is that the value in use per pound spent on its purchase will be the same across all markets, it also means that no individual can become better off without harming another (something which later on became the concept of Pareto-efficiency). Therefore, the principle of competitive decentralisation, or the pursuit of competitive markets, promises not only that prices will reflect the true socially constructed values of goods but also that all agents will solve their individual economic problem and no single agent can become better off without making someone else worse off, which means that there is no waste in potential benefits from trading in the market.[24]

So, the great promise of modern economics' paradigmatic core is that the relentless pursuit of competitive decentralisation will lead to Walrasian equilibrium prices and, with it, to all the benefits associated with such prices as they are, of course, equal to the social benchmark for economic performance.[25] If until the neoclassical revolution, economics was about commenting on the reality of the natural phenomenon of markets from some social or ethical perspectives so that one can form an opinion about the social value of markets, in the modern era all caution has been thrown to the wind. Competitive markets not only are a natural phenomenon but also have an ideal form which is the notion of perfect competition. If the implications of Smith's analysis of markets and natural prices were that markets, even when perfectly competitive, are not always working in tandem with social objectives, the modern conclusion is that the social objective should be to make markets work.

---

[24] Naturally, to say that such an outcome satisfies a social benchmark, we must also suppose that society has means by which to direct the outcomes of competitive interactions. In modern economics, as will be explored in Chap. 2, this is done through the second welfare theorem, which allows us to achieve whatever outcome society prefers through competitive markets. In Walras, this appeared in the form of his subsequent writings about social economics in which he expects society to own all land and use the rent to fund social projects that will help adjust outcomes to whatever it is that society deems as important.

[25] In fact, even though most work nowadays is not directly conducted on general equilibrium, much of it is about finding ways (institutional or contractual) to make the dream of universal competitiveness a reality.

There are many reasons to doubt the promise of general equilibrium—which we will discuss later on—however, the reason why we consider this a betrayal is because the ideal—those promising Walrasian prices—are, in fact, not reachable. It is not because there are problems in creating the perfectly competitive markets (and there are plenty); it is because of the absence of a sensible or realistic price formation process which will lead us to these prices. Even if all markets were perfectly competitive and there was no problem of incomplete markets, there is still no realistic conception of any price formation process which will produce those prices that promise all the benefits encapsulated in the social benchmark.[26] Worse still, not only that there is no process to lead us towards the Walrasian prices but even if we can approach them asymptotically, it is not at all clear that one can argue that as we approach Walrasian prices we also begin to reap the benefits which await us at those prices. In other words, all the benefits of competitive decentralisation will materialise at one point only, and this point seems to be beyond our reach; even if all markets were perfectly competitive, prices will forever oscillate around the values that will produce efficiency, but not even once will land at a point which is efficient (or a solution to the economic problem). So, one may wonder, what are the grounds for the insistence on competitive practices? If in the Smithian or Marxian system there was something, in principle, which could be done to make markets comply with social objectives, here it seems that there is nothing at all that can be done. Markets will always deviate from what could have been their social purpose, the benefits of competition will forever evade us and, therefore, the natural phenomenon of market should be viewed as a problem to be contained rather than an ideal to be promoted. *The betrayal of modern economics, therefore, is not so much the failure to see these difficulties—**and economists are fully aware of them**[27]—but the blatant refusal to draw from it the right conclusions.*

---

[26] And this goes well beyond the question of stability which we mentioned earlier.

[27] Being aware of these difficulties allows economics, in principle, to unleash the arsenal of mechanism design, the aim of which is to help markets reach the socially desirable solution. But there is a certain circularity here. The beauty of competitive interactions and markets is that they reveal the socially desirable prices without a need for a central authority to gather a great deal of information or guide the economy. For mechanism design to work, the designer needs to know where it is they wish to guide the economy (as it seems to go to the wrong place otherwise) and thus become a central planner. In this respect, it seems to invoke parallels with the *socialist calculation debate*; only

Instead of concluding that competitive decentralisation will never lead to a socially desirable solution, that the reality of markets is forever inefficient and cannot constitute the solution to the economic problem, we still recommend them as a universal and ethically neutral form of organisation. Instead of recognising that competitive markets are the problem, we are constantly seeking to expand them and increase competitiveness rather than struggle to contain them and look for alternative, more beneficial, forms of economic and social organisation.

Of course, one may argue that the main benefit of competitive markets is the plenty to which they give rise. But for an individualistic theory, this is not saying much. The purpose of modern economics is to solve individuals' economic problem, which is not about the mere creation of aggregate plenty but, rather, its distribution. It is for this reason that in modern economics the most important criterion of economic performance is allocative efficiency rather than productive efficiency. Moreover, if the objective of society is to maximise aggregate economic output, it is difficult to argue that such an objective is ethically neutral or value free. If fulfilling greed is the objective of market-based economic organisation, then it would be difficult to insist on it as a global platform which is suitable to all possible cultures or societies.

The first part of the book (volume I), therefore, is dealing with this aspect of what we have provocatively called the betrayal. It is about the way in which modern economics has created a false agenda which has become the main element in the public discourse about economic and social organisation. Naturally, in addition to the actual promise associated with the social effectiveness of competitive markets, there are other reasons why the organisational principles of modern economics have had such an appeal. The first is the claim according to which competitive markets constitute a natural order. If we just let nature take its course, society will always benefit from it. Given that individuals are all rational (in a particular manner), they will be able to co-ordinate their desires without the need for an authoritarian intervention. They will achieve this through their natural drive to specialise, trade and compete. The second, as we said

---

this time, this would be, paradoxically, the *capitalist calculation debate*. There is also an element of it in what is known as *Ordoliberalism*.

before, is the association of competitive markets with growth or the accumulation of material wellbeing. What, of course, is interesting in this context is to ask the question of whether growth is part of the promise of economics' paradigmatic core or is it some form of a distraction after realising—as many economists have—that the pursuit of competition will not bring the promised social benefits. To put it differently, is growth the Eldorado which replaces the Promised Land? The third issue is the liberal connection that seems to bind modern economics and the idea of natural order, with some notions of liberalism and, in particular, with civic society. We are referring here to the association of competitive decentralisation with a natural order that promises freedom and justice on top of expediency.

Consequently, this part of the book comprises four chapters in which we are trying to deal with each one of the main issues. In Chap. 1, we examine in some general and meta-historical terms the appeal and meaning of natural order either as an ideal or as a conception of reality. In early stages, the notion of natural order was more about harmony and tranquillity associated not only with the compatibility of human actions but also with the union of humanity with what is essentially good. As such, natural order is an ideal predicated on particular human behaviour, which may not be characteristic of human nature. In some sense, harmony and order will be achieved when humans overcame their nature. It is thus an order that must be pursued rather than a depiction of reality.

With the Enlightenment, the idea of a natural order, or a self-regulating system, as a reality became closer. Newtonian physics unfolded the beauty of God's creation by suggesting that the world of matter, the beauty of which we constantly observe, is nothing but a self-regulating order held together by the concept of equilibrium. This led to the belief that the same could also be true of the world of humans. However, unlike the particles of the material world, humans have opinions, reflect on outcomes and can even change their behaviour. Therefore, the only way to create a social self-regulating harmony would be through the endogenisation of these opinions, or, more generally speaking, ethics. As the latter takes longer to be formed or changed than the immediate economic interactions, we propose a distinction between 'synchronic' and 'diachronic' orders. The former is the immediate compatibility of economic interactions; the latter is the approval of the process and the outcomes. Indeed, classical economists have always been cautious about the relationship between human behaviour in the economic sphere and the way in which their moral opinions are formed. The implications of this for economic analysis was that while there was a recognition that there is some form of a natural order in the sense that economic interactions would be compatible, it was not enough to crown it as consistent with moral values. This, in turn, can either lead to a change in moral values or change in behaviour which would aim at undermining the working of the natural (synchronic) order.

Modern economics chose a different route altogether. Instead of accommodating the complexity of the relationship between the synchronic and the diachronic order, it opted for the path which completely separated economics from ethics. Namely, everywhere in the world people face the dilemma of scarcity. Therefore, regardless of what they want, they will need to allocate resources and economics offers them the principles of how to do so. As these principles are independent of what they wish to achieve, they are both universal and ethically neutral.[28] However, regardless of whether this is true, what it implies is that competitive decentralisation is now an ***idealised reality***. It fully exists nowhere but if societies adopted it, the outcome will be an order which is both synchronic and diachronic.

In Chap. 2, we examine the way in which economics proposes to achieve this status of universal and ethically neutral principles of economic organisation. We begin by identifying the paradigmatic core of the subject and we examine the logic of its construction from the conception of an economic problem, through the nature of its solution (and, therefore, criteria of economic performance [efficiency] and evaluation [opportunity cost]), to the institutional recommendation of competitive decentralisation. We show there that the way economics achieves the status of ethical neutrality is through the two welfare theorems which suggest that all possible outcomes—provided that they are efficient—can be achieved through competitive decentralisation. If the differences in the

---

[28] This is the line of reasoning emanating from Robbins (1935), who followed Wicksteed (1910). The way modern economic proposes this is discussed in Chap. 2.

social values between societies are manifested in their views about the outcomes of economic interactions, then competitive decentralisation (or markets) is a form of economic organisation which is compatible with all possible social values.

We reject the criticisms levied against economics on the grounds that the model is too abstract as this is the nature of modelling. We acknowledge that there is nothing in this analytical structure to suggest that it is a depiction of reality. Instead, as we said before, it is a logical limit of the idea of competitive decentralisation and, as such, a reference point. This means that criticisms against the theory must be aimed at either the nature of the abstraction or the ability to approach this logical limit. At this stage of our study, we focus on the latter and, again, as we said before, we will argue that the problem with this reference point is that it is irrelevant as there is no logical way to reach it if our starting point is the reality which is outside the model. As such, it becomes a meaningless reference point. If we cannot, in principle, get to the efficient outcome, then competitive decentralisation is neither a solution to the economic problem nor ethically neutral.

We also examine in this chapter the dialogue which the theory has had over the years with reality and how the model has been adjusted to take these things into account. We note that a great deal of developments in what economists actually do (like some aspects of institutional economics, contract theory and game theory) are efforts to help the paradigm retain its position as a universal and ethically neutral principle of organisation. Nevertheless, some of these developments have been quite devastating; notably, in a world of uncertainty with incomplete markets, the efficient outcome will never materialise. Hence, it no longer matters that there is no process leading to the efficient outcome; such an outcome does not exist.

Now, it is evident that many economists are fully aware of these results and what they seem to be doing is offer localised remedies as to how to make markets efficient. But this means that they believe that in spite of everything, we can slowly approach the logical limit where all markets are efficient. As we explain in this chapter, one of the conditions for competitive decentralisation to deliver is that all markets without exception are perfectly competitive. It is of limited value, if any at all, to make some markets efficient if we know that competitive decentralisation does not solve the economic problem and is not ethically neutral. Put more broadly, even though people seem to recognise that the allocation in which competitive decentralisation is a solution to the economic problem (i.e. efficient) has no way of materialising, they attribute these global properties of efficiency to every expression of competitive decentralisation. This, of course, is false as is the belief that the more there are competitive markets, we slowly begin to receive the social benefits which are promised at the general equilibrium allocation.[29]

We then discuss an interesting development which sheds some light on the way economists deal with the severe crack in the theory: the shift of focus towards growth. We show that the solution to the economic problem has two dimensions. One is to allocate existing resources well, and the other to increase the amount of resources available. The latter is what we mean by growth. We ask why in recent years there has been a shift from the question of efficient allocations of existing resources to the generation of growth. We claim that, in part, this reflects the exasperation with the ability of competitive decentralisation to solve the first problem of efficiently allocating existing resources. So instead, we use growth as a cover up of this failure. However, a shift towards growth without solving the first problem is a deviation from the agenda of modern economics. Being an individualistic theory, one cannot measure the success or failure of the system by merely looking at the aggregate level of output. More to the point, we discuss the question of whether the institutional arrangements which are conducive to growth are also those which are conducive to the efficient allocation of existing resources. We cite the facts that larger corporations tend to invest more in R&D and that there is a need to protect intellectual property rights (patenting), as possible indications for the conflict which may exist between the two.

In the subsequent chapter, Chap. 3, we extend our study of economics' failed promise to the question of its relevance. Here, we take a look at a number of empirical stylised facts to establish whether there are any empirical grounds to believe the promise of economics' paradigmatic

---

[29] If we add to this the realisation that with the progress of technology an increasing number of industries fall into the category of increasing returns to scale, the future of competitive markets as an empirical reality is seriously dampened. While we may wish to deal with this, trying to achieve efficiency by attempting to emulate perfect competition is, in the light of what we just said, an empty gesture.

core. There are three issues at stake pertaining to the conditions under which competitive decentralisation—or the ideal of a market-based natural order—can deliver a solution to the economic problem which is universal and ethically neutral. The first is that competitive markets must be complete and no aspect of economic life should be conducted outside such framework. The second and the third are part of one larger question which is whether individuals are capable of fending for themselves.

With regard to the first question we show that even though there has been a remarkable increase in gross domestic product (GDP) per capita in those countries that allowed competitive practices to be expanded, there was a remarkable increase in the share of governments in those economies. As the share of government in the economy grows, it means that an increased number of economic activities are not governed by the principles of competitive decentralisation. This in itself is enough to mean that competitive decentralisation will not lead to an efficient outcome. It is possible that the increase in governments reflects the public's exasperation with the outcomes which competitive markets produce, but if it is, it also means that as long as governments have such large presence there will be no chance for competitive decentralisation to deliver.

With regard to the second and third issues, it is important to emphasise that the question of the ability of individual agents to fend for themselves is not only a critical element in showing that competitive decentralisation solves the economic problem; it is also a crucial element behind the liberal conception of the civic society. In such a society, government must be small and limited to keeping the peace and upholding the law. Everything else should be the outcome of individuals' voluntary activities. If people cannot fend for themselves, they become dependent on collective decisions affecting their ability to access national income. When people become dependent on collective decisions, the idea of civic society runs into some difficulties as it begins to intrude on individuals' liberties.

We show in this respect two things. The first is the consistent and prolonged decline in the share of wages in national income. We argue that this is a problem because there is also evidence to show that the vast majority of the public relies mainly on wages as their source of income. Therefore, the implications of the fall in the share of wages are that the ability of most people to access national income through markets has been seriously diminished. The second element is less of a stylised fact as an anticipation. We note that in developed countries there is a consisted rise in the use of capital-intensive technologies. This, at some stage, may suggest that the demand for labour as a means of production may decline considerably, leaving individuals unable to access national income through markets, and if they do, their ability to be selective about that which they wish to do as a profession may be seriously restricted. Hence, as the ability of individuals to access their share in national income is reduced (through either smaller shares or the absence of work), the share of governments will have to increase. Both of these developments suggest that the conditions for competitive decentralisation to deliver on its promise are unlikely to be met.

In the final chapter of the first part, Chap. 4, we address the alternative reason for promoting the idea of competitive decentralisation. This reason is the association of markets with freedom and justice. If one can show that markets are associated with freedom (usually, of choice) as well as justice (as no agent has power over others), then maybe we can understand the pursuit of competitive decentralisation from a different, more liberal, angle which is independent of the ability of markets to solve the economic problem.

It is common to associate markets with freedom of choice but less so with respect to justice. Nevertheless, the pretended neutrality of economics seems to suggest that markets and justice are, if not bedfellows, at least not orthogonal to one another. The reason why we raise the question of justice explicitly is because we find that there is no convincing argument to tie freedom with markets. As both freedom and justice seem to be pillars of any ethical theory, successful association of markets with both would have given some credence to the claim of ethical neutrality as well as lend support to various forms of liberal support for markets.

Both concepts of freedom and justice are far too broad to be squeezed into a single chapter, and from the outset we say that it is not our intention here to conduct a thorough survey of both concepts. Instead, we focus in the chapter on the way in which people would normally tend to associate markets with these two concepts. In the case of freedom, it is the freedom of choice, and in the case of justice, it is the question of due share.

We show in the chapter that freedom of choice is not a sufficiently well-defined concept. We suggest, instead, to focus on individuals' sovereignty, which basically means the ability of agents to change their circumstances. It is interesting to note that there is a connection between conceiving freedom in terms of sovereignty and that which J. S. Mill calls free-will. According to Mill, the real measure of free-will is indeed the ability which individuals have to control the circumstances which determine their actions.

In our examination we discover that individuals, in the economic set-up in which they specialise and trade to better their conditions, are not really sovereign as they cannot opt out of the game when circumstances are such that they will no longer benefit from market interactions. We demonstrate this through the fact that to benefit from trade one has to specialise according to prevailing prices. While this means that the agent will specialise in that in which he or she has comparative advantage (i.e. they can do something cheaper in terms of other things they could have done, relative to others), it does not mean that it is also that which they like to do. If two people are good in playing the violin but one of them is clumsier than the other in baking bread, economic reasoning determines that the less clumsy individual should give up his love of music (professionally) and, instead, spend most of his life in a bakery. Naturally, economists would say that the material benefits which the agent will get from specialising will offset the cost of giving up his love of music but then again, they are just economists. More seriously, the idea of benefits from trade—at the individual level—means that not only is it possible for agents to end up doing that which they do not want to do, but if there is a change in price, they will have to be willing to change their occupation so that they can benefit from greater material wellbeing. But if the cost of changing occupation is too high, it means that either way they will become worse off but have no option to opt out from the economic game by, say, returning to a more self-sufficient form of existence.

As far as justice is concerned, we explain at great length why we choose to focus here on the question of due share, or contribution-based desert. We do not undermine the importance of questions on initial allocations or final distributions to the question of justice, but as markets represent a process, or a sequence of actions, the more relevant concept of justice would be the one in which he who puts more effort—other things being equal—should have a better market position in the sense that he can command more of the output of those who contribute less. We show that this view has a strong showing in public opinion but also that it has an important presence in the history of the concept of justice (in connection with economics). Consequently, we discover that competitive market interaction is fundamentally orthogonal to the idea of due share. This means that whether or not we have the right initial conditions, competitive interactions will subvert the course (and cause) of justice.

All of this leads to the inevitable conclusion that the ideal of competitive decentralisation—the promise of economics' paradigmatic core—has betrayed us. It is a logical failure both in the sense that there exists no competitive allocation which constitute a solution to the economic problem and which is ethically neutral, and in the sense that even if there were, there exists no process which can bring us nearer to it in a manner which will suggest that we begin reaping the promised benefit as we approach that point. It is also a relevance failure as the reality is that the more advanced the economy is, the more likely it is to have greater parts of economic activities conducted away from the rules of competitive markets. This means that even if all these markets were perfectly competitive, the efficiency (and social benefits) of the outcome will be eluding us. One could argue that this means that we should reduce governments and replace them with markets, but then the problem is that the vast majority of the public has its access to national income squeezed both by falling share of return on labour and by the imminent demise in the availability of work. Finally, it has been an ethical failure as the idea of markets is consistent neither with individuals' sovereignty nor with the preservation of justice. So, in summary, competitive markets are neither good from an expediency perspective, nor good from a moral one. Yet, they still dominate the public discourse about economic organisation within society, across societies (free trade) and intra-societies (globalisation).

*   *   *

The second part of the book (volume II) is devoted to the second aspect of the betrayal, namely in what way we have betrayed the idea of liberal classical economics. To an extent, the betrayal, by us, of the idea of liberal economics is the question of whether it is indeed the case that in order for society to allow individuality to be expressed and freedom to be protected, that the appropriate social institutions should be those of apparent competitive decentralised, or laissez-faire. In other words, it is about the conflation of the idea of individual freedom with the idea of freedom of individuals. The former is about allowing human individuality to be expressed in full. The latter is about allowing individuals to do what they want. The two are clearly not the same thing.

Assuming that expressing one's individuality depends both on the breadth of one's identity and on the depth of one's ability, then its full expression becomes dependent on circumstances and the environment. By the breadth of one's identity, we are referring to the question of whether sociality—relationships which we have with the others—are parts of what make us individual human beings or are they just a means to an end. In what sense are humans social being? If our humanity suggests a sociality which is not functional, then surely part of their individuality is dependent on individuals' ability to achieve sociality. In such a case, individuals may need help in achieving this aspect of their individuality and simply saying let them do what they want may not be sufficient.

By depth of one's ability, we are referring to the means available to individuals to fulfil their personal potential. If an individual has excellent analytical skills, then without access to the stock of human knowledge accumulated at any point in time, the ability of the individual to fulfil his or her potential will be limited. Therefore, allowing people to do what they want without providing them with the means to achieve that which they could, or would, want cannot constitute genuine freedom. In this sense, the idea of liberal economics is betrayed because the concept of liberalism is used in an extreme, and perhaps even a primitive, way. A more complex notion of what human sociality means would also suggest a more complex notion of freedom or liberalism. Subsequently, this would also suggest a different form of liberal economics.

Therefore, at the heart of the question of whether or not we betrayed liberal economics lies the question of what the nature of human sociality is. Modern economics, by separating economics from ethics or social values, is clearly signalling that it opted for a concept of sociality which is almost exclusively functional. By contrast, liberal classical economics, and in particular in the writings of Adam Smith and J. S. Mill, has opted for a conception of an intrinsic human sociality. This means that one cannot really separate people's social dispositions and moral opinions from the way in which they interact in the sphere of economics.

More recently, there has been some awareness among some economists that there may be something wrong with the apparent a-social conception of Homo economicus. This was mainly due to realisation that the predicted results of some basic games—and, in particular, non-cooperative games with a prisoners' dilemma—do not seem to materialise in experiments. Instead, an outcome emerges which suggests that agents co-ordinate their behaviour to ensure that they each get the better outcome. This, in turn, led to the conclusion that individuals are social and it is this sociality which ensures the beneficial working of competitive decentralisation.

What is interesting about all these attempts to add sociality to the conception of the individuals is that none of this has led to a review of the question: Would socially minded individuals behave competitively in the first place? Is the idea of competitive markets, in such a case, neither a description of reality nor a possible ideal? If we look at the example of the prisoners' dilemma, then the standard conception of the socially functional (a-social) individuals would lead to an outcome which is inevitable (i.e. equilibrium) but not the best for them. There is another outcome which they both prefer, but the problem is that such an outcome is not an equilibrium in the sense that if one agent commits to the strategy which will bring it about, the other agent will have an incentive to deviate and be rewarded for his or her defection. This means that in order for the outcome which is good for both agents to materialise, they must both commit to behave in a way that will not jeopardise the outcome.

To a great extent, the prisoners' dilemma is a demonstration of the first aspect of betrayal. The system of competitive decentralisation (the equivalent of non-cooperative games) leads to an inferior social outcome.

Namely, we do not reach the Promised Land of the socially desired consequence of economic interactions.[30] So how do we rescue the idea of markets or competitive interactions from failing us? We argue that individuals are socially minded and would therefore choose the strategy which benefits both. It is human sociality which saved the a-social world of competitive decentralisation. But would socially minded individuals be playing games?

The lessons we can learn from Smith and Mill is that when individuals are conceived to be socially minded, the natural phenomenon of competitive interaction is a reality which may need to be contained rather than an ideal we would wish to promote. The story in Smith is rather complex as nature has a way of deceiving people into believing things to be morally good so that its own purpose (as he sees it) of the multiplication of the species through the accumulation of material wealth is fulfilled. But the nature of human cognition, their conscience, will tell them that such a system is morally reprehensible and needs correction. In this respect, Smith seems to claim that there may be a synchronic order in the natural phenomenon of competitive markets but it may not be diachronic. For Mill, in particular, sociality of humans is something which is part of what he calls 'individuals' development' and is essential in making people the object of morality. Accordingly, he claims that when they develop, individual will become more co-operative in nature, which would lead to a different world of co-operatives, co-operation and material stagnation due to the fact that people would wish to spend less time producing material goods and immersing themselves in more of what Aristotle called the good life (Eudaimonia). It is not impossible to think that Smith would have reached similar conclusions except that he was writing at the beginning of what he called the commercial stage of social development. Given that there were three preceding stages, it was not supposed to be the last, but modern economics, in as much as it is an extrapolation of Smith, seems to have missed this point altogether and has the appearance of that unfortunate term: 'the end of history'.

---

[30] Of course, in the literature on the prisoners' dilemma we must distinguish between problems of oligopoly were the interest of the individuals and the larger society are not the same, and the cases where all members of society play the game (the case of the public good is a good example). We must also note that though strategic non-cooperative interaction is the equivalent of competitive market interactions, the two are not the same thing.

The second part of the book comprises four chapters in which we are trying to address some of these issues. From the outset, we say that we restrict ourselves to methodological individualism not because we consider this to be the right approach but rather because we would like to examine economics on its own terms. We begin with Chap. 5, which is focused on the question of what human sociality actually means. Here, we juxtapose two initial positions. At the one extreme, we have the individual whose sociality is purely functional. For such an individual, as social association serves a purpose, the whole question of ethics become subservient to this purpose. It is easy to see why from the perspective of modern economics this is a coherent position to take. If agents are functionally social, it stands to reason that their ethical values will be subjugated to the mechanism which allows them to achieve that which they want. In this case, the mechanism in question is that of competitive markets and, therefore, economics is not only independent of ethics but it should be the foundation of morality.

At the other extreme we have the individual who is intrinsically social. For such an individual, society is organic and ethics is derived from the natural qualities of the relationship which the individual has with others. Economics, in such a case, is subservient to the social purpose and the ethics which is derived from it. We claim that we can see human thought being spread between these two extremes. We already mentioned Hobbes and Locke at the two extremes of this spectrum, but we could also add Spencer and Durkheim where neither of them is at an extreme end of the spectrum but the former clearly tending towards the functional and the latter towards the more organic. If we were to locate economic thinking between these two extremes, we will clearly find modern economics at the functional (Hobbesian) side, while liberal classical economics sees society as more organic and is therefore located nearer to the Lockean end.

To judge which of these two approaches is the more relevant conception of the individual, we delve into research produced in evolutionary biology, comparative neurology and anthropology to find that by all accounts, the conception of the individual which seems to be most relevant to humans who are Sapiens is the one of intrinsic sociality. However, sociality as such is not unique to humans. What is unique to mankind is the extent of this sociality. The natural social circle of humans is considerably larger than that of other primates, which raises a question about the way in which such sociality is formed. In smaller group physical attributes would suffice; in human society this is no longer the case. Therefore, that which cements human ties is associated with the development of abstract language and abstract cognition.

In Chap. 6, we continue this theme by looking at the implications which such a conception of the individual will have on the nature of society. We already said that society can be either completely functional or organic or anything in between. Given the fact that society depends on human cognition and given that the latter is constantly developing in terms of both our ability to grasp social relationship and our ability to develop technology which facilitates social bonds, both the size of social association and the strength of bonds must also be changing.

To capture such developments, we expand on Hamilton's idea of inclusive fitness to focus on a concept of social distance (relatedness, in his case) which, we argue, is the key to the understanding the nature of society. Evidently, a society with loose social bonds is more likely to be more functional in nature than a society where such bonds are strong. However, the strength of such bonds depends both on the extent of association which technology permits and on the extent of association which our cognitive ability dictates. Namely, if technology allows us, effectively, to be equally connected with all people on the planet, whether or not we feel part of the global community depends on whether our cognition allows us to treat people who live so far away and have a different history, language and culture in the same manner we would treat people who are nearer to us in these parameters. Our direct cognitive ability to grasp society is always restricted by the original design of our brain. Therefore, a tension is likely to emerge between that which technology offers (which is an indirect result of our cognitive ability) and that which we can grasp. Putting all of this together in an analytical framework which relates humans' natural position (in terms of brain structure) with social organisation through the concept of social distance, we are able to conclude that in spite of the intrinsic nature of human sociality, it is possible, in principle, to end up with all forms of social organisation—including a functional one—depending on the way the concept of social distance develops.

We argue that the implications of this for our examination are that the natural position of humans is such that the relatively recent developments in technology would lead to a commensurate rise in our ability to grasp and, therefore, expand the extent of our association. This creates a gap between society within which we physically live and our social references. As we feel greater affinity with an increasing number of people, the social distance with those with whom we share social institutions (the physical environment within which we live) is increasing which makes society more functional. But as technology races ahead and our ability to catch up lagging, a certain alienation may develop which would lead to an increase in the sense of relatedness to people who are nearer to us (lower social distance) and, thus, shift social organisation away from the functional and closer to the organic.

While these issues may have far-reaching implications, they need to be developed further. In our examination, we are really interested in the implications which human sociality will have for the question of the role of economics in society. Naturally, the more functional society is (the greater is the social distance between its members), the more likely it becomes for the social sphere and the economic sphere to be completely separated. This is indeed the state of affairs in modern economics. However, given the initial biological position of mankind, we have never really been at the extreme functional end. With technological and cognitive developments, society may have moved somewhat in the direction of functionality but never all the way. Together with potential current trends of diminished social distance among those who share social institutions, the shift may be moving now in the organic direction. At the organic end, the separation of economics from society does not seem to have any meaning given that the economic organisation is subservient to social and ethical considerations. Therefore, as modern economics require the extreme end of social functionality and complete separation of spheres, the evidence we collated together in our analytical framework suggests that this is based on a fundamentally wrong conception of humanity. Liberal classical economics, on the other hand, seems to be in greater harmony with these findings.

Our betrayal of liberal economics, in this respect, is that we allowed modern economics to supersede liberal classical economics, deviate from it and falsely claim to be a continuity of it. Instead, we should have demanded that modern thinking about economics should be based on the classical conceptual framework rather than the one adopted by contemporary economic analysis. Yet, as we said before, there have been voices in modern economics who have acknowledged the need to adjust the conception of the individual and to allow for greater sociality to be taken into consideration. However, what is meant by greater sociality may still be a problem. After all, even within the functional approach, the agents have a view of society, though it is still functional. In Chap. 7, therefore, we are asking whether it is at all possible to rescue the modern paradigm by socialising its fundamental conception of the individual in a way which is consistent with the intrinsic sociality which is evidently part of the individual's constitution.

While we accept the principle of rationality—in the form of reasoned actions—as the way to abstract from human behaviour, we wonder whether this necessarily means the kind of rationality which has been adopted by modern economics. With the help of Weber, we identify at least two explicit alternative forms of rational behaviour as well as one implicit. We claim that the one chosen by modern economics—and manifested in the idea of the rational utility maximiser who always seeks the best means to an end—is the least likely descriptor of human behaviour if we listen to the way in which people tend to describe their own motivation. More importantly, however, we ask whether such a conception of rationality can be consistent with the sociality of humans we uncovered in the previous chapter.

The two concepts of rationality on which we focus our attention are the ones used by modern economics (which Weber calls instrumental rationality, or *Zweckrationalität*), where we always choose the best means to an end, and the other is what Weber called 'value rationality' (or *Wertrationalität*) and which is sometimes referred to as 'expressive rationality'. The latter is a form of rationality where people are driven more by the ends they value than by considerations about the means. What this means is that people form an opinion about which actions are conducive to the end they wish to promote and they follow it without considering the specifics of each individual action. Such a behaviour could be typical of people who would say that they would always act according to what they consider to be morally right rather than on the basis of such an action being the best means to an end. More broadly conceived, the difference between the two forms of rationality is that in the case of the instrumentally rational agents incentives are the more significant explanation to human action, while in the case of the expressively rational it is motivation which is the key to the understanding of human action. It is easy to see that market conditions which alter incentives are less significant as moderators of human interaction if people are expressively, rather than instrumentally, rational.

We then examine what would different levels of sociality mean to each form of rationality and discover that for instrumental rationality to be consistent with the level of sociality we think exists in humans, the level of computation and considerations which each individual will have to command is beyond what may be considered as reasonable. After all, if you are genuinely interested in the fate of others and you are about to act, choosing the best means to an end would require you to consider ***all*** possible effects of your actions on such a large circle of people that it may become debilitating. On the other hand, expressively rational individuals who only require a rule of behaviour which is consistent with their level of interest in the other have no problems expressing such sociality in their form of rationality.

Nevertheless, economists are adamant that their conception of the individual is sufficiently general to allow for social consideration to be taken into account. We question this by firstly examining the sensitivity of economics' rational utility maximiser to social settings that reflect the potential for social considerations. We find that the way standard economics understands human behaviour is, in its essence, oblivious to the type of environment within which the individual operates. Secondly, we question this by asking whether it is possible to adjust the instrumentally rational utility maximiser so that it will capture the sociality embedded in human nature. We argue that this will not be the case for two main reasons. The first we have already mentioned and it has to do with the ability to calculate the effects of one's action on those about whom one cares. The second reason is that within the instrumental rational utility maximiser lurks the idea of opportunism. This is manifested in two, related, ways: one through the idea of substitutability of outcomes and the other through the neutrality of means. It means that nothing has any intrinsic value and everything can always be compensated for. If one can achieve his or her objective through two actions where one is more harmful to other people than the other, then it is possible that the agent will be indifferent between them if the cost of doing the less harmful action is greater than the cost of executing the harmful action. In a non-functional sociality, the harmful action would be something you do not do as a matter of principle. Therefore, this kind of opportunism cannot really be a characteristic of intrinsic sociality.

We already mentioned the prisoners' dilemma and the claim that it is human sociality which drives people to choose the strategy in which they have to rely on the other following suit and not defecting to reach the outcome which is good for both agents. However, what is called here sociality is no other than functional sociality. People may learn, over time, that to achieve the best for themselves they have to reach a certain tacit agreement with the other. There is nothing social about this type of co-operation; it is a self-interested, self-serving type of co-operation and is by no stretch of imagination a reflection of intrinsic sociality.

This led to the final attempt at rescuing the instrumental rational utility maximiser from being deemed an inappropriate representation of human behaviour and sociality. It is the idea of Homo economicus. The way this notion is interpreted by modern economics is that the **domain of economics** is separable from the **social domain** and, therefore, it is perfectly consistent for individuals to act differently in each domain. This idea, emanating from J. S. Mill, is fundamentally flawed as it presumes that the behaviour in one domain is independent of the **character** of the agent. The way in which individuals perceive society is bound to be reflected in the way in which he or she interacts economically even if the domain of their interactions is separated. Therefore, the economic interactions of the functionally social (through the behaviour of an instrumentally rational utility maximiser) will be different from the economic interactions of the intrinsically social whose behaviour is captured by expressive rationality.

The fact that modern economics betrayed us because it wrongly conceived the individual in terms of his or her sociality is exacerbated by the fact that the relevant conception of the individuals in terms of their sociality was correctly perceived by liberal classical economics. The reason why this is an exacerbation of the betrayal is that modern economics insists that it is a natural logical progression from liberal classical economics and, in particular, from the writings of Adam Smith. In Chap. 8, therefore, we demonstrate (a) the implications of conceiving human sociality as intrinsic for the conceptual framework of economic analysis; and (b) how liberal classical economics, notably Adam Smith, has done it and that it is, therefore, fundamentally different from modern economic theory.

As far as the first aspect is concerned, the implication of our understanding of human sociality is that society precedes economic organisation and considerations. As that which draws people together is not a particular purpose as it is their intrinsic desire to be part of a group, society already entails the nature of relationships people have with one another. It also means that ethical values, which are the governing body of human interactions, already exist before we even begin to consider economic organisation or the raison d'être of markets. This, of course, is in stark contrast with modern economics where economic organisation seems not only to dominate social considerations but also to be, in a way, the essence of the functional society. Consequently, as is the case in functional societies, the criteria of economic performance are entirely subservient to the functions which the economy is supposed to fulfil. Ethical principles, therefore, must never interfere with the success of such an organisation and relationships between individuals are based on their usefulness.

For Smith, this could not have been further from the truth. His economic thinking is deeply embedded in his social and moral theory. But not only this, the society which he analyses is transient and part of a social evolution. As we said before, he did not reflect on what will be the next stage of commercial society because he was writing at the beginning of this stage, but for us, almost 300 years later, it may be time to consider the beginning of a transition. We also noted that J. S. Mill had already begun thinking about it and envisaged a future—based on intrinsic sociality—where competition is waning and co-operation becomes the rule of the day.

Again, as we said already at the beginning of this introduction, Smith considered the system of competitive decentralisation (laissez-faire) as a natural phenomenon but whether or not it served society well is a different question altogether. What we discover through a more systematic analysis of Smith's work is that in terms of the social drive which lies

behind the division of labour, the conditions under which a market economy will fulfil its social purpose are such that they are unlikely to materialise. To an extent, this is similar to Walras's understanding that finding
the allocation which serves its social purpose (in his case, solves the economic problem and, with the later additions, is ethically neutral) is not
the end of the process and one has to ask whether there exists a mechanism which leads to such an allocation. Walras thought that there is such
a mechanism; modern economists *know* that there is none, yet they still
attribute the properties of such an allocation to actual competitive outcomes which have nothing in common with the socially desirable one.[31]
Smith too realised that there exists a possibility that markets will serve the
social purpose but unlike the Walrasian system, where the obstacles were
the price dynamics in markets, in the case of Smith, the obstacle was
human behaviour. It is the behaviour of those who own the surpluses
(usually, those who own assets) on which the outcome depends. As they
are unlikely to restrain their consumption to some socially recognised
standard, natural prices will not emerge and the ability of the vast majority of individuals to achieve that, which they socially desire, will be
curtailed.

On the other hand, he also draws the attention to a corruption of
moral sentiments which may lead people to believe that competitive
decentralisation is a morally good system. Such a deception which is
triggered by nature, cannot, however, be part of what we called diachronic order as over time people will realise the nature of the deception and the moral and social failings of competitive markets will
become evident. To some extent, Smith's distinction between the purpose of the nature of things and that of human cognition is very similar to the argument we developed in Chaps. 5 and 6, according to
which the cognitive ability of humans to grasp sociality goes well
beyond the capacity which nature intended by giving us a particular
brain structure.

Having said all this, one cannot escape the question: So what next?
What are the implications of all this for the way in which we do econom-

---

[31] To remind you, as we did earlier, the market may be perfectly competitive but prices will forever
oscillate and not even once represent an efficient outcome.

ics in academia and the praxis of economics in terms of both structural organisation and public policy. Naturally, my intention was not to offer a new economic theory here; it was mainly to argue for the extent of inadequacy of current economic thinking. In so doing, I would like to persuade the many talented economists, who are, alas, engaged more in promoting themselves within the dysfunctional market of pseudo-ideas, to divert their abilities and intelligence towards something more genuinely academic in that it aims at benefitting our fellow human beings and society.

In the final chapter of this book, which I entitled **Quo Vadis**, I intend to merely give some general directions into which, in my view, academia and policy should proceed. I will not summarise this chapter here as it is, in itself, a summary. At this stage, I will only say this: by highlighting my conviction about the superiority of liberal classical economic thinking, I was not trying to say that the existing output of classical economics is anywhere near what one would need for a proper understanding of the role of economics within society. Nevertheless, they did offer us a conceptual framework which is commensurate with the evidence about human sociality and to which I think that we should adhere, and to the details of which we should now devote our attention.

In general, however, what comes out of this book is that the love affair, which dominant parts of academia and the public have had with the idea of competition and competitive decentralisation, must come to an end. For one, competition itself is more often associated with monopolistic or oligopolistic competitions—which even in terms of competitive decentralisation are inefficient and socially undesirable—than it is with the ideal of perfect competition. But even if genuine competitive structures were possible, they would still fail us. Yes, it is probably true that greater competition will lead to lower costs (and greater output), but whether or not this should be sufficiently central an objective for the society which the economy is serving is another question. When individual sociality does not permit the clean separation between the economic and the social spheres, it is highly unlikely that such considerations should be dominant. Moreover, even in terms of productive efficiency, it is not unlikely that if people's behaviour corresponds to their sociality, cost-cutting operations may be more effective under different structures than the one proposed by competitive decentralisation. The latter relies heavily on incentives but if the motivation is right, there may be a host of alternative forms of organisation which may produce plenty.

There may be some areas where it may matter more but there would equally be areas in which efficiency should not matter at all. Even if there are natural tendencies towards competitive behaviour—and we must bear in mind that behaviour is a learnt human trait—it does not mean that we, as a society, should condone it or promote it. The implications are not that we must eradicate markets or stifle competition at any cost. There is no obvious reason why there should be no competition in the production of, say, bread, but we must also contemplate possible alternatives even if their level of efficiency in terms of cutting cost is not as great. We must also not forget that an efficient allocation of resources is really about allocating people into work and professions where they will spend most of their time. Surely such decisions cannot be based on expediency alone.

We must, therefore, in general, treat markets with suspicion and constantly try to correct their adverse social effects. It is not less important to correct the social effects of a perfectly competitive market than it is to correct the inefficiency of other forms of competition. Therefore, as we should focus on the failures of markets rather than on markets' failure, the pursuit of competitive practices should be restrained. We must reconsider what is the economic problem which we would like to solve given that economics is part of a social project and we must allow for the fact that different societies may perceive the economic problem differently. Therefore, we should not measure economic performance by the standard conception of efficiency and we should certainly not measure it by a benchmark derived from the idea of a perfectly competitive market. Instead, we should begin to seriously consider alternative forms of economic organisation which are based on the understanding of the sociality which is embedded in human nature. In the light of it we should reconsider the role, extent and nature of private enterprise; the role, nature and extent of public provisions; the different criteria by which we judge them; the balance that must be established between them; and the way by which we judge this balance.

Bibliography

Atkinson, A. B. (2015). *Inequality: What Can Be Done?* Cambridge, MA: Harvard University Press.

Backhouse, R. E. (2006). The Keynesian Revolution. In R. E. Backhouse & B. W. Bateman (Eds.), *The Cambridge Companion to Keynes* (pp. 19–38). Cambridge: Cambridge University Press.

Barro, R. J., & Grossman, H. I. (1971). A General Equilibrium Model of Income and Employment. *American Economic Review, 61*, 82–93.

Benassy, J.-P. (1986). *Macroeconomics: An Introduction to the Non-Walrasian Approach.* New York: Academic Press.

Clower, R. W. (1965). The Keynesian Counterrevolution: A Theoretical Appraisal. In F. H. Hahn & F. P. R. Brechling (Eds.), *The Theory of Interest Rates* (pp. 103–125). London: Macmillan.

Colander, D. (2000). The Death of Neoclassical Economics. *Journal of the History of Economic Thought, 22*(2), 127–143.

Davidson, P. (2007). *John Maynard Keynes.* New York: Palgrave Macmillan.

Fisher, F. M. (2011). The Stability of General Equilibrium—What Do We Know and Why Is It Important? In P. Bridel (Ed.), *General Equilibrium Analysis—A Century After Walras* (pp. 34–45). London: Routledge.

Hicks, J. R. (1977). *Economic Perspectives: Further Essays on Money and Growth.* Oxford: Clarendon Press.

Hoover, K. D. (1995). Relative Wages, Rationality, and Involuntary Unemployment in Keynes's Labour Market. *History of Political Economy, 27*(4), 653–683.

Laidler, D. E. W. (1999). *Fabricating the Keynesian Revolution.* Cambridge University Press.

Leijonhufvud, A. (1968). *On Keynesian Economics and the Economics of Keynes.* Oxford: Oxford University Press.

Marglin, S. (2010). *The Dismal Science: How Thinking Like an Economist Undermines Community.* Harvard University Press.

Patinkin, D. (1965). *Money Interest and Prices* (2nd ed.). New York: Harper and Row.

Pigou, A. C. (1920). *The Economics of Welfare.* London: Macmillan.

Piketty, T. (2014). *Capital in the 21st Century.* Cambridge, MA: Harvard University Press.

Polanyi, K. (1944). *The Great Transformation: The Political and Economic Origins of Our Time.* Boston: Beacon Press.

Robbins, L. (1935). *Essay on the Nature and Significance of Economic Science*. London: Macmillan.

Robinson, J. (1974). History versus Equilibrium. *Indian Economic Journal, 21*(3), 202–213.

Shackle, G. L. S. (1967). *The Years of High Theory: Invention and Tradition in Economic Thought 1926–1939*. Cambridge: Cambridge University Press.

Skidelsky, R. (1992). *John Maynard Keynes, Volume II: The Economist as Saviour, 1920–1937*. London: Macmillan.

Solow, R., & Stiglitz, J. (1968). Output, Employment, and Wages in the Short Run. *The Quarterly Journal of Economics, 82*(4), 537–560.

Townshend, H. (1937). Liquidity-Premium and the Theory of Value. *Economic Journal, 47*, 157–169.

Wicksteed, P. H. (1933 [1910]). *The Common Sense of Political Economy*. London: George Routledge & Sons Ltd.

1

An Illusion of Order

Synopsis: The idea of natural, self-regulating order is one of the key elements underlying contemporary discourse about economic and social organisation. However, what exactly is meant by this is not altogether clear. Most of the time, when people refer to natural order they imply that if people were left to do that which they naturally are inclined to do, their activities will spontaneously be synchronised in the sense that they will all get that which they have reason to expect out of the system. We call such an order synchronic order as it synchronises the activities of individuals. However, there are two other elements which must be explored for such an order to have any meaning. Firstly, there is the question of whether natural synchronisation works with all sorts of human behaviour or that it only works with a particular type of behaviour. If so, is there a natural process which will equip individuals with the kind of behaviour necessary for such synchronisation to work? Secondly, once activities were synchronised, would individuals be content with the process and the outcomes (that which they have reason to expect) to an extent that they would feel the need neither to change their own behaviour nor to change the system? We call both these elements, which are required to support the synchronising ability of a natural order, 'diachronic order'. We use this term to tell us whether that which co-ordinates individual behaviour is something which is

© The Author(s) 2019
A. Witztum, *The Betrayal of Liberal Economics*,
https://doi.org/10.1007/978-3-030-10668-3_1

*sustainable over time (broadly conceived). Clearly, if there is a natural process which equips individuals with behaviour that will lead, without any intervention, to a co-ordination of their activities and where agents do not find the system as morally unacceptable, we can clearly declare that there is a natural, self-regulated order. In this chapter, we take a somewhat cursory meta-historic perspective on the evolution of the idea of natural order. We begin our journey in ancient times and find surprising similarities between some Chinese and Christian thinking about the idea of natural order. We argue that in both cases natural order is in the end an **ideal** and that individuals are required to behave in a manner which may not be natural to them so that natural order can lead to a co-ordinated outcome. As that which dictates how individuals should behave is derived from the ideal (and hence, constitutes a moral decree), such a system can be sustainable only if morality prevails and is unchanging. In such a case, there will be both synchronic and diachronic orders, but we must note that human nature is not part of the natural order itself. The Enlightenment in Europe changed all that as it brought to the fore the search for endogenous explanations such that were produced for the world of physics. In the social sciences, this amounts to an effort to emulate the notion of equilibrium in Newtonian Mechanics in the analysis of social interactions. However, now both human actions and the formation of morality become endogenous, which means that for a natural order to become both synchronic and diachronic, we must find a process that not only co-ordinates actions but also produces moral norms that support it. The difficulties are exposed at the outset when we begin by identifying Mandeville's famous paradox which juxtaposed the necessary conditions for an order to produce plenty with moral principles which are perceived to be natural too. We claim that classical economics responded to this dilemma by creating a system which closely connects the emergence of ethical ideas with the working of the system of natural liberty. This endogenisation of ethics—which I believe to be a logical imperative embedded in the idea of social natural order—allowed thinkers like Adam Smith to conclude that for all the wrong reasons, the system of natural liberty could work and temporarily appear as morally acceptable. However, in the long run, namely diachronically, such an arrangement is not sustainable as it will offend the foundation of our moral reasoning: our conscience. Modern economics chose a different route altogether. It simply chose to divorce itself from ethics. By claiming the economics is ethically neutral, it* *suggests that the idea of natural liberty in the sphere of economic activities is compatible with all possible social values or ethical principles. This very appealing idea led to the dominance of the modern economic paradigm which culminated in the spread of globalisation. However, even modern economics recognises that the conditions for the natural order to deliver a synchronised outcome, which is also ethically neutral, are not formed naturally. Therefore, the relentless pursuit of competitive decentralisation within economies and globally is more akin to a desire to implement an **ideal** rather than a plea to allow nature to take its course.*

*   *   *

Perhaps more than any century before it, the twentieth century was a stage for a colossal battle of ideas, the lines of which were clearly drawn in the second half of that century. From the perspective of economic and social organisation one can summarise this as the struggle between two extreme conceptions of economic (and social) order. At the one end stood the idea of a planned and controlled order subjugated to a perceived (usually, metaphysical) collective will as was manifested in the working of the Soviet bloc and China. At the other extreme lay the idea of a self-regulated system, a system of laissez-faire or natural order, an order that emerges naturally as individuals pursue their own natural interest and interact in a natural way (assumed to be competitive) with each other. The complete manifestation of the latter idea may not have fully materialised anywhere—and certainly not at all times—but it has been the clear aspiration and the driving force behind most Anglo-Saxon economies and in particular the USA and the UK.[1] The ultimate manifestation of this idea can be seen in the recent spread of globalisation, which is a clear attempt to expand this principle of economic organisation from individual

---

[1] Even though Krugman (2009b) laments the shifts in US politics towards neo-conservatism, even at its most compassionate form, the USA has always been totally and utterly committed to the idea of natural non-interventionist order. The New-Deal, it must be remembered, was not a change of *Weltanschauung* but an attempt to push the economy back to where the natural order can be restored. Equally, in spite of short outbursts of social interest, at the heart of the British system lies the idea of self-regulation and natural liberty.

societies to the world in its entirety.[2] In between, there were all those economies where an attempt was made to reconcile the two extremes by producing some form of a managed, or corrected, natural order in which the perception of the guiding collective will was neither metaphysical nor timeless.[3] Such forms of economic organisation—captured by the general heading of social democracy—could be found in most other Western European economies.

Towards the end of the twentieth century, with the collapse of the Soviet bloc and the adoption of some form of State Capitalism by China, it seemed that the battle had reached a conclusion. The winner, no doubt, has been the idea of natural, self-regulated order. But as the ideological battle lines had to be redrawn, an inevitable shift occurred even among those who were committed, as it were, to the middle ground. The political left in Western Europe, to some degree, had to redefine its opposition to the idea of natural order. In the past, the political battle lines seemed to have been drawn between those with total commitment to natural and spontaneous order and those who sought to limit it. The former saw no domain in the economy which could not be best dealt with by markets (perceived as the ultimate manifestation of the natural order). The latter argued that the market should be limited and that there are areas in the economy which would be best dealt with through government provisions which are more akin to the idea of planning and control—subject to a collective will—than to any notion of natural or spontaneous order. However, much of this has changed since the end of the war of ideas. Now, there remains a difference about whether there are areas in the economy for which markets may not be the right institutional framework, but instead of thinking of genuine institutional alternatives, the view seemed to have changed into public institutions that emulate the

---

[2] Recall that by globalisation we are referring in particular to the increase in the mobility of factors (capital and labour) rather than free trade in goods and services.

[3] The distinction between the Anglo-Saxon world and Continental Europe may not be entirely accidental. In very broad terms one can observe that the intellectual heritage of the former is far more empiricist in nature, while the latter tends more towards the rationalist. Subsequently, the individual plays a much greater role than the collective in the Anglo-Saxon traditions than it does in continental ones.

markets.[4] Namely, yes, there are areas where greater public involvement is required but such involvement should not be judged by other criteria than those we use to judge market performance. The extent to which this change took roots in different countries may be different but with the onslaught of globalisation—which is in itself a mark of the success of the natural order paradigm—it has become almost impossible to politically commit to any idea which is not market based or consistent with the rule of the markets. When a French president committed himself to increase the marginal tax rate for redistributional purposes, his critics argued that this will drive away all the entrepreneurial talent, which is exactly the reason why the UK government refuses to follow suit and which led a French economist to call for a global tax on capital.[5]

What were the exact reasons for the collapse of the Soviet bloc—and the victory of self-regulation—is not a simple question to answer and I have no intention of dealing with this here. There was evident economic decline in those countries, but it is not clear whether this decline and the prevailing general disaffection were due to the failure of the economic paradigm behind such systems or the fact that they seemed to have been coupled with extreme centralisation that is a necessity for tyranny. Be this as it may, we should focus our attention on the winning paradigm and here there are three immediate questions which follow from the success of the natural order doctrine: (a) What is actually the meaning of this idea of a self-regulated system or natural order paradigm? (b) What is the secret of its broad and apparently, almost universal, appeal? (c) What is the relationship between the principles of *economic* organisation and the principles of *social* organisation? Put differently, can any form of social organisation—which inevitably contains broader issues than, say, wealth creation—be consistent with the narrower concept of an economic

---

[4] There is, perhaps, no better example for this than the rise of New Labour in the UK. But there have been similar shifts among like-minded parties in other European countries. Though, in more recent times, the prolonged effects of the use of austerity as a means to resolve the problem created by the recent financial crisis have led to a revival in increased public spending, the idea that such monies should be spent according to efficiency and other markets criteria has not been abandoned.

[5] Thomas Piketty (2014) makes this call in his *Capital in the 21st Century*. The problem with such a call is that for a global tax to be levied there has to be a form of global governance. This, alas, is a question which goes well beyond the remit of economic expediency.

natural order? This third question is really part of what this book is all about and I will therefore defer dealing with it until later. At this stage, however, I would like to dwell a bit longer on the significance and appeal of the paradigmatic core behind the economic notion of self-regulated systems or, as it is sometimes referred to, the idea of natural liberty.[6]

1.1   Early Conceptions: A Conditioned Order

The idea of a natural order itself is not altogether new.[7] But what exactly is meant by natural order can sometimes be misleading. Lao-Tzu, who wrote the *Daodejing* and is considered one of the founder of Taoism (and was a contemporary of Confucius in the sixth century BC), argued that **the way** (the meaning of Dao) to a fulfilled life (happiness, or rather, contentment) is through a concept called *Wu-Wei*, which may literally translate as non-action but actually means acting in harmony with nature, being part, as it were, of the flow of reality. In Taoist philosophy, nature is, in essence, a balanced self-regulated system which through constant flows between opposites corrects and mends whatever needs to be brought back to harmony. So, the idea of a self-generating order is embedded in nature. By being one with nature individuals, as well as communities as a whole, would become part of this self-regulated and balanced system. In other words, the actual working of nature—that self-regulated natural order—constitutes both a *reality* and an *ideal*. As humans endeavour to become part of the flow, the ideal becomes a reality and nature succeeds in producing the balance between its various opposing forces. If, however, people choose to temper with the natural flow of things, the attempt will fail and will lead to ruin.[8]

---

[6] 'Natural liberty', the term more commonly used by classical economists, is perhaps a more accurate description of the idea. It simply means an order where things are left to themselves: where they are free to act naturally. It is important to understand that liberty here has nothing to do with the notion of human freedom. It is simply the idea of non-interfered order. At the same time, it is important to remember that an interfering order may itself be natural.

[7] See a discussion of the history of the idea in M. Rothbard (1990) and a more recent exposition of a more modern version of the idea as manifested in the notion of spontaneous order in Bowles (2004).

[8] See Chap. 21 in Daodejing (Ivanhoe, Philip J. (2002). *The Daodejing of Laozi*. New York: Seven Bridges Press).

But while there is no doubt that within this philosophy, nature is a self-regulated order that does not require any intervention, it is nonetheless an *ideal*. It is thus not entirely clear how people stand in relations to this order. If people too were part of nature, then people too would be subjected to the same forces of nature and would *naturally* tend to behave in a way which is consistent with it. In such a way, the harmony of nature (taken here in its physical sense) would naturally extend to human society. Nevertheless, at the same time, there is in Taoism a clear set of rules identifying the 'right' form of behaviour, that which would ensure both the order of nature and its extension to human society. However, if humans need to be instructed as to how to behave, one must wonder whether it is at all clear that people are *naturally* inclined to behave in this way. Would not this be an admission, that had people been left to themselves they would not have necessarily behaved in the 'right' way? Either way, even if people too were part of nature's balancing forces but still needed help, then it follows that nature, in general, needs a helping hand to achieve its apparent self-regulated order. Can this really be interpreted as a self-regulating system?

The evidence for this difficulty can be found in Lao-Tzu's baffling guidance to rulers. On the one hand, rulers are expected to be passive; they are expected not to seek prominence and to be, as it were, on the sidelines of society.[9] This is perfectly consistent with the view that the harmony of nature extends to humans and that they will naturally behave in the way which is consistent with the self-regulated natural order. On the other hand, however, rulers are also expected to keep people fed, keep them without knowledge and remove desires from them.[10] This, of course, suggests that people are exposed to temptations which may threaten the harmony of nature and lead, as we said, to ruin. Therefore, they seem to be, somehow, outside the domain of the *ideal* notion of nature's balancing order.

The implication of this is that of all the creatures of nature, humans are the only ones who have the capacity to ruin the natural balance, or order, which would have been created—naturally—without them. As they need to be taught how to behave in a 'natural' way, natural order can exist but will only materialise if people *believed* in it as an *ideal*. This, in turn, will

---

[9] See Chaps. 17 and 66.
[10] See Chaps. 65 and 3 respectively.

create a **moral duty** for them to behave in a manner which will allow this ideal to materialise.

Of course, one could argue that the development of the moral understanding of the natural ideal is in itself a natural process, but while this may be so under some interpretations of what one may mean by 'natural', this is far from intuitive or obvious to the modern observer. If it were natural for people to adopt the ideal of nature and to act in a way which supports it, there would be no need to guide, explain or intervene in the creation of the natural order. So there is a difference between natural order being an ideal or an ethical principle and the notion that a self-regulated order is indeed natural.[11] As far as this stage of human thought is concerned, it seems that the idea of self-regulation was more an aspiration—taken from the apparent reality of the natural (non-human) world—than a natural reality of human affairs.

This idea that there exists a self-regulated, or harmonious, social order which could be reached only if people acted in a particular way is intriguingly similar to the way scholastic thinking developed at the beginning of the Middle Ages in Europe. Perhaps the clearest manifestation of this is in St Augustine's *The City of God*.[12] St Augustine wrote his treaties after the fall of Rome to the hands of the Visigoths in 410 AD and it is believed that he wrote it in part as a response to claims about the role of Christianity in the demise of the eternal city. For St Augustine, there were two cities: an earthly city (Rome) and a Heavenly city (Jerusalem). The former was a city governed by human desire, wants and need, which are dominated by **human nature**. The latter was a city governed by the *ideal* of human behaviour dictated by the **author of nature**. When human behaviour diverges from the form of its ideal, the earthly city disintegrates and collapses. The nearer would human behaviour follow its ideal form, the longer will the city subsist.

While there is clearly a fundamental difference between the conception of the ideal in Taoism and Christianity, both ways of thinking seem

---

[11] The conundrum here is about the significance of a moral edict in a deterministic world. This problem, within the social sciences, reappeared centuries later in connection with the idea of scientific socialism.

[12] *The City of God Against the Pagans*. Translation by R. W. Dyson. New York: Cambridge University Press, 1998.

to face a similar kind of a problem: How does human nature fit, or relate, to that ideal? In Taoism, the ideal is nature itself but though it may be a natural process by which people discover the ideal, if things were left to themselves, it is not clear that this would indeed happen. So in a somewhat Rousseau-like fashion, in Taoism, people are expected to be forced to behave 'naturally'.[13] According to Lau-Tzu any deviation from the 'right' form of behaviour amounts to an attempt to temper with nature and, therefore, would only lead to ruin. In Christianity, the ideal lies outside of nature and is therefore more certain and stable than the turbulent nature we observe through our own eyes. But like Taoism, where nature seems to have difficulties taming human nature, here too the author of nature has difficulties taming humans.[14] Indeed, there are very clear rules of behaviour in Christianity which give humans the opportunity to depart from that which may be natural to them and to approximate that which they 'should' desire: the life of the Heavenly, eternal city. The behaviour of individuals without guidance or indoctrination, which leads to ruin in Taoism, will also cause the Christian earthly city to move further apart from its *Heavenly* blueprint and, thus, disintegrate and suffer the same fate as Rome. Therefore, one can conclude that in both traditions it is only through guidance and the adoption of a pattern of a preordained form of behaviour—which may not entirely be natural—that the social order can achieve its balanced and harmonious state.[15] In other words, in both traditions there seems to be a need to control what we would now consider to be human nature in order for a self-regulated system to emerge.

Both these cases help to highlight an important issue associated with the idea of a self-regulated order or any other idea of social order: its compatibility with human nature and its subsequent endurance. To help clarify this potential difficulty in understanding the idea of natural order,

---

[13] Paraphrasing on Rousseau's expectations that sometime one has to 'force freedom' on individuals. See, Rousseau, 1762, *The Social Contract* in (Gourevitch 2004) (1.7.7).

[14] We must not forget that the symmetry of the problem does not suggest symmetry of ideas. In Taoism, people have to be one with nature, while in Christianity we have to rise above nature.

[15] In Taoism, self-regulation is more evident as there is a constant balance between opposite forces. In Christianity, while in the earthly life there is a constant battle between good and evil, in the Heavenly city there is only harmony, which is by definition a self-regulated system though of a different nature.

I would like to propose a distinction between two important aspects of any idea of self-regulated social system, or natural social order. The first one I wish to call *synchronic order* and it is the one most people refer to today when they speak of 'natural order'. A synchronic order simply means that at any given social unit of time[16] the activities of all individuals[17] (namely, behaviour and interactions) coincide in such a way that people get from the system what they expect (or think they deserve), and there is no one who would wish to change the arrangement or interfere with another. For both Lao-Tzu and St Augustine, if people behave as they are supposed to behave, the order that will emerge will be such that it will be balanced as nature, or harmonious as Heaven. Individuals will find contentment and fulfilment, which is what they would expect from the system, and none of them would attempt to change the arrangement. It will be an order which synchronises human activities and it is for this reason I chose to call it synchronic order.

As we already noted, in both traditions there were some conditions for the self-regulated system to emerge. The question that arises is whether there is any natural (unguided) process which will ensure that these conditions are met. I would like to call this process *diachronic order*.[18] What I mean by this are two related issues. Firstly, I refer to whether there exists a process over a long period of time which explains the natural emergence of the synchronic order.[19] Secondly, I refer to the question of

---

[16] By synchronic I do not necessarily mean instantaneously or contemporaneously but rather a more 'socially' conceived unit of time which is more likely to be spanned over a number of years where agents can act, observe the outcomes of their actions, reflect on them and then either stay as they are or choose to change and act differently.

[17] Which we assume to be the atoms of the social system but this is by no means obvious and we will have to refer back to this question later.

[18] Notice that I use diachronic here to distinguish this from the 'dynamic'. To use modern terms to which I will return later, an economic system can be self-regulated in the sense that there exists a vector of prices where all rational wants coincide. There would also be a dynamic aspect to the system which will refer to how the system grows over time. By diachronic I am referring to the real long term when after living for a generation or so in a system which was in equilibrium and growing, we find ourselves in a position where the agents are unhappy about the outcomes of the system and as they change their attitude and behaviour, the synchronic order ceases to hold.

[19] An example of this can be seen in what has been happening more recently in economic analysis when scholars have tried to explain why people behave in a way which prevents the emergence of a prisoner's dilemma in a non-co-operative game. Some (Bowles and Gintis (2011)) suggest that there has been an evolutionary process which taught people to behave in a way that will avert a prisoner's

whether the synchronic order is sustainable over long period of time. What I mean by this is the question of whether once we are in a state of self-regulated order, changes could occur in individuals—who observe and experience the system—which could lead to its collapse.

As far as the first aspect of the diachronic order is concerned, the question is whether or not there is a natural process that will lead people to behave in such a way as to meet the necessary conditions for a self-regulated system to emerge. As Taoism takes its ideal from nature, one could argue that as people are part of nature they will naturally learn how to behave. Had this been the case then Taoism would be not only a synchronic order but also a diachronic one of both types. But as we said before, this is not really the case. People face temptations and they need guidance and indoctrination to grasp how they can live in harmony with nature. This means that there is no real natural process that will create the self-regulated system promised by the ideal of nature. It is true that Lao-Tzu gives clear instructions to rulers how to behave, but we are all aware of the fact that rulers in China did not act in this manner. They were greedy, interventionists and oppressive. Does this mean that the system created through such behaviour is not really natural? I suppose that one can say that it is not natural in the sense that it is not compatible with the idea of nature but there cannot be much doubt that it did develop naturally, or spontaneously.[20]

The same is true of the Christian system. As the ideal here lies outside of nature, there cannot even be pretence that there exists a natural process through which people will naturally acquire the right form of behaviour which will allow the earthly city to come closer to the Heavenly one. The actual development of political regimes across the globe that are not in the least associated with the development of the right form of human behaviour is, in fact, far more natural than the development of those institutions which may support either the ideal of nature or the Heavenly city.

---

dilemma and, thus, make the non-co-operative order work for the interest of the agents. The outcome of the game is the synchronic order while the process of learning to collude is the diachronic order. Whether this is a satisfactory story is something which we will discuss in detail in Chap. 7.

[20] A process where someone decides that he will make the decision for the group and others agree either because they think that person to be smart or because they are afraid of him is still a spontaneous natural order.

From the perspective of the second element of the diachronic order, in both Taoism and Christianity it is assumed that once we are in a self-regulated system of either nature or the Heavenly city, there is no obvious force which should undermine the system. In the Taoist world, the sustainability will be there due to the balancing actions of the opposite forces in nature. In Christianity, the order will be sustained because God will reward the behaviour at its core and there is nothing an individual can want more than God's approval. Therefore, in both systems there is clearly a synchronic order and diachronic order of the second type, but not necessarily of the first type.

The relationship between synchronic and diachronic orders is, in my view, of general significance to the question of the relevance of self-regulated systems. Leaving aside the two specific systems we briefly examined earlier, when we think that a system exists where the actions and interactions of all its elements (individuals) lead to an outcome where everyone gets what they can reasonably expect and no one has an incentive to instigate a change (i.e. synchronic order), we must always be able to answer the question of how such a system emerged and whether it is sustainable (diachronic order). As far as any social system is concerned, we need to explain how desires, opinions, character and subsequently institutions (broadly conceived) evolve and change over time. It may, on the one hand, explain the natural evolution of institutions which ensure and support a synchronic natural order but it may also explain the emergence of institutions which deliberately stifle synchronic natural order. Indeed, it is this evolution of institutions that many refer to when they speak today about the idea of spontaneous order. Most of the time, however, they connect spontaneous order with the evolution of institutions which support synchronic natural order.[21] Perhaps they do so because of a presumption that the diachronic and the synchronic must have the same logic. If there is a natural order in the sense that the behaviour and

---

[21] In modern discussions, spontaneous order is an alternative to the exogenous nature of laws and regulations as perceived in the Taoist tradition. In fact, it represents an extension of the idea of natural order to the diachronic aspect. By implications, institutions like Feudalism or prolonged dynastic rules are deemed as unnatural in essence and, therefore, not spontaneous. This is a complex issue which we will not explore here but the reader is encouraged to reflect on. In contemporary debates, the idea of spontaneous order is closely connected with the thinking of the Austrian school and, in particular, Hayek.

interaction of all elements are compatible, some may think that there will necessarily be a natural process that will recommend such behaviour to individuals. In other words, there may be a presumption that if institution develop naturally, they are also likely to support natural behaviour. However, as we saw in the two early examples we discussed above—not to mention looking around us today—this does not seem to be such a convincing conclusion.

Moreover, while in our example we saw that in both systems there would have been diachronic order of the second type—that once we are in the system there will be nothing to change the way people behave—in a more general context this is by no means a foregone conclusion. We must at all times be conscious of the possibility that a system, which may be in some kind of a synchronic order, may nevertheless disintegrate. The disintegration of the earthly city does not mean that there could not have been points in time when the earthly city was running smoothly in a well-co-ordinated order. However, the presumption in St Augustine's approach is that because people could not morally approve of the behaviour which is not following God's prescription, such a system cannot be sustained because people will find moral impropriety in that which facilitates the smooth running of the earthly city.[22] We can see similar issues today. For instance, the debate about self-regulation at the wake of the 2008 crisis has been mainly focused on the fact that market economies are dominated by large corporations which generate increasing inequality in both income and wealth. Some demand a response in government intervention and some would argue that these malaises (of large corporations and inequality) can be rectified. In other words, they do not believe that the presence of large corporations is a natural development within a system which offers synchronic order.

To some extent, one can compare the relationship between synchronic and diachronic orders to the relationship between mechanics and thermodynamics in physics. The simple equivalent to the idea of social synchronic order is the notion of equilibrium in mechanics. However, if this

---

[22] In the Appendix to this chapter, I provide an exposition of this point within the more traditional way in which the idea of spontaneous order has been more recently analysed, that is the framework of evolutionary games.

is a closed physical body, the laws of thermodynamic dictate that there will be a constant rise in entropy (the relationship between free energy and potential energy) which is a measure of dynamic disorder. It is true that physical elements are not going to have an opinion about the significance of the change in the level of entropy. But as the change in entropy is a significant change in the nature of the system, when the elements of the system (in the social system) recognise this, it may lead to the collapse of the order portrayed by the concept of equilibrium we borrowed from physics. This kind of process may very well be the one we currently observe with regard to the environmental debate. If we suppose for a moment—and this is something which we will discuss further in Chap. 2—that the economic system of the market is indeed a well-functioning, self-regulated natural order, then this is the equivalent notion to the physical concept of equilibrium in mechanics. The discovery that natural resources are overused is exactly and equivalent to the rise in the ratio of free energy to potential energy of the Earth. When the elements of the social system discovered that entropy is rising, they started to take measures to disturb the perceived well-functioning, self-regulating economic system.

Having said this it is important to bear in mind that in the early conceptions of self-regulated natural order, this latter development would have been considered as inconceivable. The second aspect of our diachronic test was guaranteed given the certainty attributed to nature or Heaven as an ideal. But when the ideal promises a self-regulated harmonious world, we must not overlook one important question: How had the *ideal* been formed in the first place? To be sure, this is part of what I have termed as the 'first aspect of the diachronic order', but so far we only focused on the question of whether there exists a natural process that will lead individuals to behave according to the blueprint of either systems. However, the far more fundamental question is whether the ideal itself was formed in some kind of a natural process or was it just the whims of someone yielding immense powers over others. In the latter case, it is not very reasonable to suppose that there will be any form of diachronic order. People would rather behave differently and are very likely to be unhappy with the outcome of their interaction within the dictated system. Maybe this is what happened in the Soviet bloc. But would people naturally come up with an ideal of nature, or Heaven, in the way Taoism and Christianity suggest?

While in the early stages, self-regulated natural order was an ideal, we have very little to go by in order to establish how did this ideal emerge. In more modern terms it is clear that the early conceptions of self-regulated natural order constituted a ***moral system***. They encompass in them what is good and right and what people ***ought*** to do in order to achieve that which the systems ***dictate*** as the fulfilment of life. Being an ultimate truth, it is easy to see why either Lao-Tzu or St Augustine would have concluded that people must naturally see the light and adopt the right form of behaviour. The fact that both required teaching and indoctrinating may be attributed to their impatience rather than their lack of confidence about the ultimate command which nature and Heaven will have over human thoughts or actions.

To some extent, one can see the difference between the ideal as a preordained or dictated principle, and a naturally created process, in the writings of the Greeks. Both Plato and Aristotle were concerned with the creation of the just society. In this sense, both of them recognise that the moral acceptability of social organisation is, perhaps, the most important element in its sustainability and success. Unless society is believed to be just, it will not endure (the second aspect of our concept of diachronic order). This, I hasten to say, is not very different from Taoism of Christianity. In both of these systems of thought, society will not subsist unless it is organised according to the ideal, which is, of course, the equivalent of the just society.

However, due to epistemological differences, Plato and Aristotle had very different ideas of (a) how the ideal, the just, is being identified and (b) what kind of institutional arrangements can be derived from it that will support the just, or good (in Aristotelian sense), life. Plato, who believed that we cannot trust our senses, contended that as the just is elusive we have to allow the people who can see it (the philosophers) to run society. The organisational principle of a hierarchal society which followed was as far as possible from the idea of a self-regulated natural order. At the same time, it is not clear, in Plato, whether people will naturally learn to trust the philosophers to tell them what is the just society. In this respect, Plato is still very much part of the early conception of social orders, though not with the early conception of self-regulated natural orders. He has an ideal and would wish people to be indoctrinated into it believing that once they are in such a system, though not a self-regulated system, it will nevertheless be sustainable. And like Lao-Tzu before him, or St Augustine after him, he cannot tell us whether there is a natural process which would lead for the ideal to emerge spontaneously.

On the other hand, Aristotle begins his inquire into what is just by trying to engage with public opinion. In other words, he is trying to establish the first aspect of our diachronic order by inquiring how moral opinions are being formed and by asking what is the prevailing moral opinion. When he discovers that the key to moral approbation is what he calls 'lying in the mean', or moderation, he sets out to create the institutions which will encourage the behaviour which is consistent with it. In his case, such a system is more akin to a self-regulated order but it is not clear whether the institutions of such a system can emerge spontaneously. Nor, for that matter, do we have enough to judge whether that which is considered as morally good may or may not change over time.

Nevertheless, in essence, Aristotle represents a change. In spite of the fact that his methods were adopted whole heartedly by scholastic thinkers, it is the case that in Aristotle there is at least an attempt to extract the ideal from reality rather than to presuppose it. In this respect, Aristotle contains the seeds of what is going to become the most important part of the modern conceptions of self-regulated natural order: the endogeneity of ethics.

1.2   Post-Enlightenment Developments: Internalised Conditionality

The roots of the modern conceptions of self-regulated natural order are derived, no doubt, from the revolutionising effects of the Enlightenment. One aspect of this revolution can be characterised as a move away from preordained ideals which serve as an exogenous reference point towards a more endogenous analysis based on reason or experience. Within the European traditions this meant a move from explaining nature and natural phenomena as a manifestation of the will of God to an explanation of nature which is intrinsic to nature itself. For instance, explaining the movements of objects in space based on gravity rather than God's will or, in a more prosaic way, explaining tempests as a result of pressure differences rather than God's wrath. None of this has any direct implication for the question of God's existence but it does allow humans to interfere more easily with the working of nature without a sense of impropriety.

At first, the move towards endogenous explanations was focused on the physical (non-human) world. But inevitably it spread into the social world too. In exactly the same manner as the physical world can be explained—by experience and reason—as reaching a sustained and clearly observable order through the balance of the activities of all its components (equilibrium), so can, perhaps, sustained social order be explained—again, through experience and reason—as resulting from the balanced interaction of its own elements.[23] Nevertheless, the starting point for the social order analysis is somewhat different from that of the physical world. Emancipating human thinking from the perception that the physical world is a manifestation of God's will is not exactly the same as emancipating it from the claim that the social world is a manifestation of it. While the elements of the physical world have no will of their own, humans are perceived to be in possession of such a will. This, inevitably, complicates things immensely.

Now, in both examples of the early conceptions of self-regulation and harmony we saw that a problem existed with regard to the relationship which individuals had with the ideal system. While a synchronic order is always conditioned on the diachronic one, we could not identify a clear natural process that will ensure the first aspect of the diachronic order in formulating the ideal. Namely, there was no clear explanation, based on reason or experience, which could tell us why individuals may or may not subscribe to the behaviour which will allow the self-regulated system to emerge. This was true of both systems, the one in which nature constituted the ideal and the other where the ideal was outside nature.

The moment we move away from any ideal, or an exogenous explanation, we must find an endogenous explanation, based on reason and expe-

---

[23] This does not necessarily mean that the elements themselves are individuals or that the analysis should be based on empiricist epistemology.

rience, which ties together the two aspects of the diachronic order with the synchronic one. We must find an internal explanation that will connect human nature with the traits in human character that allow the compatibility of all actions and interactions such that individuals will be naturally content with the outcome and would not wish to bring about a change.

The development of Newtonian mechanics gave the impression that emancipating the world from divine or exogenous explanations would lead to ideas of self-regulated systems (embedded in the notion of equilibrium). But this is not really the case when we come to deal with the social world. Finding a reasoned explanation to the way in which people interact with each other—the equivalent of the Newtonian idea of classical mechanics—is not enough to form a social theory. One would also need to find an intrinsic theory of how people form moral opinions and, subsequently, social institutions.[24] It is difficult to imagine a social order emerging where people are content with the material—physical—results of their interactions but are at odds with the morality of the actions which govern the system and lead to its material success. In other words, it would be difficult to sustain a social order when there may be a synchronic order in the world of material wellbeing but not a diachronic one.

Having said this we must bear in mind that the move towards an endogenous social theory does not necessarily mean that religion-based morality becomes obsolete. As I suggested earlier, spontaneous orders do not necessarily lead towards institutions and morality which support a natural synchronic order. When Hobbes proposes a reasoned argument for why people may enter a social contract in which they forgo most of

---

[24] One example of this difficulty can be seen in the distance between the application of the idea of spontaneous social contract in Hobbes and in Locke. The former assumes the atoms of society to be individuals who have particular properties and enter a social contract as a means of escaping the dangers of living alone and at each other's mercy. The morality that stems from this is very limited indeed and is only encapsulated in the right to rebel against the tyrant if he does not provide the security for which people entered the social contract. At the other end, we have Locke where the agents of society, again the individual, have a Spinozian property in the sense that they enter the social arrangement to allow the divine reflection in them to be fulfilled. Spinoza, which led the way directing human inquiry from universals (like God) to the particular (like individuals), insisted that the move away from the universal (i.e. the divine explanation) can only work if the manifestation of that universal in the particular (individuals) is taken into consideration. There was no such universal in Hobbes but there was one in Locke. The kind of social contract which logically emerges from these two extremes is quite different.

their rights—interpreted here as those things they had in the state of nature—the morality which must be embedded in it will be such that will, as he himself did, support the institution of absolute monarchy. While the natural state is hypothetical, it is still an explanation of morality and society which is based on reason and experience. In other words, the fact that society may emerge as a result of some sort of spontaneous order does not mean that the morality that will develop within it would necessarily support a synchronic order or natural liberty. Unlike the world of physics, while discovering new explanations to how a system can work may be easy, changing the contents of morality may prove to be more difficult. This is particularly so if one allows for the fact that, say, religion-based morality in itself developed spontaneously.

Not surprisingly, therefore, at the very early stages of the development of the idea of social self-regulation or natural order this tension between the moral and the effective, the diachronic and the synchronic respectively, immediately came to the fore. In 1714 Mandeville published his famous *Fable of the Bees: or Private Vice, Public Benefits*, which was considered scandalous at the time. In it, Mandeville claims that it is only through the **uncensored** vice of private desires that prosperity can be **naturally** achieved[25]:

> Fraud, Luxury, and Pride must live;
> Whilst we the Benefits receive. (p. 23)

Though Mandeville is not directly concerned here with the question of a co-ordinated outcome, he clearly believes that an unregulated system (i.e. a natural order) would be beneficial in the sense that it will create wealth which everyone desires. Morality here is clearly a restrictive regulatory force. But the question one faces is, on what grounds do we think that these are indeed private vices? If society can only produce prosperity by allowing people to behave in a particular manner—which seems to be natural to them—would this manner of behaviour not become morally

---

[25] Mandeville is not directly concerned with what we may call spontaneous order but his claim is basically synonymous in the sense that he suggests that allowing people to behave as they are naturally inclined without condemning it morally will produce an unintended outcome of a desired social consequence: prosperity.

good? Naturally, the answer to this question depends on where morals come from. From the religious perspective, it is difficult to see how 'fraud, luxury and pride' can be anything but vices. But the origin of the morality in this case is perceived to be exogenous, divine. Moreover, even though it may have been derived in some natural process (probably based on fear), it may not have been based on what we now understand. But if we move towards a more endogenous morality which is based on what we observe or experience and about which we can reason, would this lead us to change our views about luxury and pride? One could argue, for instance, in a somewhat utilitarian fashion, that the moral value of things depends entirely on their consequences. In such a case, if our experience tells us that fraud, luxury and pride produce prosperity, which we observe to be desired by everyone, should they not be deemed as virtues rather than vices?[26] This, of course, is not the only way to form an endogenous theory of ethics, and Mandeville's own position on this is not entirely clear, though he was clearly understood by many at the time as a sceptic who thought that reason and experience cannot be reconciled with religion.[27] In somewhat less deterministic terms, what he actually observed was that the diachronic order—that which emerged from the process that formulates the moral views of individuals (and, subsequently, social institutions)—was incompatible with the synchronic order which reason discovered. But the reason for Mandeville's sneers is probably due to the fact that we have not endogenised morality yet; we have not made morality the subject of experience and reason.[28] Would this necessarily harmonise

---

[26] Of course, we assume that the desire for the accumulation of material wealth (to neutralise the moral significance of 'prosperity') is indeed widely spread. Had this not been the case, 'fraud, luxury and pride' could become—endogenously—moral vices.

[27] It is not simple to ascertain Mandeville's real intention, who in addition to the *Fable* also wrote *An Enquiry into the Origins of Moral Virtues*. His position between the *Deists*—who saw no contradiction between experience, reason and God—and the *Sceptics* of his time has not been well established. See for instance, H. Munro. (1975). *The Ambivalence of Bernard Mandeville*. Oxford: Clarendon Press as well as the introductory comments on Mandeville's thought by F B Kaye in the *Liberty Classic* edition.

[28] It is interesting to note here that much later Weber seemed to connect Protestant ethics with the emergence of the capitalist system. On the face of it this seems to be an opposite position to the one taken by Mandeville but we must bear in mind that what Weber had in mind is the work ethic of individuals. However, willing to work hard does not necessarily mean that the system would produce the appropriate or just rewards. So the question Weber had posed is the reversed one: Would

the ethical with the expedient? Would this necessarily produce a synchronic order which is consistent with the diachronic one? The idea of natural order developed rapidly since the time of Mandeville through the works of scholars like Quesnay, Turgot and the physiocrats in France. But Mandeville's gauntlet—juxtaposing social norms and natural order—was picked up by members of the Scottish Enlightenment and in particular by Adam Smith, who is, no doubt, the pillar of what became to be known as classical economics. What is particularly interesting about this is the way in which modern economists see Adam Smith. Being mostly unaware of Mandeville's paradox, they nevertheless see in him someone who has effectively resolved it and opened the way for economic analysis to be conducted in the way that it is done today.[29] For contemporary economists, Adam Smith is first and foremost the father of economics as an *independent* discipline. As such, it may offer a potential solution to the tension between morality and expediency by separating the fields altogether. The understanding of how the natural order works in creating wealth could be done independently of any moral or social considerations. As such, modern economists see in Smith's theory and classical economics in general as precursors to their own understanding of how the system operates.[30] However, even those economists who seek to isolate the study of economics realise that it cannot be a sustainable arrangement if it is based on what is considered by everyone as moral

---

natural liberty of hard-working and honest individuals produce a morally acceptable distribution of rewards?

[29] On the occasion of the bicentennial of the *Wealth of Nations*, James Buchanan wrote: 'Adam Smith's system of natural liberty, interpreted as his idealized paradigm for social order, embodies justice as well as economic efficiency' (Buchanan 1978, p. 77). On a similar occasion, George Stigler of the Chicago school is quoted to have said: 'I bring greetings from Adam Smith who is alive and well and is living in Chicago' (Meek 1977, p. 3). Ronald Meek, who accounts for Stigler's declaration and can by no means be associated with the mainstream of economic thinking, goes on to say: 'Smith's great message of good cheer that competitive capitalism is, if not the best of all economic systems, at any rate the best of all possible systems' (ibid., p. 4). Milton Friedman, whose views on natural liberty need no proof (see his own book on *Capitalism and Freedom*), has taken Smith's ideas ad absurdum. He wrote, 'on the moral level, Smith regarded sympathy as a pervasive human characteristic, but it was unlimited and thus had to be economized. He would have argued that the invisible hand of the market was far more effective than the visible hand of government in mobilizing, not only material resources for immediate self-seeking ends, but also sympathy for unselfish charitable ends' (Friedman 1978, p. 18).

[30] Robbins, for instance, goes as far as to suggest that Smith's system stands 'in harmony, with the most refined apparatus of the modern School of Lausanne' (Robbins 1935, pp. 68–69).

vice. As Smith was first and foremost a moral philosopher, he is also considered by many as the person who resolved the Mandevillian paradox by demonstrating that not only can natural order produce wealth but that the individual trait which is the engine behind it—self-interest—is not really a moral vice.

There can be little doubt that Adam Smith is the right place to search for the origin of the resolution of Mandeville's paradox as well as of some elements of the modern position on the relationship between synchronic and diachronic order. Being part of the Scottish Enlightenment, Adam Smith conceived philosophy in general and moral philosophy in particular, as science. This means that at least from a methodological perspective he was in a position to endogenise not only the order which creates wealth but also the order which generates—in a natural way—social values, conventions, morality and, subsequently, institutions.

For this reason, Adam Smith is not exactly what modern economists make of him. Indeed, the question of the relationship between ethic, social institution and the economic order in his writings has been a subject of intense debates which are still going on today but of which most modern economists are completely oblivious. Perhaps the simplest way of understanding the complexity of Smith's position is by referring to two quotes from his *The Theory of Moral Sentiments* (published in 1759). In the first one Smith argues that human beings are naturally social creatures who 'stand in need of each other's assistance' (TMS, p. 85). But it is the way in which this 'necessary assistance' is being provided that tells us about human character and the kind of society that will emerge. Smith proposes two possible frameworks of social organisation which are both natural and **viable**. The first is where the 'necessary assistance is provided from generous and *disinterested* motives', and the second is where such assistance is provided for its utility, by means of 'mercenary exchange' (in other words, from *interested* motives). The former is an 'agreeable and happy state', and the latter is viable but unhappy state. A third, non-viable state is when individuals are willing to hurt each other at all times.

It is important to say that while all three states are possible and natural, only one of them will materialise. Put differently, Smith was aware of the complexity of the human character and the different forces which operate on it. According to him, people have in them the capacity to provide the mutual assistance out of benevolence, self-interest as well as in harmful ways. Social conventions which give rise to the idea of justice will deter the latter form of behaviour to take roots, but the two other forms of behaviours are subject to competing influences. Our morality—formed in a natural process—may direct us towards the benevolent provision of mutual assistance, but nature itself—the physical world, or the instinctive side of humanity—may push us towards the self-interested kind of behaviour which will ensure an accumulation of wealth consistent with nature's own evolutionary goals. Put differently, it is all a question of rewards: harmful behaviour is punished and, therefore, deterred; self-interest is naturally well rewarded but benevolence is not. It is, perhaps, the role of the human spirit to reward that which nature itself fails to reward and Adam Smith was quite explicit in his argument that the natural outcomes of the natural pursuit of self-interest is not consistent with good morals.

There can be little doubt that the *Wealth of Nations* (1776) is an exploration of the 'mercenary exchange' rather than the 'reciprocally afforded' assistance 'from love, from gratitude, from friendship, and esteem'. It is therefore a description of the less happy of the only two viable social states. Does it resolve Mandeville's paradox? It does in the sense that Smith seems to reject the idea that it is the excesses of one's pursuit of one's interest which are the necessary building blocks of the wealth generating natural order. Instead, it is the moderate pursuit of one's own interest which will yield the *natural*[31] accumulation of wealth and which would not be morally condemned. But while its economic benefits may be clear, it is the same kind of human character which will also create a society that is in principle viable but not particularly happy (and, therefore, may not be sustainable).[32] It is also the trait which nature—the physical world in Smith's eyes—rewards handsomely, though humanity may not wish to be so generous with it. So, while Smith resolved the Mandevillian paradox in the sense that prosperity does not have to be a

---

[31] Meaning here, without any intervention.

[32] In this context, being a 'happy state' is a necessary condition for the second element of diachronic order. Alternatively, if a natural self-regulated system of self-interested people generates wealth but people are unhappy, they are likely to produce changes that may interfere with the natural order of things.

result of a moral vice, he proposed a new difficulty: prosperity may be costly. By rewarding the behaviour which generates material wellbeing through the system of natural liberty, society confines itself to the less happy of the two possible social states[33]? Whether such costs are sustainable over time (diachronically) remains an open and debated question.

Indeed, even if the pursuit of self-interest yields a prosperous coordinated outcome (synchronic order), whether or not such a system becomes acceptable does not rest only on whether the motives behind the pursuit of wealth are morally acceptable; it also depends on whether the outcome of the system is morally acceptable. From Mandeville's perspective, there was no need to be concerned about it as the system was condemned from the outset. But removing the illegitimacy of the driving force behind the system requires clear answers about the moral acceptability of the system in terms of its consequences. While people may morally approve the pursuit of one's self-interest or the pursuit of wealth, the distribution of income and wealth which will be generated through such *free* pursuits may not necessarily be morally acceptable.[34] In other words, the fact that we may approve of allowing people to pursue their own interest does not necessarily mean that we should allow such behaviour to be unregulated or uncontrolled.

In the case of Smith there were at least two reasons why the free reign of unregulated pursuit of one's self-interest may not command moral

---

[33] The idea of social cost exists, in a different format, in modern welfare economics where we are sometimes paying in efficiency terms to get what is socially desirable. However, this is normally the case when we have no means (like lump-sum transfers) to achieve what is known as the first best where expediency and social choice coincide. In other terms, it is still the case that at the limit, social desires and efficiency coincide. In the case of Smith, it was not a question of degree. The free rein of mercenary exchanges which facilitates prosperity comes at the expense of social cohesion and a potential chronic dissonance between our moral principles and that which generates prosperity. The difference between this and Mandeville is that the forces behind prosperity are not deemed as vice but the good is not achieved either.

[34] Some may argue that if the outcome is not morally approved, then someone may try to change it. Namely, if there is synchronic order, it means that no one is trying to change the outcome. This seems to suggest that synchronic order implies a diachronic one. While there is some truth in it, there is a difference between one's moral opinions and one's immediate actions. People may not like what the economy dishes out to them but they will nevertheless play along as the alternative may be much worse for them. This does not mean that they approve the outcome, but they may not be able to act against it in the short run. In the long run, of course, the accumulation of resentment is bound to have an influence on the system and, subsequently, on the question of whether we accept the synchronic order.

approbation. The first is Smith's dismissive views on the meaning of 'wealth', and the second is his approach to its natural distribution (i.e. the distribution that results from natural liberty). Wealth is trifle, he argues, but its apparent appeal serves as a means by which nature, in its physical manifestation, *deceives* people to want it, to pursue it and, consequently, to advance the purpose of nature: the multiplication of the species. However, people's interests are not necessarily the same as those of nature: 'man is by Nature', writes Smith, 'directed to correct, in some measure, the distribution of things which [nature] herself would otherwise have made' (TMS, p. 168).[35] This means two things: firstly, that the smooth functioning of nature (the distribution that results from natural liberty) is not necessarily consistent with what people might perceive as the desired distribution[36]; secondly, that which people think as desirable may be a result of a *deception* by nature. Smith the observer is not imposing his own idea of what should or should not be. Instead, what he does is to say that if people took to the logical limit the way in which they form moral opinions, they will find that what they should think is not always the same as what they do think.[37]

The consequence of all this is that while Smith resolved the Mandevillian paradox by saying that there is a connection between the way people form moral opinions and what drives their behaviour in their pursuit of their own interests, he posed a new problem. A natural order driven by self-interest may be considered as socially desirable by corrupt moral sentiments of its members. Yet it would not have been approved if they had

---

[35] It should be noted that Smith uses three concepts of nature: 'nature of things', 'nature of sentiments' and 'Nature'. The first two are the more frequently used and they refer to the physical world and the spiritual world of mankind respectively. The third form, Nature, is probably the uniting force which is God or, as some would interpret it, the 'Great Design'. The important thing here is that the objectives of nature and those of Nature—our spiritual ones—are not necessarily compatible.

[36] 'Thus he who as it were supports the whole frame of society and furnishes the means of the convenience and ease of all the rest is himself possessed of a very small share and is buried in obscurity' (*Lectures on Jurisprudence*, p. 341).

[37] To some extent this is similar to modern economics. Firstly, we presume that people would have acted rationally even if, as a matter of fact, they do not. And, more importantly, as will be explored later, the existence of the synchronic order (general equilibrium) is also demonstrated at the logical limit. Interestingly, this idea is much closer to what Kant called later the Categorical Imperative, which is, of course, more rationalist than empiricist in nature.

followed their conscience (the reasoned views of an 'impartial observer'). In other words, while he suggested that self-interest may be morally acceptable, accumulating wealth through natural liberty may nonetheless, in the long run, become an unsustainable social order when people begin to realise the powers of nature's deception.[38] In terms of what we said earlier, it means that the redemption of the motives that produce a natural (synchronic) order does not guarantee the diachronic order.

The relationship between economics and the other dimensions of social theory have been the subject of considerable developments during the nineteenth century. At the one end, we have the subsuming of all aspects of social life into economic reasoning as manifested in the thinking of Marx. At the other end, we have J. S. Mill with the idea of ceteris paribus, which acknowledges that there are conditions and circumstances which may justify an isolated examination of economic relationships but not without reference to and, in the long term, interaction with, those other elements of social analysis which, ostensibly, are held constant.[39] In fact, in Mill we can find the clearest expression of the dialogue between the economic and the social spheres through his conception of ethology (or character formation) and individual development. Accordingly, human character develops in response to circumstances and the competitive phase is only an early expression of it. As people's individuality develops, he claimed, so will their co-operative tendencies as well as their appreciation of non-material aspects of their wellbeing. These, of course, will have tremendous implications for the way the economic system should be organised.

In between the two extremes of Marx and Mill, we have August Comte and the German Historical School, which denied the possibility of separating the various elements of social phenomena (Mill) and would certainly object to subjugating everything to economic reasoning (Marx). But whatever position one held, there was a clear understanding that one cannot conduct economic analysis without any reference to the social and ethical context. This was obviously true for those whom we

---

[38] Smith's position on these matters is much more subtle and complex and we will return to it in greater details in Chap. 8.

[39] We will explore this issue in more details towards the end of Chap. 7.

would call socialists but it was equally true for those whom we would call liberals.

1.3 The Modern Era: Idealised Realism

Jumping ahead to modern times and all the complexity and subtlety of Smith and the classical economists have disappeared. We find ourselves dominated by a rather elegant yet fairly narrow extension of the treatment in the *Wealth of Nations* of those mercenary exchanges without any reference or resort to the moderating powers of *The Theory of Moral Sentiments* to guide us in an attempt to understand and evaluate the social context or the social cost of allowing a natural order in the creation and accumulation of wealth. Instead, the *Wealth of Nations* is perceived to be a depiction of a self-contained natural order where its sustainability is rooted in its own beneficial outcomes (the accumulation of wealth). The transition, one must note, is quite recent. With the development of neo-classical economics, even Walras—who developed the mathematical theory of general equilibrium—insisted on the broader context of economic analysis. He saw his *Economie Sociale* and *Economie Applique* as essentials in the study of economics as much as his *Elements d'Economie Politique Pure*. Interestingly, to date only the *Elements of Pure Economics* has been translated into English. Not much remains of Walras's excursions into social and moral issues in the contemporary discourse over his idea of general equilibrium—the modern conception of synchronic order or the co-ordinating power of the natural order. Arrow and Debreu (1954), who gave the final touches to the idea of general equilibrium—the point where the idea of social natural order at last meets (at least in name) the full achievement of Newtonian Physics—have not really added volumes which can constitute the equivalents of either *The Theory of Moral Sentiments* or Walras's *Economie Sociale* and *Economie Politique et la Justice*.

But this has not been entirely a sin of omission. While there are good reasons to question the scholarship of many modern economists and their familiarity with the Smithian or Classical project, in the end there was a plan behind this development. In 1932 Robbins wrote *An Essay on the Nature and Significance of Economic Science*. In it, he implicitly proposes a way out from all the agonising deliberations embedded in the Mandevillian dilemma and the Smithian attempt to form a social theory where the diachronic and synchronic orders emanate from the same origins and interact with each other. He proposed the complete divorce between economics and any other aspect of social studies. The study of an economic synchronic order is universal and neutral to ethics and, therefore, consistent with all possible conceptions of the latter. After all, an effective use of limited resources is what every society needs regardless of its culture or social values.

This, of course, was an entirely novel approach. Unlike Mill who was content to allow the separate study of economics conditioned on the properties of the other parameters representing social life that are held constant, for Robbins those parameters did not matter at all. Economic analysis, according to him, is both universal and value free and, by implication, relevant to all possible forms of social organisation. While it took some time for economists to adopt this approach, it has very much been present in most economic textbooks for a very long time.

Perhaps one of the most recent expressions of this very same idea can be found in the publication by Acemoglou and Robinson (2012) of their book about *Why Nations Fail*[40] in which they claim that there is only one kind of economic institutions that can guarantee economic (and, by implication, social) success and that these institutions are, in principle, suitable for all societies. In other words, societies must have the right political institutions which will allow for the right form of economic organisation to emerge and that this 'right' form of organisation is both universal and independent of specific social values (or culture).[41] They

---

[40] They are, of course, not the only ones to celebrate the great success and universality of the idea of natural liberty. See also Phelps (2013) and Deaton (2013).

[41] While Acemoglou and Robinson make much of their claim for the endogeneity of institutions, what they really mean by this is political machination. In other words, they acknowledge that different societies will not have the required institutions because of political reasons, but they also suggest that any society, the moment it acquires these specific institutions, would flourish regardless of whether the cultures of all societies are conducive to the success of such institutions. In their 2016 paper they berate Piketty as well as Marx (?!) for their determinism and lack of attention to the endogeneity of institutions but they themselves think that competitive institutions will make all societies flourish regardless of their cultural differences. They are clearly not deterministic but they are very much monolithic.

argue that throughout history it has been repeatedly observed that societies that adopted what they call non-extracting, or inclusive, institutions succeeded in the sense that they generated prosperity. In general, the idea of non-extracting institutions is aimed at the prevention of corrupt elites from stifling the engine of growth by securing the property rights of innovators and the competition between able citizens. Put differently, the main element of non-extractive institutions—which connects them with prosperity—is that they protect the returns which people may receive for the application of their personal abilities, or that they do not allow elites or people with power to command the fruits of other people's labour. In other words, non-extractive institutions are really none other than the institutions which allowed the natural order to prevail in the sense that people should be allowed to act freely on their natural interests and keep the returns on their actions (and, in particular, their entrepreneurial activities) without fearing anyone extracting any surplus from them.[42] On the face of it, this looks like an innocent positive statement but this is quite misleading. First of all, we have to accept that material prosperity is indeed a universal objective.[43] Secondly, by claiming that in whatever circumstances societies which adopted such institutions succeeded, the authors are implicitly saying that given that at different times and differ-

---

[42] Non-extractive institutions are really about the absence of rent-seeking, which means that the institutional set-up is such that neither the institutions nor anyone else can extract the returns which are specific to the activities and abilities of an agent. The general gist of this requirement is indeed a code for natural order as it suggests a world where the returns to individuals' specific actions should be protected. This also implies that governments' ability to raise taxes should be restricted. While taxation is not really rent-seeking, it does affect the returns to efforts and to the application of human capital. Therefore, it is inconceivable to imagine non-extractive institutions with high level of taxation even if the decision to tax is reached democratically in what they call inclusive political framework. After all, even modern economics admits that when people vote for higher tax, they will still respond in the same manner to its application: reduce their effort (at both ends of the redistribution cycle). This means that effectively a collective decision to tax or an elite commandeering someone's due share will amount to the same thing: extracting institutions; unless, of course, one is willing to distinguish between motives and incentives—which will be discussed later on in this book—but then the presumption of universality is less likely to hold.

[43] In their analysis, Acemoglou and Robinson claim that the reason why there are so few societies that adopted these institutions—and, therefore, are not prosperous—is because the elites are bound to lose from a change that will shift economic power away from them and, therefore, they will object to such changes. However, they do not contemplate the possibility that some societies may not value material prosperity in the same ways as others. And if they did, this may not be enhanced through private enrichment.

ent places there would be different social and cultural environments, the success of *proper* laissez-faire (embodied in the idea of non-extractive institutions) is guaranteed irrespective of cultural and social differences.

In Mandevillian terms this means that societies which allowed at least luxury and pride—associated with the idea of selfish or self-interested behaviour—to reign freely will always prosper and flourish.[44] Or, to put it in Mandeville's own terms[45]:

> Millions endeavouring to supply
> Each other's lust and vanity ....
> Thus every part was full of vice
> Yet the whole mass, a paradise

The novelty embedded in the modern approach is that Acemoglou and Robinson would have removed the third line. They make no claim about whether endeavouring to supply each other's lust and vanity is a moral vice. In fact, they do not seem to be in the least interested in what people may think of allowing others to pursue their own interests undisturbed. By claiming that *throughout history and across cultures* it is only in the presence of non-extractive institutions (and, by implications, the prevalence of proper laissez-faire) that prosperity has been achieved, they are implying that the success of the natural (synchronic) economic order is independent of any particular moral or cultural position and, thus, morally neutral. Without explicitly admitting this, they have adopted Robbins's approach to the resolution of Mandeville's paradox rather than the Smithian or Classical one. It is as if they are saying that Mandeville was right to suggest that allowing the free reign of selfish behaviour would produce prosperity but he was wrong to think that this poses a dilemma. In fact, they seem to be completely oblivious to the problem of diachronic order or the need for moral acceptability of a synchronic order for it to

---

[44] Naturally, the question whether one can distinguish between self-interest and selfishness is crucial and we shall deal with this later, but it is clear that for modern economists this does not matter at all.

[45] The first two lines are from page 18 and the remaining two from page 24 in Mandeville (1988 [1732]).

persist over time. A possible explanation to this is that in their mind synchronic order generates its own persistence. In the long run, when people see the benefit of allowing the free rein of self-interest, they will learn to love it. Unlike Smith where that which drove the material world was closely associated with that which drove the moral one, here, all of a sudden, we have a sequential approach: the origins of moral values are in the successes of the material world. The mere achievement of synchronic order generated a diachronic order. After all, who can object to prosperity? So, if we started with Mandeville, who expressed concern about the co-existence of morality and material expediency, we ended up in a place where expediency implicitly took over morality.

But it is not really that Acemoglou and Robinson claim that ethics should be subjected to economic expediency. This may have been outrageous but at least, to some extent, potentially logical. Instead, they follow Robbins's line. In their story—where natural order was effective throughout history and across cultures—the natural order is consistent with all possible forms of morality as it is independent of them. At the same time, however, they do not believe that the non-extracting institutions emerge spontaneously. Namely, not all societies would naturally develop these institutions. In part, this would inevitably be so due to cultural differences which may as well entail different moral systems. But they do believe that if such institutions were imposed on these cultures, they would nevertheless be successful regardless of their moral systems and corresponding institutions. Presumably, the argument behind it is that all cultures can adjust to the benefits of natural order. Mandeville may have mocked the religiously based ethical system but he knew that as long as it is in place prosperity which emanates from what is considered as vice will not materialise or, at least, cannot be sustained (it is not a natural diachronic order). If we take the argument of Acemoglou and Robinson to the limit, then they would have us believe that even if the engine of prosperity is morally reviled, the system can still succeed.

So, the question is how did we get from an understanding that social order is a delicate balance between various aspects of human interactions and values to a belief that we can treat one aspect of it in complete isolation from the rest[46]? But not only that, that thing—the natural order in the pursuit of wealth—is universal and should be applied in all societies as well as become the foundation of a global order. Have we really resolved Mandeville's dilemma by following Robbins and simply separate completely expediency from ethics? Alternatively, are we really prepared to completely subjugate ethics to expediency? Have we decided to completely ignore the contributions of Smith and the classical economists to this question? In other words, what is it that allows us to separate the question of synchronic order from that of the diachronic one? I am not asking these questions from a historical perspective, which is, of course, tremendously important, but rather from an analytical one. What is it about our understanding of the world that led to this dramatic change in the way we understand the working of economics and its position within society? Is it a reasonable way of thinking both in the sense of its internal logic and its applicability? Is it a more convincing way of thinking than the logical systems, like that of Smith and the entire classical school, which stuck with the Mandevillian underlying understanding that there cannot be synchronic order without a diachronic one? That the application of reason to the way in which people behave cannot be isolated from the application of reason to the way in which they form moral opinions and social institutions? Are we, today, better thinkers than those who insisted that economic institutions cannot be divorced from ethical systems that underlie all social institutions?

Some economists may argue that this is all a storm in a teacup. They would insist that they have nothing to say about the Mandevillian dilemma nor have any views about ethics. The only thing they claim is that certain institutional arrangements, which allow people to do what they normally desire, will lead to prosperity. Whether societies wish to adopt such institutions is entirely up to them. This, ostensibly, is the 'positive' nature of economic reasoning. But there is a strange implicit assumption here that ethics—or the formulation of normative judgements—is not as natural as the pursuit of one's own desires or that we

---

[46] I am not referring here to the methodological debate about whether one can analyse economics while assuming other things being equal (the *Methodenstreit*) but to the question of whether the contents of those other things matter or not. I shall explore these issues in detail in later chapters.

cannot make positive statements about ethics. While it is true that ethics is about what is good or bad and, hence, normative, there is a real, positive process—an emerging, and sometime spontaneous, order—whereby these ideas are formed. To suggest that allowing the natural order in the pursuit of wealth to prevail will neither be affected by prevailing social values nor influence them means that economists would like to believe in 'half positive' statements. The interaction of the institutions which provide wealth with other social norms and institutions is inevitably part of the social phenomenon. We may, as J. S. Mill suggested, analyse different aspects of the social phenomenon separately but we cannot simply ignore its other components.

Indeed, Mandeville was juxtaposing two positive statements about a social phenomenon: vanity and pride produce prosperity; vanity and pride are perceived to be vices. It was not necessarily his own judgement, and he may have implicitly suggested that if we realised that those things we learned to condemn generate material wealth, then we may have changed our views about their moral values. But whatever it is, his paradox pointed at the need for the two positive statements about a social phenomenon to generate consistent notions of both synchronic and diachronic orders. It is difficult to imagine a natural process which produces simultaneously the behaviour which produces prosperity and the social norms and moral values which denounce them. Such an order cannot be sustained unless one aspect of it is altered. Obviously, while economists wish to pretend that they are indifferent to ethics, actually they seem to expect that the adjustment would come from ethics. To some extent, the position which states that economists have nothing to say about ethics implies a somewhat childish reaction to Mandeville's paradox: if ethics is inconsistent with expediency, change ethics.

But there is another strange anomaly in the position which economists take about the consistency of their proposed synchronic order and ethics. It is the absence of time or evolution. The synchronic order proposed by modern economists represents a certain stage in the development of technology, the economy and society, but it seems to be unaffected by the possibility (nay, certainty) that this stage is itself a result of a long process or that this stage will in the end be transformed into another, different, set-up. This, again, is closely associated with the departure of modern

economics from its classical roots. Following Turgot, Adam Smith specu-
lates about the anthropological developments which led society to the
'commercial state' which is depicted in his *Wealth of Nations*. The explanations for much that is going on in this stage cannot be fully understood
without an understanding of the social process which led to this, commercial stage. It is true that Smith does not go beyond this stage but this is not
because he saw in it a final stage of development. It was simply too far in
the future for him to be concerned about it at the time he was writing. So
when economists today spend a lot of energy and skills to refine the model
behind the *Wealth of Nations*, they seem to suppose that, as we said earlier,
the commercial stage is, to use an unfortunate analogy, the 'end of history'.
While one can understand why modern economists are reluctant to follow
the more deterministic route of Marx in describing the evolution of society, they could have paid more attention to liberal economists like Mill,
who spends a great part of his book to try to speculate where society is
heading. Naturally, his understanding and evaluation of the state of affairs
in his own time must have been influenced by these insights.

An alternative possible explanation for the modern perception that
natural order in the economic sphere could go with everything and
should therefore be applied globally could be the presumption that the
system of natural liberty is *universally moral*. If this is indeed the case,
then it makes sense to argue for laissez-faire, or natural order, to be
pursued irrespective of *other* (ostensibly unrelated) elements of one's
moral theory, which may account for cultural differences. And it also
makes sense to recommend these institutions to all societies at all times.
This would also be consistent with the modern take on Adam Smith,
though not really with what Smith himself suggested. But can one really
argue that the relentless pursuit of one's own interest—the vanity and
pride of Mandeville's depiction—is universally moral? The fact that
Mandeville pointed at a given system of morality—albeit, exogenous in
essence—where this is not true should be a sufficient proof that such a
position is not obvious unless one wishes to argue that religious beliefs
cannot evolve naturally or spontaneously.

There is, however, another, more powerful manifestation of the universal morality of the natural order. It is the close association between
liberalism and the idea of decentralised decision-making (laissez-faire)

and markets. The term 'liberalism' is, of course, complex but in its most basic conception it is about freedom and the protection of the individual. On the face of it, what can be more conducive to freedom than allowing people to behave in a way that is natural to them? What can be more protective of such a freedom than a world where the only purpose of society is to prevent people from harming one another and to make sure that people fulfil obligations which they voluntarily took upon themselves?

However, the objection we raised earlier about the universality of such an idea still stands. Firstly, for liberalism to be a meaningful ethical system we must accept the supremacy of the individual as the agent in social theories. When Mandeville was talking about the prevailing admonition of the natural tendencies of individuals, he was referring to religious doctrines where the individual is not the supreme agent in the social or ethical analysis. As religions have proven to be part of sustainable diachronic orders, we cannot dismiss them as unnatural. Secondly, there is the more complex question of what it means to be free. The association of individual freedom with a natural order must be based on the presumption that the natural order does indeed allow people to be free. But is it really so? Even if it were potentially so, there would always be the question of whether it is also a universal principle.

In general, even if one argues that natural motivation and personal drives are morally good and should therefore be allowed a free rein, it does not follow that a natural order would necessarily produce a distribution of rewards which is consistent with good morals. The fact that such activities may produce wealth is in itself insufficient to rescue the universal morality of such a system. Could people be considered as genuinely free if they are unable to extract from the system what they may reasonably think is due to them? If we refer to Weber's argument about the role of Protestant Ethics as the origin of capitalism (i.e. that natural order which produces plenty), we would still need to show that people who work hard are naturally rewarded more than those who do not. While it may be possible for religion-based-ethics to recommend hard work with earthly rewards which are consistently inversely related to one's contribution, this may be more difficult for a system which is dominated by the individual and where ethics is intrinsic. This, of course, is a problem which did not concern Mandeville as he was more concerned with the morality of the natural drives. But it did concern Smith—who was certainly a liberal—and as Jacob Viner observed, the *Wealth of Nations* is full of statements which would service many socialist orations.

So far, however, we assumed that the natural order is indeed successful in achieving something but we questioned its sustainability when it is based on morally repugnant principles. But there is another, not unrelated, question concerning the meaning of a ***successful*** natural order. In the Taoist case, this was very clear: each individual would be happier in a de-regulated world. Whether or not this is true or whether people may develop other objectives in life once they are happy is really an empirical question.

In the Mandevillian case and what followed, the natural order was, ostensibly, about prosperity. The question is, of course, what does it mean and can we take it for granted that the natural order would always deliver? I suppose that the most instinctive answer which modern economists would give is gross domestic product (GDP) per capita (both levels and growth rates) as measures of the success of the system. But from an individual perspective this may not be as simple as that. If people engage in the production of wealth for its own sake, then the question is whether every one of them gets what they (reasonably or rationally) expect to receive. If someone puts a lot of effort to become wealthy, will he be successful in the sense that he will be wealthier than someone who made less effort? Would his success be measured in absolute or relative terms? Will he or she be successful at all? Namely, we cannot just look at aggregates and we must ask the question about the ability of individuals to fulfil their plans (within reason) through the natural working of the system.

But what if prosperity is just a means to an end? What if the reasons we would like to acquire wealth are social (say, social approbation) or personal (self-fulfilment)? In such a case, the success or the failure of the system will depend on what precisely these ends are. This is far more difficult to establish than the mere measure of wealth production and the fact that the system may produce greater wealth would mean nothing at all. Evidently, if most people fail to fulfil the aims which they seek to achieve through the accumulation of wealth, the system of natural order would fail in spite of the wealth it generates. Even though people may not attribute such a failure to any specific moral wrongdoing, their morale will falter. At some point, when the number of people whose morale has been affected by the failure of the system to deliver their real objectives has reached a certain proportion, this low social morale may turn into a moral indignation which could create the split between what people consider as morally acceptable and the working of the system.

For Mandeville, as I argued before, this could not have been a concern as he was primarily concerned with whether or not the motives behind the system are acceptable even if it is successful. But in Adam Smith, for instance, this is already a concern. Yes, he may have argued that self-interest (being the moderate care for one's self) is morally acceptable but does the system deliver? We will, of course, have to go into more details about this further down the line as this is a crucial point, but at this stage I would only point to two issues. Firstly, while Smith appreciated that the overall production of wealth will benefit everyone through some kind of a trickle-down process, he did consider the possibilities that the natural order would fail and produce stagnation or even regression. Secondly, there is the question of what it is that people are trying to get from the system. For Smith, this was social approbation and not wealth as such even though there was scope for confusing the two. But whether or not this—social approbation—can actually be delivered through the accumulation of wealth depended on the moral system which people will adopt.

In as much as the delivery of the system is concerned, modern economics poses a strange anomaly. On the one hand, there is the belief that the natural order will give everyone what they can reasonably expect. On the other hand, however, there is also a recognition that in reality the conditions for this to materialise will not be formed naturally and there is a need to assist, as it were, either in law or policy, the system for the 'natural order' to succeed. So is the natural order in such a set-up really natural?

We will need, of course, to explore further and in greater details the logic of current economic theorising in order to better understand the position which modern economics takes with regard to the idea of natural order. We will need to establish whether economics is indeed ethically neutral or whether it is based on a universally accepted morality. The answers to these questions will allow us to understand the relationships between economics and society which are embedded in modern economics. It will also help in explaining the policies and ideologies to which it gives rise and which seem to have convulsed the world in a frenzied pursuit of some kind of a universal synchronic and diachronic order which is based on an almost-unbounded notion of laissez-faire (tied with liberty and freedom) and the sanctity of material wellbeing and growth.

Most importantly, we will also be able to understand the position of modern economics relative to the analytical framework which is embedded in classical economics. This will allow us to pose the question not only whether the progression between classical economics to modern economics has been anything but linear, but also whether we lost vital elements in the understanding of economics as a social theory. As we shall see, the institutional and policy recommendation we can derive from classical economics are very different from the ones modern economics purport to suggest.

Appendix: About Synchronic and Diachronic Orders

One possible way of explaining the difference between synchronic and diachronic orders is through the examination of the more traditional tool used in the analysis of spontaneous order. I refer here to the idea of evolutionary games.

Imagine for a moment that society is made up of two types of individuals: Those who behave like Hawks and those who behave like Doves. Notwithstanding the real nature of these two birds, let us suppose that the former behaves competitively and aggressively while the latter, the Doves, behave more co-operatively and moderately. Each individual is seeking a livelihood which brings him or her in contact with the other. The following table provides the information about the outcomes of such interactions:

	Hawk	Dove
Hawk	(h,h)	(H,d)
Dove	(d,H)	(D,D)

This means that when a Hawk meets a Hawk, they are both aggressive and competitive. As a result, the battle between them will reduce the amount left to each one of them in the end. Each one of them, in such a case, will get h which is the gain they will get from the encounter. This gain can be just physical units of food but it can also include less tangible things like sense of humiliation or exhaustion. By comparison, if a Hawk meets a Dove, the Hawk will take home H (which is clearly greater than h) and the defeated Dove will go home with only d. When a Dove meets a Dove, then they co-operatively share the food and may derive a sense of pleasure from their collaborative activity. In such a case, each one of them will get D, which is clearly greater than what they will get if they met a Hawk (d).

What remains for us to do is to ask whether the Hawk gets more when he meets a Dove than what a Dove will get when he meets another Dove. Namely, we need to establish whether $D > H$ or $H > D$. Let us begin by assuming that $H > D$ and also assume that p is the proportion of individuals who behave Hawk in society. Therefore, the expected gains for a Hawk will depend on the number of encounters he will have with other Hawks or with Doves. As p is the probability that he will meet another Hawk, the expected gains for the Hawk can be described as follows:

$$E_H = p \cdot h + \left(1 - p\right) \cdot H$$

The Dove too will meet a Hawk with probability p and another Dove with probability $(1 - p)$:

$$E_D = p \cdot d + \left(1 - p\right) \cdot D$$

We assumed that $H > D$ and we would like to add an assumption that $d > h$. Namely, we would like to assume that the bruised encounter of a Dove with a Hawk provides a greater gain for the Dove than the violent encounter between two Hawks provide each one of them. This is not an unreasonable assumption as the Dove, by submission, may avoid injury, but the Hawk, in fighting the other Hawk, is more likely to incur real cost which will make his benefit negative. If this is the case, the following picture will follow:

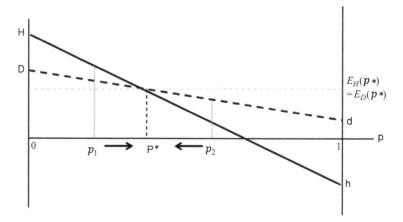

The heavy line describes the expected gains of the Hawk when the proportion of Hawks in the population increases from 0 to 1 according to the equation above. The broken line describes the expected returns for the Dove when the proportion of Hawks in the population increased from 0 to 1. Suppose now that at first the proportion of Hawks in the population is given by p_1 ($<p^*$). In such a case, as can be seen in the diagram, the expected return of the Hawks is great than the expected return of the Doves. Given that the return each type of individual brings home will determine the amount of offspring they can rear, it is clear that the Hawks, with their higher returns, will have greater abundance to rear more Hawks than the Doves. This, inevitably, will increase the share of Hawks in the population and p increases. This will continue until we get to the point where the share of Hawks in the population reaches p^*. Here, the return for either type of individuals is the same so the rearing will be such that each type will produce enough offspring to maintain a stable population where p^* will stay the proportion of Hawks in the population for generations. Had we started at a distribution where Hawks make up a proportion p_2($>p^*$) of the population, then the reverse would be true. The expected return on being a Dove is greater than on being a Hawk and this means that the offspring rearing activities of the Doves will be more successful than that of the Hawks and the share in population of the Hawks will diminish until we get to point p^*.

This is a stable evolutionary equilibrium which was formed spontaneously. At this point we have a combination of synchronic and diachronic orders. For each type of individual, behaving as they naturally do in order to survive will naturally produce an outcome where they will survive (the proportion of either group will not change). It is also a diachronic order because there is nothing about their circumstances which would recommend to any of them to change their behaviour or do something else (as long as the issue at hand is survival).

What makes the difference between what I am calling diachronic order and this form of spontaneous order is that it is based, not accidentally, on animals. So yes, in a world of Doves and Hawks p^* will create a spontaneous order which will be both synchronic, in the sense that at each period each of the species would survive in the sense that it will sustain its share in the population, and diachronic in the sense that there is nothing internal to lead to a change.

However, if we are dealing with humans and if the Hawk and the Dove are just metaphors to how different people tend to behave naturally, then the interpretation of the evolutionary stable equilibrium becomes more complex. If we assumed that people who are naturally inclined to behave in these different manners will pass on to their offspring the same traits, then the previous biological interpretation remains the same. But, if by talking about humans we suppose that the behaviour is a matter of choice (in the sense of habit formation), then the game we described should be interpreted slightly differently.

Individuals can choose whether to behave Hawkishly or Dovishly. If p, then, represents their belief about how many Hawks there are in the world, then the equilibrium would mean that the proportion of people choosing to act Hawk in the population will be p^* (or, in a more abstract manner, that the probability that the person you encounter would act like a Hawk is p^*). This equilibrium will represent a synchronic order in the sense that if people are out there to get the best deal for themselves (which is a problematic issue in itself as it assumes that the objectives of the Doves and the Hawks are the same), the fraction p^* will behave like Hawks and $1 - p^*$ will behave like Doves. As long as there is no exogenous change, this distribution of characters, or behaviour, will stay the same. So far, this is not really much different from the idea of spontaneous order which we used before.

People, unlike real Hawks and Doves, will form an opinion about the outcome or even about the process. The question is, of course, whether the process whereby they form their moral opinion is independent of what happened here. We will come to this question later in the book, but let us suppose that the public view is that behaving like a Hawk is morally bad, that it is like Mandeville's 'fraud, luxury and pride'. It is not inconceivable that people in society choose to act in a morally bad way even though they know it to be so. What is more difficult to accept is that this is a long-term sustainable situation as is implied by the model above.

So, what is it that will bring about a change? If we assume that people care about morality and that the outcome of their action is not just a reflection of their material success but also of their perception of their social standing, the matrix of payoffs may look somewhat different. Suppose that if one acts Hawkish one would have to take into account the cost of being morally blamed (B), whereas if someone behaves Dovishly, one would also bask in praise (P):

	Hawk	Dove
Hawk	$(h - B, h - B)$	$(H - B, d+P)$
Dove	$(d+P, H - B)$	$(D+P, D+P)$

Therefore, we could end up with the following situation:

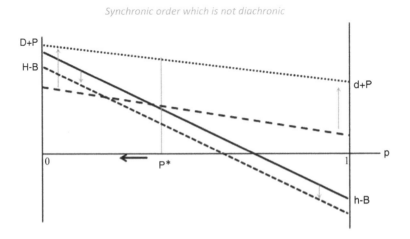

Synchronic order which is not diachronic

This means that at p^* the equilibrium, which emerges synchronically from the compatibility of choices made by individuals, will not be an equilibrium in the long run as the moral/social dimension will affect the returns (construed in broader manner than just the material gains). At p^* now, the expected return on being a Dove is greater than that of being a Hawk. This means that there is one equilibrium only and that is to behave Dovishly. If we wish to think about it in more evolutionary terms, we will need to show that the social standing of an individual (which is bound to affect his or her morale) will also be significant in ensuring successful breeding of offspring.

If moral opinions are formed by simple majority rules, then the question whether we all become Doves or Hawks depends on the value of the synchronic order (p^*). If $p^* < 0.5$, then majority are Doves and Hawkish behaviour will be deemed as evil. This, when translated into social penalties B and P, will make us all Doves. But if $p^* > 0.5$, the reverse will happen and we will all become Hawks. So, can p^* which is not a corner solution (i.e. neither 0 nor 1) still be a synchronic order which holds diachronically? The answer depends on how ethics is being formed. One can imagine a world in which being a Hawk and being a Dove are treated as equally valued expressions of human behaviour. In such a pluralistic society, $0 < p^* < 1$ could constitute both a synchronic and a diachronic order. However, it is important to emphasise that this pluralistic idea works only as long as a Dove can always be a Dove and a Hawk can be a Hawk. In other words, it will work only if the message is not just that it is morally acceptable to be one or the other but that it is something which you can effectively do. In other words, will the economic system support whatever it is that individuals want to be or would it force them to change and adapt. This problem will become to the fore when we discuss the apparent pretence of modern economics to uphold such pluralistic views of morality.

An alternative way of thinking about the relationship between the synchronic and diachronic orders could be demonstrated by assuming that the achievement of the Hawk from meeting a Dove is not as great as the result of the collaborative interaction between two Doves. Implicitly, it suggests that the collaborative meeting between two Doves generates an overall benefit which may include more than just material outcomes but could also be suggested by a notion that collaboration is more productive. At this stage, we shall just assume this without explaining this further. In such a case, the following picture will emerge:

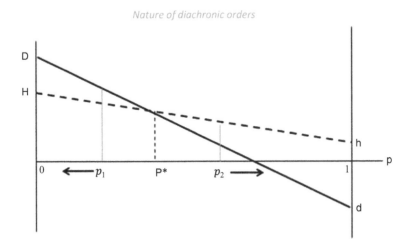

Nature of diachronic orders

In this case, if we start at p_1 the Hawks will have too many seriously bruising encounters with other Hawks and the Doves will have enough collaborative encounters with other Doves so that the expected returns of the Doves are greater than those of the Hawks. This means that the number of Doves will increase and the proportion of Hawks in the population will diminish until they completely disappear. The evolutionary stable equilibrium in this case will be for $p^* = 0$ and everyone is a Dove. In human terms, this may indeed generate a happy society which is predominantly collaborative. Alternatively, one can think of the synchronic order as the order which generates what scholars like Locke or Hobbes called a natural state. So, in the natural state here everyone is a Dove, which, in turn, corresponds to Locke's view. Nevertheless, in Locke, in spite of the natural state being a sustainable natural order, individuals do enter a social contract. This contract, in our case, becomes the framework of the diachronic order. It preserves the natural traits in human behaviour which generated the synchronic order but it goes further to ensure the fulfilment of social (or Divine, in Locke's case) objectives.

If we started with p_2, then the expected returns on Hawkish behaviour exceed those on Dovish behaviour and the natural process of propagation or choice of behaviour would lead to an equilibrium at point $p^* = 1$: everyone becomes a Hawk. This, again, is the synchronic order which creates the natural state which is more akin to the one conceived by Hobbes. This synchronic order is an order in the sense that there is nothing which can change the individual traits of the agents but, if we follow Hobbes, the Hawks themselves become frustrated as they would have had more if some of the agents were Doves or because it is far scarier to live in a world of Hawks. Consequently, they may all join a social contract (a diachronic order) which is not changing who they are but is removing their freedom to act.

In addition to the fact that adding social or moral considerations may affect the kind of order that emerges, we can also see from this account that the success of the synchronic order in achieving its declared objectives (survival or social preservation in our two stories) are not guaranteed. The synchronic order where $p^* = 0$ (everyone a Dove) is not only a diachronic order in the sense that the individual traits which created it would still be encouraged but it produces the best expected returns in terms of survival or social preservation. When $p^* = 1$ (everyone a Hawk), the synchronic order is certainly not manageable over time and diachronic order may dictate the stifling of individuals' natural traits. But not only that, the synchronic order which produces the expected return of h is clearly the worst possible outcome.

Bibliography

Acemoglou, D., & Robinson, J. (2012). *Why Nations Fail: The Origin of Power, Prosperity and Poverty*. London: Profile Books.

Arrow, K. J., & Debreu, G. (1954). Existence of an Equilibrium for a Competitive Economy. *Econometrica, 22*(3), 265–290.

Bowles, S. (2004). *Microeconomics: Behaviour, Institutions, and Evolution*. Princeton, NJ: Princeton University Press.

Bowles, S., & Gintis, H. A. (2011). *A Cooperative Species: Human Reciprocity and Its Evolution*. Princeton, NJ: Princeton University Press.

Buchanan, J. M. (1978). The Justice of Natural Liberty. In F. R. Glahe (Ed.), *Adam Smith and the Wealth of Nations: 1776–1976 Bicentennial Essays* (pp. 61–82). Boulder, CO: Colorado Associated University Press.

Deaton, A. (2013). *The Great Escape: Health, Wealth, and the Origins of Inequality.* Princeton, NJ: Princeton University Press.

Friedman, M. (1978). Adam Smith's Relevance for 1976. In R. G. Fred (Ed.), *Adam Smith and the Wealth of Nations: Bicentennial Essays 1776–1976.* Boulder, CO: Colorado Associated University Press.

Gourevitch, V. (2004). *Rousseau: The Social Contract and Other Later Political Writings.* Cambridge: Cambridge University Press.

Mandeville, B. (1988 [1732]). *The Fable Also Wrote an Enquiry into the Origins of Moral Virtues.* Liberty Press.

Meek, R. (1977). Mr. Sraffa's Rehabilitation of Classical Economics. In *Smith, Marx and After* (pp. 119–136). London: Chapman & Hall.

Phelps, E. (2013). *Mass Flourishing: How Grassroots Innovation Created Jobs, Challenge, and Change.* Princeton, NJ: Princeton University Press.

Piketty, T. (2014). *Capital in the 21st Century.* Cambridge, MA: Harvard University Press.

Robbins, L. (1935). *Essay on the Nature and Significance of Economic Science.* London: Macmillan.

Rothbard, M. (1990). Concept of the Role of Intellectuals in Social Change Towards Laissez-Faire. *Journal of Libertarian Studies, 9*(2), 43–67.

2

The Power of Beliefs: The Organisational Principles of Economics' Paradigmatic Core

Synopsis*: To claim that the co-ordinating powers of the market constitute a natural order, there is a need to show not only that such an order exists (i.e. synchronic order in the sense that it achieves a co-ordinated outcome to economic interactions) but also that it does not offend people's moral sensibilities (i.e. that it is also a diachronic order). One way of achieving this is by making the system universal and ethically neutral. The way modern economics proposes to do this is by adhering to strict methodological individualism and by removing the 'other' (except as someone whose actions may affect us) from all economic considerations. As individuals exist in all societies, and as it is the attitudes towards the 'other' which may distinguish one society from another, economics claims to have produced an idea of an order which is universal and independent of ethical or social dispositions. In this chapter, we examine how economics proposes to achieve this outcome and whether it has been successful in its endeavour.*

We begin by identifying a paradigmatic core where the economic problem is perceived as the problem of reconciling unlimited wants with scarcity; where the individual is rational and competitive; and where the institutions which solve the problem are those of competitive decentralisation. We also explain how the two welfare theorems transform this solution into a universal

© The Author(s) 2019
A. Witztum, *The Betrayal of Liberal Economics*,
https://doi.org/10.1007/978-3-030-10668-3_2

and ethically neutral one in the sense that all socially desirable distributions of outcomes can be achieved by the same competitive institutions. We note, however, that ethical neutrality here is predicated on ethics being consequentialist, which already compromises the claim.

A great deal of the criticism against economics has been levied at the realism of the model (the paradigmatic core). However, this is a futile attack as the model, by definition, is not supposed to be a depiction of reality. It is, instead, a logical limit of the idea of competitive decentralisation. As such, it offers a reference point for the evaluation of economic performance and for the formulation of policies regarding economic and social organisation. Nevertheless, the ideal (the model) has some relationship with the world it conceptualises, and this is where the difficulties lie. In this context we identify two types of difficulties. One, which is a question of whether the abstraction is relevant, requires a constant re-evaluation of the message of the core by incorporating (abstractly) the fundamentals of reality which cannot, in principle, be ameliorated through policy or legislation. Among the issues here are the questions of uncertainty and incomplete markets. The second type of difficulty is associated with those things which could, in principle, be resolved through policy and legislation and, therefore, allow reality, in principle, to asymptotically fulfil the necessary conditions for the promise of the core to be valid. Here we are referring to problems of asymmetric powers like, for instance, monopolistic powers (including strategic interactions).

We discuss at some length the first difficulty and point out that in a world of uncertainty with incomplete markets, the message of the paradigmatic core is altered completely. Spontaneous order based on competitive decentralisation will no longer solve the economic problem. While there are some remedies which may, at best, salvage productive efficiency (i.e. the provision side of the solution to the economic problem), the distributional dimension of the solution (i.e. allocative efficiency) cannot really be salvaged in a way which will allow the theory to remain ethically neutral or universal.

Given this blow, we ask why it is that the academic and the public discourse have not moved away from the ideal of competitive decentralisation. We suggest that this may be so because of an implicit presumption that though the ideal may not be reachable, taking the road towards it—namely, expanding competitive practices—is beneficial to society as the promised benefits of the paradigmatic core are strewed along this road. In other words, even though competitive decentralisation, at the limit (when there are missing markets and in a state of uncertainty), is inefficient (in the sense that it does not constitute a solution to the economic problem), expanding competition will nevertheless make society better off. We argue that this line of reasoning is seriously flawed as it assumes the presence of a well-defined measure of social wellbeing. But even if such a measure were possible, we argue that it is not possible to claim that increase in competitiveness will necessarily lead to such an improvement. Moreover, the problem of the relationship between the ideal and the world is much more serious than this. Even if we contemplate a world with certainty and without missing markets (which fulfils all the characteristic of a solution to the economic problem that is neutral), we will not be able to find a meaningful price formation mechanism that will produce those prices which constitute the solution to the economic problem.

These realisations, we claim, can help explain the rise in interest in growth. Being an aggregate concept, which is defined in terms of material wellbeing, growth allows us to circumvent the need to consider distributional consequences. But, given the individualistic nature of modern economics, there is no meaning for a solution to the economic problem which does not take into account the distributional consequences. Nevertheless, if we can at least claim the accumulation of material wellbeing, why should anyone object? Both the traditional solution to the economic problem and growth use the language of competitive decentralisation. However, while the former demands allocative efficiency (as well as productive efficiency), growth only looks at the latter. Therefore, the kind of competitiveness needed for growth is very different from the one required for the solution of the economic problem. The two, in fact, may have problems of compatibility. Yet, there seems to be a conflation between the two in the sense that people approve of competitive practices because they think that they are efficient in the sense of being a solution to the economic problem (as promised by the core). But they think that they solve the economic problem, just because they produce plenty (growth).

*   *   *

Whatever one may think of economics as an academic discipline or as an intellectual endeavour, one cannot but marvel at its enormous success and powers of persuasion. Not only have its organisational principles guided the organisation of increasing number of societies, they are also gaining grounds as the pillars of a global order. Moreover, as an intellectual project, economic thinking has dominated the social sciences. From sociology through political science to international relations, economic analysis—be it in the form of rational and competitive behaviour or strategic interaction—has been at the forefront of a considerable part of the intellectual developments in those disciplines culminating in the emergence of the new amalgamation of what is now known as the new political economy. The latter, paradoxically, exemplifies both the success and potential failure of economics as an intellectual project. As Political Economics is not in the least a new concept, there are, evidently, different ways of conceiving it. Indeed, the difference between the old version and the new one shows more than anything else how economics may have conquered the social arena, but at the same time it also shows how, potentially, it may have been a hollow victory. While in the old version of political economy—also known as classical economics—scholars were interested in how other aspects of social life affect economic analysis, in the new political economy we now ask how economic analysis affects all other areas of social life. Had we been able to compare economics to an emperor, he would have clearly repeated Caesar's famous declaration: Veni, Vidi, Vici.

But whether the expansion of economic analysis into other areas of the social science together with the rise of the new political economy can be considered a success depends on whether one accepts the view that economics is indeed universal and ethically neutral. It is evident that a theory which holds these two attributes is more akin to science and in this respect it is not a surprise that all social disciplines absorb into them the main tenets of economics. Nor would it be a surprise that the organisational principles which are derived from the economic paradigm are universally applicable to all societies.

So, what is this 'economics' to which I have been referring repeatedly and which seems to be such a success story? And how did it manage to persuade us that it is an expression of universal principles which are also ethically neutral? The answers may appear complicated if one wishes to address these questions by sifting through the mountains of articles published in 'leading' economic journals. Economists seem to be writing a lot and about an enormous variety of issues. It is, to a great extent, a reflection of their confidence in the scientific nature—also a code for universality and ethical neutrality—of their subject and to its wide applicability. Nevertheless, it is not difficult to notice that there is a rather conspicuous common thread to all their writings which is dominated by four elements (not necessarily all of them present at the same time). Firstly, explanations are usually derived exclusively from the analysis of actions and interactions between rational individuals (i.e. an individualistic approach). Secondly, individuals are considered to be rational in the sense that they always seek the best means to an end (whatever that end may be). Thirdly, individuals are considered to be competitive, which, in general, means that no matter what objective they wish to achieve, if anyone can do something at a lower cost (broadly conceived), they will act on it, and lastly, and closely related, that efficiency—in all its manifestations—is both an implicit driving force behind the system and a criterion of its successful performance.

To understand the significance and centrality of these elements in economic thinking, it would have been useful to extract a paradigmatic core from this mountain of work produced by academic economists. But there is an easier way of doing this. I suggest that the best way to discover the paradigmatic core of the subject is not to ask what economists *do* but rather to ask what economists *teach*. While the daily application of theory may take some academics to strange and wonderful lands, in the end if they do not go back to the classroom and tell their students that they need to teach them something completely different from what they have been teaching up to now, then there is no change in paradigm. Indeed, the reality is that in spite of an explosion in the number of economists and in the quantity of their academic output in the last 40 years, hardly anything of substance has really changed during that period in the textbooks which are used in educating the next generation of economists at both graduate and undergraduate levels.[1]

---

[1] At the undergraduate level, it is enough to take a look at the multitudes of editions of books like Samuelson's, Lipsey's and Dornbusch and Fischer's, as well as intermediate books from Stigler's Price Theory to contemporary ones. At the graduate level, one can compare books like Varian's *Microeconomic Analysis* from 1977, Mas-Colell, Whinston and Green from 1995 and Kreps from

Yes, there have been plenty of additions and more chapters showing the breadth of interests which economists now have and the extent to which they now apply their paradigm but the heart of the subject has not changed at all. Given the four elements I mentioned which dominate the expanses of economists' interest and given the nature of economics textbooks, I do not think that it will be audacious on my part to conclude that there is a very clear and well-established paradigmatic core. This core, I claim, is made up of three fundamental components: firstly, the conception of the economic problem; secondly, the conception of the individual; and thirdly, the conception of the interactions between individuals. In the last 40 years the first has not changed at all; the second was extended to include behaviour in uncertainty but not changed in essence[2]; and the third was broadened to include strategic interaction captured by game theory as well as institutions but it has not really *replaced* the standard framework of competitive interaction which remains, to date, the main point of reference.

2.1   The Paradigmatic Core

In a nutshell, the core argument nested in economics' paradigmatic core is that in a world of sovereign individuals who are naturally competitive and rational, competitive decentralisation (i.e. truly competitive markets) is the best way to organise economic activities as it would yield a co-ordinated outcome (i.e. equilibrium) which would solve each individual's economic problem—reconciling wants with scarcity—in the sense that each agent would get out of the system that which he or she could rationally expect. The individualistic nature of the theory, which also entails a purely functional conception of society (corresponding to the modern liberal idea of civic society), also means that such an outcome should always be consistent with whatever it is society, as a collective, may desire.

2013 to see that not much has really changed in what economists teach as the core of their subject.

[2] Developments emanating from behavioural economics like, for instance, prospect theory have not yet reached the core chapters in textbooks as the debates about them are still raging.

To understand the logic behind these statements, it is important to systematically track the development in the way of thinking from the conception of the economic problem to the institutional recommendations. We shall do this in a brief, though comprehensive, manner (*this may be a bit tedious for professional economists but essential for those who are not economists and need to understand the logic behind economics' paradigmatic core*):

The Economic Problem

a. We all *desire* things which are *scarce*, and our **economic problem** is therefore to reconcile this unlimited desire with the finality of scarcity.
b. A solution to such a problem will have the characteristic that resources are allocated in such a way that we cannot have more of one economic good without forgoing another. We call such an allocation **efficient**.
c. We now need to find institutional arrangements that will resolve this problem for the individual as well as for the collective.[3]

The Individual

d. We assume that society—or the collective—is no more than the sum of its components. This means that the atom of social analysis is the individual.
e. To find the right institutional arrangements, we must begin with how the atom of society—the individual—can solve the problem for himself or herself.
f. We assume agents to be **rational** in the sense that they will always seek the best means to achieve any end. As far as the economic problem is concerned, this simply means that he or she will always wish to

---

[3] The question of whether solving the individual problem is sufficient to solve the collective one or, alternatively, that individuals cannot solve the problem by themselves is a very important question pertaining to the relationship between the individual and the collective (society) and the methodological issue regarding the way in which we choose to analyse society. The assumption regarding this in modern economics is spelt out in point (d). But it is important to bear in mind that this is only one way of conceiving the methodology of social analysis.

employ resources in such a way that will leave them with as many opportunities for more usage of these resources. In other words, an individual will always minimise the costs (broadly conceived) in terms of resources whatever objectives he or she would like to achieve. In alternative formulation of the same idea, we can say that individuals will try to maximise the value of what they can obtain from their limited resources. Logically, this will indeed lead to allocations which are efficient in nature as far as each individual is concerned.

g. But individuals live in society and people are different. Therefore, it stands to reason that people should concentrate on things which they are 'good at'[4] doing. If, for instance, one person's engagement in activity, say, x, means that he has to forgo five units of another good, say y, which he could have obtained had he been engaged in another activity, while another person can engage in activity x while forgoing only two units of y, it would be better for the second person to engage in x and for the first person to engage is something else where the units of other goods he has to forgo from other activities are the least. We call this **specialisation** which is based on **comparative advantage (the ability to obtain something at lower costs—measured in loss of economic goods (also known as opportunity cost)).**

h. Specialisation, however, means that people become **dependent** on each other. Though we specialise, for instance, in producing commodity x, this does not mean that we would not like to have commodity y or z too. As a result, to solve our economic problem we must not only specialise but also **trade**, or **exchange**, with the others. The same principle of specialisation should also be applied to society as a whole which inevitably exists among other societies. As societies are different, each one will have a comparative advantage in providing different goods. If societies specialised and traded, then societies as a whole can be made better off through international trade.

---

[4] To be 'good at' something should not be confused with wanting to do that thing. A tall person may have some advantages in some employments over a short person, but it does not mean that the tall person likes to be engaged in that employment.

Nature of Interaction and Synchronic Order

i. We now need to establish what should be the nature of trade, or exchange, if individuals as well as society in general were to solve their economic problem through specialisation. The answer is given by the idea of *competition*.

j. There are two aspects to competitiveness. Firstly, it is a behavioural trait associated with rationality and corresponds to the desire always to choose the option with the lowest cost (broadly conceived). This means that all agents in society will at all times seek to employ the cheapest option. Secondly, it is a description of a market, or conditions of exchange. As such, by competitiveness, or competition, we mean that markets are sufficiently large for agents to become price-taker in the sense that they act as if their action will have no impact on the market outcome. In other words, agents do not have any power over other agents.[5]

k. The outcome of competitive interaction is what we call *equilibrium*. However, while the concept is borrowed from physics, it is not really the balancing act of opposing forces. It is simply a situation, usually depicted by a vector of prices, where all agents—as price-takers—manage to fulfil their rational plans in attempting to resolve their individual economic problem.

l. But as all economic activities are interconnected, we find that competitive equilibrium across all markets (what we call *general equilibrium*) ensures the solution of the economic problem for all agents involved in the sense that (i) everyone managed to fulfil their rational plans; (ii) we cannot obtain the same amount of economic goods by a different allocation of resources that would allow us to produce even more goods—namely, the allocation is efficient; (iii) from the social perspective we note that with such an equilibrium we cannot

---

[5] It has to be observed that the term 'competition' here is used in a very well-defined, yet limited, fashion. Intuitively, and perhaps colloquially, competition may, and will, prevail among individuals who are not necessarily equal. Indeed, even in a monopolistic set-up there is still a degree of competition taking place among consumers and even the monopolist who is trying to keep others out of its turf. But we use the term here in its purest form where the most important assumption is that competition is where all agents have the same power (fair, if you will). A case where no one has any power is, perhaps, the fairest of all set-ups.

make anyone better off without making someone worse off—which means that in terms of each individual's wellbeing (which is in itself an economic good as it is scarce as well as desirable), the allocation of 'wellbeing' is also efficient. We call this **Pareto-efficiency.**[6] We have thus created a distinction between efficiency which is applied to commodities or tangible services (which we call *productive* efficiency) and the one applied to less tangible economic goods like wellbeing (which we call *allocative*, or Pareto, efficiency).

m. As a by-product, we get an additional benefit which is that competitive prices reflect the true social/technological cost and, therefore, allow individuals and society to specialise and trade in that which they truly have comparative advantage.

n. Therefore, the best institutional arrangement which solves the economic problem at the individual and the social levels is that of *decentralised decision-making based on competitive interactions.*[7]

o. Competitive equilibrium—which is a form of a synchronic order—solves the economic problem through the mechanism of prices. This means that each equilibrium is associated with specific distributional parameters (as wages and the return to capital are prices too). Society may not like the distribution associated with a particular equilibrium, does this mean that we should abandon competition? The answer which economics provides is very powerful and is known as the *two welfare theorems*. According to the first theorem, competitive equilibria as we said before are always efficient. But the second theorem provides an answer to the question of what happened if society prefers (for cultural or any other social specific reasons) a different distributional outcome. In such a case, the second theorem promises that

---

[6] After the Italian economist-turned-sociologist Vilfredo Pareto, who inherited the Chair of Leon Walras in the University of Lausanne.

[7] Notice that we discuss here an ideal world, a benchmark or a reference point. It is clear that economics realised that the reality of competition is more complex. This gave rise to the idea of incomplete markets which was somewhat resolved by the introduction of property rights into the discussion. While this is an important issue, it is not really part of the core as it is part of the application. I shall discuss these issues further down the line. Here, I am simply trying to delineate the core, the logical limit of the idea of decentralised decision-making.

all efficient outcomes can be achieved by competitive means.[8] This means that if society prefers a different social distribution of wellbeing, provided that this allocation is efficient—and why should society ever prefer an allocation which is not efficient[9]—it can always be achieved by competitive means, through, for instance, a redistribution of wealth (which is not the same as the income derived from it).

Diachronic Sustainability and Economic Dynamics

p. The implication of the previous point is that the idea of decentralised decision-making which is based on competitive interaction is **universal and ethically neutral**. The reasons for this is embedded in the following two arguments:

(i) The principle of making an efficient use of resources is independent of what each individual or society would like to achieve.

(ii) Competition is consistent with whatever distribution society wishes to adopt and as social differences manifest themselves in different distributional consequences, competition is consistent with whatever society may rationally choose to achieve.

q. The conclusion at (p) ensures that the synchronic order described in (k)–(n) is also a diachronic order. If what society would like to achieve morally is consistent with efficiency and therefore with competition, it is unlikely that social disapproval could be directed at the institutions of competition and decentralisation. Instead, the social debate should be focused on what distribution society should wish to support. But while this clearly entails a certain ethically pluralist element—as different societies may wish to have different distributions—it also reduces ethics to consequentialism. The differences between

---

[8] There is a proviso here as this is only true in the presence of lump-sum transfers. These however, are not really possible in reality which led to the development of what is known as the 'second-best' approach. But these are details which, although of great importance, will not alter the main thrust of the argument.

[9] In spite of appearances, we will see that this is not as obvious as it may seem.

societies are only measured in terms of the differences in their attitudes towards the consequences produced by the system.

r. From the dynamic perspective of solving the economic problem, the question that remains is whether the same institutions also support either the accumulation of resources or the technological improvements which allow a greater use of the existing resources. Leaving aside the question of capital accumulation (increase in resources) which is predominantly a question of social choices (in terms of savings and consumption) and, therefore, not an institutional question, the issue of technological development may have some institutional elements. We know that for R&D (the source of technological development) we would need funds and incentive to invest. In a perfectly competitive environment where information is readily available to everyone and where profits, above the normal rates of return,[10] are squeezed, firms may be less inclined to invest in R&D than, say, monopolists who have both the incentives (to keep ahead of potential entrants) and the funds (profits are not eroded by competition). This was part of a conjecture by the Austrian economists Schumpeter about whose claim the debate is still raging[11] but it is not a problem that cannot be dealt with by the introduction of things like intellectual property rights.[12]

s. In general terms, the idea of decentralised decision-making coupled with competitive interaction is still the dominant view of effective generation of R&D and, subsequently, technological change. If individuals are allowed to invent ideas and exchange them in a competitive

---

[10] In principle, profits are made up of the return to capital which is comprised of what we call normal profits and profits above the normal. The normal profit is what the firm pays to those who forwarded capital to it, which is equivalent to what they would have received elsewhere (the market rate of return). Any profits above it can be used by the firm either to be distributed to its shareholders, who then receive a return on their capital which is higher than the market rate, or to be invested in the firm itself. Competition usually erodes the latter part which means that firms will have no funds to invest in R&D.

[11] The evidence seems to support the argument that larger firms tend to invest more in R&D than smaller firm, but this in itself does not mean that monopolist will invest more. Monopolistic power does not necessarily mean larger firms.

[12] For instance, by protecting patents, the innovator has limited monopolistic power which allows him or her to recoup the return on their investment by preventing competition from eroding their gains.

market where no one can cream off the return on their investment (non-extracting institutions), the circumstances for innovation and technological change would be best met.

To make this story simple, the following diagram offers a visual representation of the main ideas embedded in the narrative of the paradigmatic core of modern economics:

The economic scheme of society

The story thus begins with the individual (in the diagram we have two: i and j). Each one of them faces the same economic problem. If you allow individuals who are rational in the sense that they seek the best means to an end and behave competitively to act as they choose, they will specialise and become dependent on each other. Their dependency will pay off if their natural competitiveness (always to undercut a more expensive option) will be matched by market institutions where no one individual has the power to influence the outcome by himself. The outcome of their interaction will then solve each agent's economic problem and, by implication, society's economic problem. It should be added here that while individuals' competitiveness is aimed at giving them advantage over others, the role of competition—as an institution—is to erode all such advantages. In so doing, competition ensures that everyone gets that which he or she rationally desires and we reach a point (named equilibrium) where all these rational plans coincide. No one, therefore, will have an interest to undermine the outcome or to try to alter it. It is in this sense that such an equilibrium represents the idea of order. The word 'natural', usually attached to the word 'order', signifies that it is an order created without any intervention or manipulation. It is an order generated by individuals acting on their own interest without impediments. Whether or not it is really *natural* is a complex question as the idea of perfect competition is by no stretch of imagination natural. If societies have to create the environment within which the pursuit of self-interest will lead to an order (co-ordinated outcome) among such people, then a case should be made to explain why society should create these institutions. It cannot be justified, however, on the grounds that it is a natural arrangement. Consequently, the whole project becomes the subject matter of ethics and social norms. One could say that as each individual naturally aims to solve his or her economic problem, then creating the conditions of perfect competition facilitates a solution to the problem seems natural. But this is only true if society is only here to facilitate the solution of individuals' economic problem and if individuals have no other issue which requires social assistance. Neither of these issues is ethically neutral, nor the answer to the questions universal.

In summary and to recap on the main points, economics' paradigmatic core is a promise that in a world of sovereign competitive rational utility maximisers there exists a ***spontaneous order*** which solves both the individual and the social-economic problems. This conclusion is ***universal*** because the economic problem and the rationality of agents—in the sense of seeking the best means to achieve any end—capture human nature everywhere, and because the order that emerges is in fact spontaneous. Everywhere in the world if you allow individuals to interact *freely*,[13] it will lead to a co-ordinated outcome in which agents solve their individual economic problem. For societies, being in essence functional, this is a necessary building block of social organisations regardless of what social values different societies may wish to promote.

---

[13] Also meaning that they compete on equal footing and with full information. What exactly is meant by freely will be further discussed in Chap. 4.

To some extent, the universality claim is in itself a claim for ***ethical neutrality***. If everywhere in the world people need competitive decentralisation to serve their interests—whatever these may be—then the successful co-ordination generated by markets is independent of what it is that people seek and should be seen, therefore, as neutral. However, ethics is not about what individuals may or may not wish to achieve for themselves. It is about the relationships between them. After all, the outcomes of competitive systems provide each agent with that which he or she can rationally expect, but this is predicated on what they had had at the beginning of the process, which may be different from what others had. While people's rational plans may be fulfilled through competitive decentralisation, their ethical values about what the outcomes mean for their relationships with the others may not be fulfilled. Therefore, universality alone is not sufficient to explain ethical neutrality which led us to discuss the *second welfare theorem*.

However, there is an important proviso here which already sheds some doubt over the ethical-neutrality claim. As the second welfare theorem claims that all efficient allocations can be reached by competitive means, its extension to ethical neutrality is predicated on all socially desirable allocations being also efficient in the sense that we cannot make anyone better off without making someone else worse off. This is far from obvious and already a restriction on the kind of ethical values permissible in the discussion about social values.

But there are more serious issues behind the claim of ethical neutrality associated with the second welfare theorem. For the theorem to provide for ethical neutrality, social values must be confined to either initial allocations or final distributions (outcome) but not to the relationship between them or the actual process of market exchange. We either choose an initial allocation which satisfies our moral requirements and claim that as all subsequent interactions (exchanges) are done voluntarily, they should also be morally good, or define the properties of the final distribution which satisfies our morality and, according to the second welfare theorem, adjust the initial one to allow competitive decentralisation to produce it regardless of the nature of the process, or of the possible relationship between them. But what if we think that a particular initial allocation merits a particular final distribution? What if we think that the process of exchange must fulfil certain moral requirements? Would the ethical neutrality of competitive decentralisation still hold? We will explore this in greater details in Chap. 4.

Notwithstanding these difficulties to which we will come back as we progress in our analysis, this, in a nutshell, is the way in which economics' paradigmatic core presents itself as natural, universal and ethically neutral principle of economic organisation.

2.2   The Nature of Theoretical Obstacles and Developments

Theoretical developments in economics (like institutional economics, game theory and behavioural economics) raise questions with regard to potential impediments on the road between decentralised decision-making and the holy grail of efficiency (the solution to the economic problem), but they have questioned neither the competitive nature of human interaction nor the idea that with the right institutional support (notably, the proper allocation of property rights and the curtailing of agents' power asymmetries), such behaviour would indeed lead to the resolution of the economic problem. As a result, the relentless pursuit of competition and markets, the relentless demand for small governments and the relentless proliferation of the idea of competitive decentralised decision-making have never ceased in the last 40 years.

There have been many attacks on the realism of economics' paradigmatic core. But these have been thoroughly misguided and it is not surprising that they have not really dampened the power of its attraction. The reason for this is that the purpose of such a paradigmatic core is not to *describe* how the world really looks like. Instead, it is an insight into the principles of how the world (the social one) works. It begins with a few generalised, and ideally, agreed, observations (known as premises) and through the use of logic leads us to some logical limits which are logically true but not necessarily empirically true. Therefore, the argument according to which, in a state of perfect competition, the outcome of decentralised decision-making that is based on an agreed observation about the economic problem which individuals face, and the way in which they will go about it (i.e. rationality and competitiveness), will lead to efficiency and hence, a resolution of the economic problem, is not a description of the world. Instead, it provides us with principles of organisation. It simply says that at the logical limit, namely if all people were indeed perfectly rational and the environments of exchange were truly competitive, the outcome will be efficient. Though we all recognise that this may never really happen, we extract from it the idea that by pursuing competition while allowing individuals to pursue what is best for them (decentralisation), we will *asymptotically* approach this state where the outcome of free voluntary interaction will lead to a resolution of the economic problem for the individual and for society. In other words, *in the world of rational individuals who seek the best for themselves, the more competition there is, the nearer we get to an efficient outcome (and hence, a solution to the economic problem)*.

Therefore, the paradigmatic core of economics is merely a logical guide from which many practical institutional recommendations as well as social policies can be derived. It is not the reality of the description—which is not the purpose of a model—that provides the power behind the ideology of laissez-faire. It is the power of logic; it is the power of persuasion. There is nothing more universal than the use of logic. Descriptions of the world change over time and across space. But logic is eternal (well, at least on the Earth and for those of us who are not postmodernists).[14]

In this respect, the developments in economic theory since the middle of the twentieth century should simply be seen as a constant dialogue between the model—the logical limit of the idea of competitive decentralised decision-making—and the more complex reality which we face in different places and circumstances. However, there are two very differ-

---

[14] Bearing in mind epistemological differences across culture (and in particular between rationalist Continental European thinkers and Anglo-Saxon empiricists), the argument can be slightly modified to say that the abstract—non-descriptive—part of the theory produces testable claims about the world which, if confirmed, would increase the belief about the empirical truth behind the model. While this is a view, which empiricists would subscribe to, it has serious difficulties as even the empirical confirmation of testable claims derived from the model can in no possible way lend empirical truth to other components of the model. Namely, even if we can empirically confirm that, say, demand schedules in the world are downward sloping, we will not be able to conclude that a competitive equilibrium is empirically efficient because it does not lend empirical truth to the utility function which is the analytical tool needed to interpret the area below the demand schedule.

ent threads to this dialogue; two different types of potential difficulties facing the paradigmatic core. The first type is concerned with its logical validity and the second one with its relationship with reality or implementation difficulties. By logical validity we are referring to the question of whether the promise of the core still holds when we consider some underlying fundamentals which have been missing from its abstract logical structure. It has to be borne in mind that the logical nature of the paradigmatic core is of interest to us only if it is based on a *relevant abstraction*. The fact that a particular model—the abstraction—is not descriptive does not mean that any abstraction, by virtue of being one, has the licence to serve as a paradigmatic core. An example of this line of difficulty is the case of uncertainty. The fact that we could show that decentralised decision-making based on rationality and competitive interaction (i.e. spontaneous order) resolves the economic problem in a world of certainty does not necessarily mean that this is a relevant conclusion in a world where there is uncertainty. But is it really just a question of the reality being different from the abstraction? The answer must be negative as uncertainty is a sufficiently fundamental component of the environment which the paradigmatic core proposes to represent that no serious abstraction can really ignore it. In the same vein, it is inconceivable that there exists a process—even conceptually—that can turn the paradigmatic core of certainty into the logical limit of a world where there is uncertainty.[15] Therefore, recognising such fundamentals requires not just their explicit presence in the core but also a *reconfirmation* of the paradigmatic promise while taking them into account. Indeed, this is exactly how economics dealt with the issue. Recognising that uncertainty is a sufficiently fundamental aspect of human existence, it became apparent that we need reassurance that what we thought to be true in the abstract world of competitive decentralisation (without uncertainty) still holds when we consider the abstract world in the light of uncertainty. Incorporating uncertainty into the model is not a step towards making it more realistic. The model of general equilibrium with uncertainty is, to

---

[15] Some would correctly point out that markets may help in alleviating uncertainty and even allow individuals, through insurance, to live, potentially, in a world which seems certain (what is called full insurance), but this is still the result of a recommendation emanating from a model, or an abstraction, which was based on recognising the presence of uncertainty.

an extent, even more abstract than the one in the world of certainty[16]; nevertheless, the abstraction itself is now more relevant to the world it is trying to capture. Not shying away from the challenge, economics managed through the contributions of Debreu and Arrow[17] to reassure us that even in the face of uncertainty competitive decentralisation will still yield a co-ordinated outcome (equilibrium) which is efficient and, hence, solves the private and the social-economic problem (still assuming society to be purely functional).

It is important to emphasise that had this not been the outcome of the exercise, we could no longer have claimed that competitive decentralisation is a force for the good in the sense that the more we pursue it, the nearer we get to a co-ordinated outcome where the economic problem would have been solved. In fact, there would have been no grounds at all to argue that even logically, let alone empirically, competitive decentralisation can ever constitute a solution to the economic problem. Competitive decentralisation, or spontaneous order, as a benchmark for universal and ethically neutral economic organisation, would cease to be a meaningful policy reference point.

The second type of difficulty, the more common one, is directly related to the dialogue that takes place between the abstract core and reality. Here, the issue is whether or not it is conceivable, in principle,[18] to influence reality so that it would asymptotically approach the ideal: the paradigmatic core. If competition in the core—the one that solves the economic problem—is between individuals who cannot, by themselves, affect the outcome, what is the meaning of it in a reality where they can do so? Naturally, we would first of all use the benchmark to claim that such a situation is inefficient and, therefore, not a solution to the economic problem. But such an assertion would be meaningful only if we could

---

[16] For instance, while in a world of certainty, that which defines an economic good is fairly straightforward, in a world of uncertainty we deem the same commodity in different states of nature as completely different economic goods. This, by no stretch of imagination, is a simple abstraction.

[17] Debreu has formalised this idea in his *Theory of Value* which was an attempt to modernise, mathematically, Walras's *Elements of Pure Economics*. All of this led to the application of Walrasian General Equilibrium to the world of what is known as 'state-contingent-claims' in the form of the Arrow-Debreu Securities model.

[18] This should be seen as somewhat more akin to the idea behind Popper's principle of falsifiability.

devise means that in reality will either bring us closer to the competitive interaction as envisaged by the paradigmatic core or allow us to influence the outcomes so that they will lead to the ones we expect in a truly competitive world. If we cannot do either of these, the problem we observe in reality is, in fact, a fundamental one and needs to be treated in the same manner as the problem of uncertainty. This means that it would require a reiteration that in its presence, the promise of the paradigmatic core still holds at least logically.

The kind of problems to which we are referring here are those where agents have asymmetric powers in their competitive interaction. These are cases like monopolies, monopolistic competition, oligopolies and other problems associated with asymmetric information. However, while the presence of asymmetric powers may indeed be a feature of reality, it is conceivable to think about a world where such powers are curtailed or eliminated altogether. By contrast, it is inconceivable to consider a world where uncertainty can be curtailed. Thus, in the case of uncertainty, it is meaningless to talk about what would have happened in a world without uncertainly, but it is still meaningful to discuss a world where agents' powers are curtailed.

Therefore, in problems of the second type, there is no need to revisit the paradigmatic core. Whether or not one is fully successful in curtailing asymmetries in the power of participants, the idea that promoting competitive practices as a means of asymptotically approaching the beneficial outcome embedded in the promise of the paradigmatic core is still valid (in principle). Nevertheless, even here there is another issue lurking under the surface which may be a source of difficulty and to which we will relate further below. We are referring here to the meaning of asymptotically approaching the core. In principle, there are two characteristics to competitive decentralisation as imagined by the paradigmatic core. The first is the institutional set-up in the sense that (a) there is a large number of agents or, which is the same thing, agents have no power to individually affect the outcome; (b) information is equally and widely available; and (c) that agents can enter or leave the market freely. The second is the mechanism of competitive *interactions* within this institutional set-up that produces the equilibrium prices that are, in fact, the guarantor that the outcome is indeed efficient and, hence, solves the economic problem.

Attempting to curtail individuals' power is equivalent to an institutional approach to the question of asymptotically nearing the ideal. As we create conditions that facilitate (a)–(c) the institutions of competitive decentralisation in reality will, in the end, approximate well the ones conceived in the paradigmatic core. However, this does not tell us much about the actual process, or the nature of competitive interactions, that creates those equilibrium prices which embody all the benefits of competitive decentralisation. As we already noted in the introduction, the existence of a set of prices where all markets are in equilibrium and the economic problem solved is not a guarantee that there exists, even in theory, a process that brings us to these prices. If there exists no conceivable process that produces such prices, there will also be no real process whereby we can asymptotically approach the core even if we were to proliferate the institutions of competitive decentralisation. We will return to this problem below.

In what follows we will not say much about the second type of problems. We shall accept that there are, in principle, ways to curtail asymmetries in agents' power—at least at the institutional level—and, therefore, would argue that the fact that we still observe such a phenomenon is in itself not a reason to question the logical benchmark embedded in economics' paradigmatic core. We will, instead, focus on the first type of problems which pose a threat to the logical validity of the core as a reference point. We shall also discuss the implications of the absence of an appropriate price formation process which threatens to turn the second type of problems into unresolved problems of the first kind.

2.3 The Hard Problems

With the exception of the case of uncertainty where economics pursued the right methodological protocol and revisited its core, most issues in the dialogue between the abstract core and reality, have been of the less-severe nature surrounding the construction of institutional bridges between reality and the ideal, assuming all the time that in principle it is possible to conceive a reality where these difficulties can be eradicated. However, there were two other developments which are as serious as the problem of uncertainty and, therefore, require the re-evaluation of the core's promise, but where economics stopped short of drawing the necessary conclusions. We are referring here to the problems of missing markets and the question raised by the problem of the prisoner's dilemma.

2.3.1 Missing Markets

The significance of missing markets to the logical relevance of economics' paradigmatic core cannot be overstated but their treatment in the context of certainty and uncertainty has been dramatically different, which could explain why there was a failure to re-examine the core as should have been done given the nature of the problem.

What we mean by missing markets is the fact that some aspects of economic interactions have no expressions in terms of economic values. The most obvious example is what has been known as externalities. For instance, if a boat sheds its refuse into a river while providing a luxury cruise which is purchased through a market, the fishing communities along the river will have their harvest affected by such an activity, although neither the cruising company nor the fishing community trade with the refuse (i.e. a result of one's agent action which affects another). The owner of the boat will perceive no cost for dumping the refuse in the river, while for society (including the fishermen) there will clearly be a cost in terms of lost fish. Namely, the cost of the cruise for society is much greater than it is for the people who take the cruise as the price they pay—which in a competitive environment will reflect the cost of the cruise to the cruise company—does not include the cost of dumping refuse into the river. This is a sign of inefficiency. Naturally, had it been known that one can use the refuse from the boat to, say, fertilise the land along the river, there might have been a market for this refuse, and in such a case, the opportunity cost of shedding the refuse to the river will not be zero for the boat provider. Their profit maximising behaviour will now take into consideration that they can earn money from the refuse which will help to realign the private with the social cost.

In this example, it seems evident that there may be another use for the refuse dumped from the boat but most of the time this is not the case. The cruise may generate other externalities like, for instance, disturbing the peace of the people who live by the river and who are engaged in creative writing. Therefore, we will ignore for the moment the intuitive understanding that refuse from the boat may have a usage and suppose that there is no such usage. In such a case, the cost to society of the cruise is much greater than it is to the company providing it so that even in a perfectly competitive environment where individuals pay for a cruise its apparent cost, the outcome will be inefficient.

It should not be too difficult to imagine why this is a hard problem—or a problem of the first type which questions the logical relevance of the core—as missing markets are everywhere. It is difficult to imagine a world where an economic activity of one agent does not affect other activities or the activities of other agents without anyone being fully aware of it and, consequently, for its effect being taken into account by anyone. It is, thus, very similar to the case of uncertainty. There is nothing one can do to rid the world—as opposed to the individual—from uncertainty which, as we said before, is not the same for the powers which agents manage to acquire. Equally, there is nothing we can do to rid the world from the problem of missing markets. Therefore, in order for the belief in the promise of economics' paradigmatic core to be maintained, there is a need to review the core and to ask the question of whether competitive decentralisation in a world where there are missing markets would still logically lead to efficient outcomes (i.e. solve the economic problem).

To fully appreciate the significance of the problem, we depict below, in an extremely simplified manner, the issues embedded in the dialogue between the abstract paradigmatic core and reality:

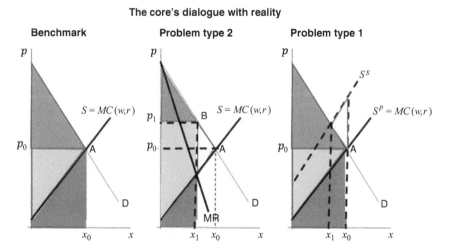

The core's dialogue with reality

The left-hand diagram depicts the most broadly known conception of modern economics. This is the demand and supply for a commodity (x), the quantities of which are given by the horizontal axis and the price by the vertical one. Markets where the institutions of competitive decentralisation are properly established are expected to yield the price p_0, which is the equilibrium price where the quantity rational agents would want to buy is the same as the quantity rational agents would want to sell. The efficiency of the outcome can be seen in two different ways. The first is the presumption that the supply schedule represents the true cost of each additional unit. It is rising because of the diminishing nature of productivity for a given set of means of production. In equilibrium, individuals pay the price for the good which is the same as the cost of producing its last unit. What we mean by true costs is the fact that we could not produce this quantity with fewer resources even if there was a benevolent and all-knowing central planner to replace the market. This means, more seriously, that the cost of the good for producers is the same as it is for society. In this respect, we cannot transfer any of the resources allocated to x into another employment without losing x. This is what is meant by productive efficiency. The powers of competition will force producers to work at these levels of cost. But this is only one aspect of the solution. We must also make sure that the benefits produced by the system are not wasted. In principle, the area under the demand schedule (blue + green + red) represent a proxy in money terms for the wellbeing (utility) generated by the market. These benefits materialise in three different forms. The red area represents that part of it which went to pay for the production of the goods. To some extent, this is of no interest to us as it is a transfer from one pocket to another. Consumers pay this to the producer, who in turn pays them this in a form of return for their services in the production process. What remains are net benefits which are distributed between consumers (blue area) and producers (green area). We can see that at equilibrium these benefits have been (a) maximised and (b) efficiently distributed. If we produced beyond the level of x_0, the additional costs (area under the supply schedule) will have to be subtracted from the net benefits as no one is willing to pay the higher prices corresponding to the higher levels of cost. It is also efficiently distributed in the sense that we cannot increase consumers' benefits without reducing producers' one or vice versa. This is the allocative efficiency (Pareto) nature of the outcome. So, the equilibrium price of the perfectly competitive market represents an efficient outcome and a solution to the economic problem.

Before we continue dealing with the two types of difficulties, it would be worthwhile referring here to the other difficulty of asymptotic convergence about which we talked earlier. Even if we knew what the demand and supply schedules looked like and were able to calculate the price at which the socially desirable equilibrium will materialise, there is a question whether there exists a competitive process which produces these prices. The standard economic abstract is a static model which by definition does not entails any dynamics that can persuade us about the existence of a process through which this price will come about. Therefore, even when all the institutional conditions are fulfilled, we still have no idea whether or not the efficient prices will emerge. In the literature about general equilibrium—considering multitude of markets—this is known as the stability problem, but we can extend it to the more general issue of price formation. We will say more about it later.

The second type of difficulty which we mentioned was the one that is not fundamental in the sense that we can do something to bring us nearer to the ideal. This is the case of market power which we can see in the middle diagram. When there is a single monopolist in the market, the producer would be aware that for every extra unit he sells, and which would lead to a fall in price, he will lose revenue he could have had from all those who were willing to pay the higher price and now pay less for the same good. Therefore, the equilibrium will be at point B (where the price is greater than the marginal cost). The first use to which we put the paradigmatic core is to declare this outcome inefficient and socially undesirable. Assuming that in the production process, the monopolist is still behaving in a manner consistent with productive efficiency, the inefficiency of the outcome will become evident from the loss of wellbeing as measured by the yellow triangle. It is easy to see that if we curtail the power of the monopolist either by introducing more competition or by legislation, we can push the outcome towards point A where all the benefits promised by competitive decentralisation will materialise.

However, for the problem of missing markets—the first type of a problem—things are considerably more complicated. Notice that here, from an institutional perspective, the market is perfectly competitive. However, given that the social costs are greater than the private ones (as we saw in the case of the cruise dumping refuse into the river), the outcome would still be at point A with the competitive prices which we would normally expect to be efficient, but which are, in fact, as inefficient as in the case of the monopolist. The yellow triangle, which is the cost not covered by consumers' willingness to pay, will have to be deducted from the benefits generated and leave us with the same amount of benefits as those created by the monopolists that we have clearly deemed as inefficient and socially undesirable. One cannot overstress this point. In the presence of missing markets, everything that appears to be perfectly competitive and efficient is, in fact, far from it.[19]

The question that arises is whether there is something we could do about it as was the case in the asymmetric power (monopoly) situation. Naturally, the case of a boat dumping its refuse in the river may be too obvious, which may lead some to conclude that it is easy to identify the missing market and, therefore, resolve the problem.[20] However, we must bear in mind that there are numerous forms of missing markets or externalities, both negative and positive, which are not so easily noticeable, but that may nevertheless affect the outcome. If we accept that not all missing markets can easily be identified or detected, then we face a real conundrum: How can we tell whether the paradigm is true or false (logically as well as empirically)? We may observe an economy where all perceived markets are perfectly competitive (in terms of both their institutional set-up and the existence of an appropriate price formation mechanism). This should lead us to conclude that such an economy resolved its economic problem (in a co-ordinated manner where no one

---

[19] We are leaving out at this stage personal distributional matters as they are present everywhere in our story. Even at the perfectly competitive case, there is always the question who receives these benefits. In general, as individuals are both consumers and owners of firms, we cannot learn from this anything about the personal distribution of benefits. The second welfare theorem is a means to ensure that we can change the distribution of these benefits without affecting the total sums produced. Nevertheless, we do have a distributional element here too as we focus on the distribution of benefits in terms of returns for economic activities.

[20] But even this is not straightforward. Suppose that we know that dumping refuse will affect the fishing industry, how do we evaluate the damage? The government would want to tax the cruise owners according to the damage they create. This will lead their supply curve (the marginal cost of a cruise) upward in line with the social cost (it is also known as Pigouvian Tax). But the government does not know what the damage is and will have to rely on reports from fishermen—who are likely to exaggerate the damage—and the cruise operators—who are likely to undervalue it.

can become better off without anyone becoming worse off) and that market prices reflect the true social cost of all goods. However, if we believe that there are always missing markets somewhere in the system, then the only conclusion we can draw is that even with perfect competition the economic problem will not be resolved. In such a case, a dark shadow will be casted over the idea of spontaneous or natural order. Also, all our attempts to encourage decentralisation and competition through regulation or otherwise will be a misguided policy. It is one thing to encourage an institutional change that will, in principle, lead to a solution of the economic problem but quite another matter to encourage institutional changes which would lead, well, nowhere. In our three diagrams case, we may wish to correct the monopolist's situation by legislation and greater competition only to find ourselves in the situation depicted in the right-hand diagram which is equally inefficient as the case we started with. In other words, the underlying reason why we may pursuit competition would no longer exist, and we would need to think of other ways for solving the economic problem than simply allowing people to act according to their own interest in a perfectly competitive and ostensibly spontaneous manner.

However, in a world of certainty there is a way to resolve this problem without having to significantly review the paradigmatic core. Coase's important contribution to this debate was the claim that the problem of missing markets can be resolved by allocating property rights. However, this in itself would have created a serious problem for the claim of *ethical neutrality*. The distribution of property rights will necessarily have an impact on the kind of distributions of income that will emerge from competitive interactions. As such, the idea that all possible distributions—thus reflecting all possible cultural and social differences[21]—can be achieved by competitive means can no longer be true because only specific distributions of property rights (ownership) support the resolution of the economic problem. But luckily, there was a relief in what has become known as the *Coase Theorem*. It is true that the allocation of

---

[21] I do not for a moment suppose that cultural differences can only be manifested in the choice of the distributional outcomes but within the terminology of modern economics—which is a consequentialist theory—this is the only way in which such differences can be well captured.

property rights is necessary to deal with the problem of missing markets but, in the absence of transaction costs (to which we will soon return), it does not matter how property rights are allocated for the competitive model to produce the desired outcome. If the distribution of property rights does not matter, the idea that competition can support any kind of social values as manifested in different distributions of income is upheld.

The reason why allocation of property rights resolves the problem of missing markets is very simple. In the case of our story about the boat, the only question we face is: Who owns the river? If it is owned by the fishermen's community, then the owners of the cruising boats will need to seek permission to dump their refuse in the river. Therefore, the owners of the boat are likely to have to pay to do this,[22] which will, of course, increase their cost of running the cruise to match the social cost (i.e. in the right-hand diagram, there will be only one supply which is the social one (S^S) reflecting the social marginal costs) and, subsequently, be reflected in the price of a cruise. In such a case, as the price of the cruise reflects its true social cost, it will lead us to the efficient outcome. If, on the other hand, the river was owned by the owner of the cruising boat, then they can dump their refuse as they please. However, as the fishermen are affected by this, they will find it profitable to offer the owners of the boat money so that they do not dump endless quantity of refuse in the river. Here too, the payment that will be agreed will balance the interests of both parties and, therefore, will lead to a price which reflects the social cost. If there are no transaction cost in the sense that there are no costs involved in the different forms of negotiating and signing such a deal, then it really does not matter who owns the river. The cost of dumping the refuse in the river will affect the amount of cruising as well as the level of fishing in such a way as to reflect the social optimum where the market prices of the goods reflect their true social cost.

So, the meaning of this is that with regard to the benchmark of certainty, the problem of missing market should not shake our confidence in the ability of competitive decentralised decision-making to solve the eco-

---

[22] We assume that the fishermen are interested in maximising their own value and will therefore accept money for the right to dump the refuse in the river. The price that they will determine will be such that the quantity dumped will be consistent with the social optimum of bruising and producing fish for the market.

nomic problem. It does however add an element to the conditions which need to be satisfied before we can establish that such organisational principles will indeed lead to an efficient allocation. The potential of missing markets requires that to ensure the efficiency of competition we must be sure that property rights have been allocated but it does not matter how. As this is something which is not difficult to imagine, our confidence in the competitive paradigm should not be shaken. Having said this, we must bear in mind that even when property rights have been fully allocated, there would still be externalities which are difficult to detect. It does not matter who owns the river, the creative talents living along it may not realise how disruptive is the noise of the boats and the tourists travelling next to their place of work. If we take this line of reasoning, then there can be only one conclusion: competitive decentralisation will always lead to an inefficient outcome which is not easily discernible from the inefficiency created by a monopolist or other forms of what is known as market failures. There would be nothing—in terms of our definition of the economic problem and the conception of the individual—about competitive decentralisation which would recommend it as a desired form of economic organisation. Economics, of course, chose the former path. The Coase Theorem was celebrated and the problem of missing markets, temporarily, was hastily shoved under the carpet.

However, we already discussed the realisation that uncertainty requires a restatement of the paradigmatic core because an abstraction without it is an *irrelevant abstraction*. This means that when we recognise the endemic nature of missing markets, for the abstraction to remain relevant we cannot really stop at examining the core in the case of certainty and we must reconfirm it with a simultaneous reference to both uncertainty and missing markets. And here, as will become apparent, there will be a complete failure in restating that competitive decentralisation would lead to a co-ordinated outcome which solves the economic problem. If we find that at the logical limit spontaneous orders based on competitive decentralisation do not solve the economic problem and are not ethically neutral, we can no longer use this organisational principle as either a reference point or a guiding line.

We did not say much about the changes in economic analysis that followed the introduction of uncertainty, but we did mention (in a footnote) the principle that the same good in different states of the world constituted different economic goods. This means that agents will not only trade in commodities (or goods)—the analysis of which was covered by the certainty case—but will also wish to trade goods in different states of the world. A simple story to explain this can be described as follows: suppose that there is only one commodity (say wheat) and that there are only two individuals: A and B. Both of them grow wheat, but A's farm is on a top of a hill, while B's farm is at the bottom of a valley. Suppose too that there are only two possible states of the world: sunny or stormy. If it is stormy, the entire crops of A will be decimated as his farm is on top of the hill and exposed to the winds. The crops of B will flourish as the valley is protected from the winds. If it were sunny, the crops of A will flourish but B's crops will be decimated due to the frost that will settle in the bottom of the valley when there is no wind. So, each agent wants two economic goods: wheat in sunny weather and wheat in stormy weather. Naturally, only one state of the world will materialise, which means that one of them will find himself without any wheat. Therefore, they will trade wheat in one state of the world for wheat in another. This is what we mean by insurance. In an ideal world, they could trade with a promise—or a *state-contingent claim*—that A will sell so much wheat to B at such a (money) price if it is sunny, in return for which B will sell so much wheat to A at such a (money) price if it is stormy. But in reality, where there are many such individuals and many such commodities, there are no clear markets for such kind of a trade so instead, A and B can trade in their *assets* to ensure the consumption of wheat in either states of the world. If they exchange some of each other's land, they can achieve what they desire. Namely, if A sells half (or any other fraction) of his lands to B in return for half (or any other fraction) of B's land, both of them will have assets which yield wheat in either states of the world.

Indeed, once we generalise this idea, we discover that for such a system to work and achieve a distribution of assets that would have obtained, for all agents, that which they would have wanted to have in any state of the world, the number of assets should be the same as the number of the possible states of the world. This is what we mean, in this context, by a state of *complete markets* or no missing markets. In our example, we had two states of the world (stormy and sunny) and two assets (the plot of land on top of the hill and the one at the bottom of the valley). To see what would have happened had the number of assets been less than the number of states of nature, we should simply think of a situation where there was only one plot of land (say, on top of the hill) but still two states of nature. This means that if A—who owns the plot—could have trades in state-contingent claims, he would have wanted to have less wheat in the good state in return for some wheat in the bad state. However, without such a market, there are not enough assets to trade with. Consequently, he will have to be satisfied with what his assets provide him in each state of the world without being able to alter this outcome. It is quite obvious that this outcome is inferior to the one which the person would have preferred when he can consume wheat in either states of the world. This is what missing markets (or *incomplete markets*) means in the context of uncertainty.

Given the almost-infinite number of states of nature which are possible, it is next to impossible to believe that there could be an equivalent number of assets in society. Therefore, the efforts people will make to insure themselves—the role of financial markets—will necessarily lead to economic inefficiency which, through the interrelated pricing mechanisms of general equilibrium, will permeate into the trade in actual commodities to lead to a complete breakdown of efficiency.[23] In such a case, the outcome of competitive decentralised decision-making will fail to resolve

---

[23] Some economists take an extremely narrow view of what economics does and for them economics is the art of reaching an agreement between rational agents. Therefore, the problem of missing market is just a problem of constraint. If we do not have enough assets, individuals will still be able to trade and reach an equilibrium which is Pareto-efficient in the sense that one cannot make anyone better off without making someone else worse off. However, it is clear that this is not what people would have wanted had they been able to trade in state-contingent claims. The outcome of such a trade would have constituted the solution to the economic problem. The solution that will materialise failing this may be such where we cannot make one person better off without harming the other, but it still is not a solution to the economic problem. Namely, it will not correspond to the benchmark of efficiency. To show the absurdity of this claim, imagine a world in which there are monopolists. This is clearly a world where the value of what has been produced is not maximised and there are clear deadweight losses in terms of efficiency. Yet, according to this narrow view of economics, agents may trade in secondary markets that which has been allocated to them and, in so doing, reach an allocation where no one can be made better off without harming another. This may, in principle, allow some gains in utility for both agents but not enough to offset the loss of utility emanating from the presence of monopolists. Surely no one would argue that such an equilibrium, in spite of its apparent efficiency, constitutes a solution to the economic problem in the way in which we defined it.

the economic problem. There will no longer be a reason why the spread of competitive decentralisation is a desired course of action if we strive to resolve our economic problem.

It is important to emphasise that this is not a question of reality versus ideal; it is not about the fact that the actual world does not look the same as the ideal. Instead, it is about the role of the ideal. We already acknowledged that we do not expect the ideal to be descriptive, but it has to be a *relevant abstraction* in the sense that it captures the fundamentals of the reality it is modelling. As such, it is a logical limit of an idea. As long as there were no logical problems to prove that, logically, competitive decentralisation leads to the solution of the economic problem, it made sense to use it as a guiding principle of organisation and a means for evaluating that which we observe in reality, even if reality seemed remote from the conditions of the model. But the moment that this logical proof breaks down—due to significant updates of fundamentals—and becomes more like an *impossibility theorem*, that which collapses is not the descriptive power of the model but the validity of its logical instructions. It is thus no longer true that competitive decentralisation either solves the economic problem or is ethically neutral; why, then, pursue it with such vigour? Why then, evaluate organisation against the principles of competitive decentralisation? And why jump into conclusion that if an arrangement does not coincide with the principles of markets, it must be failing the economic agenda of society?

But is it possible that like in the case of certainty we can find something similar to the Coase Theorem which would help resolve the problem? The answer is, alas, negative. Allocating property rights will still be a necessity but unlike the case of certainty, now, the distribution of these rights matters a great deal. By implication, as property rights affect the flows of income in the system, it means that the theory would lose its ethical neutrality which was achieved through the second welfare theorem and the Coase theorem. But things are even more complicated than this. To understand it better we must be very clear here about what exactly it is that we are talking about. In the beginning of our narrative we said that in modern economics a solution to the economic problem will be an allocation which is efficient in the sense that we cannot have more of one economic good without forgoing another. We mentioned the distinction between productive efficiency, where the economic goods in question are things tangible like commodities or services, and allocative (Pareto) efficiency, where the economic good that we cannot have more of, without forgoing another, is a less tangible good like utility or wellbeing.[24] We normally tend to lump the two together in the sense that we are not interested in solutions which are merely productive efficient. If we can still make one person better off without making someone else worse off (where wellbeing is the economic good in question) we—from the modern and individualistic perspective—cannot be satisfied that society has resolved the economic problem. After all, in this modern, individualistic set-up, the purpose of society is to facilitate the solution of the economic problem by all individuals. The absence of allocative efficiency—which is, effectively, the distributional aspect of the solution—would clearly mean that we have not fully resolved this problem for everyone. We may have produced enough goods, but we have not distributed them properly.

Nevertheless, given that commodities or tangible economic goods are desired by everyone, it seemed reasonable to expect that the choice of allocative (Pareto) efficient distributions would come from the set of productive efficient allocations. If an allocation is Pareto-efficient but not productive efficient, surely we can increase the quantity of one tangible economic good, or commodity, without forgoing another and give it to one person. If we could do this, that person would become better off without anyone becoming worse off. So, on the face of it, it seemed quite sensible to condition allocative efficiency on productive efficiency. Put differently, not all productive efficient allocations are also allocative efficient but we would like all allocative efficient allocations to be productive efficient.[25]

---

[24] In other words, productive efficiency is about allocating resources in such a way as to fully utilise the existing resources while allocative efficiency is about the distribution of that which has been produced.

[25] In Chap. 7, we discuss a case where two agents in society with different abilities choose to divide the work between them according to a principle of equity rather than expediency (in this case, the issue was the distribution of burden). In such a case, it is clear that the productive inefficient allocation is allocatively efficient, which contradicts what we have just said. However, it is important to bear in mind that from the perspective of the organisational principles of the paradigm there are no clear organisational rules that will lead to such an allocation. Competitive decentralisation is highly unlikely to lead us to such an allocation. Therefore, such a case is a case where moral values precede

In our discussion of the effects of incomplete markets in the presence of uncertainty, on the efficiency of the outcome we were primarily concerned with allocative efficiency and not so much with productive efficiency. When A and B, in our example, wanted to trade in their respective output to smooth their consumption over the two states of the world, we assumed that the output each one of them will produce is given and is the maximum they can do (hence, productive efficient). But once they trade their assets, a new problem—which is an extension of the missing market problem—arises. This is the problem of incomplete contracts. If A now owns half the plot on top of the hill and half the plot at the bottom of the valley while B owns the other halves, the question that arises is who works for whom?

When they could trade in state-contingent claims, each one owned his entire plot and the entire output of that plot would have gone to the owner (A will have the entire output of the plot on the hill, while B will have the entire out of the plot in the valley). They only traded in the output depending on the state of nature. But when they divide the ownership of the plots and each one of them continues to work the same plot, they become employee of the other when they cultivate the other's share of the plot. This means that the output they produce on that part of the plot does not belong to them but rather to the person who owns it. Now will they put the same amount of effort in cultivating the part of the plot they own and where the entire produce of their labour goes to them and the part of the plot where the produce of their labour goes to someone else? Of course, they may earn a wage for it, or even get an agreed fraction of what they have produced, but the owner always has residual claims which he can use to reduce the amount available for the division between him and the employee.[26] This is known as the problem of **_incomplete contracts_**, which is another expression of the problem of

economic considerations which cannot be the case of a universal and ethically neutral system. This point too will be further discussed in Chap. 8.

[26] Residual claims are the basis upon which an owner can argue for a smaller share of the produce to be available. If, for instance, the agreement between the owner of the plot and the worker is to share the produce of the employee effort 50:50, then if the produce is a 100, the employee will get 50. However, the owner can say that he must keep 10 aside because he has extra cost emanating from his ownership of the land, which means that instead of receiving 50, the employee will get only 45.

missing markets, and which gives rise to the significance of the distribution of property rights for the question of productive efficiency. In our case, it is clear that as rational agents the amount of effort they will put while working their own part will be greater than the amount of effort they will put in working the part which belongs to the other. Therefore, the total amount of output (in either states of the world) would be lower than in the case where they could have traded in state-contingent claims and hence, the outcome is productively inefficient.

But while the problem of allocative inefficiency cannot be resolved due to our inability to generate sufficient number of assets, the problem with productive efficiency may be somewhat ameliorated. In our story, we assumed that after they trade in shares of their plots of land they continue to work on their original plot. This made them worker-owner as well as employees. But if they only worked the land they owned, the productive efficient outcome may be salvaged. Namely, if A now worked half the time on this share of the plot on top of the mountain and half the time on the share of his plot at the bottom of the valley, he will only be working on the land which he owns. This means that his effort will be maximised. The same would be true for agent B. As we have only one good in our story, the differences in their skills does not matter and the total output after trade in assets will be more or less the same as it would have been in the case when they could trade in state-contingent claims. In such a case, the outcome will maintain its productive efficiency, and as the number of assets is the same as the number of states of the world, it would also be allocative efficient. But the problem of incomplete contract will still be there when the number of assets cannot match the number of states of nature. This means that allocative inefficiency is inherent, but productive efficiency may somewhat be salvaged if the distribution of property rights is optimised to maximise output.

In other words, in the case of certainly, the distribution of property rights could be anything and, therefore, the competitive system, in spite of the requirement to allocate property rights, could still continue to support all possible distributions of income (and hence, stay ethically neutral). However, in the uncertainty case there is a very specific distribution of these rights—and hence, income—which facilitates productive efficiency: broadly speaking it is the one where agents own the assets which they operate.[27] This means that even if we could match the number of assets with the states of nature so as to establish allocative efficiency as well, the restrictions imposed on the distribution of property rights limit the scope of the system to accommodate all possible distributions of income. We thus lose the ethical neutrality of the system that was an essential component in the argument for its compatibility with all societies and cultures.

Altogether, the picture that seems to emerge from the complication of missing markets (in uncertainty) is that allocative efficiency must be abandoned, and productive efficiency can only be preserved under very restrictive rules for the distribution of property rights. Put differently, incomplete markets have logically overturned the idea that competitive decentralisation can ever lead to a solution of the economic problem. At first, we thought that property rights would save the day, but we soon discovered that this is not the case if we consider the other fundamental (uncertainty) which the abstraction has to take into account in order to remain relevant. Still, through specific forms of ownership structures, we were able to recover some of the generation of plenty (productive efficiency) aspect of the theory but failed to salvage that which is most important for the solution of the economic problem in an individualistic theory: allocative efficiency.[28]

So, the question that arises is whether the loss of allocative (Pareto) efficiency should be a reason to abandon the whole project altogether. Could it be sensible for us to say that while it is true that competitive decentralisation will not produce an allocative efficient solution, it may

---

[27] It is interesting to note that the modern conception of the connection between ownership and productivity has already been fully articulated by Nassau Senior and J. S. Mill.

[28] Notice that entailed in this story is also an explanation to the existence of corporations (which has also been the concern of institutional economics). In principle, in a purely competitive environment, all activities should be conducted through markets. The presence of corporations suggests that this is not the case and some transactions take place, as it were, in-house. Clearly, the reasons for this are both the presence of missing markets (which make some market transaction inefficient) and the salvaging power of specific ownership structures (like corporations) which make these transactions efficient (for a more complete discussion, see, for instance, Hart (1995)). This means that corporations are here not to impede competition but rather to support markets in the face of the disturbance generated by missing markets. Notice that corporations are in essence the union of capital. The implications of all of this are that in modern economics unions of capital are beneficial for society while union of labour is not (as it gives power to a group of agents which distorts efficiency).

still produce a productive efficient one which is both a condition for allocative efficiency and, more importantly, a real step in the direction of creating plenty and hence we should continue pursuing competitive decentralisation? On the face of it, this does not look a promising avenue to take. The word 'efficiency' itself means very little, and when it is not dealing with all members of society, it may tell us even less. For instance, it is possible to show that in the case of fixed-proportions technologies in production (where the two factors of production are labour and capital) productive efficient allocations will include allocations where only capital is fully employed. This means that labour is not fully employed but because there is not enough capital, we cannot produce more of one good without forgoing another and hence, some labour will remain unemployed. According to the definition of efficiency, this will be a productive efficient allocation. Could we simply ignore this fact and celebrate the productive efficiency of our arrangement? Surely a situation where some people do not participate in the production process cannot be the base for a solution of the economic problem unless there are clear **social** mechanisms which ensure the access to national income for those who are unable to achieve this through the market. Alternatively, if society is producing efficiently but most of its resources are directed to the production of luxury goods while most of the people are poor, the productive efficiency of the allocation of resources is unlikely to impress anyone as a solution to society's economic problem. In other words, the production of plenty is by no stretch of imagination a sufficient condition for the economic problem—as it had been conceived by modern economics—to be solved. And if it were, it would, by no possible account, be either universal or ethically neutral.

However, in spite of these quite serious blows to the idea that competitive decentralisation either solves the economic problem or is ethically—and, therefore, socially—neutral, the vigour in the pursuit of such (competitive) institutional arrangements has not been dampened. If anything, it became even stronger in recent years and the question we must ask ourselves is whether there could still be a reason to universally pursue competitive decentralisation even when it is clear that it does not deliver on its original promise.

2.3.2   The Issue of Approximation

In part, the resilience of economics' paradigmatic core stems from its somewhat vague methodological position. There can be no doubt that the ideal of an efficient general equilibrium is the heart and soul of the idea that spontaneous order works. But it is a logical claim which, as we emphasised before, is not, and should not be, expected to be a description of reality, though one should have some expectations regarding the relationship of this abstraction with the world it claims to conceptualise.

Indeed, when we identified the problem of incomplete markets as a reason to discredit the claim about the promise of a spontaneous order based on competitive decentralisation, it was part of the discussion about the relationship between the model and the world. To remind the reader, in this context we distinguished between aspects of reality which could, in principle, be ameliorated and, thus, lead the observed world on an asymptotic trajectory towards the ideal and those which are too fundamental, and therefore, must be part of the abstraction itself. Namely, it is no longer a question of approximating the ideal but whether the relevant ideal still suggests the same claim.

Agents with power or the asymmetric distribution of it are all issues that can be dealt with through legislation or policy which, in principle, can lead to an institutional set-up where the reality of economic interactions increasingly resembles that of the ideal. The presence of uncertainty cannot be changed, and this required a restatement of the claim that competitive decentralisation is a socially beneficial spontaneous order. So, is the phenomenon of missing markets (or contracts) such that can be ameliorated or is it fundamental? We have argued that it is the latter, but some may feel that it is the former.

It is evident that if it is the latter, there can be no claim that competitive decentralisation can solve the economic problem even in its most abstract form. This means that competition must cease to be a reference point for economic analysis. It may indeed capture reality—something which we will question too—but as such, it is a reality that should be contained rather than promoted. The only way people may keep their belief in the promise of economics' paradigmatic core is if they insist that the problem of missing markets can be ameliorated. We argued that in the case of certainty this may appear to be possible. After all, with the help of Coase Theorem (and the allocation of property rights), the tenets of the core remain unchanged. But in the case of uncertainty, whether or not it is possible is entirely dependent on one's views about the relationship between the number of assets and the number of states of nature. We argued that the latter will always exceed the former and this is why competitive decentralisation will always be allocative inefficient and even for productive efficiency it would lose the ethical neutrality. Nevertheless, someone could argue that there are no limits to financial innovation and in reality the number of assets is constantly growing, which means that we are on an approximation trajectory which could lead us nearer to the ideal (unreasonably assuming that the number of the states of nature is both finite and constant).

However, the fact remains that even when we consider problems that can be ameliorated (like the imbalance in agents' powers), we know that through policy and legislation we can only approximate the conditions stipulated in the core for the claims about the benefits of competition to be true. Namely, we will never really fulfil the necessary conditions for the claim in the model to be logically true (let alone, empirically). So, can the process of approximation really be considered a reason to maintain our belief in the promise of economics' paradigmatic core?

2.3.3 The Promised Land: On the Significance of Unreachable Dreams

At such a junction when we begin to realise that we are in the pursuit of the unreachable, one cannot but get biblical. In the book of Deuteronomy, chapter 34, verse 4, God says onto Moses after 40 years of wandering in the desert on the way from Egypt to Canaan: 'And the LORD said unto him: "This is the land which I swore unto Abraham, unto Isaac, and unto Jacob, saying: I will give it unto thy seed; I have caused thee to see it with thine eyes, but thou shalt not go over thither".' The paradigmatic core, here, plays the role of the Promised Land; the current theory (the culmination of the process of the dialogue with reality), on the other hand, plays the role of Moses and all other Israelite who came all the way from Egypt. It is clear in this biblical reference that the Promised Land exists. But not for Moses and all those who were the desert generation, namely those who were born slaves in Egypt and who have roamed the desert on their way to this Promised Land. They would never enter it. This means that while the Promised Land may or may not exist for the next generation, for the older generation it did not exit; it had only been a promise. Similarly, economic theory has been taking us on a journey to a Promised Land which will never ever materialise (and we have no equivalence here for the next generation).

So, in some sense, for the desert generation the Promised Land was just a point of reference rather than any concrete reality. It was, of course, useful as it gave them both direction and a sense of purpose. But when they died before reaching it, can we say that they had enjoyed its promised benefits? Can we say that they saw any of its promised benefit as they approached it? The answer to both questions must be negative. The land which was promised was of milk and honey and none of those wanderers of the desert generation will ever feel the taste of milk or honey.

Similarly, when we say that the paradigmatic core promises a solution to the economic problem when all markets are perfectly competitive and there are no missing markets (or enough assets to match the number of states of nature), we are actually saying that the benefits of competition, like the milk and honey of the Promised Land, will never be experienced by those who are seeking it. The process of approaching the conditions required for the benefits of competition to be accrued does not entail a single point which is genuinely efficient. It only entails the *hope* of efficiency.

But would the Israelites have agreed to wonder 40 years in the desert if they knew that they will never enter the Promised Land? The bible does not tell us and the answer could be yes if we consider the possible altruism of the generation of slaves. They would have probably gone all this way without benefitting themselves if they believed that their children would benefit from it. But from our perspective, there are no generational issues and the hypothetical question we should ask is whether they would have wandered the desert for 40 years if they knew that they (or any of their children) would never get to the Promised Land. To this the answer would be clearly no. Therefore, the route to the Promised Land was merely a reference point which provided a sense of purpose, but only as long as it was believed to be a reachable goal; when it was believed that they would all enjoy the milk and honey of the land. In the same vein, why should societies choose the path of competition if it will never ever yield its promised benefits? Yet, it is difficult to imagine people who would not associate the term 'competition' with efficiency and efficiency with the good of society. In other words, either people are deluded or they realise that things are not good, but believe that we are on the right path!

There are, therefore, two separate issues. The first is the question of convergence and the second the question of reference. We will take them in turns. By convergence we mean that there exists, in principle, a process which brings us closer to the logical limit of the idea of competition and where the paradigmatic core resides; and where the benefits attributed to this limit can be better felt the nearer we get to it. In simple terms and ignoring now the problems of incompleteness, we know that the benefits of competition will be accrued in a world where all markets are perfectly competitive. Will the expansion of competition to markets which until now were, say, monopolised, make us, so to speak, *more* efficient? If we can make sense of the word 'more efficient' and if this is indeed the case, then it is possible to say that there is a process whereby we are monotonically approaching the efficient outcome; we will, sometime, enter the Promised Land.

However, from our perspective, the idea of being 'more' or 'less' efficient is a hollow one. Recall that efficiency means not being able to have more of one economic good without forgoing another. Therefore, we are either in this situation or we are not; we are either efficient or we are not. We cannot be half efficient or a quarter efficient so what would 'more' or 'less' efficiency mean? By implication, we also cannot compare or evaluate degrees of inefficiency. We cannot say that one allocation is more or less inefficient than another.[29] If this is indeed the case, there exists no asymp-

---

[29] Previously, we used the area under the demand to approximate the money value of the utility generated by the consumption of commodity x. In this particular case, we managed to argue that the inefficiency of the monopolist will be the same as the inefficiency generated by missing markets. However, this was a very simple case of one market and where we had no information about the

totic process which leads us to the benefits of the paradigmatic core; these will only be accrued at the logical limit and not a moment before. So, unless we can demonstrate that we can actually reach the ideal of competitive decentralisation, it will not be possible to justify the drive for greater competitiveness.

A possible way to pour some contents into a notion of a level of efficiency would have been some measure of social welfare. If we could say that there is a social welfare function which measures the collective well-being of the public, then we could meaningfully talk about the move from one inefficient allocation with lower social welfare to a different inefficient allocation with higher social welfare. We may indeed call the latter allocation a 'more' efficient one or, better phrased, 'less' inefficient one as it is, after all, not really efficient. In such a case, if we can demonstrate that the competitive drive increases the level of efficiency, then even if we know that we will never ever get to the ideal of a perfectly competitive system, we may claim that we are *asymptotically* approaching it. It is in a case like this that the paradigmatic core—which will never materialise—becomes what I shall call a *reference point*, a form of 'spiritual' guidance as the promise land was for the lost Israelites in the desert.

Altogether, if we were to distinguish between the institutional question and the question of benefits, we will end up with four main possible situations. By the institutional question, we are referring to the process whereby the economy moves towards the required conditions for competitive decentralisation to yield its benefits (i.e. efficiency, both productive and allocative). This refers to the process we mentioned earlier, where in the absence of missing markets the number of economic activities conducted through perfectly competitive markets increase. By the question of benefits, we are referring to the question of whether the institutional change which leads us towards the fulfilment of the required conditions by the paradigmatic core is accompanied by an improved efficiency (which, of course, depends on whether this can indeed be measured).

---

distribution of the benefits among all participants. We assumed the demand to be derived from the utility of a representative agent and, consequently, lost all the information about the distribution of these benefits across all those who participate in the market. To do this, we run into the difficulty of comparing utilities between individuals.

From the perspective of the institutional change, there are only two possible situations: either the process of expanding competition can lead us to a world which is completely competitive or not. But in each of these situations there are two corresponding situations with regard to benefits: either benefits are measurable and improve when we move towards complete competition or they are not measurable or not monotonically improve. We thus have the following four positions:

The road to the Promised Land

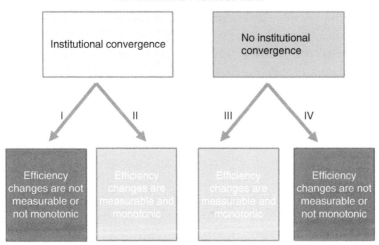

In situations I and II, we assume that there is institutional convergence in the sense that by expanding competitive practices we will, in principle, get to a position where all economic activities without exception are conducted through fully competitive interactions (markets).[30] This corre-

---

[30] If there are also missing markets—in the case of certainty—then the allocation of property rights regardless of their distribution will solve the problem (this is the case of certainty). Also, we may add to this the assumption that natural monopolies are state owned and produce efficiently at marginal cost pricing with a designated lump-sum tax to cover their losses. However, it is not inconceivable to consider the possibility of institutional convergence even in the presence of missing markets. Recall that part of the effects of missing markets was to form corporations and, therefore, require certain ownership structures to ensure productive efficiency. In a digitised world, it may be the case that when individuals are less concerned about job security—being able to derive income from other sources—they may work more on a freelance base which may be a way to solve some of the missing market problems (in the sense that operators own the assets with which they work).

sponds to what we have said about the world of certainty with and without missing markets as well as the world with uncertainty and complete markets. In all these cases, there is nothing which in principle prevents reality to converge to the ideal as depicted by the abstract model. In the case of uncertainty and incomplete markets (and contracts), this would only apply if one believes that it is conceivable that at any time the number of assets will be the same as the number of states of nature.

Now if efficiency changes are not measurable or if they are, they are not monotonic (situation I), then we may still desire to pursue competition even though there are no immediate benefits, because we know that when we reach the end state, the benefits (i.e. productive and allocative efficiency) will be accrued to us. In other words, we will get to the Promised Land, though the journey may be long and hard.

In situation II we still have institutional convergence as before, but here efficiency gains are measurable and monotonic. This is the best of all possible worlds. Not only are we on an ever-improving path, in the end we will also be showered with all the benefits which the system promised. The pursuit of competitive practices not only makes sense but is an imperative.

In situations III and IV, we assume that there is no institutional convergence. This is particularly true in the case of missing markets in the world of uncertainty. Here, it does not matter how many more assets we create, as we cannot know how the set of possible states of nature changes, we cannot say whether we are closer or further from the situation where the number of assets is the same as the number of states of the world which, in our case, is the equivalent to having more economic interactions conducted in less than perfectly competitive conditions. Put differently, it does not matter what we do, we will never find ourselves in a situation where the conditions required for the paradigmatic core to deliver the solution to the economic problem are met.[31] So, we are now in the domain in which the competitive paradigm is no longer the objective as it becomes a *reference point*. It is what the Promised Land meant

---

[31] Elul (1995), for instance, demonstrates how financial innovations—the equivalent to an increase in the number of competitive markets—does not necessarily lead to an improvement in welfare. This, of course, is the case of situation IV.

to those Israelites who would have never reached it. However, whether or not this reference point should play the role of a guiding principle depends on whether the journey towards it is socially beneficial.

In situation III, we can measure efficiency gains as we move across inefficient allocations. This means that even though we will never experience the full benefits of the paradigmatic promise, the process itself bring us *asymptotically* nearer to it. The logic behind the pursuit of competitive practices in this case should be based first on accepting that the paradigmatic core encapsulates something which is socially desirable even if it is institutionally unreachable, and second, on the progress of these benefits as we expand competition. In situation IV, on the other hand, the reference point becomes mute. It is the case where not only do we know that competitive decentralisation will never yield a solution to the economic problem, but also there is nothing in the attempts to reach it which yields any benefits. It is the scenario where we have the ultimate rejection of the paradigmatic core as it is neither reachable institutionally nor is the process of trying to get there, beneficial in any meaningful way.

So, we can see from the above that the mere difficulties in fulfilling the institutional conditions which are embedded in the logical limit of competitive decentralisation are not in themselves a reason to abandon the project. This may explain why in the case of certainty or uncertainty with complete markets, the logic of the pursuit of competitive practices was based either on the possibility that the ideal will materialise or on the process that brings us nearer to its benefits, or both. But in the case of uncertainty with incomplete markets, neither holds. As there is no persuasive argument that by pursuing greater competitiveness we are reaping some of the benefits which await us at the end of the process, we can, at best, adopt the paradigmatic core as a reference point. However, for this to be a valid reference point we do have to accept that it is possible, in principle, to equate the number of assets to the number of states of the world. This, we feel, is far too much to expect. There is no dispute that in the case of certainty, the ideal, in principle, could materialise and therefore we may believe in it even if there is no asymptotic process. But there will always be a disputation about the possibility of complete markets in uncertainty. Given that there is also no asymptotic process, one cannot really accept such a severely contested presumption as the foundation of economic and social thinking. This means that the model that correctly captures uncertainty and incomplete markets as fundamentals of reality will bring us to scenario IV. The significance of this scenario is that it suggests that there is no logical reason why society should believe that spontaneous order based on competitive decentralisation should yield a solution to the economic problem. Nor should society use competition as a reference point or a guiding principle for social or economic organisation.

But there is another reason why there should be serious doubts about the possibility of any convergence towards the ideal either in the case of certainty or in the case of uncertainty with incomplete markets. It is the problem of price formation. Recall that in the diagrams above we identified an equilibrium price where the outcome is efficient. But the only thing we know is that there exists such a price (where demand intersects supply). However, we do not know the nature of competitive interaction and therefore we have no clear idea about the process which produces these equilibrium prices. The truth is that to date no convincing process of competitive interactions which is sufficiently general has been produced to explain the emergence of these prices which solve the economic problem.[32] This means that even though there may be institutional convergence, it does not mean anything at all. The fact that the conditions of perfectly competitive markets are fulfilled may still not yield the solution to the economic problem if we do not know whether this will also lead to those prices where we expect the problem to be solved. Hence, the conclusion should be that there is never a convergence. This reduces our options to scenarios III and IV and whether or not we can uphold the message of economics' paradigmatic core relies heavily on whether there exists an asymptotic process in terms of benefits.

On this front, it seems, there has been very little progress. As we said before, the only obvious way of ranking inefficient allocations would have been through some measure of social wellbeing which is defined over these allocations. With ordinal individual utility functions, we have become aware of the difficulties associated with aggregating measures of wellbeing. Arrow's impossibility theorem has created insurmountable problems for any attempt at creating social preferences which could have

---

[32] See Appendix.

been the basis for a non-utilitarian social welfare function. We are, therefore, on very weak grounds when it comes to the question of ranking inefficient allocations. Moreover, even if we accept that there may exist a social welfare function which behaves as nicely as an individual's utility function, we will find that expanding competitiveness does not necessitate monotonic improvement. This means that an allocation with larger set of economic activities covered by proper competition is not necessarily 'more' efficient—in the sense of generating higher social welfare—than an allocation with fewer such practices. If this is indeed the case, we are left with situation IV, which, as we said, suggests that there is no obvious reason why societies should so vigorously pursue competitive decentralisation. In fact, this may give us a reason to abandon the competitive project altogether and begin thinking afresh on the questions of economic and social organisation.

In other words, even if we accept the proposition as if the number of assets may correspond to the number of state of nature, we are still left with the universal problem of convergence emanating from the problem of price formation. Against this background, it is difficult to reach any other conclusion than that irrespective of how one interprets the institutional convergence there will never be convergence and there is no process of asymptotic acquisition of benefits. Hence, we must reject the conclusion which has been repeatedly drummed into the head of countless generations of students who became citizens, politicians, captains of industry and academic economists and instead clearly state that competitive interaction is a problem rather than a solution.

All of these tie well with what we have been discussing in the previous chapter. Recall that one of the questions we posed there was whether or not the idea of natural order, or self-regulating systems, was a perception of reality or an ideal. In early days of human social thinking, a working natural order was an ideal predicated on human behaviour (which needed to be improved and was not, in principle, natural). With the Enlightenment, the question changes into whether, given the (natural) behaviour of individuals, there will be a natural, or spontaneous, order. Following physics, it was believed that there may indeed be a social natural order. But unlike physics, while there may always be some form of a natural order (what we called synchronic order), whether or not this could be a sustainable arrangement depended on whether it fulfilled people's moral expectations (what we called diachronic order). What we have been discussing here is the question of whether the reality of natural order could be considered as sustainable (i.e. diachronic order), given that the conditions for such sustainability only reside in the logical limit of the competitive idea or the paradigmatic core. This, in turn, depended on the relationship between reality and the ideal. Therefore, if we are in situation IV above, it means that the reality of natural order will never have the attributes of its ideal form. Notice that this does not mean that there are no societies for which competitive decentralisation may indeed constitute the morally supported solution of the economic problem. It only means that the claims for its universality and ethical neutrality as the basis for its diachronic order are ill-founded.

2.3.4   The Shadow of a Dilemma

So far, our discussion of the difficulties which the paradigmatic core faces was focused on the validity of its conclusions when some fundamentals of reality—in an abstract form—are *added* to the existing abstraction. But we have not questioned at all, the premises of the system. Thus, we asked what would happen in a world where there are rational agents who behave competitively if they also faced uncertainty and incomplete markets. Namely, we have not changed or contested the premise of the system in terms of its conception of the individual. In the end, a great deal of what we are trying to do in this book is just that, but at this stage we would like to make just a short comment about this, in the context of the dialogue between the abstraction (the model) and the world which it purports to conceptualise.

We already mentioned that one of the issues within the domain of the second type of dialogue—the one where deviations from the model could, in principle, be ameliorated by legislation and policy—is the question of powers which agents hold in the market. For competitive decentralisation to produce the spontaneous order which solves the economic problem, agents should have no powers over others or the markets and certainly should have no asymmetric powers. We briefly mentioned the simple example of the monopolist. But associated with the presence of such power was the development of the notion of strategic interaction, which is a more realistic depiction of competitive behaviour when agents have powers to influence outcomes.

The contributions of game theory to this question are quite interesting as in part they increase our confidence in the promise of the paradigmatic core even when agents have powers. In this respect, this is all truly in the domain of the second type of problem. In game theory, competitive behaviour is extended further by adding strategic consideration to the power which agents already possess. By strategic behaviour we are not departing from the basic notion of competitive behaviour, but agents are now aware of the others' possible choice of actions and the effect that this would have on the outcome. This mutual awareness has given rise to a new concept of equilibrium depicting competitive interaction. It is the concept of Nash equilibrium.[33] Unlike competitive equilibrium where agents have no individual power to influence the outcome and where the equilibrium is really the coincidence of all their rational plans, in the Nash equilibrium we have a situation where no agent can find a better course of action given the other agents' possible choices, but the outcome may *not* be the best the agent could have hoped for in the context of the game. In such a set-up, also known as the prisoner's dilemma, the only way the agent can reach the most desired outcome for him, from all possible outcomes, would be by *colluding* with the others. But relying on others may be risky if this were not the best strategy the individual would have chosen without such reliance. In other words, the rationality and competitiveness of agents would make such a collusion an irrational choice and therefore not a sustainable one. Consequently, as those who have the power are undermined by their competitiveness, the economy in general would gain.

In this respect, strategic behaviour in game theory allowed us to strengthen our beliefs in the promise of the core. Even without a legal apparatus or policies to curb the power of participants, there are clear market forces which will work to undermine the power of agents. When agents interact

---

[33] On the fascinating history of how the concept emerged from von Neumann through Morgenstern and, subsequently, Nash, see Giocoli (2003).

strategically, the ultimate inefficiency of the outcome—the greatest monopolists' exploits available to the participants—would only happen when agents collude: when they agree to hold back output so as to keep the price well above its perfectly competitive benchmark. But as each agent is rational they have an *incentive* to deviate and take advantage of the higher price. In so doing, they lead the market nearer to its competitive benchmark. In some cases—as it is in the classical Bertrand Model—the competitive interaction of agents, who have power but behave strategically, will lead to the very same competitive outcome that would materialise if they had no power at all. In other words, as is the case in the paradigmatic notion of competitive decentralisation, competition erodes the power of agents and, in so doing, directs us towards the efficient outcome.[34]

But if competitive behaviour—as embedded in the Nash equilibrium—leads to an outcome where participating agents are not capable of achieving the outcome they desire through competition, it may have broader implications. In the oligopolistic kind of games which we described, it is indeed the case that the prisoner's dilemma represents the failure of agents to exploit others (in this case, customers who are not taking part in the game). However, it also means that competitive interaction does not yield the desired outcome for those who participate. If we expand the game to include all members of society as may be represented in the public good or social choice types of games, then a prisoner's dilemma means that competitive decentralisation leads to an outcome which is not the solution to the economic problem (i.e. it is allocatively inefficient). Namely, competitive interactions (or spontaneous order) fail to solve the economic problem.

---

[34] Of course, there are mountains of attempts to analyse conditions under which the agents will stick to their collusion rather than deviate but in many of these studies the distinction between what is an abstraction and what is a reality has been somewhat blurred. One can always create sufficiently complex and specific imaginary structures where outcomes will be different, but in the dialogue between reality and the model we are more concerned with simplified and fairly general rules. Indeed, the story I tell is the one that managed to enter the textbooks even though some allowances are made to the other forms of analysis (like infinite horizon and the likes), but if they take us further from the paradigmatic core, they make the latter irrelevant and leave us without any clear idea about what would be the best form of social organisation that will resolve the economic problem.

In the public good case agents have a choice of contributing something to the public purse and as a result, share—equally with everyone else— the benefits created by the public good to which they have all contributed. However, it will be strategically rational for agents to freeride. Namely, if others contribute to the public good and you do not, you will still benefit from it (this is the nature of a public good like, for instance, defence) while keeping all your income for yourself. Of course, if everyone does this, the public good will either not come to being or be inadequate. Evidently, like in the oligopolistic case, if agents colluded (tacitly agreed not to freeride and stuck by it), the socially desirable outcome would have emerged. This means that the prisoner's dilemma has not only demonstrated the failure of competitive decentralisation to solve the economic problem—something which is similar to the case of uncertainty with incomplete markets—but here it also tells us how such a problem could be solved: co-operation.

In other words, unlike previous problems which only demonstrated how the system of spontaneous order based on competitive decentralisation may fail to achieve the socially desirable outcome, game theory suggests an alternative form of behaviour. But would the required behaviour for the solution to the economic problem to emerge be something that a rational competitive individual would do? As we already mentioned earlier, the prisoner's dilemma is the result of the rationality of the competitive agents—which is the way in which modern economics conceives the individual—so to circumvent this, we may need a revaluation of the way in which we conceive the individual and subsequently, of the nature of human interaction.

It is, of course, possible to show that there are circumstances in which the choice of 'co-operation' may become an expression of rationality as it is conceived by modern economics. In some forms of repeated games or evolutionary games, competitive interaction may not lead to a prisoner's dilemma and, thus, exonerate economics' paradigmatic core. However, the evidence that seems to be accumulated through experimental economics appears to suggest that the 'co-operative' option may be the one more often used by players even in a one-off game. This may raise the question of whether this means that people co-operate for other reasons than those suggested by standard rationality. We will revisit this issue in

Chap. 7, but at this stage we only point out something which we believe is important. If competitive decentralisation does not lead to a solution to the economic problem, could this be because we have wrongly conceived the individual? And if we did, would competitiveness be the right attribute to describe their economic interaction and if not, would competitive decentralisation remain a relevant principle of organisation?

2.4   Growth: The New Holy Grail

In spite of all these difficulties, neither the teaching of economics nor the public discourse about it seemed to have absorbed the understanding that there is nothing about the reality of competitive interactions which has any of the wonderful features that such exchanges possess at the limit of the idea of competition (i.e. the paradigmatic core). Moreover, as we noted earlier, the tendency has been to abandon the complex question of allocative efficiency and instead focus the attention on productive efficiency as the solution to the economic problem. However, as we said already, it is difficult to see how productive efficiency can be seriously taken as the sole criterion of economic performance. The fact that society has fully utilised its resources does not tell us anything about the ability of all individuals to solve their personal economic problem. In an individualistic theory, this is quite a significant qualification as would be any attempt to consider an aggregate as a measure of economic success.

To be sure, so far, all we said was directly related to the question of whether there exists an institutional arrangement that can solve the *static* economic problem, namely the arrangements that would lead society to make the most of the resources it already possesses. Yet, in our original narrative we also discussed, within the framework of solving the economic problem, the question of economic dynamics, or growth (points (r) and (s) in Sect. 2.1). While it does make sense to first make use of the resources which are at one's disposal, solving the economic problem does contain a dynamic aspect which is the increase in the productive capacity of society. Is it possible that the continuing commitment to the idea of competitive decentralisation reflects the recognition that while these institutional arrangements may not solve the static problem, they are nevertheless useful in the solution of the dynamic one? After all, what can be so wrong about a system that may not make full use of existing resources but is doing so well in augmenting them?

Actually, quite a lot is wrong about this. For one, even in terms of economics' own criterion, it is inefficient to augment resources if one is not making full use of existing resources. Surely the resources directed at the augmentation of resources could have better served different social purposes had these had any significance which was in the slightest greater than or even equal to growth itself. Moreover, the idea that a spontaneous order based on competitive decentralisation is mainly aimed at the provision of plenty is not very different from what Mandeville or even the Greek Sophists suggested. After all, allowing the few who are more ambitious, ruthless and maybe even more talented than the rest to charge ahead with no impediment will surely generate plenty. But then we should admit that social organisation is based on morally dubious principles and that the attempts to curb the freedom of the ambitious who would stop at nothing, is merely, in the spirit of Greek sophists, a conspiracy by the weak to pervert the course of nature.[35]

However, one cannot but suspect that the belief in the supremacy of growth as a social objective is indeed the case when one notices how the economic discourse has been altered in recent years. Indeed, the rise in academic interest in growth[36]—the dynamic solution to the economic problem—can be viewed as a move from the less tractable problem of static solutions (Pareto-efficiency) to the apparently easier problem of growth. When I say easier, I mainly refer to the aggregate nature of growth which makes distributional matters less obvious and concepts like allocative efficiency (Pareto) somewhat trivial or redundant altogether.[37] This is a serious drawback given that in the context of our formulation of the

---

[35] Recall that the attraction of spontaneous order was predicated on the diachronic nature of that order. By this, to remind the reader, we are referring to the moral acceptability—and, thus, sustainability—of the system.

[36] Growth has been part of the interest of economists all the time since the days of classical economics and Adam Smith. So, I am not suggesting that interest in growth as such is new but rather that growth has become the main part of the academic and, subsequently, public, discourse.

[37] It is true that on many occasions theorist examines the 'efficiency' of growth by comparing it to a benchmark of a social planner who is maximising some form of a social welfare function. Whether or not this is a measure of ethical goodness is highly contentious and I will not spend time discuss-

economic problem distributional matters are of considerable significance as only when allocations are Pareto-efficient can we be content that the institutional arrangements we adopted actually solve (or have a potential of solving) the economic problem. There is no social, or aggregate, economic problem in the methodologically individualistic world of modern economics. The social problem is only to solve each individual's economic problem. So, when we observe an economy grow faster, is such an economy solving its economic problem better than one that grows slower? In other words, if we accept that competitive decentralisation does not solve the static economic problem even in theory, is there any purpose at all in seeking to maximise growth as a means for solving the very same intractable economic problem? If, for instance, the distribution of outcomes which results from the failed attempt to solve the static problem by competitive decentralisation is left as it is, would growth help ameliorate, or will it exacerbate the situation?

If, instead, we abandon the desire to help individuals solve their economic problem and embark on seeking growth, do we not have to redefine the economic problem as we now move from methodological individualism to some form of collectivism where the purpose of society is merely to augment the amount of collective resources available irrespective of their distribution? One can see that in principle accumulated wealth, or resources, could be seen as a good substitute for the solution of the economic problem.[38] If markets fail individuals in the sense that people could have been made better off without anyone becoming worse off given the resources available to society, then a simple increase in resources could stand in good stead in the attempt to solve the economic problem. But the aggregate nature of growth does not really mean that. We just move from one inefficient situation to another; we are always in a situa-

---

ing this here. It would be sufficient to say that even in such a framework, real distributional matters are never near the surface.

[38] To some extent, the focus on growth seems to be an extension on Robbins's attempt to make economics an ethically neutral discipline. Following Wicksteed, Robbins's basic claim is that the domain of economics is the creation of plenty which is a necessary condition for whatever values society may wish to implement. In the same way that the presumption of competitiveness in the sense that individuals will always choose the cheapest option (broadly conceived) whatever it is they are trying to achieve, the pursue of growth is merely a collective attempt at creating the plenty upon which all social and moral values can be implemented.

tion where society betrays individuals who could have been made better off at no one's expense and they are not. Growth does not mean that *all* individuals, frustrated by the failure of society, will now be, so to speak, compensated by having an increase in their resources, or wealth.

This, of course, is where the famous question about trickle-down comes to the fore. Trickle-down simply means that when wealth is created by the few, they still buy services from the rest of society and, in so doing, allow this wealth to trickle down to everyone. If this were the case, then one could say that the compensation provided by growth is indeed universal. It is quite true that in a *closed system* accumulation of wealth is bound to trigger a trickle-down of this wealth to all members of society. Nonetheless, it is important to note that trickle-down only means *compensation* and not really a solution to the individual's economic problem in the way we defined it at the beginning of this chapter.[39] More importantly, there are two main issues which arise from this. Firstly, for the trickle-down to work, we need the economy to be a *closed system* which in the world of globalisation[40] it is not; secondly, we must perceive the solution of the economic problem as being pursued in isolation to the rest of social considerations. Namely, the fact that someone has now more than his parents had had is in itself compensation regardless of the fact that his parents' position in society was much closer to the wealthiest person in it than the individual who is now much more relatively, worse off than the wealthier person in his society. One could say that this, of course, is of no consequence when we adopt the individualistic nature of the theory and the absence of any social dimensions in the life of the individual. However, it is also of no consequence in relation to the ability of the system to solve the economic problem. Why should it matter how poor or rich you are for the realisation that you could have been made better off without affecting anyone else if society did not allow the

---

[39] By compensation we mean the general increase in living standards which people may experience as a result of the greater affluence. This, however, does not mean that society managed to reach an allocative efficient allocation commensurate with the socially desirable distribution of income.

[40] Which is in itself the result of our belief that competitive decentralisation is both the right way of solving the original economic problem and ethically neutral. Some may argue that in the context of the globalised world (i.e. the whole world is one economic system) the rule will work but this may raise questions about whether individuals, *in their lifetime*, enjoy the compensation of not being able to solve their individual economic problem.

betrayal of the markets or considered other institutional arrangements to solve its economic problem?

In fact, it is quite possible that a society which is more concerned with ensuring that the benefits of growth reach everyone (in good time) will end up growing slower than other societies. So how can growth itself become the criterion of economic performance if it tells us nothing about the ability of individuals in society to solve their individual economic problems?

There is, of course, a substantial amount of literature in economics which looks at the relationship between growth and inequality. While this is, no doubt, a worthy subject, it is more circumstantial than substantial. The reason for this is that theories of economic growth are still basically aggregate in nature. This means that they do not take into consideration the question of how growth is related to the success of individuals in solving their own individual economic problem.[41] The fact that the benefits of growth may be more equally divided may mean that more people are compensated for not being able to solve their own economic problem, but this still leaves us with the question of whether compensating for the failure of solving the economic problem is the best society can do in these circumstances.

But even if we do wish to pursue growth as a way of compensating for the failure of the economic system we created, we would then face two main questions: firstly, the more complex question to which we alluded earlier about the consistency between the institutions which solve the static problem and those which solve the dynamic one; secondly, there is the question—which we already touched upon—of whether society should adopt the institutions which promote growth irrespective of whether or not they solve the static economic problem. Moreover, will the idea of competitive decentralisation prove to be the most growth promoting in spite of its disappointing ability to universally resolve the static economic problem?

---

[41] What we are referring to here is the presence, or absence, of Pareto-efficiency. But in growth models, the presence of efficiency criteria is usually through a comparison between the rate of growth which society—as a collective (a social planner)—desires and the one which would be otherwise generated by the model.

I would not want to spend too much time on the question of whether the institutions which solve the static problem also solve the dynamic one. For one, we already saw that the recommended institutional arrangements which should solve the static problem fail to do so. Therefore, as things stand, we do not know which institutional arrangements best solve the static problem. Nor do we have a recipe which is sufficiently universal and neutral as to be recommended to all societies everywhere and at all times. So, we are left with two sub-questions: firstly, which institutional arrangements are most conducive to growth? Secondly, should the pursuit of growth by itself constitute a universal and ethically neutral objective?

At first, the focus of modern growth theory was on the question of accumulation of resources and in particular the accumulation of capital. The approach was aggregate, the assumption of competitive institutions widely accepted and the determinants exogenous. However, soon enough there was a change of focus from the exogenous accumulation of resources to the endogenous explanations focused on innovation and technological progress. If technological innovation is a function of the level of scientific knowledge in society, then it makes sense to think of the growth in capabilities of the economy as a function of the exogenous rate in which this knowledge changes. However, if innovation is also a matter of the motivation or incentives of the agents to implement or innovate for their own benefits, then the story becomes endogenous. Here, of course, the question of the institutional arrangements has been far more important.

From the institutional perspective, an early conundrum came to the fore due to Schumpeter's speculation (which we mentioned before) about whether investment in R&D—the key to technological development—would come from firms in perfectly competitive markets or from those firms which have direct power over the market outcomes. One can think of this in simple terms: to invest in R&D one needs both incentives and funds. If perfect competition is doing well its job, then the profits which firms (as legal entities) make will be eroded over time so funds, in the long term, are more precarious here. For competition to fulfil its promise of eroding profits and reduce costs and prices, information must be readily available. This means that no one could have an incentive to innovate (and thus lead to a reduction in the cost of production) as such innovation will soon be available for everyone else. The monopolist, on the other hands, has the funds (profits which are not under immediate danger of being eroded) as well as the incentive given that monopolistic power no longer stems from personal corrupt relationships with rulers but from the ability to prevent others, lurking at the margin of the market, from entering. To be able to prevent others from attempting to enter and contest the monopolist's position, the incumbent must be able to threaten in a credible way. This means, among other things, to be able to engage in a price war for which a cheaper technology would come in quite handy.

In the same spirit that is underlying Coase Theorem (but, of course, much earlier than his contribution), a solution to this problem has been to provide the innovators with the protection of property rights or, to be more precise, intellectual property rights. By patenting ideas, society allows innovators, even within a perfectly competitive market to command a return on their innovation which is protected at least for a limited period of time. This, in principle, should provide the incentives (and, though not immediately, the funds) for R&D even within a competitive environment and thereby resolve the problem posed by Schumpeter but does it really? By giving agents the rights to exclusively enjoy the fruits of their endeavour, we introduce monopolistic power into the competitive set-up. Assuming that at any point of time some agents will be enjoying these rights, the market ceases to be competitive in the original sense and we find ourselves saying that the only form of competition which is conducive to growth is monopolistic competition. While there is no question that competition is present in such a framework, this is not the idea upon which we based the conclusion that the economic problem will be solved. From the point of view of solving the economic problem through allocatively efficient outcomes, monopolistic competition is as good a solution as is a pure monopolist. But there is, nevertheless, a semantic conundrum here. Both the solution to the static and the dynamic economic problem require competitive decentralisation. On the face of it, there seems to be a consistency between the institutional set-ups which solve both aspects of the problem. However, what we mean by competitive decentralisation in the solution to the static problem is not the same as what we mean by competitive decentralisation in the dynamic sense.

But firms or entrepreneurs can always raise specific funds for a particular innovation outside the internal funds available within an organisation. Indeed, the question of writing a contract in a world of uncertainty between an innovator who has specific skills and a financier has been the subject of extensive research. The major concern which economists have here is whether arrangements will, on the one hand, be conducive for people to become innovator and, on the other, encourage financiers to take the risk and invest in such endeavours. Much of the property rights literature to which I alluded earlier is dealing with such problems as well as broader questions of legal systems which become particularly important in the world of incomplete contract. In such a world, where contracts do not specify all eventualities, the fate of many of these projects will depend on the disposition of the courts. For instance, in the common case where the project is delayed and there are liquidity problems should the court rule in favour of the financier who might wish to terminate the project or should the court rule in favour of the innovator who may need a bit more time—and money—but could, in principle, bring the project to fruition?

While this literature is specific and ad hoc, the general gist of it is rather clear and is encapsulated in the idea behind the concept of non-extractive institutions to which Acemoglou and Robinson relate in their book and which I briefly discussed in the previous chapter. To promote technological development, entrepreneurs and innovators should be able, at will, to seek funds in a competitive market (for which they should pay the going rate (taking risk into account)) and be sure to retain the return on their specific innovative activity. Notwithstanding the problems of hidden actions and incomplete contracts, this still is not really the same idea of competition which we discussed earlier as individuals must have some direct command (power) over the outcomes for them to be willing to invest their time, skills and money. But the idea that they can acquire funds at a competitive rate (taking the risk of their project into account) and keep the return on their investment which is above that rate, is very much embedded, in the eyes of many, in the nature of competitive markets. But this is not the competitive benchmark which economics was trying to sell to the world as an organisational principle which can resolve the economic problem for all possible societies and at all times.

Also, there is something somewhat misleading here in terms of the ability of such competitive environment to promote growth. It may be true that there is more likely to be greater availability of funds for innovation in competitive markets but the projects for which funds like this are more likely to be available are those with an immediate and significant promise of return in the market (albeit protected for at least a limited period of time). It means, among other things, that the *applications* of knowledge rather than its *development* are more likely to be the recipients of funds through the market. Accumulation of *generic* knowledge—which is the true source of all innovations—is less likely to be funded by the market. Nor, for this matter, will the desire to allow innovators to keep the return on their innovation be conducive to competitive practices. In a somewhat paradoxical way, the idea which seems to be emerging from the growth literature is contradictory. We want competition to allow to channel funds to innovative activities, but to create the incentives for the entrepreneur we would like to protect them (at least for a period of time) from the market and the eroding powers of our abstract notion of competition.

Moreover, the competitive streak (such as it is) behind the growth literature is also dependent on other factors. In particular, public investment in education—assumed to be raising the level of human capital as well as investing in generic knowledge—is considered to be conducive to growth. Is the expectation of public investment in education consistent with the desire to have competitive decentralisation? The answer seems to depend, to some extent, on the nature of education. This, of course, is a separate topic about which we will say more later on, but at this stage we will simply distinguish between functional and intrinsic education. The former perceives education as a means to a direct end which is defined by being economically useful (finding a job). The latter presumes that there are intrinsic benefits to learning even if they do not have obvious or immediate apparent use. I would postulate that the latter entails the former but will not make the case for it here. I will say, however, that the organisational implications of pursuing education for its functional purposes are different from those derived from wishing to provide intrinsic education.

It stands to reason that the functional approach to education may propose that markets should have a role in the provision of education. Thus, while public provision means that education should be available to everyone and will therefore be funded by government through taxes, the actual provision of education can be outsourced within a competitive structure. However, while such an approach may ensure that the education is provided in a productively efficient manner, it is still the case that the government will have to raise the money through taxes which, in the absence of lump-sum taxes,[42] are always a source of allocative (Pareto) inefficiency. Namely, the inefficiency created by taxes is not, in principle, different from the one creating by having monopolies in the economy. Therefore, it is not clear how the idea of public investment in education is consistent with the working of competitive decentralisation which requires the completeness of competitive practice across the whole economy without anyone interfering with relative prices and therefore uncompensated choices.[43]

To reiterate, the language of current discussions is quite misleading. In the context of growth, the competition to which people refer to is that of monopolistic competition which may be conducive to growth but is certainly not the universal and neutral recipe which hid behind the idea of competitive decentralisation as a solution to the economic problem. In this context, providing universal education may be important (for the solution of the dynamic problem) but should we care at all about the productive efficiency of its provision if we know that this can anyway only emerge under very specific ownership structures (and, therefore, specific flows of income)? Well, some will argue that whatever we think of the efficiency of private provision of education, it is clearly less inefficient than the provision of education by the government. Notwithstanding the validity of this claim, even if it were true, how can a dynamic objec-

---

[42] Lump-sum taxes, which were mentioned earlier, are a form of tax where payments are due irrespective of what a person does. This means that the relative value of different choices remains the same. For instance, with a lump-sum tax, the opportunity cost of leisure remains the same so rational agents will not change their choice of how to split their time between leisure and work. Moreover, as their overall income falls, they may wish to have less leisure and consequently work more. At the same time, as the money is given to someone else, in the same form, that person would also not change the relative choice of time allocation but may work less as his, or her, income increases. This form of transfer is the condition under which the second welfare theorem would hold. Non-lump-sum taxes create not only the income effect but will have an additional substitution effect as, say, leisure becomes less expensive.

[43] By this I again refer to lump-sum transfer where the loss of labour—due to what economists call, income effect—is compensated by a gain of labour from those who receive the tax as benefit.

tive of growth be better served by an efficient education system which erodes generic knowledge and emphasises application of existing knowledge?

The meaning of all this is that if the dynamic solution of the economic problem requires both a different form of competition and a public involvement which is greater than what is, in principle, required for the solution of the static problem, then it is yet another feature that distinguishes the institutional arrangements supporting the dynamic solution from those conducive to the static solution.

If, however, education is perceived to have intrinsic value, it is far from obvious that the idea of providing education through the markets (by outsourcing the service) will be an effective choice to achieve this end. In fact, I do not believe that even functional education can be achieved through markets unless by 'functional' we mean really basic skills. If this is indeed the case, then not only will there be allocative inefficiency due to the distortion created by taxes, but there might also be productive inefficiency due to the possible absence of competitive pressures in the provision of the service. This, by the way, may not be a bad thing for education, though it is clearly bad news from the perspective of the attempt to solve the economic problem through competitive decentralisation.

All of this leads to the following conclusions. Firstly, for agents to have an incentive to innovate, agents must command some power in the market to ensure their gain from an investment in technological development. This means that we immediately move from the domain of competition among equals (who are, in fact, powerless)—which was the necessary condition for solving the static problem—to a domain of monopolistic competition, namely a domain of competition between agents who command some power (not necessarily equal) and who are competing for these powers. In some sense, it is still competitive decentralisation but the notion of competition here is different from the one we employed in the solution of the static problem. We also know that the outcome of competitive decentralisation where competition is about monopolistic powers is outright inefficient. This means that in such a world agents may think that they have solved their individual problem, but it would be clear to the observer that this is not the case. All agents could have become better off (and found a better allocation to solve their economic problem) had there not been any monopolistic power in the markets.

2.5   Conclusion

In Chap. 1, we argued that the idea of synchronic, or spontaneous, order requires diachronic sustainability. This means, among other things, that the synchronic order—even when working well—must not offend the moral sensibilities of the public. One way of achieving such a system is by making it both universal and ethically neutral. And the way to achieve this is by removing the 'other', or society, from our considerations. Methodological individualism can help to achieve this end, though it does not necessitate it.

In this chapter, we asked the question of whether the exercise of using methodological individualism for the removal of the 'other' or society from our consideration will actually work.[44] Namely, we are asking here whether modern economics succeeded in creating a theory which is both universal and ethically neutral and which works. By works, at this stage, we are only referring to the logical validity of the system. In other words, we are asking whether based on the proposed conception of the world the proposed institutional arrangement serves its own expressed purpose.

We identified a paradigmatic core in economics by looking at what economists teach, and we found that there is a well-defined core which goes as a thread through everything economists do. It is based on the presumption that people are rational and competitive. It therefore follows that decentralised competition will yield a natural order which does not require any intervention. We also saw that this paradigmatic core presents a theory which, in principle, is indeed universal and ethically neutral provided that we accept that ethics is confined to a selection of outcomes or consequences. Naturally, this last proviso immediately tells

---

[44] I hasten to say that the removal of the other is not an inherent trait of methodological individualism but simply a specific characteristic of the way in which economics employs the concept. I shall come back to this question in Chaps. 7 and 8, where I will discuss the conception of the individual in modern and classical economics.

us that the pretence of ethical neutrality is from the outset just that: a pretence.

Nevertheless, we found that even within its own world, the idea that competitive decentralisation solves the economic problem is false. Though we rejected the critique of economics' paradigmatic core which is based on the realism of the abstract model, we argued that the relationship between the abstraction and the world it conceives matters a great deal. We noted that there are two issues at stake. First, there is the question of whether it is conceivable that in principle the institutional set-up required by the theory can asymptotically be obtained in reality. Second, there is the question of whether the proposed benefits which await us at the logical limit of the ideal can be felt in the process of approximating the limit.

Through a distinction between two characteristics of the relationship between the model and the world, we reached the conclusion that while it is possible to talk about institutional convergence when we discuss deviation from the model which could, in principle, be ameliorated through legislation or policy, when the problem is more fundamental, we need to re-examine the core. This meant that while we can consider the possibility of convergence in the case of certainty with or without missing markets, and in the case of uncertainty with complete markets, this was not possible in the case of uncertainty with incomplete markets (and contracts). Moreover, we also queried the possibility of monotonically experiencing an improvement in terms of the promised benefits of the core. This meant that at best the limit can be considered as a reference point, but for this to hold, there will also have to be an institutional convergence. In the case of uncertainty with missing markets, we had neither of these.

In addition to this, we noted the problem of price formation which suggests that even when we expect an institutional convergence, this will not materialise because there is no sufficiently general and realistically relevant process which will produce the prices upon which the benefits of the system are predicated. Consequently, both because of the extent of competition (i.e. the fact that not all markets could be perfectly competitive) and because of missing markets, the outcome of competitive decentralisation will forever be inefficient. But not only will it not resolve the economic problem by failing to lead towards allocative efficiency, productive efficiency (the necessary condition for allocative efficiency) becomes dependent on specific ownership structures which significantly limit the span of distributions which are consistent with it. Therefore, even the pretence of ethical neutrality must be conceded.

In the face of these theoretical failures, it is not at all surprising that we observe a shift in the economic discourse from allocative efficiency to growth. However, we argued that growth, which relies on a different form of competitive decentralisation, cannot be considered a good substitute for the solution of the economic problem which lies at the core of economic analysis. In many respects, the shift to growth is a return to the basic Mandevillian dilemma: greed (embedded in the inefficiency of monopolistic competition, the excessive protection of individuals' gains and the social objective of maximising material wellbeing) is the only way to achieve wealth. While some may feel that greed is morally good if it promotes the accumulation of material wellbeing, under no circumstances can such a view be considered as either universal or ethically neutral.

It is, perhaps, worthwhile noting that some economists would claim to have abandoned this paradigmatic core altogether and argue that what they do is to examine the interactions between rational agents. Emboldened by evolutionary biology[45] many would argue that the self-interested rational agent (which they would now admit to be selfish in the spirit of evolutionary biology) is a universal trait of all things, including humans, and therefore, the purpose of economic research is to either explain observed outcomes as a result of the interaction between such agents or predict the outcomes of such an interaction given certain institutional constraints. Notwithstanding the difficulties associated with identifying social with biological evolution, it is not clear what could be the purpose of such a research agenda. Suppose that one can explain something which may appear to be social (say, co-operation) as a selfish act, what would be the implications of this? Does it tell us anything about how we should organise society? In fact, the only purpose of such a research would be to argue that the self-interested rational agent is the

---

[45] See, for instance, Dawkins, R. (1976). *The Selfish Gene*. Oxford: Oxford University Press or Maynard Smith, J. (1982). *Evolution and the Theory of Games*. Cambridge: Cambridge University Press.

correct conception of individuals and, therefore, the paradigmatic core is right. In other words, as economic theory is a theory of organisation (otherwise, it would have been psychology), one cannot really have the luxury of abandoning the paradigmatic core. The only thing one can do is trying to change it but to claim that one is no longer interested in it is, I fear, not genuine.

Appendix

Walras, the rationalist, discovered in his *Elements of Pure Economics* that as the essence of goods is utility, there exists a vector of prices for which all rational plans coincide and all markets, without exception, are in equilibrium. This vector of prices, the Walrasian prices in their modern transformation, has all the properties of efficiency required by the solution to the economic problem. However, for Walras, the rationalists, these prices were actually the essence of values but not necessarily the actual market price. In this respect, Walras was following the traditions of economic thinking, according to which there is always a difference between 'value' and 'price'. They did not all mean the same thing, but one can trace such a distinction all the way back to Aristotle. In his theory, he distinguishes between what he calls a 'just price' and the actual market price that will emerge. By 'just price' Aristotle was referring to something akin to labour theory of value by expecting this price to reflect the relative difficulties of attainment. As the objective of Aristotle's theorising was to find the conditions which would support what he called the just, or good, society (alternatively, the society which would support the good life understood as eudemonia). In such a society, material wellbeing is not the objective and, therefore, the production and exchange of it should be based on needs. Trade for the purpose of wants is immoral. Therefore, to some extent, the just price was the measure of how well the system operates. Without the middlemen, who will appear when trade becomes wants-based, prices of good will correspond to the just price. Therefore, just price is a form of value against which one can measure prices and decree whether the system is working well.

St Thomas of Aquinas followed suit and even in Adam Smith one can find a similar concept in what he calls the 'natural rate'. Natural prices, for Smith, were a benchmark for whether or not the system of natural liberty is consistent with morality and justice.[46] When market price deviates from their natural rate, there is something not right about the system. Ricardo too was looking for an absolute value but the purpose of this was somewhat different. In Marx, however, the use of the distinction between values and prices becomes more acute. Marx, being a rationalist like Walras, finds that the labour is the value embodied in all commodities. This led to his famous labour theory of value, which was, like that which Walras did later, a search for the essence of things. Marx was very much aware of the fact that market prices deviate from labour values and it is through this deviation that the exploitative nature of the system is revealed. Many interpreted the labour theory of value as the explanation for prices and were therefore concerned with the most intricate of problems: the problem of transformation. How do labour values explain market prices? Not much good came out of this exercise and for a good reason. The labour values were a benchmark, a reference point, rather than an explanation of prices.

So, Walras too was concerned with the question of how actual market prices relate to the values of goods which are the general equilibrium prices. In some sense, this is similar to the problem we have posed in the text. Here, the Walrasian prices are the paradigmatic core and actual market prices represent reality. Therefore, the question of whether there is convergence is really a question of whether there exists a process, in principle, which will lead actual market prices to their Walrasian values.

Walras himself was baffled by this and proposed a somewhat peculiar process known as the Tatonnement (or groping). But there have been many questions raised both about the realism (i.e. whether it is really a possible process) of the process and about its convergence. Scarf (1960)[47] demonstrates the problem in a very simple context. The fact that we have no convergence in such a simple case raises serious doubts on the general-

---

[46] I know that many equate the natural rates with long-run equilibrium prices in Marshall, while market prices are the short-run equilibrium. I believe that this is a misguided reading of Smith which ignores the social—and moral—context of his theorising. This point is more directly explored in Witztum (2008), but it will also be explored further in Chap. 8.

[47] Scarf, Herbert. (1960). "Some Examples of Global Instability of Competitive Equilibrium," *International Economic Review* 1:157–172.

ity of any other account. There were also attempts to devise simple sequential bargaining processes, but these too did not seem to lead to Walrasian prices.[48] Mandel and Gintis (2014) propose that a solution can be found if we adopt an evolutionary game approach, but this raises a serious question about what we mean by the idea of competition. Moreover, the conditions of the structures which may generate convergence are far too specific to make this a sufficiently generalised proposition.

In any case, to demonstrate the problems of convergence and reference, let us look at a very simple example: the Cobweb model. Suppose that we have a simple competitive market for good x with standard demand and supply schedules:

Competitive equilibrium in a single market

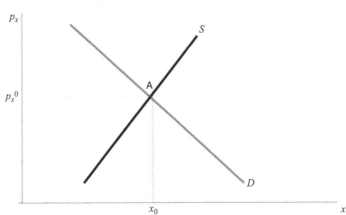

This, of course, is only one market but assuming all other markets in equilibrium (their prices would affect the position of both demand and supply), the price where this market too is in equilibrium—and thus the entire system—is, of course, the price corresponding to point A. So, we know that there exists a price for which there will be a Walrasian general

[48] Rubinstein, Ariel and Asher Wolinsky. (1985). "Equilibrium in a Market with Sequential Bargaining," *Econometrica* 53:1133–1150.

Rubinstein and Wolinsky. (1990). "Decentralized Trading, Strategic Behavior and the Walrasian Outcome," *Review of Economic Studies* 57:63–78.

equilibrium and where the allocation of resources and distribution of outcomes are efficient.

Now, the question is, how do such prices form? Clearly, the demand and supply schedules do not really exist; they tell us what we think would happen, had people been rational, when prices change. But in the real world, there is a price and that is it. But the model does not tell us how the price is being determined. Let us, therefore, devise a very simple and intuitively appealing story to describe this dynamic.

Suppose that the good x is sold in a weekly market. The suppliers who bring the goods to the market in the morning must decide how much to bring that would be consistent with their rationality as producers, that is, profit maximising principle. The principle which guides them is to bring a quantity to the market where the marginal cost (the cost of the last unit) equals the price. However, they do not know what the price tomorrow will be. They do know, however, what the price was at the end of today's trade. A simple form of expectation would be for them to think that the price of tomorrow will be the same as the closing price of today. This is what should happen when we have convergence:

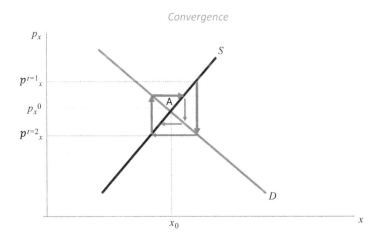

Convergence

If the price at the end of today ($t = 1$) is where it is, producers who maximise profits will bring to the market the quantity dictated by the marginal cost curve (supply). But during the day they will discover that at this price the quantity demanded is less than that. This means that they will find that there is excess supply in the market. As they cannot keep their goods from one day to another, sellers will declare a sale and prices will fall to the level at $t = 2$, where the sellers will be able to sell all their goods.

Next day, the sellers know that the price was at the level it stood at the end of $t = 2$ and they would therefore want to sell the quantity suggested by the supply curve. But at this lower price, quantity demanded will be greater—the opposite of yesterday—so there will be excess demand and consumers will bid up the price to get what they wanted. As price increases, quantity demanded will fall until it matches the quantity supplied. What we can see in the above diagram is that the difference between the prices in each day is falling and after a while the prices will converge to the Walrasian level if nothing else changes.

This is what we mean by convergence. There is a process which, in principle, can lead to us to the Walrasian prices. The reason I say, in principle, as even the story I told was quite stylised and assumed that nothing else changes throughout the process. Nevertheless, as a process exists in principles,[49] we are willing to accept that the Walrasian prices are meaningful and that we are in a constant motion towards them.

But can we say that we are also monotonically becoming better off as we approach the Walrasian price? The answer will be clearly not:

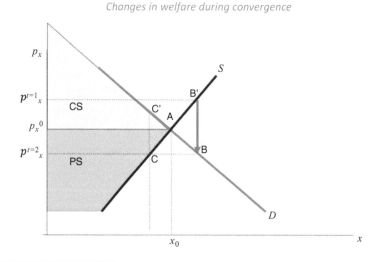

Changes in welfare during convergence

---

[49] Recall what we said earlier about the 'in principle' idea which is very similar to the Popperian notion of falsifiability.

The partial equilibrium representation of the efficiency of Walrasian equilibrium can be captured by the yellow and green areas which represent consumer and producer surplus respectively. The former is a proxy to the money measure of the utilities accrued to consumers at point A, and the latter is a measure of the utility generated by the market which ends up in the hands of producers. Point A is allocative efficient as we cannot increase one without reducing the other.

When we find ourselves at point B (after the first day), it is easy to see that consumer surplus will be increased but at the expense of producers. Moreover, producers will have an extra cost which is not covered by the benefits generated in the market and this would be the triangle CBB'. Therefore, point B is inefficient. A similar argument can be made about point C where we find ourselves in the following day. In other words, none of the points before we get to A can be deemed as efficient. So, while we know that we will be approaching the efficient outcome, we cannot attribute the efficiency of the limit of the process (at point A) to any point on the way. Nor can we clearly see the overall net benefits monotonically increasing.

But this is not the only possible outcome of the simple story we have been telling. It is quite possible that the process will actually not converge:

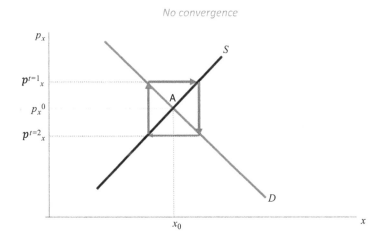

No convergence

In this case, we have the same story as before except that prices always fluctuate around point A but will never get to it. This is the equivalent to the Israelites who roamed the desert and who were destined not to get into the Promised Land. While it is true that the path which the prices will take as they fluctuate will be influenced by the position of point A, there will never be efficiency in this market. There was no efficiency throughout the process when it converged and there is no efficiency when they do not. But while in the previous story we could pretend that at some point—when we get to A—we will benefit from the promised efficiency, we can no longer make this claim.

Can we consider A as a reference point? Well, we could but only for the purpose of being able to predict how prices will fluctuate. But, as before, we still cannot attribute any of the good properties of point A to any of the prices we observe in this very competitive market. So, the benefits are all concentrated at a point which we will never reach and there is clearly no monotonic progression in our wellbeing. What, then, is the point of pursuing greater competitiveness?

That which determines whether prices will converge or not is a set of conditions on the slopes of demand and supply (and, hence, their elasticities). These conditions require a very specific relationship between the two schedules. This means that for all markets without exception, such conditions should be present. It is enough for one of the market in the economy not to have converging prices for the general convergence of the system to fail. At the same time, there is no plausible reason why all the markets should have this particular relationship between the slope of demand and the slope of supply. This is, therefore, another reason to believe that Walrasian prices, like Marx' labour values, are merely a benchmark for the system rather than an explanation of how prices are being formed. Marxian values exposed exploitation. Walrasian values condemn competition as an eternally inefficient form of economic and social organisation.

This last point is strengthened once we add to this the realisation that with missing markets, point A in the above diagrams does not constitute an efficient point either. As the social marginal costs of producing x are greater than the private one—represented by the supply schedule—an equilibrium at point A means that the price does not reflect the social cost of the good and, hence, will generate allocative inefficiency. To some extent, failing to gravitate towards an inefficient outcome may be a good thing but not when every other point is equally inefficient.

Bibliography

Elul, R. (1995). Welfare Effects of Financial Innovation in Incomplete Markets Economies with Several Consumption Goods. *Journal of Economic Theory, 65*(1), 43–78.

Giocoli, N. (2003). *Modelling Rational Agents: From Interwar Economics to Early Modern Game Theory*. Cheltenham: Elgar.

Hart, O. (1995). *Firms, Contracts and Financial Structure*. Oxford: Clarendon Press.

Mandel, A., & Gintis, H. (2014). Stochastic Stability in the Scarf Economy. *Mathematical Social Sciences, 67*(C), 44–49.

Scarf, H. (1960). Some Examples of Global Instability of Competitive Equilibrium. *International Economic Review, 1*, 157–172.

Witztum, A. (2008). Social Attitudes and Re-distributive Policies. *Journal of Socio-Economics, 37*(4), 1597–1623.

3

A Sense of Irrelevance

Synopsis: *After exploring the logical pitfalls which raise question marks over the validity of economics' paradigmatic core as a theory of social organisation, we will explore in this chapter some of its relevance. For a theory to be relevant, it must capture the essence of the world both about which it makes pronouncements and into which it feeds back. We noticed that for the system of competitive decentralised decision-making to deliver a solution to the economic problem which is also universal and ethically neutral, competition (in its perfect form) must be complete and total. All economic activities must be conducted through perfectly competitive markets that will attach a competitive price (which reflects the true social cost) to all goods so that an allocation can emerge which is both productive and allocative efficient (and, thus, a solution to the economic problem). The absence of such completeness may produce an impression of competition but not a solution to the economic problem with the properties of universality and ethical neutrality. Therefore, we set out in this chapter to explore some stylised facts about the world which may give us the confidence that the model we created, in spite of its logical difficulties, is nevertheless relevant. There are two basic areas in which the question regarding the extent (and limitation) of competitive practices come to the fore. The first is the role of government in the economy and the second*

© The Author(s) 2019
A. Witztum, *The Betrayal of Liberal Economics*,
https://doi.org/10.1007/978-3-030-10668-3_3

the ability of individuals to solve by themselves their economic problem through market interactions and without a need for collective intervention.

Naturally, for the competitive paradigm to deliver, governments must be minimal. They should keep the peace and uphold the law. At best, they could adjust distributional outcomes but only through the use of lump-sum transfers which do not interfere in the market mechanism. The reality is that while there may be some truth in the claim that gross domestic product (GDP) per capita *rose dramatically in those countries and those periods where competitive practices have been spreading, it is also true that the unprecedented increase in material wellbeing was accompanied by an unprecedented increase in size of governments. The meaning of it is that in economies with high material prosperity a significant share of economic activities is conducted outside the domain of the market. Consequently, as all markets and all prices are connected, the fact that such a large proportion of economic activities are priced in a different way to the one which the market would dictate, the overall outcome is bound to be inefficient both productively and allocatively. Notwithstanding the question whether large governments promote the increase in material wellbeing or are the result of it, we also find evidence that the public, in general, is almost as much in favour of private market enterprises as they are in favour of public provisions. This leads to a conclusion that not only are there no conditions for competitive systems to fulfil their promise— unless aggregate accumulation of material wellbeing is one's only concern— but it is quite possible that the public is not at all interested in the economic problem which the competitive paradigm proposes to solve.*

The second element is the position of individuals in such a form of economic organisation. For the paradigm to deliver, all individual should be able to fend for themselves and through market operations. In simple terms, individuals can access national income either through their labour or through ownership of assets (capital). The way the decentralised system affects the distribution of income is by affecting the distribution of returns between labour and capital. Classical economists thought that individuals are identified according to their economic position and this meant the competition between the returns to capital and the returns to labour translated into a social tension. Modern economics blurred the distinction by claiming that we are all both workers and owners of capital. While true in principle, the evidence seems to suggest that the classical distinction is still relevant and that the majority of the public derive their current income from labour alone. Hence, the way economics affects the distribution of returns also influences the actual distribution of income in the economy and, consequently, the access which individuals have to national income.

In the light of this, looking at some basic evidence we discover the following reality: (a) the share of wages in national income has been falling for a while now and this means that the larger share of the population receives diminishing shares of national income. This does not mean that they are necessarily poorer in absolute terms but they will certainly find it more difficult to acquire the income which will allow them to live in accordance with prevailing standards which are suggested by the overall measure of wellbeing (i.e. GDP per capita); (b) at all times there are a considerable number of individuals who are outside the labour force and who are defined as economically inactive. While some of those who are inactive are in education, there are enough individuals in society who are neither in the labour force nor in education and who are unable to access their share in national income by themselves or through the markets. Therefore, the fact that there are always some individuals in society who are in this position and the fact that those who are able to access income through labour find this an increasingly difficult task (as share of wages is falling) suggest that the presumption behind the competitive paradigm that all individuals can fend for themselves and, thus, allow markets to direct economic activities, is unfounded. If we add to this the concerns with regard to the future of work in the light of the new technological (or, rather, digital) revolution, the difficulties which an increasing number of individuals will have in accessing national income through markets in a manner that is sufficient to solve their private economic problem, completely erode the relevance of economics' paradigmatic core.

In the previous chapter, we suggested that the failings of economic theory to find a way to make the paradigmatic core—the logical limit of competition which is the universal and ethically neutral solution to the economic problem—a meaningful reference point led to its replacement with a dynamic problem, that of growth maximisation. Leaving aside the contradiction embedded in an individualistic theory which measures its performance in aggregates, we also find evidence that the uncontrolled pursuit of growth is a lost cause as growth rates in advanced economies having been slowing down considerably over the last 50 years, and the prominence of such cause can only be explained, as we did in the first chapter, as a means to avoid the subject of distribution.

All in all, reality dictates that all outcomes of competitive interactions are bound to be inefficient. As we have no meaningful way to distinguish between inefficient allocations, it is not clear on what grounds we can judge inefficiency associated with, say, 20% of activities conducted by government to be superior to the inefficiency created by, say, 40%.

∗   ∗   ∗

One might have thought that the theoretical difficulties which we highlighted in the previous chapter would have been enough to merit an extensive soul-searching and, possibly, some shift in paradigm. We noted that even from a theoretical perspective there are no reasonable conditions which would make competitive decentralisation a universal and ethically neutral form of organisation. In fact, if there was anything to learn from economic theory, then it must be that competitive structures will never ever solve the economic problem (in terms of the allocative efficiency, or distributional, dimension of the solution) and, therefore, cannot possibly be considered as ethically neutral. Nevertheless, we noted the shift in the justification for this form of organisation. From being a universal solution to an economic problem which encompasses the problem of both production and distribution—through the concept of allocative efficiency which is predicated on productive efficiency—it became a solution to a much narrower problem confined to efficient production and growth. In this latter framework, competition and the vigorous protection of property rights appeared to have been the key to the production of plenty the subsequent distribution of which was left, at best, to the nebulous concept of trickle-down.[1]

The commonality of the principle of competition—albeit in different forms—adopted by both approaches led to an implicit confusion of the two. Namely, the support for competitive institutions as a means of promoting growth was lumped together with the support for it because of its

---

[1] Piketty (2014), whom we mentioned earlier, provides a comprehensive collection of evidence to the elusive nature of the hope that wealth would trickle down.

universality and ethical neutrality which were the properties of the ideal notion of static competitive decentralisation. We want to have competitive institutions both because they produce solutions which are allocative efficient (the static solution to the problem) AND because they are growth maximising (its dynamic side). Evidently, this is not possible. Firstly, it is not possible because the allocative efficient solution to the static problem does not really exist (even logically in the absence of meaningful converging mechanism). Secondly, it is not possible because the competition which promotes growth is more akin to monopolistic competition (that is, in essence, allocatively inefficient) which, coupled with restrictions on the distribution of property rights that supposedly promote growth and productive efficiency, guarantees that the outcome will have none of the properties attributed to the one associated with perfect competition.

However, none of this seemed to have mattered at all. Economists continued to teach microeconomics as a story about the wonders of competition in the static framework of the problem and to teach growth as part of the macroeconomic problem falsely claiming for it to be the bridge between micro and macro analyses. The two, of course, are perceived as complementary and therefore there is nothing which seems to affect the greatness of the message coming out of the paradigmatic core. A most striking expression of this complacency, if not downright blindness, can be detected on the very occasion which, in itself, should have triggered much soul-searching even within a successful paradigm: the turn of the millennium. In a special issue of the *Journal of Economic Perspective*, devoted to this tumultuous psychological occasion, a host of economists reflect on the state of the subject. In general, they seem to be quite pleased with themselves. Easterlin (2000) points to the continuous and rapid growth of GDP per capital since the industrial revolution and the spread of democratic and decentralised competitive institutions which, it seems, is a form of vindication of the paradigmatic core. Kornai (2000) finds universalism in the compatibility of capitalism with all possible political systems as opposed to the totalitarian necessity of socialism. Thaler (2000) offers a prediction according to which Homo economicus will become more realistic (bounded in rationality and emotional). However, this is not because he sees anything wrong with the way economics is done but simply predicts a more sophisticated way of doing the same thing. Solow (2000) is concerned about the medium range. Namely, he accepts the economics of the short run (Keynesian) and the long run (neoclassical) but would like to see a new branch of the medium run. Lucas (2000) sees no problems at all and predicts (with, of course, yet another economic way of modelling) that growth will be diffuse around the world.

Perhaps only Colander (2000) makes the point that there has been some shift in the way people do economics (from the 'right price' question based on the two welfare theorems to the 'right institution' question). However, it is not clear to me that he is right to suggest that the shift is reflecting any real change in the way people think about the subject. In 2010 he will be agonising again about the rise of Dynamic Stochastic General Equilibrium models in macroeconomic analysis[2] reflecting, if anything, the rising dominance of the 'right price'—or general equilibrium—approach. In any case, whatever were the reservations expressed at the turn of the century, as we said in the previous chapter, judging by textbooks throughout all these years one can indeed detect little, if any, real change in the way economics is being taught and, subsequently, discussed and executed.

Then, of course, came the financial crisis of 2008, which forced economists to defend their discipline but has not really led to any serious attempts at revising it. It is interesting to note that the focus of protest in the immediate aftermath of the crisis was the excesses, or abuse, of the system rather than the system itself. The theoretical response was almost entirely concentrated on the role of government in dealing with the effects of the crisis rather than with the role of governments in the economy in general. The opposing views here were the usual suspects. At the one end were those who claimed that in the spirit of the competitive paradigm, governments should reduce their spending further to allow for the reduction in sovereign debt which resulted from the crisis. At the other end were those who thought that governments should increase their spending to stimulate the economy and help those who have been most affected by—though not triggered—the crisis. These types of

---

[2] Colander (2010).

Keynesian arguments are not really a denouncement of the competitive paradigm; they simply reflect the idea that the system needs help in steering it to the right position but once it is in the right position, the neoclassical model comes to its own (to paraphrase on Keynes's own statement) and government should pull out of the economy.[3] In between there were those who are neither here nor there and wanted a more targeted government intervention in the form of quantitative easing. In so doing, even more tiptoeing around the competitive paradigm in order to better position it without disturbing it in its blessed work. However, none of the discussions seem to be aimed at asking whether or not the pursuit of competitive decentralised system has lost its appeal.[4]

It should be evident to the reader of this book that there was no need for a crisis to trigger a reconsideration of the competitive paradigmatic core and its derived organisational principles. Economic theory has always recognised the fundamental inefficiency of financial markets (the problem of incomplete markets which we briefly discussed in the previous chapter) so there should not have been any surprise that the more competitive and less regulated these markets are, the more likely they are to give rise to inefficiencies which may, on occasions, lead to a crisis.[5] The anger aimed at economics was, to a great extent, unjustified. Robert Lucas, an economics Nobel Prize laureate, was right, in my view, to say that the nature of a crisis is that no one can predict it. The failings of economics have nothing to do with their predictive power or with the crisis but rather, with the logic of their system of thought and their subsequent organisational recommendations.

It is thus the logical difficulties of defending the organisational principles derived from the paradigmatic core which should have been the cause of genuine and radical soul-searching, not the failures of economics to predict. The question is, therefore, whether we can find support for

---

[3] I discuss this issue in connection with Keynes in Witztum (2013).

[4] I am referring here to arguments and discussion within the discipline. There were, of course, the usual voices which consistently denounce capitalism and usually, from the specific Marxian perspective (and there is nothing better than a crisis to give rise to such arguments).

[5] As there is no mechanism to asymptotically lead us from a world of incomplete markets to the efficient world of complete markets, so will financial innovation fail to bridge this gap in the world of inherently incomplete markets.

our theoretical doubt about the merits of the competitive paradigm in empirical evidence other than predictions. Namely, is there anything about the economic and social realities which make the attempts to abstract from the world into the competitive paradigm the way it is understood by economists an irrelevance? After all, for the competitive paradigm to serve as a yardstick for that which is socially desirable, it must resonate with the world from which it abstracts and into which it feeds.

Beyond the complex issues of missing markets, there is, perhaps, one major observable feature which is vital, if not detrimental, to the relevance of the competitive paradigm—whether in its static or dynamic forms—as an ideal of economic organisation. It is the principle according to which the domain of economic activities should, *in its entirety*, be governed by competitive interactions.[6] It is, of course, a statement about the world in the sense that no one would wish to model a society where only a fraction of economic activities *could* be conducted through markets by using a conceptual framework which requires all of them to be conducted in this manner. Naturally, for the theory and its promise to be relevant, there is no need, at all times, for all economics activities to be actually conducted by competitive means but there must be an understanding that it is at least possible for all of them to be so conducted as well as a tendency for competition to be the preferred form of organisation.

Put differently, by abstracting from the world in which people are assumed to behave competitively in *all areas* involving the subject matter of economics (i.e. economic goods), the paradigmatic core suggests that if such behaviour were allowed to reign free, the outcome of such interactions will be efficient in the sense that it will solve all agents' individual economic problem. But if not all areas are governed by the conditions of perfect competition, the outcome of these very same organisational

---

[6] It goes without saying that the more fundamental principle of which competitive interaction is predicated is that of rational behaviour. However, this is far less an observable reality than the presence of competitive interaction which could, of course, be triggered by other forms of behaviour. We will, of course, devote a considerable amount of space later in the book to the issue of rationality but at this stage, as we are concerned with observed interactions rather than their causes, we shall not be discussing it.

principles will fail to solve society's economic problem.[7] In other words, for us to theorise about a world where all economic activities are channelled through perfectly competitive markets, there must be at least a tendency for the domain of perfect competition to continuously increase. There are two obvious empirical implications to such a position. The first is that the share of government in the economy must be minimal (or, at least, falling). As governments are unlikely to participate in economic activities which could be otherwise provided through the rule of the market, their presence in the economy is either a reflection of a serious failing by markets, or a social desire for provisions which markets cannot provide, or a social preference for public provisions even when markets could provide them. Either way, the fact that part of the economic domain is not conducted through competitive principles will, inevitably, affect the entire economy and would make the efficient outcome—the desired solution of the economic problem—an empirical impossibility.[8] Therefore, in a perfectly competitive economy one would expect government to be minimal, funded by lump-sum transfers and confined predominantly to keeping the peace and upholding the law (contracts).[9]

---

[7] Recall that as there is no clear mechanism which can asymptotically lead towards the efficient outcome, such inefficiency is not, in principle, very different from the one that would have emerged if, for instance, all markets were monopolised but subjected to competition in ownership (thus ensuring productive efficiency).

[8] There are, of course, aspects of economic activities where the role of government can be seen as an attempt at assisting the competitive streak. For instance, the fact that only a publicly owned natural monopoly is likely to price the good at marginal cost though critics would say that there would be a problem with productive efficiency. But other than that, when government is expected by the public to take over the provision of goods, it is because the public believes that competitive principles should not be applied (like, for instance, education or health). In other words, the presence of a large government may suggest that there are areas of economic activities where competitive behaviour does not rule. In turn, this will make a model which assumes all areas of economic activity to be governed by competition irrelevant.

[9] The fact that governments' presence in the economy is understood to be an obstacle for the efficiency of competitive decentralisation, as well as that the objective of achieving allocative efficiency is important, can be drawn from the drive to make governments' provisions more competitive. As we mentioned in Chap. 1, one of the expressions of the rise of the competitive paradigm as the ideal form of social organisation was manifested in the change which some social-democratic political parties have gone through. The idea of new labour in Britain was nothing else than an attempt to reconcile the need for government together with the desire that government should not upset the potential order promised by allocative efficiency. Whether this is at all possible is a separate question but had governments' been able to operate like the markets there would be no need for governments' presence in the first place.

The other, related, empirical implication is that we would expect in such economies all agents in society to have a way of accessing their subsistence (their share in national income) through competitive means (i.e. markets). Namely, agents can acquire income either through their labour or through their ownership of assets by trading them in the market. If this is not the case it would mean that some agents in society rely on non-competitive organisations to acquire their share and this, in most cases, would mean a form of collective decision (government) upon which a rule—different from a market rule—can be established to determine the way in which such necessities will be provided. In such a case, as the government will also need to raise funds to achieve such redistribution, and as lump-sum transfers are not really possible, the system will become inevitably inefficient. In other words, in a world where agents rely on non-competitive means to acquire their share in the national income, the paradigmatic core will fail to deliver the promised solution to the economic problem.[10] From the point of view of the dynamic agenda, the significance would be similar as government intervention—which is what would normally happen in such cases—would lead to interference with the returns on innovative entrepreneurial activities which would, ostensibly, stifle growth.

As the switch of agenda from the static to the dynamic solution of the economic problem effectively means a change in focus from the distributional benefits of competitive interactions to the mere accumulation of material plenty, we will also want to say something about the empirical relevance of such an agenda. Namely, even though we already discussed, in the previous chapter, the ethical implications of the pretence of neutrality behind Robbins's agenda, we will try to explore here whether this is, empirically, a sustainable and meaningful one.

---

[10] Allow me to emphasise here that while this may appear similar to a welfarist argument according to which we are always willing to pay in terms of efficiency to acquire what is equitable (second-best principle), this is not at all so. Here, we are not discussing changes in a distribution which would have come about without intervention. We are discussing here a case where there is no efficient outcome as individuals cannot acquire any income through the markets. So, it is not a question of correcting the markets but rather a question of replacing them. It is in this sense that if there is evidence to suggest that individuals are unable to acquire their share in national income through markets, the promise of competitive decentralisation will be deemed as false. Put differently, when we move from one inefficient outcome to another, the idea behind the second-best principle becomes vacuous (unless, of course, we believe that we can measure the benefit changes as we move from one inefficient outcome to another. We argued earlier that to do this requires considerable leap of faith).

3.1   Share of Governments

Easterlin (2000), Solow (2009) and many others draw our attention to the almost exponential rise in GDP per capital since the industrial revolution. In the eyes of many, these developments seem correlated with the spread of competitive practices coupled, almost inevitably, with democracy and respect for property rights. More to the point, the evidence seems to suggest that the main beneficiaries of the exploding rise in material wellbeing were those societies that went furthest in adopting the market as the prime mechanism for economic organisation.[11] On the face of it, this seems to give some impressionist credence to the idea that competitive decentralised decision-making is the right recipe for successful organisation of economic activities in society.

Indeed, if we look at the evidence by focusing on a limited number of developed economies—so that we see how economic changes occurred in a well-defined place—we may find some confirmation of this position:

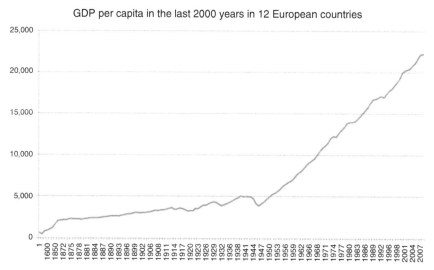

GDP per capita in the last 2000 years in 12 European countries

Source: A. Maddison *Historical Statistics of the World Economy: 1-2008*

---

[11] This all chimes well with Acemoglou and Robinson (2012), whom we have mentioned before and who claimed that throughout history societies which adopted non-extracting institutions (i.e. respected property rights) succeeded. Namely, those societies where decision-making was dispersed, property rights respected and governments which did not over extract any of the rent on economic activities in the form of tax, flourished.

This is, of course, a phenomenally interesting graph which requires much greater attention than it seemed to have received. We will not explore the issues here but merely make some passing comments. What is particularly remarkable about it is that it demonstrates that there are, in fact, two distinct periods within the era in which GDP per capita rose significantly.[12] The first is the period immediately following the beginning of the industrial revolution until the Second World War, and the second is the post-war period. Clearly, the most impressive jump in GDP per capita occurred after the Second World War in a period which is clearly marked, in these countries, by peace, democracy and the spread of market economy both internally and internationally in the form of the European Common market and the global push towards greater freedom of trade as manifested in the General Agreement on Tariffs and Trade (GATT) rounds and the World Trade Organization (WTO). Between 1850 and the eve of the Second World War, we can see 'only' a gradual increase which led to a more or less twofold level of GDP per capita in those countries. These roughly 100 years, though years of the industrial revolution and the establishment of property rights, were also the age of empires and concentrated monopolistic powers. In the subsequent 60 years, GDP per capita increased by almost fivefold.

There is, no doubt, an accumulation effect of technological development which in itself may provide a reason for the unparalleled increase in GDP per capita in the last 60 years.[13] But at the same time, if indeed the post-Second World War period is more clearly marked, in these countries, by the spread of competitive markets and democracy while the period before it is only marked by rapid technological changes coupled with limited democracy, widespread monopolistic powers and considerable social upheavals, then it is the rise and spread of market economics (carried on the shoulders of the fruits of the industrial revolution) that

---

[12] It is true that there was a considerable rise between 1600 and 1850 but as this rise is spread over 250 years, while still respectable and deserving of attention more than is general given to it, it pales in terms of the rate in which GDP per capital changes annually in comparison with the subsequent periods.

[13] If we add to this the contribution of wars to the development of new technologies, we can see why at the end of the Second World War there is a kink in the diagram suggesting that the rapid growth in the last 60 years cannot simply be attributed to the accumulation process.

had much to do with the incredible rise in material wellbeing in those countries.[14]

It is important to bear in mind, however, that there are at least two major forces at work when it comes to the rise in GDP per capita. The first is an increase in utilisation of existing resources, which is what we earlier called the static problem and for which, the idea of decentralised competitive interactions seems to provide a universal and neutral solution. This includes both a better utilisation of resources by those already operating through markets and an increase in activities which go through markets.[15] The second is the increase in the amount of resources available (i.e. growth through capital accumulation) or an improvement in what we can do with existing resources (i.e. growth through technological change). This, of course, is the dynamic problem for which competition was essential but only from the point of view of productive efficiency. This also means that the distributional elements have been removed and, consequently, the solution of the economic problem cannot be deemed to be either universal or ethically neutral. So, in some sense, the earlier period is where there was a significant increase in the *potential* output due to technological change but that the full impact of it could only have come to the fore in a world where resources are also fully utilised. This, of course, is the role of the static notion of competitive decentralisation.

---

[14] Indeed, as we mentioned in Chap. 1, some of the arguments about the industrial revolution have also been based on the claim that better protection of property rights in England, which was claimed to be the result of the glorious revolution of 1688, is associated with the limitation of governments (and, hence, more market economy). However, it is important to note the debate about this question as some scholars claim that the level of protectionism in England was greater than in France during the industrial revolution, which is a counterargument for the effects of government on promoting technological change.

[15] Whether or not an increase in activities which are channelled through the market is an improvement in the wellbeing of the public is a complex question. In part, the argument would be that the market would provide such services efficiently but would we really wish to commercialise all our activities? For instance, replacing an evening of reading, discussions and games with family or friends with a consumption of entertainment through, say, TV channels or through senseless shakings of the body in a nightclub may suggest a greater efficiency in provision (and definitely an increase in GDP per capita), but is it necessarily an improvement? To some extent, when we look at the sharp increase in GDP per capita after the Second World War, one cannot but wonder whether this is a result of the complete destruction and decimation of community lives in these countries. The war has displayed millions and destroyed communities in which a great deal of social activities would not have been commercialised. Once by themselves, people had no choice but to act through markets and this in itself would have led to a sharp increase in GDP per capita.

From the perspective of our investigation into the relevance of the paradigmatic core, we are, of course, mainly interested in the static problem which represents the more fundamental concept of a solution to the economic problem as it entails not only the full utilisation of resources but also their allocation in a manner where the distributional consequences are also taken into considerations (allocative efficiency). But the data does not tell us much about this. It only suggests that there must have been an improvement both in the utilisation of resources and in increasing them (mainly through technological change). In other words, it only tells us that economies have become more productive efficient. But this, as was suggested earlier, could be the result of monopolistic competition associated with growth—due to the protection of the property rights of innovation and entrepreneurial activities—and would therefore not necessarily constitute an allocative efficient outcome or a universal and ethically neutral solution to the economic problem. Nevertheless, as productive efficiency is a necessary condition (though not sufficient) for allocative efficiency, attributing the remarkable increase in levels of GDP per capita to greater competitiveness may still strengthen our belief in the power of the paradigmatic core. Either way, whether competition contributes to the dynamic solution alone or whether it contributes to the static one, one thing is clear, a greater share of economic activities should be conducted through the markets and governments should be smaller.

However, if we look at what happened to government involvement in these economies during the period in which output increased most, we will find that it has increased. Now, as most of these countries have undergone political upheavals, it would be particularly interesting to take a look at the British government which is the one most clearly to have transferred without a break from a mode of industrial revolution with an empire (the period between 1850 until the Second World War), to a mode of market economy which became particularly competitive with the rise of Thatcherism in the 1980s of the previous century. What we will discover is a strange anomaly: during the height of the empire and when the fruits of the industrial revolution were most ripe (the turn of the century), we find the British government uninvolved in the economy and government's expenditure stood at around 15% of GDP:

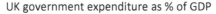

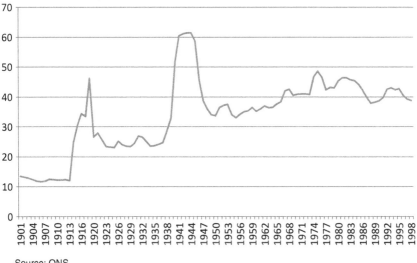

Source: ONS

The two wars give a push to this level of spending which could be construed as some form of a ratchet effect but the reality is that even in the years most devoted to the promotion of competitive practices, the level of government spending as a share of GDP rose to around 40%. In other words, as the economy moved from a historical age of empire and monopolistic powers to an age of ruthless pursuit of competitive practices (Thatcher's years), government share in the economy increased. Clearly, the overall level of government expenditure includes a great deal of transfer payments which may not be considered as part of the direct involvement of the government in economic interactions. However, even transfer payments are a sign that there are domains of economic activities which are not governed by competition or the markets. Transfer payments will normally be associated with the failure which some individuals face in extracting their subsistence from the national economy by competitive means. But even if we wish to focus on the rates of direct involvement and assume this rate to be a fraction of the overall expenditure, there is still a considerable increase in that level during the period in which GDP per capita has risen dramatically.

A similar picture will emerge for the USA, and if this is the case for those economies where the idea of competitive decentralised decision-making is most popular and deeply rooted, one can imagine the situation in other economies. If we look more specifically at government consumption (not including investment or direct transfers)—namely, more direct government involvement in the markets—we will find that in general those countries where government is relatively large do better than those where it is small:

Government consumption as percentage of GDP

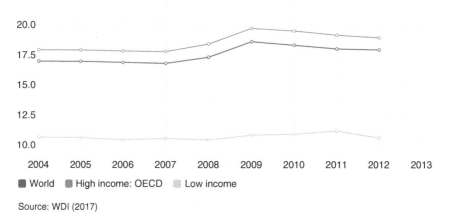

● World ● High income: OECD ● Low income

Source: WDI (2017)

High-income economies have governments which are more directly involved in the economy and even more so if we added the social spending by way of transfer payments. This means that the share of economic activities conducted under the rules and guidance of competitive decentralisation is significantly lower in economies that are supposed to have benefited from the promise of the paradigmatic core.[16]

It is, of course, difficult to measure the extent of the competitive nature of an economy but if we use, as a crude measure, the index proposed by

---

[16] This, of course, is not a proof that low-income economies are poor because they have small governments and market economies. In fact, poorer economies have no tax base from which to derive government revenues that will allow authorities to get involved in the economy. This may mean that (a) a considerable amount of activities are not conducted through markets and (b) wherever there are markets, they may not be competitive at all (i.e. corruption, monopolistic power).

the US-based Heritage Foundation, we can confirm the view according to which larger governments suggests that the extent of competition—and, hence, the relevance of the paradigmatic core—is limited. If we take a snapshot look at some advanced economies at a year which would be more or less neutral in the sense of being sufficiently distant from the brewing crisis of 2008 and sufficiently far from the Asian financial crisis (of 1998) as well as before the institutional change in Europe, where 15 East-European economies joined the European Union (EU), we would want to look at a year like 2004. What we are looking at is the share of social spending (as percentage of GDP)—which is a measure of the level of government involvement in the economy—and the level of economic freedom as proposed by the Heritage Foundation index (the lower the index the freer is the economy from regulation or other impediments to a true world of laissez-faire-*laissez-passer*). We find the following result:

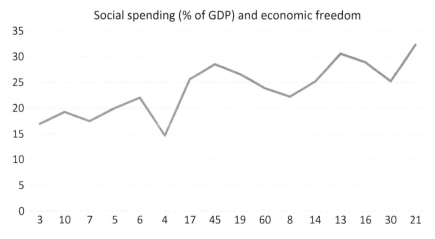

Source: Heritage Foundation (n.d.) and OECD (2017)

This means that the more involved is the government in the economy, the less will be the level of economic freedom (i.e. the index will be higher). In terms of our discussion this means that the less economic freedom there is, the less likely it will be for markets to be genuinely competitive so that they can deliver the promised efficient outcome where all agents solve their individual economic problem.

Not surprisingly, one can clearly see from this set of data that all the Anglo-Saxon (AS) economies will have significantly higher level of economic freedom.[17] The mean value of economic freedom for those countries is 5.8, while the one for Continental European economies is 24.3. At the same time, it would be interesting to note that while the level of competition in the economies with more government is lower, this did not seem to have a significant impact on the level of GDP per capital which, to some, will be the ultimate measure of success:

GDP per capita and economic freedom

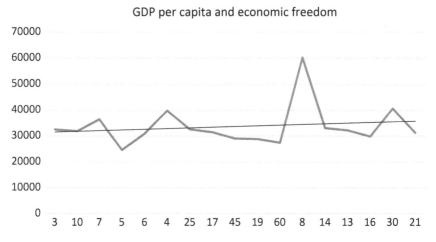

Source: Heritage Foundation (n.d.) and OECD (2017)

The slightly upwards trendline (mainly influenced by one exceptional case) suggests that economies with higher government involvement do not necessarily pay a price in terms of their GDP per capita. If they do, this price does not seem to be considerable. So, while it is clear that more government means less proper competitive decentralisation, it does not mean that this will lead to less successful economic performance even if one uses, solely, the crude measure of GDP per

[17] Countries included are: Anglo-Saxons: Australia, Canada, New Zealand, Ireland, the UK and the USA. Continental economies included Austria, Belgium, France, Germany, Italy, Luxemburg, the Netherlands, Denmark, Finland, Norway and Sweden. We deliberately excluded the more problematic southern European economies for the purpose of proper comparability. Namely, we chose advanced and successful economies so that one could argue that the only real difference between them is institutional.

capita. In other words, it is not clear that a less competitive environment means less success in economic performance.

If we return to the longer-time perspective, we can see that in general, though the period post-Second World War is clearly a period of prosperity the world over, it is also marked as the period with almost unprecedented levels of government involvement the world over (the data below is for all countries):

General government final consumption expenditure (% of GDP)

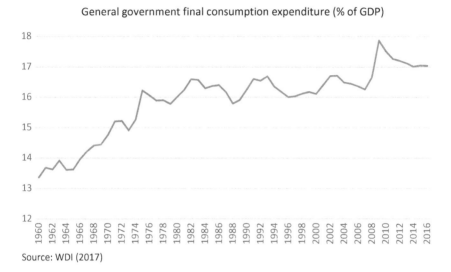

Source: WDI (2017)

It is therefore evident that prosperity in general—when measured in terms of GDP per capita—seems to be associated with relatively large government involvement in the economy. More to the point, we clearly live in a world where government share in the economy is not minimal and if anything, it is growing (in terms of long term trends). While this clearly means that the promise of the paradigmatic core cannot be delivered, it also raises the question as to why this is the case and as one would expect, the answers are divided.

A different way of phrasing this question is to ask whether the rise in government spending is the result of higher levels of GDP per capita, or is it the reason for it. This, of course, is a formidable question which merits a full and separate investigation and is beyond the scope of this book. However, as we are merely trying to make sense of some of the more obvious and undisputed evidence, it would be enough to see whether there is an agreement about the explanations of this observation.

Wagner (1893) provided a fundamental explanation in the form of Wagner's law, according to which it is the increase in GDP which triggers a greater demand for government services. This, of course, is a demand-side explanation to why government's share in GDP increases with the rise of GDP. However, there are also opposite arguments to suggest that it is government size which affects the rise in GDP. These are, of course, arguments about the relationship between government size and growth, which, from our perspective, are the less interesting aspect of the problem as they only deal with the dynamic (and aggregate) aspect of the solution to the economic problem. In general, the view seems to be that there may be a certain threshold of government size which is essential for growth. This may correspond to the minimal state we were discussing in the context of the static problem and which upholds the law and protects property rights. But large governments are seen as bad for growth. In Afonso and Jalles (2011), they look at 108 countries and conclude that large governments are, on the whole, detrimental to growth. However, there are other voices too. For instance, Loizidis and Vamvoukas (2005) find evidence that at least in the UK and Ireland government size can Granger-cause the growth rate of GDP. However, as the authors admit, there is a wealth of studies which produce conflicting results and, in many cases, the results for different countries would be different.[18]

From our perspective, it does not matter much whether or not government causes growth or otherwise. If the hypothesis that government size causes growth is true, then the argument in favour of markets would have been dissolved and the belief in the promise of the competitive paradigm would have been severely undermined. But the evidence on this is far too sketchy to make any serious claim along these lines. On the other hand, the demand-side explanation of the share of government in the economy is quite interesting as it raises the question of whether governments are indispensable for achieving wellbeing. If so, the promise of the competitive paradigm which requires all economic interactions to be channelled through perfectly competitive markets cannot be true. Neither the world from which we abstract to build the theory nor the logical conditions for the theory to hold will make the theory relevant. In other words, the fact

---

[18] See, for instance, Ram (1986, 1987), Cullis and Jones (1987).

that people demand greater government activity the wealthier they get seems to suggest that they are not really content with what the markets are able to provide.[19]

As for the universality of any of this, it would be interesting to note that when we examine people's attitudes towards the role of government in the economy, two things come to the fore. Firstly, the number of people who have a positive attitude towards greater governmental involvement is considerably higher than that which one would expect from a world upon which the abstraction was drawn for the model of economics' paradigmatic core; and secondly, there are differences between the attitudes of people in Anglo-Saxon economies and those who are in, say, Continental Europe. The reason I chose to look at the two groups in separation is because Anglo-Saxons, in general, are better disposed towards the competitive paradigm than their continental counterparts. The reasons for this are complex and I do not wish to discuss them here. But if we look at the data, this assertion would be confirmed.

To examine the attitude towards government involvement in the economy, I chose to look at a particular question which appears in the World Value Survey (WVS) from 2005.[20] The question I chose was phrased in terms of private versus public ownership of business, which is even a stronger indication about the attitude towards government involvement in the economy as it does not entail any particular form of market failure (like, for instance, public goods or natural monopolies) and simply asks whether in general, people would like to see the government more active in the normal life of the economy. By implication, the more people wish to see public ownership in the economy, the less people trust the working of competitive decentralised decision-making, or natural liberty. The results were as follows:

---

[19] Government provisions are more likely to be in the form of public goods than they are to be in the form of private consumption. This would be somewhat reminiscent of J. S. Mill's claim that as society progresses the ideal would be stagnation in terms of the growth of material wellbeing as people will move away from such concepts of wellbeing to more abstract and spiritual notions of wellbeing.

[20] I deliberately look at evidence from before the financial crisis in 2008 as the upheavals of the crisis, the remnants of which are still felt today, are likely to influence what people would have considered to be true at more settled times.

Private ownership—Anglo-Saxon

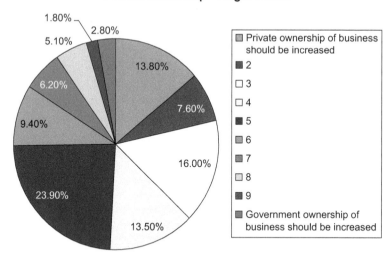

Source: WVS (2005–2009)

The answers were given on a scale of 1–10, where 1 represents the idea that private ownership of business should be increased—which means total distrust of government and complete faith in natural liberty—while 10 represents the idea that public ownership of business should be increased. This, in turn, represents the exact opposite: total distrust of markets and a complete trust in collectively based considerations. For a world where the promise of the market is widely received, one would expect most people to wish greater private ownership and a withdrawal of the government. In the Anglo-Saxon economies for which I found evidence (the USA, the UK, Canada, New Zealand and Australia), about 50% chose a number between 1 and 4 (which is clearly on the private ownership side). Number 5 is those who cannot decide and 6–10 are those who distrust the market and wish for greater public ownership of business. About 25% in the Anglo-Saxon economies chose a number supporting public ownership.

The conclusion from this is that even in those societies where the idea of liberal market economy is deeply rooted only 50% express a tendency to trust markets more than they trust the government. Only about 21% are really committed to the market (chose 1–2), though those committed to the government (chose 9–10) are, as expected, only 4.6% of respondents. In Continental Europe, the picture is slightly different:

Private ownership—Continental

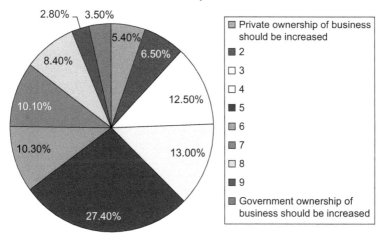

Source: WVS (2005–2009)

Here, there seems to be a balance with about 35% supporting either greater public ownership or greater private ownership. This means that fewer people in the continent trust the market (the number for Anglo-Saxons was 50%) and many more trust the government (35% as opposed to 25% among Anglo-Saxons).

Therefore, the fact that governments have a large share in the economy may have nothing to do with the level of income or the rate in which it grows. It may well be the result of a more fundamental truth that the public has either never had or has lost the confidence it had in the ability of liberal economics to produce an outcome which would be socially acceptable. Indeed, it was at the time of democracy when the increase in governments' involvement in the economy took roots and if democracy is a form of natural liberty we can see in this the seeds of a potential contradiction: political natural liberty may lead to a rejection of economic natural liberty.[21] In any case, these findings would support the argument that the increase in governments' share is more of a demand pull. It does not mean that such increases will have no effect on growth rates but it may very well be the rise in affluence which, in a very Millian way,[22] deflects interest from the production of plenty (i.e. growth) or increases the disillusionment of the public with the promise of economics' paradigmatic core. Needless to say, economic theory has little to tell us about a world where there is a division of labour between the public and the private interests. In a world of large government involvement in the economy, modern economics becomes an irrelevance.[23] It is therefore not at all surprising that economics is fighting a rear-guard battle to have market replace government or have government abide by the rules of the market. In the light of what we have seen thus far, the logic of such a position is most peculiar indeed.

3.2   The Share of Wages in National Income

So far, we have argued against the relevance of the competitive paradigm by trying to demonstrate that in the world we live in the question of large or small governments is, at best, academic (pun intended). Given the actual size of governments—which seems to be linked to material prosperity—the neoclassical model of the competitive paradigm becomes an illusion in the sense that we cannot really conclude that competitive

---

[21] One must add here that what I mean by political natural liberty is not really the simple mechanism of representative democracy. To a great extent, political systems may impede the will of the people (whatever that may be) to come through even if the system is labelled as democratic.

[22] As was mentioned before, J. S. Mill's vision of stagnation was based on the presumption that as humans develop they will lose interest in material wellbeing and develop greater interest in more spiritual aspects of human life (reminiscent of Aristotle's eudaimonia).

[23] This will be so because efficiency will no longer be the criteria of economic performance. If the public desires large governments—demand pull—the notion of productive efficiency loses its significance as a criterion of performance as the public is clearly no longer interested in having endless quantities of material goods. Nor would the idea of allocative efficiency mean much as large government means collective interests, which implies that making one agent better off without making another worse off cannot become an overriding principle. The universality and ethically neutrality will be lost as (a) public in different societies may view the role of governments differently and (b) the way the government raises revenue and distributes its services may vary too in different societies according to their specific ethical or social values.

organisation will actually produce a solution to the economic problem, let alone an outcome which is universal and ethically neutral. Moreover, if governments are large because of demand as captured by the Wagner's Law and public opinion about ownership (and, hence, government involvement), not only can the competitive model no longer be conceived as a solution to the economic problem but the economic problem itself, as perceived by the public, may altogether be different. To simply rely on the power of competition to produce productive efficiency in specific industries and to promote growth means that the economic problem is no longer to facilitate a universal reconciliation of unsatiated wants with scarcity but, rather, a mindless pursuit of material wellbeing with no reference at all to its distributional consequences.[24]

However, there is another aspect of the competitive paradigm which, to an extent, is far more significant than the previous one in the sense that it touches upon the main building block upon which the theory is constructed: fundamental individualism (and, consequently, liberalism). It is evident that an idea of decentralised decision-making works only if all individuals in society can take care of their own needs (and wants) through market operations. What this means is that every individual is capable of fulfilling his or her objectives—and, in particular, the acquisition of life's necessities—through impersonal and unorchestrated interactions with other participants in the economy.[25] In other words, individuals are not dependent on the collective (i.e. government) to achieve their objectives.[26] Anonymous bilateral interactions are all that it takes for agents to achieve their economic goals.

---

[24] Note that to claim that one can independently address the problem of redistribution is false as any attempts at redistribution will have material effects through the impact it will have on incentives and consequently, on productive efficiency itself.

[25] I deliberately do not use the term 'society' here as this implies many other things. The civic society, which is closely attached to the paradigmatic core, defines society as a mere framework for keeping the peace and facilitating prosperity. As such, it is predicated on members being able to fend for themselves. If not, then the reason why and how people may wish to support others may undermine the working of decentralised decision-making and require a clearer conception of the collective. We shall explore these issues later in the book.

[26] This does not mean that they may not choose to achieve some aspects of their desires through collective action but only that they do not depend on it for their survival (broadly conceived).

Put differently, the distributional outcome of the competitive decentralised decision-making system must be such that all individuals can solve their private economic problem, which in effect means that they can *socially subsist*. What we mean by this are basically three general themes:

1. Individuals acquire enough income to be able to physically survive in line with the conditions which prevail in their time (in terms of health and longevity).
2. Individuals acquire enough income to allow them to function socially. What we mean by this is that the standard of living which should be available to all members of society is at least an acceptable fraction of some notion of a social average.[27]
3. Individuals find dignity in their position in society in the sense that there is some correspondence between what they do and the return they get. We shall discuss this point in more details in the next chapter, but what we mean by this is that when people live in a social setting, they are naturally observed by others. Whether or not there is dignity in their position will depend on ethical values held by society. In particular, as will be explained later, we find the principle of proportional remuneration as one of the foundations of that dignity. If a person works hard and gets a disproportionately low return, he, or she, may appear as a fool, while another who works little for a high return may appear as a knave. This, of course, is only relevant when the system of decentralised decision-making is believed to be the right way of solving the economic problem. Otherwise, these issues would have been dealt with by the collective which would have, presumably, preserved (or at least attempted to preserve) social values. In the decentralised system, however, there is a belief (which we will show to be wrong) that everyone is the sole author of their fate and as the system is believed to be consistent with all social values, individuals are unlikely to be humiliated except by their own doing.

---

[27] This idea corresponds, to some extent, to the capabilities approach developed by Nussbaum (1988, 1992) and Sen (1985, 1992, 1999).

In the competitive decentralised system, income is distributed, like everything else, through markets. Indeed, one of the attractions of the paradigmatic core is that markets provide a simultaneous solution to both the problem of resources allocation and the issue of income distribution. It is for this very reason that the collective, or the government, has no role in the economy other than—by virtue of the second welfare theorem—to correct such a distribution without interference in the working of the markets.

However, the association of the distribution of income with the allocation of resources means that the contribution of the market to the distribution of income comes through the determination of the distributional parameters which represent the returns on productive services. These services, broadly speaking, can be either human labour (enhanced by human capital) or the use of assets which are owned by humans (i.e. capital (or land)).[28] Hence, what the markets, so to speak, decide upon is the flow of returns to the different categories of resources. The return to labour is in the form of wages while the return to capital is divided between the returns for the use of capital in the production process, and the returns one earns in the form of rent which is derived from ownership. Naturally, it is these flows which also determine the allocation of these resources. The appendix to this chapter provides a diagrammatic illustration of this point.

The question that arises is whether the distribution of returns between capital and labour also tells us something about the distribution of income in the economy. Classical economists like Smith, Ricardo, Mill and Marx saw a clear and strong association between one's income and one's position in the productive process. Namely, people were, in general, either workers who lived of their labour (and hence, wages were their sole source of income) or capitalists, which meant that their income was derived almost exclusively from the returns on capital (or assets more broadly conceived).[29]

---

[28] The distribution of these productive services constitutes what we called in the previous chapter the initial allocation. We will, in general, focus our discussion on labour and capital, leaving out land as a special category. One of the reasons for this is given in the following footnote.

[29] In classical economics, there was also the category of landlords who derived their income from ownership alone in the form of rent, but this has become superfluous in our discussion as we

Consequently, there was a clear tension between the two main categories of returns—which, in the case of Marx, led to the idea of class struggle. As the value of what is produced in an economy always dissolves into these two major categories, the greater is the one, the smaller is the other (again, this point is also explored in the appendix). To wit, the greater is the return on capital in all its forms, the lower will be the return on labour and vice versa.

Modern economics circumvented this dichotomy by blurring this distinction. Accordingly, each agent in society owns some assets and, therefore, is able to derive income both from his labour and from his assets. In such a case, whether returns to capital increase at the expense of wages or the other way around, the effects on the income earned by agents may not be so obvious. Naturally, the tension between the two categories of returns disappears as agents should not mind whether their income comes from their wages or from their earnings on the assets which they own. Nevertheless, it is clear that if there is an increase in returns on capital, for a given level of output, at the expense of wages, the income of those who rely more on labour than on capital is more likely to fall.

But is it really true that the separation of the returns to factors from the distribution of income has become a characteristic of the economy, in the sense that we can no longer identify individuals with their position in the economic (or productive) process? Can we not learn anything about the distribution of income from the behaviour of the returns to factors of production which are determined by the markets? The data on this matter is quite confusing. As many own their homes and have pension schemes or other forms of savings, the majority of the public would own some forms of assets and thus, in principle, justify the separation of returns to factors from the distribution of income. However, these assets do not normally generate an annual flow of income which can be seen as playing an equivalent role to that of wages in servicing daily lives. Instead, the returns on assets held in these forms will mainly be used to augment

---

included returns from ownership—what in textbooks is named as profits above the normal—in the returns on capital.

savings and pay for their management, but these sums are not available to the individual as a source of immediate earnings.[30]

Indeed, if we look at the share of capital income in the earnings of families in the USA—the economy with probably the greatest access opportunities to capital—we will find that, for most, income from capital is almost insignificant. Looking at data from the Survey of Consumer Finances (SCF), the following picture emerges:

Share of capital income in family earnings in percentile of net worth

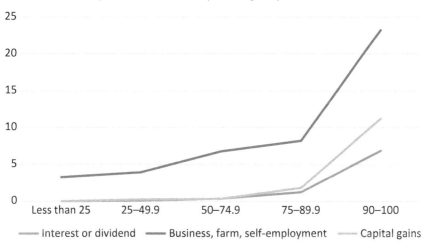

Source: Survey of Consumer Finances (2016)

Families are arranged from bottom to top in terms of their net worth (i.e. their wealth). Thus, on the left-hand side we have the 25% of family with the lowest net worth, while on the right we have the 10% of families with the top net worth. If we first focus on the two lower lines depicting capital gains and interest or dividends, we can see that even for the top group of the lower 75% of families (the bottom 50–74.9%) capital income is virtually nothing (0.67% of earnings, to be precise). These shares become more significant in the top 25% of families and in

---

[30] We are, of course, aware of the fact that wealth and future earnings have an effect on the availability of funds at each period of time, but given the cost of borrowing we do not think that it has the same role in individuals' consideration as the readily available flow of income emanating without any strings attached.

particular, for the top 10% for whom this share stands on about 18% of earnings.

The higher line is somewhat less clear. It depicts the earnings from business, farm and self-employment. This, too, is relatively low for the bottom 75% but not as insignificant as the previous, more obvious, returns to capital. The problem with this parameter is that it conflates returns from pure ownership (like a farm or a small business) and returns from labour in the form of self-employment. One can speculate that the composition of this line, as we move from the families with lower net worth to the higher, would shift from being mostly returns on self-employed labour to becoming increasingly more returns from profits of owning small businesses and farms. But even here, for the top group of the bottom 75%, this rate stands on no more than 6.78% of earnings. By contrast, it stands on 23% for the top 10% of families. Therefore, it is hard to conclude from this that most individuals indeed have access to income in all its forms, whether derived from capital or labour. Consequently, changes in returns to factor are more likely to reflect significant changes in income distribution.

Further evidence for the fact that most people derive their earnings from only one distributional parameter—wages—can be found in the way in which capital income is distributed. Saez and Zucman (2016) show that the top 0.1% of earners in the USA capture around 43% of all taxable capital income (around 34% if we exclude capital gains). This, by the way, is a dramatic increase from around 14% of taxable capital income in the early 1960s (around 10% excluding capital gains), which in itself raises questions regarding the workings of competitive decentralisation. Hence, if the top 0.1% captures around 40% of capital income, it is not very likely that the remaining 60% of it would be equally distributed over the remaining households. The logic hidden in this and the previous findings suggests that probably no more than the top 20% of household would command almost all the income generated by capital. This seems to suggest that the number of households which do not have any access, or any meaningful access, to capital income is quite considerable.

The same conclusion is also borne by looking at the composition of wealth of the majority of the population. Saez and Zucman (2016) suggest that in 2012 the bottom 90% of households held less than 25% of the total household wealth. If we look at the internal composition of that wealth, we find that most of it is, as we suggested earlier, held in pension funds and, as such, is not a direct source of daily earnings. From those assets which can generate a usable flow of earnings (i.e. business assets), the bottom 90% hold about 2%. Equity and fixed claim amount to almost nothing in their portfolio. Bearing in mind that the bottom 90% includes very rich households, it stands to reason that as we go down the groups of households we will find a considerably reduced ability to rely on income from capital as an equivalent or alternative to labour income.

A slightly less aggregate perspective can be gained by looking at the US Census from 2014, where we can find the percentage of household in each quintile which has, potentially, access to a regular flow of capital income:

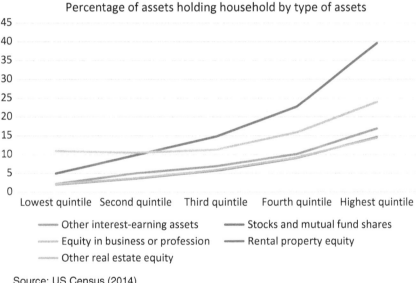

Percentage of assets holding household by type of assets

Source: US Census (2014)

It is easy to see that for the bottom 60% of household (measured in terms of their monthly income) the percentage of household with access to untied income generating capital in each quintile is well below 15% and, for most such assets, not much more than 10%.[31] Therefore, it will

---

[31] While the data does not specify this, we assume that one should not add the percentage of household holding all assets. In other words, it is probably the case that all these assets are held by more or less the same households.

be perfectly reasonable to suppose that among this group of households more than 85% of them will have no access to flow of income from capital that can seriously be considered as a steady annual flow of income equivalent to that which comes from labour. If we include the fourth quintile, the numbers of those with access to capital income is not much greater (around 23%) and by implication the percentage of households which can rely on capital income is, again, very small. Assuming that there is a correspondence between low net worth and low monthly income, we can conclude from this that most households have very limited access to capital income and the income which they do derive from the few assets they do hold is almost insignificant.

All in all, one can deduce from this that the presumption as if one can ignore the association of individuals' income with the behaviour of the returns to factors is false. The majority of the public derive their income from wages alone. There are those who derive income from both and probably very few who derive their income only from capital. And this is all based on US data which, perhaps, is the economy with the broadest access to capital markets. In other countries, and in particular non-Anglo-Saxon one, it is very likely that the association between returns to factors and individuals' income is even stronger. Consequently, the way in which the markets associate efficient allocations with income distribution—that is, the distribution of returns to factors—is something of great significance to the question of individuals' ability to access *enough income* that will guarantee their *social subsistence*.

Let us now examine more closely the way in which markets affect the distribution of the returns to factor so that we can say something about the significance of empirical evidence to the relevance of the paradigmatic core. Looking at the economy as a whole (in terms of aggregate labour, capital and output), that which determines the basic distribution of returns between labour and capital is the equilibrium conditions of the generalised and aggregate labour market (again, see the appendix for a diagrammatic exposition of most points discussed here). In other words, for any given level of capital, there will be a demand for labour reflecting the profit maximising considerations of producers throughout the economy. As the productivity of labour—namely, the contribution of a unit of labour to output—is diminishing for a given level of capital, the more labour employers would wish to hire, the lower would be the real wage. The supply of labour which is a reflection of the rational considerations of individuals will be rising with wages as the opportunity cost of leisure is rising. The equilibrium level of wages which will be determined at the wage level where the quantity of labour supplied equals the quantity of labour demanded will therefore determine the efficient allocation of labour (for a given level of capital) as well as the share of wages in national income (which is the real wages per unit of labour multiplied by the number of units allocated) that supports it. By definition, the remainder of the income will constitute the returns on capital.[32]

This means that in part the distribution of returns on factors of production is affected by their productivity. For higher level of labour productivity, the demand for labour will increase and for the same supply function of labour, wages (as well as output and income) will be higher. However, as was mentioned before, the distribution of income, from the perspective of modern economics, is not the same as the distribution of returns. As people access national income through both labour and assets (i.e. capital), their share of national income is fed through both the return on labour and the return on capital. The idea of the second welfare theorem can easily be demonstrated here as the government can (if it were possible) use lump-sum transfers to change the distribution of ownership of assets and, in this way, alter the distribution of income without interfering in the efficiency of the allocation determined through the market returns on labour and capital.[33]

But if it is the case, as we have endeavoured to persuade, that people are, as a matter of fact, divided in terms of their access to national income between those who mainly derive their income from labour and those who mainly derive their income from assets (and we will say more about it soon), the distribution of these shares will tell us something about the ability of agents to access income in a way that will guarantee their social subsistence.

---

[32] We assume, for simplicity of argument, no intermediate goods and these returns include profits above the normal.

[33] Recall that this freedom to redistribute ownership without affecting the efficient outcome is lost when we consider the presence of missing markets in a world of uncertainty. In such a world, the distribution of ownership is crucial for achieving productive efficiency.

It is, therefore, interesting to note that there has been a consistent, and in some cases relatively sharp, decline in the share of labour in national income during that period in which there has been a spread and consolidation of the markets and an improved protection of property rights. In an International Monetary Fund (IMF) report—World Economic Outlook—from April 2017, they provide a diagram depicting the evolution of labour share in national income since 1970.[34] The figure shows a consistent decline in that share in both advanced economies, and emerging markets and developing economies. In the advanced economies, the share of labour in national income has fallen from around 55% in 1970 to less than 51% in 2015. Developing countries and emerging markets mimic that movement but at a lower share of national income.[35] One should note, however, that the significant decline in the share of labour in national income, in advanced economies, began towards the end of the 1970s and the beginning of the 1980s. This corresponds to the time when competitive decentralisation (or market economics) declared its final triumph in the struggles of ideas to which we referred in the first chapter. It was the time when Thatcher and Reagan came to power in the UK and the USA respectively, the Soviet Union and the Eastern European bloc had begun their final collapse and when globalisation became the heart of a new world order.[36] It is also worth noting that this fall in the share of wages also corresponds with the rise of the internet.[37]

---

[34] Chapter 3, Fig. 3.1 on page 122.

[35] The numbers may vary slightly in different studies mainly because of the question of self-employed income. In an OECD report from 2015, which adjusts for self-employed income, the share of labour in national income ends up slightly higher, at around 55% in 2011. Altogether, the OECD schedule is very similar except that it is slightly higher by around 5%. Note too that the picture is much grimmer when it comes to emerging markets and developing economies, but this is a subject beyond the scope of this book.

[36] To remind the reader, we use the term 'globalisation' in this book to describe the increase in the free movement of factors (capital and labour) rather than the spread of free trade in goods and services which preceded the 1980s. In fact, the lifting of restrictions on the mobility of capital—which for our purpose is the beginning of globalisation in recent times—was triggered by the collapse of the Bretton-Wood regime during the 1970s. It is therefore very likely that the real effects of this change will first be felt during the 1980s. With regard to the data, it is also clear from US data we reported earlier that between 1947 and 1981 (more or less the era of restrictions on the mobility of capital), the share of wages remained more or less stable.

[37] Which, among other things, facilitated greater incursion of markets to areas of life which earlier would not have been seen as fertile ground for markets.

In the face of this decline in the share of labour in national income, one cannot fail to observe that if it is indeed the case that the majority of people (roughly around 80% according to our previous account) derive their income from wages alone, having an average share around the 51% mark is quite alarming. Moreover, if we take into account that the wages of those who also derive income from capital (i.e. high earners) are included in the share of labour, that which is left for the majority for whom labour is the sole source of earning becomes even smaller. In an OECD (2012) report on employment outlook, they show that the share of labour would fall by 2.9% more for Canada and by 2.2% more for the USA, if the wages of the top 1% of earners were excluded. The picture is going to be much more pronounced if we excluded the top 10% earners. In such a case, the fall in the share of labour in national income would be much more dramatic. Therefore, one can quite safely conclude that for the majority of individuals, those who rely on labour income alone—and who are likely to be low earners—as a means for accessing national income, it has become increasingly difficult to maintain the standard of living—the solution of their own individual economic problem—which is commensurate with the level of GDP per capita in their own economy.

Some may argue that in spite of the fact that labour shares are falling, the overall level of income is greater and, therefore, even those at the bottom of the wage scale can still derive an income which would facilitate a standard of living much higher than in the past.[38] This, in turn, invokes two fairly complex questions. The first is whether poverty is an absolute or relative term. The second is whether trickle-down is working. There can be little doubt that to be poor in a rich economy is not the same

---

[38] Indeed, the fall in the share of wages in national income may be associated with an *increase in real wage*. This means that when both demand and supply of labour increase, the increase in output is much greater than the increase in the total wage bill and, thus, the share of wages in total income may still become smaller (see Appendix). Nevertheless, this wage to which we are referring is an *average wage* which may be higher mainly because of the influence of those who are well paid in the economy. We have seen in the above figures that once we remove the top 1% the fall in the share of labour is much greater and this will be more pronounced with the top 10%. Therefore, the actual wage of most people who rely on labour alone may be lower even if the average wage increased. But even if there is an increase in everyone's wages, the fact that the share of capital has now increased so much will make these people in their own society relatively poorer (see point (b) in the previous discussion).

experience as being poor in a poor economy. We are not suggesting now—as it seems to be widely believed—that the former is better than the latter. To be poor when everyone around you is poor may not be as unsettling as being poor when there is so much wealth to make everyone better off. Life has more than one dimension. From the beginning, when we suggested the idea of *social subsistence*, we emphasised that this is not just about physical survival—the conditions for which may indeed be absolute—but, rather, it is about the ability to conduct a social life based on the norm. Such a norm is more likely to be dictated by a certain concept of mean income (or GDP per capita) and, therefore, is relative in nature.

Consequently, whether or not the fall in labour share—even when real wages increased—will have a detrimental effect on the ability of those who rely on wages alone to achieve the socially defined standard of living depends on whether they become relatively, rather than absolutely, poorer. So far, we have established that the labour share in national income is falling. We have also established that the vast majority of the public depends on labour alone as a source of income. At the same time, we know that income increased and that the number of people in the working-age group who depend on labour also increased. On the face of it, this leaves the question of whether those who rely on wages become worse off undetermined. However, we already argued that the drop in the share of labour is probably much more pronounced as we remove the relatively few high earners from the data. This should increase our confidence that most of the wage earners, as a whole, have become relatively worse off. The clearest manifestation of this would be if we discovered that there is a connection between the fall in the share of labour and the rise in inequality of income distribution. Increase in income inequality clearly means that the distance between agents in terms of their earning has increased. In particular, the distance of the many who derive their income from the dwindling share of wages in national income from all other earners will increase and, consequently, make it more difficult for those people to obtain the standard of living they would have been able to obtain had income been equally divided.

This, in part, leads to the second question of trickle-down. In the eyes of many, the benefits of the competitive system of decentralised decision-making is that it generates a trickle-down of income from those who, as it were, make it, to the rest of society. Already in Adam Smith there is a reference to this phenomenon. In his implicit argument with Rousseau, who saw private property as an inherent cause of inequality, Smith famously invoked the invisible hand of *The Theory of Moral Sentiments* to argue that this is not entirely true. Smith's argument was that as the stomach of the rich is not greater than that of the poor, there is a limit to how much the rich can consume of the income generated by their assets. That which they do not, so to speak, eat they will use to buy services and other goods which are provided by other people in society. Therefore, the surplus of the income generated by their assets will inevitably flow towards everyone else. It will thus be true that if the income of the rich increases, the surplus will also spread and the income of everyone else should also improve. In other words, trickle-down means that increases in income will inevitably flow down all levels of income and make the poorest better off. It may also suggest that the distribution of income should become more equal. Consequently, if the fall in the share of labour in national income leads to greater difficulty in acquiring social subsistence by those who rely on it because the distribution of income becomes more unequal, then there must be a problem with the mechanism of trickle-down.[39]

Indeed, the expectation that diminishing labour share will have a detrimental effect on the ability of agents to use markets for their social subsistence is borne out by the observation that not only has there been a rise in income inequality, but this rise is correlated with the fall in the share of wages. In the same IMF report from April 2017[40] which we mentioned earlier, we can find a clear and significant negative correlation between the changes in the share of labour and the changes in the Gini coefficient which measures the level of inequality. The higher is the Gini coefficient, the more unequal is the distribution; hence, a negative correlation means that the fall in the share of labour in national income is

---

[39] This will not discredit Smith's argument as he did not suggest that trickle-down will make the distribution of income more equal as increase in wages will lead, in his story, to increase in labour supply and wages will sink back to subsistence. His invisible hand only guarantees that life's necessities—the bundle associated with avoiding absolute poverty—will always be equally distributed. We will return to this issue in Chap. 8.

[40] Figure 3.2 on page 122 (panel 3 in particular).

correlated with a rise in the Gini value (i.e. inequality). A similar picture can also be found in the OECD (2012) report which we mentioned before.

There is, of course, no surprise in this when one adopts the classical perspective which equates individuals' source of income with their role in the productive process. When there are people who derive their income from labour alone and others who derive it from both labour and capital, it stands to reason that a fall in the share of labour will increase inequality and make it more difficult for those individuals to solve their economic problem (determined by the general level of output) by relying on the way in which markets distribute the returns on productive services.[41]

In summary, if the share of wages is negatively correlated with inequality, this is an indication that even though the share of wages may have fallen at a time of increase in income, the income which each individual worker could extract from the market was relatively smaller. This could be a result of the fact that the increase in productivity (which would have increased the share of wages, as well as income, for a given workforce size) was not sufficient to offset the increase in the workforce, or in those who are dependent on wages alone (which would have reduced the share of wages for a given level of productivity—see the appendix for diagrammatic exposition). But also, it could be the result of the fact that no matter what happened to the equilibrium wage level, the fact that the relatively few high earners (who usually have other sources of earnings) make up a significant share of the wage bill, the share in income of those who rely on wages exclusively will go down.

This kind of explanation to the fall in the share of wages is, of course, based on the presumption that labour markets are working and that the economy is in equilibrium. It is, however, very difficult to find the exact explanation as the labour market—as we explained in the previous chapter—is a conceptual framework rather than a description of the world. To calculate the change in the share of wages, one would need to find the

---

[41] Indeed, the explanations cited in the IMF report amount to very much the same thing. Accordingly, the proposed reasons are named as the actual decline in the labour share of the lower-skilled workers together with the somewhat-puzzling fall in the share of middle-earning occupations in total employment (see also Autor and Dorn (2013) and Goos et al. (2014)) as well as the concentration of capital income among the high earners.

elasticities of demand and supply, both of which have been (a) aggregates which make their empirical decomposition next to impossible and (b) are subject to continuous changes. The demand for labour represents the demand by all producers who fluctuate in number and reflect the technology (i.e. the marginal product) which is continuously changing. The supply too is made up of a changing number of individuals who are subject to changing preferences.[42]

If we were to find an explanation consistent with the requirements of an equilibrium in the labour market, the significance of the fall in the share of labour—and the subsequent reduction in the accessibility of income through markets—would be that the workings of the competitive decentralised system undermine its purpose: that all agents can solve their economic problem by themselves (through market interactions). Naturally, in such a case, one could argue that through lump-sum redistribution of assets it could be possible for such an equilibrium in terms of returns to factors not to have increased inequality. If those who rely on wages alone were allocated assets, the fall in the share of wages would have no real significance.

But as we said before, there are a few difficulties with this assertion. Firstly, lump-sum transfers are not possible, which means that any attempt at redistribution will lead us to an inefficient allocation. As we cannot compare different inefficient allocations, it would not make sense, in such a case, to insist on the competitive paradigm as there is no obvious benefit to it. Secondly, even if assets could be redistributed, we would still have the problem of incompleteness in uncertainty where the allocation of assets (and property rights) is crucial to the productive efficiency of the system. Allocating assets to individuals just because they cannot access enough income through labour will ensure that the incentive sets of the economy are not going to be optimal and, therefore, the outcome will be inefficient. Thirdly, experience with mass privatisation when gov-

---

[42] According to OECD data, between 2000 and 2015, the number of individuals in the labour force (which would constitute the supply of labour) had risen by 7% in the G7 countries and by 9% in the EU. Given that over the same period of 15 years, population in the G7 grew by 9% and in the EU by 3.9%, the increase in the labour force in OECD cannot be deemed to be sufficiently large to offset the evident technological development. We should have expected the share of wages to increase, had markets been in equilibrium.

ernments attempted to increase ownership (popular capitalism) led to all the poor people who bought assets to get rid of them immediately afterwards simply because they desperately needed the money.

Either way, we are not really in this position because there is evidence to suggest that the reason behind the fall in labour share has more to do with the failure in conceiving the labour markets than with the outcome of its proper functioning. Namely, it is not the competitive equilibrium which will help us understand this development. Recall that equilibrium in the labour market means that the real wage is equal to labour productivity or the contribution to output of the last unit of labour. If we assume that there was an increase in labour productivity (due to both the accumulation of human capital [and, hence, innovations] and the increase in the stock of capital), then for the equilibrium condition in the labour market to ensure both a fall in the share of wages in national income and an increase in inequality there should have been a sufficiently large increase in the labour force to push down real wages. As this equilibrium level of real wages should reflect labour productivity as measured by the contribution of the last unit of labour, it should also fall.

However, we already noted in Footnote 42 that the increase in the labour force was not very large over the last 15 years, which makes this outcome, empirically, not very likely. In fact, with the kind of technological change we have observed in recent years and the rise in the stock of capital, one would expect both productivity and wages to increase. With it, one would also expect the share of labour in income to increase. However, what we observe is something which raises serious doubts about both the workings of the labour markets and its relevance as a model, which is supposed to capture the way in which markets allocate resources and distribute income.

There is considerable amount of evidence to suggest that there is an increasing gap between labour productivity and real wages. An example of such evidence can be found in the International Labour Organization (ILO) *Global Wage Report 2014/15: Wages and Income Inequality.*[43] There, they show the gap between labour productivity and real wages as it evolves from 1999, which is used as the base year. Thus, between 1999 and 2013,

---

[43] Page 8, Fig. 7.

the index of productivity increased from 100 to about 117, while that of real wages increased from 100 in 1999 to only around 106 in 2013. Had the labour market worked properly, the increase in both indices should have been the same.[44] Therefore, it will not be unreasonable to conclude that as the gap between what workers contribute and what they receive in return increases, the share of wages is likely to fall. That which workers have produced and was not paid to them was distributed to capital in the form of cost of using it and return on ownership (The appendix explores this point too). But if real wages are lower than the productivity of labour, this means that something in the market mechanism is not working well.[45] As such, this does not really discredit the labour market as the conclusion we could draw from this is that something is preventing the labour market from reaching its equilibrium point and had it been possible, there would have been no gap between productivity and real wages and the share of wages could have increased.

Indeed, in part, the Keynesian revolution was also associated with a perceived failure of the labour market.[46] In the case of Keynes, this failure was perceived to be the creation of a disequilibrium point where real wages were above the equilibrium level which gave rise to involuntary unemployment and which suggested that the mechanism of the labour market (which should have led to a fall in nominal wages and increase in employment) is not working properly. In our case, we have the exact opposite situation, as wages are below the productivity level, demand for workers should have been greater and nominal wages should have increased to fill the gap. However, this has not been happening. We are

---

[44] It is important to bear in mind that it is not the case that in 1999 real wages equalled labour productivity. It is simply that the availability of data was such that the calculation is based on the evolution of each of the two variables since. Hence, if in 1999 there was already a gap, it widened considerably. If there was no gap, then it has certainly developed.

[45] It is worth noting that the way in which productivity is calculated is more akin to what one would call average product. In theory, when markets are in long-run equilibrium, the marginal cost will be the same as the average cost which may justify using average product as a measure for marginal product. But if there is some degree of monopolistic power (as there always is), it means that the economy is producing at the downward sloping part of the average costs which, in turn, means that the marginal product is much higher than the average product and, therefore, the problem we identify here is much greater than the evidence suggests.

[46] Already observed by Marshall and J. S. Mill. See a discussion of some of these points in Witztum (2013).

sure that there are a lot of stories that can be told about why this is the situation but the persistence of such a situation over such a long period of time suggests that the equilibrium perspective maybe the one which is irrelevant.

As we discussed in the previous chapter, the relevance of these models depends on whether there is a conceivable process that can lead us, asymptotically, towards the equilibrium point, which is the only place where the promised benefits of the system can be accrued. Both the consistent presence of unemployment (the Keynesian perspective) and the evident gap between productivity and real wages suggest that our confidence in the relevance of this model should be seriously diminished. With it, our confidence that the market mechanism of allocation will produce a distribution of income where all members of society can rely on it to extract the income they need to sociality subsist should also be seriously diminished.

The breakdown in the promised association between productivity and reward (real wages) has also an effect on the third aspect of what we defined as social subsistence and that is the perceived dignity of individuals. To some extent, the promise of the market to equate the marginal contribution (i.e. productivity) of a factor to its reward sounds almost ethical. Who would not wish a system to reward people according to their contribution to it. In the next chapter, we will discuss in some details the merit (and demerit) of this apparent promise but at this stage we can only say that the fact that workers receive less than the agreed measure of their contribution is an ethical affront which could affect their dignity. Those who live by capital alone—albeit few in number—seem to receive a return which is disproportionate to their direct contribution, while those who work receive a return disproportionately lower than their direct contribution. The spectre of the fool and the knave is not too far from one's mind. In terms of our discussion in Chap. 1 and the idea of diachronic order, it is inconceivable that a system which offends such a basic notion of ethical decency would be able to subsist for a long period of time. It is far too similar to Mandeville's paradox to allow us to gloss over it. Bearing in mind that the final victory of market economy came only in the 1980s (Reagan-Thatcher axis of supply side economics) and in the early 1990s (with the collapse of the Eastern bloc), and that the spread of competitive practices has reached its most extended form (through WTO and globalisation) at the end of the 1990s, the full-blown manifestation of the idea of liberal economics has been around for a relatively short period of time. Therefore, from the perspective of diachronic order, it has no real record of prolonged sustainability, and judging by this particular affront it would be difficult to sustain it for much longer.[47]

3.3   Employment

The observations we have discussed so far suggest that the ability of individuals to access national income through labour alone is under pressure as the share of income available to an increasing body of people who depend on it has been consistently diminishing. At the same time, capital has not become more widely available to those who earn less. If the trend continues, it may lead to a situation where earnings from wages may become altogether insufficient to support the lifestyle which the level of national income could support (i.e. social subsistence).

However, while the fall in the share of labour suggests that an increasing number of people will find themselves with insufficient funds to support the appropriate level of social subsistence, the problem worsens when we consider the fact that there is a significant number of individuals who cannot access the labour market altogether (nor, of course, the capital market). The former problem is more about the way in which the system of decentralised decision-making is functioning, but the latter suggests that the decentralised system is not functioning at all as it leaves people outside the system altogether. If this is a chronic feature of such a system, this raises the question of whether a decentralised system of decision-making is at all relevant. It is important to emphasise that we are not discussing here involuntary unemployment as this may be just a

---

[47] Some may argue that the competitive paradigm has been around since the days of Adam Smith and the physiocrats' laissez-faire. While this is true that the promise of the competitive paradigm has been around for a long time, its full application into social life is only a recent and short phenomenon. The question of diachronic order does not relate to the length of time in which the promise is being repeated but rather, it is based on the experience of its application in daily life.

problem of market failure and not of failure of the market[48] but, rather, we are discussing those people who are outside the labour force altogether. Namely, people who are defined to be economically inactive and who may remain so even if the labour market is in equilibrium.

To have a rough idea on the extent of the problem, it is best to look at labour force participation rates which include both people in employment and those who are defined, according to the ILO definitions as unemployed:

Labour force participation (% of 16–65 years old)

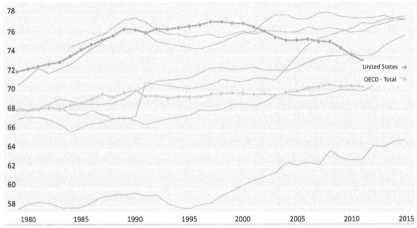

Source: OECD (2017)

If we look at all Organisation for Economic Co-operation and Development (OECD) countries, we can see that on average the rate of participation in the labour force of those who are at working age (16–65) has increased by less than 4% over the period of 35 years. As such, it has changed from 68% of the working-age population in 1980 to below 72% in 2015. The USA, which is, perhaps, the most market oriented of all the OECD economies, shows a slightly different pattern with higher partici-

---

[48] To remind the reader we drew this distinction in the previous chapter to distinguish between situations where there is something which prevents competitive markets to perform (like in the case of involuntary unemployment where nominal wages are not falling to bridge the gap between demand and supply) and situations where market may perform well but still, not achieve the objectives.

pation rates—due to fewer social protection and, thus, greater market dependency—which increased somewhat over the period but eventually has been falling since the mid-1990s to a level which is not dissimilar to other OECD economies. The rate of participation in the USA in 2015 is slightly above 72%. But even at its highest, it has been below 78%.

Before exploring the nature of this phenomenon, we must emphasise the fact that there is a substantial section of the population whose income is not obtained through market operations. One would have thought that it may be the case that these individuals have access through capital and probably some of them do, but a great number of those who are economically inactive are not in such an envious position. Hence, their absence from the labour force is not necessarily an indication of sufficient income flowing from capital but, rather, either a dependency on others—specific individuals (like spouses or family)—or an inability to fend for themselves through market activities which makes them dependent on the collective (government). While dependency on specific others like spouse or family may not directly suggest a problem for the competitive paradigm, the presence of a significant group who are dependent on the collective does. A system which is based on a promise that everyone can care for themselves cannot be relevant in a world where a significant number of people are incapable of doing so.

In 2015, the rate of those who had no access to income through markets stood on slightly above 28%! In the USA, this rate was slightly below 28%. This is not an insignificant group of people. Nevertheless, as we said, there are different reasons for why agents do not participate in the market to obtain their share of income. For one, the age range of the data includes years in which people are normally in education. This raises the question of both the educational provisions and the subsistence during the period of education. In most countries, the provision of education (at least some of it) is public (i.e. the collective) and subsistence is through family dependency. In a few, education may be provided through markets but even then subsistence may be the result of dependency. Whether or not these people have been failed by the market depends on what would have happened if there were no public provisions of education—which in themselves undermine the completeness of competitive interactions—and no family support? After all, the competitive paradigm is profoundly individualistic, and once it relies on social structures to facilitate its working, it can no longer claim to be universal or ethically neutral.

Another reason for being economically inactive, related to what we have just said, is the broader implications of relying on culture, or social institutions (like marriage or civil partnerships), to allow people non-market access to income. In such cases, a person may not be economically active but at the same time will be able to access national income through their partners. Most of the time, the dependency on one's partner would reflect social norms like, for instance, that of stay-at-home parent, but it can also be parental contributions to adult offspring and the likes. The last and most serious form of inactivity is when there are people who have no support from the social structures (i.e. family), have no assets and, therefore, rely entirely on the collective (government) to ensure access to income.

On the face of it, it may look as if the only ones who are really betrayed by the markets are the third group, those who rely on the collective. But this is not entirely obvious. As we said before, for the system of competitive decentralisation to be meaningful, it must provide every individual with the ability to acquire their social subsistence through markets. It is true that for those relying on a spouse there is no need for the collective to interfere (and, thus, government can remain minimal) but there is a need for social norms to exist, to ensure the lives of those in social institutions like marriage. If these norms did not exist, would all members of society still be able to acquire their share such that it will ensure their social subsistence? One could argue, of course, that if all those dependent on a spouse were to enter the labour force, the supply of labour would increase but the demand for it would also increase as some of the services which those individuals had provided their household with will now have to be provided through markets. The combined shift of supply and demand suggests that there may not be a change in the share of wages in national income. But if this share is low, the problem of reduced accessibility to national income remains. Moreover, there is a somewhat deeper issue here: Can we really say that the individualistic promise of the competitive paradigm is relevant in a world where we need institutions like marriage, or family, to make sure that the flows of income are such that all agents have access to sufficient income to socially subsist?

Be this as it may, the fact is that the number of individuals in the third category—those who rely entirely on the collective—is significant enough to conclude that the condition for the paradigmatic core to deliver on its promise do not exist and have not existed for a very long time (if ever).

In a study conducted by Eurostat on *Statistics in Focus: Population and Social Conditions* (authored by O Hardarson) in 2006, they examined in more details the state of inactivity in EU-25 (Denmark, Ireland and Sweden were not included) in 2004. If we look at the detailed information available there, we can separate those who are in education or with alternative incomes (either from partners or from various forms of retirements) from the population of the inactive individuals. In 2004, the total population of 15–64-year-olds (the working-age population) in the EU-25 countries was 303,226,000. The total population of economically inactive individuals in the same age group in the EU-25 countries was 92,105,000 individuals. They constituted 30% of the total working-age population. Both in percentage and in numbers, this is a very large group of people.

The interesting observation one can derive from the data is that the group of inactive people are divided almost equally between three age groups: about a third are members of the 15–24-year-old age group, who are indeed more likely to be in education; about a third in the 24–54 group; and about a third in the 55–64 group. Among the first group, as could be expected, most are in education (25,923,000 out of 30,819,000, which is 84%). In most cases, these individuals are dependent on the collective which provides them with education and are also dependent on their family for subsistence. Therefore, those who are not in education or in any employment or unable to access capital income and are directly reliant on the collective (perhaps the purest form of economic inactivity) are only 4,896,000 (or 16% of this age group of economically inactive individuals). The other two groups (25–64), if we remove all those who are in education and all those who are retired (which means that they have income from other market governed sources), make up 41,372,000. Together with the 'pure' inactive people from the first group, the total number of inactive individuals who are not in education and are not earning income from assets (retirement) is 46,268,000 which make up

15% of the working-age population. While this is clearly less intimidating than 30%, it is still a significant share of the population.

So far, we do not know how many individuals in this category rely on a partner's income and how many are completely dependent on the collective. The information here is more complicated to gauge, but the same study concluded that 24.3% of single-parent households with children under the age of 15 are economically inactive and 12.3% of people who are living alone are economically inactive and are less likely to rely on specific others (like family) for their subsistence. Alternatively, we can find corroborating information about the dependency of the economically inactive on the public by looking at data on the number of people who live in household where no one is working:

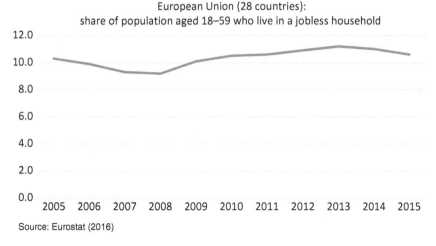

European Union (28 countries): share of population aged 18–59 who live in a jobless household

Source: Eurostat (2016)

This means that around 10% of the working-age population in the EU do not have any access to national income through either labour, capital or family relations. This percentage seems to have been more or less steady in the last 10 years although the trend in the data is somewhat upwards. Either way, it suggests that this is more of a permanent feature of the system than a temporary stage. Though the number of economically inactive people who depend on the collective is significantly smaller than the total number of economically inactive individuals, they are nevertheless a significant share of the working-age population. If we add to this those who are in education and therefore depend both on the collective and on family support (they constitute above 8.5% of the working-age population—based on the study we just mentioned), the share of those who are deriving their social subsistence by other means than markets is quite considerable (almost a fifth of the working-age population).

In the light of such findings, therefore, it is difficult to have a serious discussion about the promise of the paradigmatic core which is predicated on all individuals being able to solve their own economic problem simply by using market interactions. The problem of inactivity is not new but rather a reflection of some fundamental issues which govern social life. These are: (a) the dependency of individuals on the collective for the purpose of being able to be economically active (i.e. the provision of education); and (b) not all people are the same in their ability or disposition to take advantage of system and there are always some people in society who will end up outside the economic game.

This is not the place to get into a debate about whether education—at all levels—could indeed be provided by markets with an equivalent social reach as it would had it been provided by the public. But it is worth noting that if education were governed by market principles, it is most likely that the number of adults who would become inactive would considerably increase. The uptake of education, in the case of market provision, is bound to be lower than that under the state-governed provisions, which, in part, is governed by compulsory attendance. Those who will acquire less education will also find it more difficult to find work in an increasingly developed (technologically) workplace. Consequently, not only inactivity would increase but also inequality, which, too, reduces the accessibly of national income to an increasingly larger section of the population. But if education were publicly provided, then we are in the world where competition can never be complete, and the reign of decentralised competitive systems will necessarily produce inefficient outcomes. As we cannot really distinguish between different inefficient outcomes, we cannot honestly claim that any of them constitutes a solution to the economic problem.

To summarise, the problem of economic inactivity (excluding those who choose to do so due to alternative market source of income) is comprised of three main issues. The first is the question of social-based dependency. What we mean by this is the group of people who rely on other members of a socially constructed unit to provide them with market-based income. These people are not as such a burden to the system as all these choices are, to an extent, voluntary. It is also not clear whether the entry of all those individuals into the labour force would necessarily have adverse effects by either reducing wages or the sharing of wages in national income. Nevertheless, there may be other reasons to believe that the entry of all these individuals to the labour force may not translate into employment and economic sovereignty. Even at the current participation rates there is a significant level of unemployment suggesting both problems of matching and problems associated with the level of need for labour in the production process (we shall come back to this soon). As such, the current arrangement suggests that the apparent working of the competitive paradigm is predicated on particular social institutions. If this is the case, surely other social issues may also take precedent over economic principles and the universality of the paradigmatic core would have to be challenged.

The second issue is the role that education plays in the system. While those in education are not economically active, they are (a) dependent on subsistence from their family (the first issue we mentioned) and (b) acquire something which could either be provided by the market or by the collective. Whether education is provided publicly or through markets makes a great deal of difference both in affecting current levels of inactivity and in affecting future levels of it. As we suggested before, with private provisions there may be fewer people inactive now (as fewer people will be in education) but there will be many more in the future as the ability of agents to become economically active will be curtailed.

The third issue is the most obvious one and it involves those individuals who are not active but who have no alternative source of income other than that which is provided by the collective. Whether the collective provides such income or not, the competitive paradigm clearly fails in its promise. Either because government's interference restricts the domain of competitive practices or because individuals fail to become economically sovereign, the outcome of competitive interaction cannot be crowned as the universal and ethically neutral solution to the economic problem.

The problem of economic inactivity highlights an important element of the paradigmatic core which, in general, has not been prominent in the discussions about its relevance. It is the general question of participation. In our discussion of inactivity, the concern was that there are some people who are not able to participate in the economic game which is limited to market interactions and, consequently, their economic problem cannot be solved. The solution of such a problem would, of course, require a way to get these people into the labour market. Indeed, when one listens to the public discourse on this question, it is almost entirely focused on finding ways to bring these people into the labour force (even though there is a significant level of unemployment and the probability that these people will join the unemployed rather than the employed is relatively high). As we have already mentioned, this is all reminiscent of Keynes's intervention where the issue of participation was prominent. For him, the focus of attention was the unemployed and the objective of society was full employment. Needless to say, inactivity (in its non-voluntary form) should also invite measures for its eradication.

So, what lies at the heart of the struggle against unemployment and the one against involuntary inactivity is the (correct) understanding that for the idea of competitive decentralisation to succeed there has to be a world of full participation. This means that all individuals are economically sovereign in the sense that they can use the markets to solve their individual economic problem. They should not rely on the collective and, therefore, the collective does not have to convene, decide, interfere and consequently disturb the working of the decentralised system. Needless to say, the choices of the collective are bound to reflect social and cultural differences that are not conducive to the idea of a single, universal, form of economic organisation.

However, when we refer to economic sovereignty of the agents, there is a question whether participation is a necessary condition for sovereignty or is the ability not to participate the real sign of sovereignty. In other words, does the fact that people must participate to solve their economic problem means that they are sovereign or not? We will address this question in the next chapter (and it is, basically, a supply side question) but we would like to touch upon the question of whether the system provides the means for full participation (i.e. the demand-side question). Naturally, when wealth is equally divided, everyone in society may have equal access to income through wealth. However, this may not be enough, and people may still need labour to provide for their social subsistence. Moreover, if the reality is that wealth is unequally divided[49]

---

[49] In fact, it is extremely unequally divided, and we already provided some evidence to this effect. But the full scale of this inequality can be seen in Piketty (2014).

and, therefore, the majority of the population rely only on labour as a means for accessing their share in national income, will there be enough labour for people not only to have a job but also for earnings to be sufficient to support the appropriate level of social subsistence? In other words, for the system of competitive decentralisation to work under all possible distributions of wealth (and recall that in the case of incompleteness, even productive efficiency requires particular ownership structures), labour must be the great equaliser and therefore in sufficient demand. It is, after all, the only means available to the population for acquiring their share if they do not own assets. The more unequal is the distribution of wealth, the more available should labour be (i.e. greater demand for labour).

We have already noted the falling share of wages in national income, which raised a question mark over the ability of the majority who rely on labour alone to acquire the income needed for the basic social standard. However, the failure here was that of the labour market and not the principle behind the system. Had wages increased in line of productivity, the share of wages in national income would have probably increased. But what if the supply of labour (i.e. jobs) is dwindling? What if, in the light of enormous technological developments, there is a decreasing need for labour as a means of production? In such a case, relying on labour as the 'great equaliser' will no longer be meaningful. We are referring here to what has been recognised as the more general problem of the *future of work* in an increasingly high-tech world with a significant rise in artificial intelligence.

Since the early days of the industrial revolution, some have raised concerns regarding the possibility that technological developments and the invention of new machines will displace workers and make work, as a means of acquiring subsistence, impossible. The Luddites was the name of this movement that was particularly active between 1811 and 1813 protesting by smashing machines and equipment which they felt endanger their ability to find work.[50]

---

[50] See an interesting collection of the writings by Luddites which reveals a more complex approach than the one of machine smashing and anti-technology attitudes: Kevin Binfield, (ed). *Writings of the Luddites*. Baltimore: Johns Hopkins UP, 2004.

But the Luddites were, of course, wrong. New technologies were also a source of new industries and, hence, a source for novel ways of finding employment. The nineteenth century has witnessed perhaps the sharpest rise in employment as people moved from agriculture to manufacturing.[51] The clearest evidence for the increase in the number of jobs can be found in the increases in wages which typified the second half of the nineteenth century.[52] Nevertheless, the fact that the Luddites were wrong about the impact which the industrial revolution had had on work (in terms of its availability, not quality) does not mean that such a problem can never develop.[53] In other words, if one thinks of human life, throughout time, as being broadly comprised of three types of activities, one can make sense of past development as well as become concerned about the future. Basically, Homo sapiens have more or less always been engaged in providing themselves with food (agriculture), creating tools (manufacturing) and providing each other with services including entertainment and culture. It is also evident that on the spectrum between needs and wants, the progress will be from agriculture (clear need), through manufacturing to services (pure wants). Indeed, if the measure of time is technological

---

[51] We must be careful here as data from those days is not quite reliable. In part, this is so because many people were employed in agriculture within their own family or community. Their employment, which did not go through markets, would not have been recorded. Once they moved into cities and became the workers of a rising manufacturing industry, their labour was co-ordinated through markets. Therefore, when we say that there was a large increase in employment, we mainly refer to the presence of new vacancies due to new technologies. About this, there is not much disputation.

[52] See, for instance, an analysis in Gregory Clark (2005).

[53] Zeira (1998) suggests that the conception of innovation in modern economics has been misguided in that it was based on the presumption that innovation allows one to produce more with given inputs. However, he claims, there have been multitude of innovations (and perhaps more so today than in the past) which are directed at replacing inputs (notably labour) rather than allow the same input to produce more. Acemoglou and Restrepo (2016) accept his position but propose to expand on this model (though in my view, not persuasively) by repeating the old mantra that innovation creates new tasks and, therefore, can enhance employment. But while we may use the same argument now as we did in response to the Luddites, today we face a new problem in terms of the rate in which replacement works. By the time new tasks have been created, and hence, potentially new jobs, the machine to perform it and replace the worker may be just around the corner. They bring evidence that there is a very slight positive correlation between the change in growth rates of employment throughout a decade and the number of new jobs (tasks) at the beginning of the decade. Naturally, as we suggested before, in a world where people have no alternative but to offer themselves in the labour market, employment may grow, but as mismatch increases it means that these people may, after all, be redundant.

development, one can coarsely expect that the development of human occupation will move along the following lines:

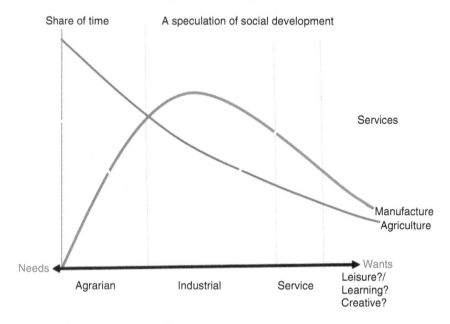

In early stages, most of the available working time would have been devoted to the production of food (agriculture) as satisfying needs were the dominant aspects of life. There will be some time devoted to services (including entertainment and culture) even before the production of tools has begun. As technology develops, it will be mainly in those areas where most human activity is focused; in the early days, this would be in agriculture. Therefore, technological developments in agriculture would lead to a reduction in the labour required for the production of increasing quantities of output. This, in turn, releases labour to be engaged in other activities, like the production of tools and machinery (manufacturing). As time progresses, technological developments keep reducing the labour requirements in agriculture but now, as they move into the new focus of human activities, they begin to replace workers in manufacturing too. The release of labour from manufacturing opens the door for its employment in services and the shift of emphasis in human life from fulfilling needs to satisfying wants. The industrial revolution is the period when labour moved from agriculture to manufacturing. The twentieth century, the second half in particular, is when labour moved from manufacturing to services. What has been happening in recent years—the years of internet, artificial intelligence and the digital revolution—is that services have now fallen 'victim' to the same syndrome. But while the shift from agriculture to manufacturing and then to services is a shift between types of occupations which have always been around, the departure from services does not point us clearly in any obvious direction. After all, the new technologies are as powerful in reducing the need for labour in industry and agriculture as they are in removing the need of labour in services.

If we look at more recent data, this trend can clearly be confirmed. Looking at the employment trends in the UK in recent years, we find the following trends:

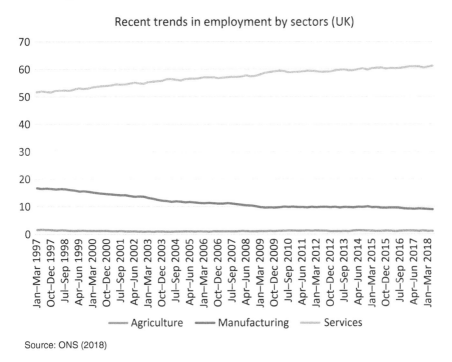

Recent trends in employment by sectors (UK)

Source: ONS (2018)

The percentage of employees who work in agriculture is continuously declining and stands on a very low rate even though output in this industry has risen significantly over the same period and is certainly at levels commensurate with fulfilling the needs of an ever-growing population.[54] The same can be said on the employment in manufacturing where the main fall in employment happened during the twentieth century but even over this last period, the rate of employment was almost halved (from about 16.5% to 8.9%). The workforce which leaves these traditional sectors ends up in the service sector. However, even here we can see a beginning of saturation as the IT revolution begins to bite. Between 1997 and 2018 there was an increase of about 10% in the share of services in employment but most of it happened in the first period. Between 2010 and 2018, the increase was around 2%. This means that the ability of the service sector to absorb employment is diminishing when technological development begins to affect it too. So, where next?

We are facing now a situation where work may no longer be widely available. If this is indeed the case, what would be the implications of this for the relevance of the paradigmatic core? Evidently, if not all individuals are capable of accessing their share in national income through markets, the distribution of income will have to become increasingly dependent on collective decisions which: (a) due to its interference in the working of the markets will ensure the inefficiency of the competitive paradigm and thus raise a question mark over the ability of decentralised decision-making to deliver; (b) will raise doubt over the *relevance* of the entire idea of decentralised decision-making in a world where individuals are incapable of finding their share—or social subsistence—by themselves; (c) will raise some questions about the dependency of the competitive model on the role which the idea of work has played in individuals' lives[55]; and (d) will raise some broader doubts over the civic society project.

---

[54] The UK is, of course, long past the industrial revolution so the real fall in employment in the agricultural sector happened a long time ago. Still, even at this advanced stage, the trend continues (from about 1.5% to 1.08%) while there is no shortage of agricultural products. It is important to note that the fall in employment is not a reflection of what happens to output or the effects of terms of trade. These patterns are the same in main trading partners.

[55] This, of course, is a reference to Weber's association of capitalism with protestant ethics.

But is it really the case that labour is becoming less significant a factor in the process of resolving the economic problem? From our perspective, there are two main issues here. The first is whether labour is becoming a less significant factor of production. The second is whether labour is an important aspect of human life and, therefore, an economic good in itself. If so, what might be the implications of treating labour as an economic good and should we indeed do so.

Let us begin with the 'easier' question of whether labour is becoming less significant in the production process. Naturally, there is an element of speculation when we come to examine the future of production as one cannot be sure of the directions which technology and the economy will take. One could, however, try to extract some trends from recent years and apply common sense to it but even this is fraught with difficulties. Therefore, we should constantly bear in mind that we are in the realm of speculation and be cautious with our pronouncements.

The data on this question is difficult to gauge. The most obvious thing to do is to look at the way in which the rate of employment developed:

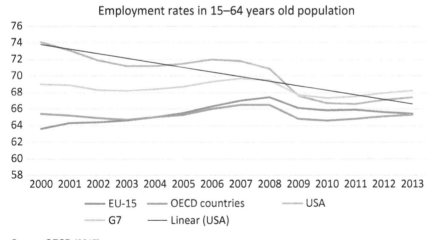

Employment rates in 15–64 years old population

Source: OECD (2017)

This is by no means conclusive. If we consider the USA as the example of the most advanced economy, then the trend in employment is clearly downwards (the trendline is in the diagram). We can see that even before the 2008 crisis, rates of employment among the working-age population were falling (from 74% in 2000 to 72% in 2006). There has been clearly a recovery after the crisis, but it is difficult to assert whether the slight rise (relative to 2008) will bring us back to a lower level than the 72% of 2006. In 2013, the rate in the USA stood on 67.4%. For the G7 group the rate is more stable, though it falls dramatically during the 2008 crisis. In the whole of the OECD during the whole period there was only a slight change in the rate of employment within the working-age population (the trend is stable). The EU-15 is the exception here with an increase in the rate of employment before the 2008 crisis.

We could say, if we treat the USA as the example of an advanced economy,[56] that there is some evidence for the claim that the rate of employment is decreasing at the time when output increases. But it is not clear whether this means less employment as there have been demographic changes in all these societies which may suggest that the adjustment in rates is merely a result of demography (i.e. increase in population and, in particular, increases in working-age population due to migration).

However, even when there is no clear trend of the rate of employment to fall, this does not mean that there is no decline in the demand for (or use of) labour as a means of production. Some evidence in support of this conjecture can be seen in the trends that exist in the number of hours worked per person (also associated with labour utilisation). If employment rates are stable—assuming no significant increase in the working-age population—but people work fewer hours, it would suggest that the total number of hours used in production has gone down. What we see is happening in terms of total hours worked per worker is indeed a continuous fall:

---

[56] The other reason why the US data may be somewhat more telling is because it is the evidence from one institutional framework. The OECD, the G7 as well as the EU-15 mean the lumping together of a multitude of systems that are neither the same nor in the same stage of development.

Total hours worked per worker

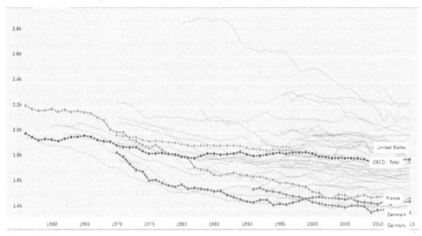

Source: OECD

In continental economies, we can see a dramatic fall in the number of hours worked per worker but even in the USA (and the whole of the OECD) we can see a trend downwards in those hours. Moreover, we also observe a shift from full-time employment to part-time employment, which suggests that the significance of workers in the production process has been somewhat diminished. It may also suggest that even a rise in number of people employed may be associated with a decline in labour utilisation. In the OECD countries over the period between 2000 and 2012, there has been a fall of 2.9% in the number of people employed full time and an equivalent increase in the number of people working part time. At the same time, there was an increase of 9% in the number of people employed but a fall of 3.6% in the number of hours per worker. The implications of this for the total number of hours worked are unclear but one can clearly see that existing trends could suggest a fall in total labour contribution to output (which is, by the way, rising). By implication, the role of capital in the production process increases. Indeed, if the labour market were in equilibrium in the sense that real wages were equal to productivity, one could argue, in some circumstances, that the fall in the share of wages in output is an indication of a technology which is much less reliant on labour.[57]

In general, to make an argument about the possible decline in the role of labour in the production process, the normal thing to do would be to suggest an increase in the capital to labour ratio, which means that each unit of output is produced by greater quantity of capital per hour worked, which means that the same quantity of output can now be produced by less labour. Equally, increased quantities of output would not require great increases in labour to generate a rise in national income.

To see what is happening to the capital to labour ratio, we have looked at data from the USA on capital deepening, which measures the annual increase in the capital per hour worked ratio. Clearly, as this ratio increases it means that the same level of output would now require less labour and, in the same vein, greater quantity of output could be produced with smaller increments in the amounts of hours worked:

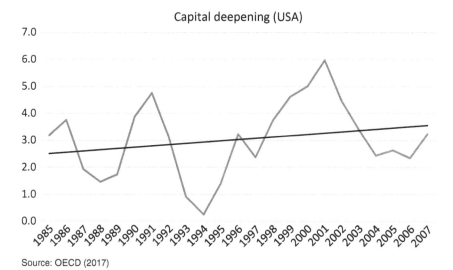

Capital deepening (USA)

Source: OECD (2017)

---

[57] This, of course, is when we assume that the aggregate production function is of a constant return to scale type where the sum of factors' contribution is unity. But as we said before, given that the wages are not equal to marginal product, we cannot make such a deduction even if the production function had this property.

We deliberately chose to look at the data leading to 2008 as the financial crisis of this year threw everything into disarray and, consequently, had a blurring effect on real trends. What we see from this graph is that throughout the entire period there has always been a positive increase in the capital to hour worked ratio. This means that in developed economies there is a continuous process in which capital replaces labour in the production process. As these are aggregate data, they fold in them the shift across industries as technology leads to improvements in production through greater use of capital. But it is not only that we can see that the capital to labour ratio has consistently increased but we can see a slight trend upwards over the years. If this trend continues, and the role of capital increases, increasing levels of output (i.e. income) will require diminishing increases in labour input.

But this is not the whole story. The capital in the data is a measure of the stock of physical capital. Therefore, the full impact of human capital is not taken into consideration. To explain this point, one only needs to think of a simple example like running a travel agency. In the past, this would have needed considerable amount of physical capital—like offices, office furniture, telephones and so on—and a certain number of individuals who sat by the phones or at desks receiving clients. With the introduction of internet, there is now no need for offices at all and in fact there is, perhaps, a need only for one computer and one operator who is managing the site. There are two things hidden in this story which are not captured by the simple discussion of capital deepening. Firstly, there is the point that if before there was a relatively high ratio of capital to labour (all the offices and furniture which are usually quite costly), now this ratio is lower as the physical capital only includes one computer. Secondly, the one computer and one worker can, in fact, produce almost endless quantity of service. This means that the adoption of new technologies may not be reflected in the increase in the capital to labour share but may be equally devastating in terms of its effects on the need for labour (and capital) in the production process.[58]

---

[58] Indeed, if one looks at the data of capital deepening beyond 2008, there seems to be a sharp fall in the rate in which it is growing (though still positive). The reason for this is that the correction of the sharp fall in the increase in number of hours worked due to the crisis, and is quite rapidly being

In terms of our earlier narrative, imagine an individual who used to work in agriculture and became redundant with the introduction of combines (which would increase the capital to labour ratio) and other new methods of cultivation. He then works in a car factory on the assembly line until robots are introduced to replace the people on the assembly line (again, a rise in the capital to labour ratio). He then goes to work as a travel agent in the agency which we have just described (and with a relatively high capital to labour ratio). However, with the rise of the internet (and the decline in physical capital to labour ratio), he loses his work there. In principle, he could have gone to work at another travel agent company as the person who controls the website. But to do this he should have acquired new skills and, which is even more important, we must assume that there is a need for more agencies. As each operation can provide an incredibly large output (measured in terms of customers that can be treated per unit of time), the number of such firms needed to cover all the needs of the population may be limited indeed. So where shall this person go now? Eating, building machines and travel have always been elements of one's life. But what comes next?

The question of the disappearance of jobs due to technological developments has been the focus of some educated speculation. Rodrick (2013, 2015), for instance, points out that in manufacturing there has been a convergence in technology due to great trade exposure. This allows one to note that the percentage of people employed in manufacturing at its peak is falling as we progress in time and income. If in the UK the peak was around 45% of employment before the First World War, in countries like India or Brazil employment had already peaked at around 15%. This seems to suggest that when a particular industry reaches its full potential of employment, this potential—measured in labour inputs—will be decreasing as technology develops. Another example is Frey and Osborne (2013), who conducted a study in which they discuss the probabilities that various jobs will be lost to sophisticated machinery. In part, the calculation is based on the distinction between routine tasks which could easily be replaced by machine and less routine tasks where humans

---

compensated in the following years, though the rate in which capital growth stayed more or less the same.

are more difficult to replace. Nevertheless, with the developments in artificial intelligence, it seems that a great deal of the less routine tasks could also be taken over by sophisticated machinery. The Chief Economist of the Bank of England, Andrew Haldane, presented their results in a much clearer fashion during a speech which he gave to the Trade Union Congress in London on November 12, 2015.[59]

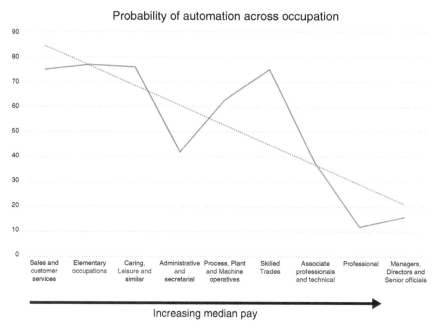

Probability of automation across occupation

There is nothing really surprising here but what we see is that as wages increase, the probability of the occupation being automated and replaced by machines is receding. The most at risk are, of course, the lower-skilled occupation where automation has a high probability of replacing human workers. Naturally, this does not mean that there will be an increase in the number of jobs available at the higher levels of earning. With greater automation, the same number of jobs at the top of the hierarchy can

---

[59] Source: ONS; Frey and Osborne (2013); Bank calculation Notes: The values show the estimated average probability of automation across occupations using the probabilities in Frey and Osborne (2013) weighted by UK employment.

produce much more than the same quantity of jobs could achieve with less automation (or capital).

So, there will be work which will always be around but the need for such workers is not going to be sufficient to replace the work which is currently done. If one takes a car factory with human-based assembly lines, there may be 5000 people working there. Once the system is automated through the use of robots, there may be a need for a computer analyst, technical support team and a manger that directs them to where they are needed. Their number may now be a 100. Will the 4900 people who were mainly menial worker be now retrain as analyst or technical support? Can they do so? Should they do so? And if they do, will they actually find work?

From the perspective of modern economics, this is all a question of prices. The analysis of profit maximisation suggests that the choice of capital to labour ratio (i.e. technology) which producers make depends on the relative price of these factors of production. Therefore, as wages increase, producers would opt for more capital-intensive technology to reduce their cost. Hence, if there is a decline in the use of labour in the production process, it means that there will be excess supply of labour in the labour market. After all, in a competitive decentralised system individuals who depend on labour for their income have no alternative but to enter the labour market. In turn, this should reduce nominal wages and make labour more attractive than capital for the producers.

But there are two problems with this argument. Firstly, wages will have to fall so low to become attractive (i.e. for a factory manager to prefer human workforce over robots) that it may not be enough as a source of income. This will create a problem similar to the one we discussed in connection with the fall of labour share in national income. In such a case, the system of decentralisation will fail as the people inside the labour market are not able to fend for themselves through the markets. This will require an increased role for the collective and, consequently, lead to inefficient outcomes and all that we have said about it.

The second problem is the personal cost from which people will suffer by working now in employments for which they may not be best suited or which they do not like doing. In the end, when our agent—who dreamt all his life of being a travel agent—was sacked from the travel agent company that went online, he cannot find work in the same industry and he will have to find work in some other industry. This means that there may be a transition period where people may still find work as they are spewed out of industries that adopt newer technologies because they would be willing to work for less. But as they are hired into jobs they are not keen on, they become less productive, but, more importantly, in some sense they also become enslaved.[60]

Even if we accept the arguments that the emergence of new technologies also produces new tasks, then besides the question of whether the rate in which technology evolves nowadays is sufficiently high to be only temporarily replaced by labour it would mean that people will have to move from one type of a job to another at an increasing rate. The presumption here, of course, is that people may be sufficiently flexible to be able to do so but this ignores the cost side of it. The fact that our individual with the dream of becoming a travel agent may be able to find a job—after further training—as a technician monitoring the circulation of sewage in the city does not mean that such a move is not stressful for him. From following his life's dream of interacting with people and discussing their holiday plans with them, he is now reduced to sitting in front of a monitor counting the volume of sewage transferred by a sophisticated system of pipelines. The job may require high skills but the only thing to match the height of his new skills would be the extent of his misery.

In other words, the progress of technology will either create something akin to what Karl Marx called the *Reserve Army of the Unemployed* in the

---

[60] The implication of our speculative story is that when the process of the decline of work takes hold, the immediate effect of it would not be a fall in employment (or rate of participation). As society is not prepared for a situation where an increasing number of people may rely on the collective—that is, it still adheres to the idea of competitive decentralisation—they have no choice by to find work. But if it is the case that work on a large scale is becoming slowly redundant, one of the symptoms we should expect to see is a rise in jobs mismatch as well as a rising levels of disaffection. The truth is that there is evidence for both. In Green and Zhu (2007), they explore the question of overqualification. They discover that for graduate men, the level of match in jobs has been steadily decreasing from 78.3% in 1992 to 66.8% in 2006. Slonimczyk (2011) discusses the rise of mismatch in the USA which too has been consistently rising. Similarly, Gallup worldwide research discovered that the percentage of people who are engaged with their workplace is very limited. The question of job satisfaction is, however, more complex as we must bear in mind that many would be satisfied having a job at all regardless of whether they are happy in what they do.

sense that there will be an increasing number of people who are not needed for the production process but who are nevertheless dependent on finding work to be able to access their share in national income, or create an army of people who have to chase new tasks before they are taken over by further technological development. The latter may not be unemployed but will have to be sufficiently empty in their mind and soul to find the multitude of jobs through which they pass as an acceptable form of living.

On the other hand, had the organisation of society not been based on the ability of individuals to access national income through labour, the problem may not have arisen, provided that work has no other function than a mere means of production. This, of course, is the subject of the second big issue which we mentioned earlier in connection with the fall of labour: Should work be such an important aspect of human life?

This is a formidable question which deserves its own treatise and I will therefore not explore it here. But it will be nevertheless useful to say something quite general about this question from the perspective of what work may mean to people in the current state of affairs. Naturally, we must bear in mind that whatever people may think about work today is itself the product of their socialisation. Therefore, it is influenced by the way in which society is currently organised and the values which it promotes through its institutions and educational systems.

Jestingly one could say that the question about the importance of work is a question about whether we work to live or live to work. The former suggests that work is a means to an end, while the latter suggests that work is an end in itself. Given the proportion of our time on Earth that is spent on work, by most people, this is not a minor issue. If work were a means to an end, what would be the significance of the fact that we are spending so much time working? The answer would have to be that it reflects the difficulties with which work provides the living one is seeking. The more meagre is the return to work, the more one would need to do it to achieve one's ends. If, on the other hand, work were an end, then it would make perfect sense to find people spending most of their lives at it but the return to work should be of little interest. Probably the reality is a mixture of the two, but this may only be an appearance. Namely, if people have to work in order to live, it means that the amount of work they invest is proportional to the living which such an investment provides. When this proportion is high, it would help if what one does is also what one would like to do. However, would one like to have done that which they do if they did not have to work in order to live? In other words, to find people who see a mission in their labour could be the result of the fact that from their early days they have been groomed to find their mission in that which they could do.

It is interesting to note that in surveys like the WVS, which we mentioned earlier (2005 wave), when people are asked what is the first thing they are looking for in a job, their answers are as follows:

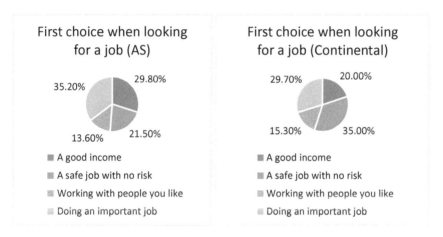

First choice when looking for a job (AS)

29.80% 35.20% 13.60% 21.50%

First choice when looking for a job (Continental)

20.00% 29.70% 15.30% 35.00%

- A good income
- A safe job with no risk
- Working with people you like
- Doing an important job

As in our previous examination, we separated the Anglo-Saxon responses from the continental ones to see whether the cultural difference between the more individualistic societies (AS) and those where the collective has greater significance, has any effect. There is clearly not a great deal of difference between the two groups but what we see in both groups is quite interesting. More than 50% of respondents in both groups say that it is the income and job's security which were the most important thing for them in looking for a job. Both these items are clear expression of the idea that people *work to live*. It is true that there was no question about the job being a manifestation of one's interest and we do not deny that framing of questions matters. But there is a possible answer which could be used as a proxy for the idea that work is one's mission; it is the answer that one wants to do an important job. Presumably, that which makes a job important can vary and may depend on objective reasoning, but one could agree that to desire to do an important job means that one is looking for a job which is more of a vocation than a means to an end. As we can see in the above diagram, only 35.2% of AS respondents (and 29.7% of continental ones) thought this to be the most important thing about a job.

To some extent, even the item of wishing to work with people one likes is an indication of the job being a means to an end. As people know that they have to work, choosing to do this in a pleasant environment will ease the pain. Alternatively, in a somewhat less generous interpretation, they see work as the foundation of their social life. Either way, if we included this item in the list of answers suggesting work to be a means to an end, then about 64% of AS respondents (and around 70% of continental ones) look for jobs from the perspective of a means towards an end.[61]

Having said this, we cannot ignore the fact that around a third of responded, those who are looking for important jobs, could be treating work as a vocation (an end in itself). It is by no means definite and there may be plenty of reasons why people may wish to perform an important job, but as the importance of a job gives work an intrinsic value, it is not farfetched to suppose that there is a vocational non-instrumental element here.

There is further evidence to suggest that people treat work differently. It comes in the form of whether people consider work to be a social duty:

---

[61] If one were to comment on the differences between the two sets of answers, one could speculate that the reason for this is the extreme individualism of the Anglo-Saxon economies. As people have no expectations from the collective, one's quality of life is derived entirely from one's own earnings. Therefore, for the AS, income is more important when work is treated as a means to an end. For the continentals, as the collective has greater significance—think of the values of the French republic—one has greater expectations from the collective and, therefore, income itself is somewhat less important. At the same time, the fact that the continentals are less interested in the job being important may be a reflection of the fact that they do, in general, work less than the AS. Therefore, whether or not the job is important (and hence, intrinsically interesting) may be less significant. This is, of course, one possible explanation, but it does not matter much for our argument as long we as can admit that in both culture jobs are seen more as a means to an end.

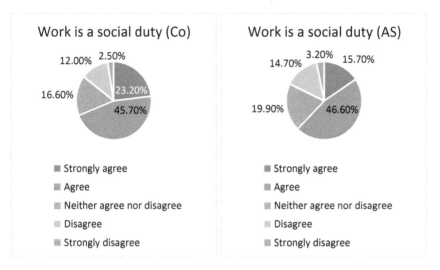

Those who agree make up 68.9% of continental respondents and 62.3% of Anglo-Saxon respondents. This means that around a third of respondents do not consider work as a social duty. We cannot tell from this why it is that people think of work as social duty but there could, in principle, be two reasons: one, that people must not be a burden to society and, therefore, they have a duty to care for themselves; the other that people have to work in order to contribute to social life. I must confess that the former seems more likely to be the reason why people may find duty in work.[62] If this is indeed the case, it would mean that those who see work as a social duty are also more likely to see work as instrumental. They must acquire income and support themselves and not become a burden on society. Indeed, the number seems to be consistent with the number of those we claimed before to be interested in work for an instrumental reason, although we cannot, of course, be sure that they are indeed the same individuals.

---

[62] Some corroborating evidence could be based on the fact that continentals are more likely to have stronger religious affiliations (and in particular, stronger protestant affiliations) which would favour the no-burden-on-society explanation. Algan and Cahuc (2006) find that countries like Denmark with the most generous out-of-work benefits—which should imply (according to standard economic theory) that people leave the labour force—have extremely high participation rates. They explain some of it by the intensity of protestant ethics in the population.

It stands to reason that those who do not see work as a social duty are more likely to have a more private and, hence, vocational approach towards it. Therefore, from both these types of responses we must conclude that there is no uniform approach to work and that both general categories of instrumental approach and vocational ones are present in sufficient numbers in each society. There are two main reasons why the distinction between those who treat work instrumentally and those who see a vocation in it should matter. Firstly, if there is such orthogonality in the way in which people treat labour, would one way of modelling their behaviour be sufficient? Secondly, there is the question of whether the disappearance of work is going to be of lesser significance if there are enough people who see in it a means to an end.

As far as the first issue is concerned, it is quite clear that from the perspective of standard economic analysis (and the paradigmatic core) work is perceived only as instrumental. In fact, it is barely even a choice as it is a residual decision. Work itself is not an economic good even though it is clearly scarce and desirable. Instead, it is the residual of the decision which agents make with regard to other economic goods like commodities, services and leisure. Hence, we only use work as a means for acquiring other goods and we have to balance the consumption of those goods with the fact that work reduced the availability of a particular economic good: leisure. We suppose that people will work more when wages increase both because it will allow them to consume more economic goods and because the opportunity cost (i.e. the price) of leisure has gone up. By the same logic, we deduce that when income increases we will want more of all economic good (including leisure), which would lead to a fall in the amount of work we are willing to do. In turn, this argument is used as one of the foundations of the claim about the inefficiency of redistribution (none lump sum) as by taxing wages we reduce them to the agents and thus make leisure cheaper. This, in turn, will lead some people to have more leisure (less work). At the other end of the cycle, when we give people money unrelated to their work (transfer payments), they will see their income increase and thus want to have more leisure. Both these effects will lead to a fall in the supply of labour (or effort), which would mean less output and inefficiency.

This kind of general attitude towards redistributive policies—which dominates the public discourse—is indeed predicated on the uniformity of the way people treat work. However, if we allow agents to treat work differently, two issues arise. Firstly, it is not evident that competition will indeed lead to an efficient labour market due to the fact that those with an instrumental attitude towards labour are more likely to be able to take advantage of those who see an intrinsic value in work. The scope for substitutability will be broader for the former than for the latter.[63] Secondly, the universal conclusion about the inefficiency of redistributive policies may no longer be true.[64] Therefore, the moment one admits to such profound differences between the ways different agents behave, one must accept that the paradigmatic core—as a logical system—is no longer a relevant abstraction. A world in which some people seek to work as a mission and others seek it for other reasons cannot be modelled on the basis of a uniform conception of individuals' attitudes and behaviour.[65]

As far as the second question, with regard to the effect that diverse attitudes to labour may have on the prospects of disappearing jobs is concerned, the news could be good. If it is indeed the case that the majority of people treat work instrumentally and only a minority (sizable as this may be) treats is as an end in itself, then the threat of a future with diminishing work can be alleviated. It is clear that for those who see a vocation in work there can be no obvious substitute and they will have to find employment (assuming, naively, that matching is not an issue). But as they are a minority, the number of jobs they need is significantly lower than the current availability. On the other hand, for those who are treating work instrumentally, the disappearance of jobs is not a problem in itself. The only thing they will need is an alternative source of income. The most obvious way for society to address this issue would be through a redistribution of assets. But there is a paradox here: if the availability of jobs declines, competitive decentralisation cannot subsist if assets were

---

[63] The way in which such asymmetry between agents can lead to inefficiency will be explored further in Chap. 7.

[64] See a discussion in Witztum (2008).

[65] It is not that we suppose that those who treat work as an end to be irrational but, as will be explored in Chap. 7, there are different forms of rationality and if one allows them all to be present at the same time, much of what economic theory has to say becomes increasingly problematic.

not distributed to those who have less access to the labour market. However, given the problems of missing markets, the distribution of assets which is necessary for the competitive paradigm to deliver on its promise (at least at the productive efficiency level) favours those who are at work and need to recoup the fruits of their efforts and productive innovation. Here lies the essence of the competitive dilemma in the face of an evolving reality for which there is no obvious solution.

But beyond the practicality of organising alternative sources of income to resolve the problem of a potential decline in the availability of jobs, there is a broader question about the meaning of work in the life of the individual. While it is true that the majority of people seem to treat work as a means to an end, it is still the case that most people spend most of their working-age lives at work. Though many of them are not seeking any particular employment, it is their employment which pours contents into their lives. Beyond the social convention which attributes dignity to work, their place of work is a source of cognitive engagement, and, in some cases, it is this engagement which ends up defining the person. In other words, work seems to be a human, rather than social, need.

On the face of it, the idea embedded in economics' paradigmatic core is supposed to serve such a need. In a world where competitive decentralisation works properly—recall the first and second welfare theorems—every individual can access the labour market even if they do not depend on it for their livelihood. The universal and ethically neutral nature of the system ensures that there should not be any direct correspondence between the search for work and the distribution of income. So, if people enter the labour market because they feel a need to work and, in so doing, they depress wages, the possibility of redistributing assets through lump-sum transfers would have taken care of any potential reduction in the ability to access national income.

However, this rosy picture of the paradigmatic core is misleading. In fact, if there are two individuals who, in the basic story told by the theory, choose to specialise and trade according to their comparative advantage, they will both benefit from it because they will have more material wellbeing. What determines what they should specialise in is the set of market prices, and as work is only instrumental (and, therefore, does not mean much to them), it does not really matter what it is they specialise in. But if one of them treats work as an end, he or she is more likely to be more specific about that which they want to do, and their choice may not be consistent with market prices. As a result, it is quite possible that the outcome of their interaction will be beneficial to either only one of them or none. So, the compatibility of the modern paradigm with the world of disappearing jobs depends on work per se rather than its contents, being that which humans need.

In any case, we already noted that even if the majority of people treat work functionally and, in this way, comply with the requirement of the paradigm, there are enough who do not. But the more disturbing question is why is it that people who treat labour as a means to an end have become so clearly dependent on it? In other words, are the organisational principles of economics responsible for the creation of this dependency or is this something more intrinsic to human nature. Has society developed in such a way as to make work a need?

People have always worked for their subsistence but from early days of modern civilisation we can find a sufficiently large number of people who engage in other activities which cannot be described purely as work. The life of contemplation aspired to by Socrates and conceptualised by Aristotle (Eudemonia) has always been an important part of human life. There may be some differences between Eastern and Western civilisations in the meaning of contemplation in the sense that in the latter contemplation seems to be associated more with the presence of material wellbeing and was based less on solitude, but this does not alter the fact that everywhere humans have desired spirituality or non-material engagements in life. We will discuss some of these issues further in Chaps. 5 and 6, but we do not think that it is unreasonable to suppose that throughout history, people have engaged a considerable amount of their time with things one would define as 'unproductive' in the sense that they are not material wellbeing nor are they clearly economic goods.

To some extent, economic success, as measured through GDP, is based on the expansion of as many activities into the domain of the market. This is also consistent with the paradigmatic core which requires all activities involving things desirable and scarce to be conducted through markets. Thus, if we idealise for a moment family, or group, life in some previous stages of society, there would have been a lot of activities involved in producing what we now call entertainment. So, if then people sat together every evening, with most of them contributing to the collective entertainment through forms of storytelling, poetry, music, acting, dancing and the like, now all these activities are, as it were, outsourced. They have been commercialised and we acquire (i.e. consume!) them through markets. It is clearly efficient for one person to write a story and for as many people as possible to listen to it rather than all of them writing stories by themselves, but this may somewhat circumvent the purpose of life. Most people become passive consumers of activities in which they could have taken part. It is this commercialisation of all aspects of life which made work—as a means to an end—a necessity, or a need.

At this junction, it would be interesting to reiterate that when J. S. Mill considered the future, he saw it as a time of *stagnation*, in terms of the growth of material (or economic) wellbeing, as an increasing number of people discover the possibility of the good life (a la Aristotle). However, from Mill's perspective this is all conditioned on human's personal development. The contemplative good life, in his view, is very much a function of people's education. Already in his discussion on liberty Mill qualifies the extent to which real liberty is an applicable concept. He clearly states in his discussion that it is not enough to be human to be entitled to rights; one must also be *consciously sovereign*. Mill's own conjecture was that as people become more educated they will better learn to appreciate the other, become more co-operative in their behaviour and learn to value the non-material aspects of life.

Therefore, for people to be able to find their own purpose in life and not through work, people must have the means by which to search for them. At any point in time, the best way society can help individuals form their life-long interests is by providing them with the knowledge of the accumulated stock of society's intellectual and cultural heritage. By doing so, society will give everyone the tools with which to forge interests in life and actively interact with contemporary experiences. The outcome of such a process will facilitate an engagement with life which goes well beyond the pleasure of becoming cogs in a productive machine.

Unfortunately, the way in which the education system has developed in more recent times is with a view to create exactly such cogs. It seems that increasingly—through the inspiration of the Anglo-Saxon economies—education is being perceived as a glorified apprenticeship. People get educated in order to become economically useful; in order for them to be able to acquire a profession and get a job in the market. In this way, they will make something of themselves as well as relieve society from the duty to care for them. It is not at all surprising that if people's education is geared up to prepare them for the life of work, work becomes a need or, worse, a life. But if the education system was entirely focused on preparing people for life (not work), people would have found alternative ways to express themselves. Such a system, one must hasten to say, will not sit well at all with the competitive paradigm as it would first of all require a considerable amount of government (collective) involvement.[66] This, as we said earlier, will undermine the conditions for competition to deliver on its promise to solve the economic problem. Moreover, as a greater number of people may now be allowed not to join the labour market and to find life in another form than through work, the dependency of a large group in society on the collective for the purpose of accessing national income will considerably increase.

3.4   A Note on Growth

After discussing some aspects of the real world which raise question marks over the *relevance* of the paradigmatic core, we would like to say something about the escape route which we mentioned in the previous chapter: growth. To remind the reader, in the previous chapter we suggested that the theoretical conditions required for competitive decentralisation to deliver a solution to the economic problem are either impossible or logically unreachable (i.e. the absence of any meaningful process which will lead us to the logical limit where the benefits of competitive decentralisation reside). As solving the economic problem had static and dynamic aspects, we pointed towards the shift of focus in economic

---

[66] In the case of purely job-oriented education, it is not inconceivable that markets could provide such education as people will need to borrow to pay for education but if there is a good return in the life of work and capital markets work well, this should, in principle be a possibility. But if education is not aimed at achieving a particular return, the only way in which education could be provided is through public provisions.

analysis from the former to the latter. The static problem meant finding an allocation for a given amount of resources where all agents solve their economic problem (allocative efficiency). Distribution was an important aspect of it. The dynamic problem, on the other hand, which is a more aggregate approach, was focused on either increasing these resources (capital accumulation) or that which can be done with them (technological development).

There is a deep and important question regarding whether growth should interest us at all. After all, when growth becomes the focus of our attention, we implicitly suggest that the only thing which matters to society—as far as its economic organisation is concerned—is the mere provision of material plenty and without any real reference to its distributional consequences beyond a belief in the vague concept of trickle-down. This, as we said before, is very much the line proposed by Wicksteed and Robbins, according to which whatever society may wish to achieve would be better fulfilled in the presence of plenty.

Notwithstanding the question of whether that which society may wish to achieve on top of material plenty may itself be related to the way in which plenty is provided, there is the question of whether setting an objective in terms of material wellbeing is indeed ethically neutral and whether or not this is something societies should wish to achieve. I do not think that it is difficult to see that to desire plenty of material wellbeing in itself cannot constitute an ethically neutral objective. In its most simple form, such a desire is nothing short of greed, and while some societies may see greed as a legitimate social and private objective, one does not need great imagination to suppose that some societies may find it morally objectionable. We are clearly not making a statement here about the legitimacy of such an objective but merely pointing out that a theory which would like to be understood as an ethically neutral theory of organisation cannot have an objective which is morally laden.[67]

Having said this, it is a fact that the focus of economic analysis (and the public discourse) has shifted from the question of how decentralised competition—a theory of allocation and distribution—allows all individuals to solve their problem to a more collective desire to produce plenty of material wellbeing. Whether or not people thought this to be a morally desirable objective is not entirely clear, but it is difficult to imag-

---

[67] I discuss Robbins's claim for economics' ethical neutrality in Witztum (2011).

ine a consistent support for growth-promoting policies without some belief in its ethical validity (i.e. diachronic order). Naturally, if people believed that plenty always trickles down, then it almost seemed to fit Rawls's principle of justice, according to which we should always adopt a rule that makes the worst-off person in society better off.[68] Whether or not this actually happens is another question—and the recent sharp increases in inequality is a good reason why we should doubt it—but the argument is still being used when people wish to justify globalisation by pointing to the lifting out of poverty of great number of people in poor parts of the world. Obviously, there will be many questions about whether or not such a lift out of absolute poverty has not come at the expense of increasing relative poverty and, if so, is this a necessity and, if so, whose choice was it[69]?

In recent years, there has been an increasing interest in the significance and legitimacy of the growth in material wellbeing (measured through GDP) as a measure of economic performance.[70] Recall that in the static problem, efficiency was the measure of economic performance. In the dynamic problem, it is simply the rate of growth which needs to be maximised. But scholars have realised that this cannot be enough.[71] The United Nations, for instance, developed a Human Development Index (HDI) to provide a broader prism on what may constitute the successes and failure of an economic system.

---

[68] But even if it did, it would only mean that it has a particular ethical value rather than ethical neutrality. It is interesting to note that the association of growth with ethical principles already exists in Adam Smith (we will discuss it at some length in Chap. 8) but then there is no ethical neutrality in his world and the reason why growth mattered was that it salvaged competitive decentralisation from an ethical abyss.

[69] The main issue here is where the limits of society lie. We will discuss this further in Chaps. 5 and 6.

[70] See, for instance, Stiglitz, Joseph E., Amartya Sen and Jean-Paul Fitoussi. (2009). *Report by the Commission on the Measurement of Economic Performance and Social Progress*. http://www.stiglitz-sen-fitoussi.fr/. But much earlier than that there was a warning from Kuznets about the deceptive nature of single numbers (Kuznets, S. 1934. National Income 1929–1932. A report to the U.S. Senate, 73rd Congress, 2nd Session. Washington, DC. US Government Printing Office). He writes: 'With quantitative measurements especially, the definiteness of the result suggests, often misleadingly, a precision and simplicity in the outlines of the object measured. Measurements of national income are subject to this type of illusion and resulting abuse, especially since they deal with matters that are the centre of conflict of opposing social groups where the effectiveness of an argument is often contingent upon oversimplification' (ibid., pp. 4–5).

[71] See Fleurbaey, Marc. (2009). "Beyond GDP: The Quest for a Measure of Social Welfare." *Journal of Economic Literature*, 47(4): 1029–1075 and Marc Fleurbaey and Didier Blanchet. (2013). *Beyond GDP: Measuring Welfare and Assessing Sustainability* OUP.

But whether or not these alternative measures have proven to measure things differently than the way it is done by GDP per capita remains disputed. Recently, Charles I. Jones and Peter J. Klenow (2016) claimed that by expanding measures to include inequality, mortality, consumption and leisure they find such measures to be closely correlated with the GDP per capita. Nevertheless, they do acknowledge that there are often large deviations.[72] But while these approaches attempt to add dimensions to what is considered a measure of economic success, there are alternative methods where income remains the main measure, but it is subject to corrections which are based on some measures of the social cost of inequality, crime, environmental degradation and leisure. This measure, developed by Daly and Cobb (1989), is called *Genuine Progress Indicator* (GPI) and it seems to produce a startling difference between GDP measures and GPI. For instance, according to Talberth, Cobb et al. (2007), while GDP per capita in the USA rose from around $12,000 in 1950 to around $37,000 in 2004, the GPI—the GDP per capital after a deduction of the social costs mentioned—rose from around $9000 in 1950 to around $15,000 in 2004. Namely, while the GDP per capital increased by a bit more than three times, the GPI increased by just a bit more than one and a half time. It is easy to see that if we take into consideration the cost of social failings when growth is pursued vigorously, then the measure of economic success over the period of 54 years looks less impressive than if we only looked at GDP per capita. In fact, since the 1980s, while there is a remarkable increase in GDP per capita (associated with globalisation and the tightening of the grip by market economy under Reagan), in term of GPI per capita—as measured by Talberth, Cobb et al. (2007)—there was hardly any improvement at all.

In many respects, all these attempts to argue against the use of GDP per capita as a measure of economic performance are reflections of the frustrations which people feel with the reduction of the economic problem into a problem of collective value maximisation. They are, in many respects, a call for a return of focus to the static problem with which the

---

[72] In fact, there is something misleading in this. According to their own results, it is interesting to note that all Continental European economies are clearly on one side (in the sense of less GDP per capita than the USA but considerably high welfare index), and the other countries in the sample are less developed and are all on the other side of the line. We therefore remain unconvinced by the apparent correlation between welfare indices and GDP per capita.

paradigmatic core was predominately concerned. It is the problem of organisation—allocation and distribution—and the ability of all agents to solve their individual economic problem. The fact that there is deviation between GDP per capita and alternative measures suggests that there is something wrong with the solution to the static problem. But in spite of all these attempts to move away from material wellbeing as the single measure of economic performance, it is still the dominant feature of public and professional discourse. Claims for high correlation between alternative indices and GDP per capita (like those which can be found in Jones and Klenow (2016)) are strengthening the hands of those who wish to stick to the single measure. In this book, we do not wish to get involved in this argument. We do not even wish to get involved with the question over its legitimacy. What we would like to argue here is for its irrelevance.

If we return to the concept of growth in material wellbeing (GDP), we know that this can be achieved through either increasing the amount of resources (capital accumulation) or through technological developments which allow us to do more with the same amount of resources. However, this way of growing is referring to the production frontier of the economy. Namely, at each point in time for any given level of resources and technology, there is a limit of what the economy can produce. If the economy were efficient, it would choose an allocation which is located on that frontier (the limit) and where it is no longer possible to produce more of one economic good without forgoing another. This is exactly the promise of competitive decentralisation which lies at the heart of the paradigmatic core. But in reality, not all economies have reached their full potential, or their frontier. This means that they have not yet fully utilised the resources which they already possess and that they have not fully expanded economic activity into the domain of the market. Consequently, these economies can still increase the amount of resources available as well as improve technology but they mainly grow by simply utilising the so-far-unused existing resources. Or, they can better allocate existing resources as well as expand the domain of market-dominated economic activities. Either way, these economies will be growing but it is not really growth in the sense of the dynamic solution to the economic problem. Namely, it is in principle possible for these economies to grow in the sense of increasing their GDP per capita even without any move of their frontier or the potential of their output.

As different countries in the world are at different stages of development, which also means that many of them have not yet reached their
frontier (or limit) where all their existing resources are efficiently utilised,
at any point in time there are diverse growth rates. This, sometimes, leads
to a confusion when people compare a fast-growing economy, which is
merely utilising existing resources, with the growth rates of advanced
economies, which are already on their frontier and are engaged in the
very difficult process of shifting their frontier.

For an advanced economy to grow, there are only the routes of capital
accumulation and technological development. Savings rates in these economies—which are the source of capital accumulation—are known to be falling and to stand on relatively low levels. This means that the main push
towards increased potential output should come from investment in research
and development (R&D; i.e. technological development) rather than from
capital accumulation. This is a far more complex route to ensure growth. It
is therefore not surprising that advanced economies have experienced in the
last 50 years a consistent fall in the annual rate of growth of GDP per capita:

Average annual growth rates (GPD per capita) of 12 Western European countries

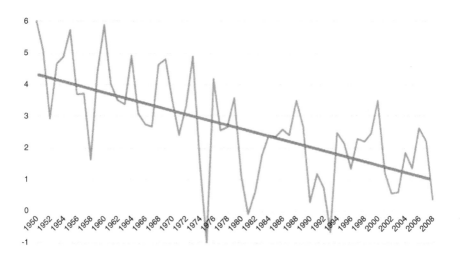

Source: A. Maddison *Historical Statistics of the World Economy: 1-2008*

The very high growth rates in the period after the Second World War included, in these countries, a great deal of recovering lost resources, which means a period in which the utilisation of existing resources or their replacement could have explained a great deal of this growth. These high rates could have therefore given the mistaken impression as if one could indeed replace proper utilisation of existing resources (i.e. allocation and distribution) with a bonanza of greater quantities of material wellbeing. Ever since, there has been a steady and continuous decline in these rates of growth which are more representative of the real difficulty embedded in genuine growth.

Therefore, if annual rates of growth are low in advanced economies, they are unlikely to serve as a proper substitute for the proper organisation of the economy, which is aimed at solving individuals' economic problem. Even if there were any truth in the idea of trickle-down, such low levels of growth are not going to promise a proper compensation for the failures of competitive decentralisation in providing an allocation which is both productive and allocative efficient. Declining rates of growth which reflect the reality of real growth make the crowning of growth as a social objective, hollow.

3.5   Conclusion

The purpose of this chapter was to highlight the empirical irrelevance of economics' paradigmatic core. We try to establish this by examining the presence in reality of processes which would raise confidence in the way in which economics conceives the world and the conditions it proposes for the successful resolution of the economic problem. The way economics conceives the world is a form of extreme methodological individualism. The world, in principle, is made up of individuals who seek what is best for themselves. They know best that which they want, and they know best how to acquire it. In other words, each agent is assumed to be fully sovereign and capable of resolving his or her own individual economic problem.

Upon this conception of the world, modern economics proposes that the best way to organise society in order that there will be no conflict between agents and everyone will be able to solve their personal economic problem is through competitive decentralisation. If agents pursued that which is best for themselves (as far as economic goods are concerned) through impersonal and mercenary interactions (markets), everyone will be able to solve their economic problem and society too will be able to adjust solutions to whatever values the collective of individuals would wish to uphold. However, for this plan to succeed, competition must be total in the sense that all economic activities should be channelled through competitive markets and all agents should be in a position where they can use the markets to achieve their aims.

We began by asking whether in reality the domain of market-dominated economic activities is expanding or shrinking. There are two elements upon which the reach of the market depends. The first is the presence of activities which individuals are conducting through other forms than markets (like family, friends and the like) and the second is the presence of impersonal interactions which are not dominated by the rules of the market. The former is very difficult to gauge, and we have therefore not said much about it. To some extent, the very sharp increase in GDP per capita in the period following the Second World War could have been a reflection of the collapse of the traditional social frameworks (like family and friends) in the face of the enormous uprooting of people which had been caused by the war. When people are no longer in the same place and where the traditional social fabric disintegrated, they will tend to seek through markets a great deal of those things which in the past were provided through the social network of family and friends.

But while there are empirical difficulties to establish the extent of non-market activities which are based on personal relationship, this is less of a problem when we come to address the second element of impersonal interactions which are not conducted through markets. Here we have the case of public involvement. Sometimes, the public gets involved in the economy due to market failures (like natural monopolies and public goods) but also for other reasons (like education, or health). But whatever it is, it is clear that within the public provisions the rules of the market will never be implemented in the way the market intended. Consequently, the presence of public involvement in the economic domain suggests that some economic goods will be priced differently than what they would have been had they been provided by a competitive efficient market. As all aspects of the economy are connected, the presence of some goods which are valued in a non-market manner is bound to influence the values of all other goods, including those which are determined in purely market circumstances. In other words, once a single aspect of the economy is not conducted through markets, the outcome could, in principle, still be productive efficient but will not be allocative efficient. As there are many inefficient allocations, there is not much the theory can tell us about that which distinguishes one inefficient allocation from another.

We have noticed that what typifies the rapid increase in GDP per capita, which is seen by some as a measure of economic success since the end of the Second World War, was a rapid increase in the share of government in the economy. Focusing only on consumption we noted that this rate is currently around the 20% of GDP mark. If we add all other aspects of government activities (i.e. investment and transfers), this share will rise considerably. From a theoretical perspective, the significance of this is very simple: the conditions under which competitive decentralisation will provide a solution to the economic problem which is both universal and ethically neutral are unlikely to be met.

As such, this is not really a claim for irrelevance. One could still argue that no matter how successful these economies may appear, if they reduced government or expanded the rules of the market into public affairs, they would be even more successful and, therefore, allow competition to fulfil its promise. Indeed, this is what we hear when we listen to the public discourse about the economy. This raises the question of why governments have become so big and what we have noticed is that there is enough evidence to suggest that the public is not averse to non-market economic activities. By implications, this may suggest that the public has been frustrated by the failures of the markets to offer a genuine solution to their individual economic problem. In such an environment, for economic theory to choose an abstraction of the world, which is predicated on total market-based provision, is a form of irrelevance.

But the real blow to the relevance of economics' paradigmatic core comes from the conception of the world where individuals are sovereign and can solve their economic problems by themselves or, as theory recommends, through markets. What we have tried to establish is that both the conception and the recommended organisational principles have no relations to what is happening in the world. Allocative efficiency is a complex notion representing the distributional consequences of the system. A solution to the economic problem (allocative efficiency) means that all agents have access to their share of national income which will allow them to lead a life commensurate with the standards of their social group. We have observed that the way in which the economy distributes income is through the returns to factor. Whether or not the way in which these returns are governed matters, depends on the dependency of individuals on these returns. They will be dependent on it only in a world where their income is closely associated with their position in the economic process. While classical economists believed this to be the case, modern economics assumes that all agents derive income from both labour and assets. In such a case, that which governs the returns to factors would have no social significance. However, we looked at some evidence to form the claim that in reality the vast majority of people have no access to a flow of income other than through the return on their labour. Therefore, when we observe a consistent decline in the share of wages in national income, we are observing a squeeze on the ability of an increasing number of people to access their share in national income in a satisfactory manner. The fact that overall income increases may mean that they are not becoming absolutely poor, but their relative poverty will most likely increase.

If we add to this the observation that there is a group of people who are altogether outside the labour market and have no ways of accessing national income other than through socially constructed institutions (like marriage, or partnership) or public provisions (welfare), then a doubt must be raised not only over the possible success of economics' organisational principle but also on its conception of the world. Surely if there are people who have no way of accessing national income, the presumption that society is made up of sovereign individuals who can solve their individual economic problem by themselves is profoundly misguided.

Moreover, when we observe the technological trends and their significance to the question of employment, we find that growth—this ubiquitous measure of economic success—may be enhanced with an ever-decreasing reliance on labour. This suggests that the problem of people being unable to access national income through markets may worsen in years to come. It is, of course, true that such a problem could, in principle, be resolved through the redistribution of assets, but in a world of incomplete markets even productive efficiency is dependent on a particular distribution of ownership. Therefore, one cannot solve the problem of access without undermining efficiency and, consequently, the ideal of competitive decentralisation becomes an empty aspiration.

Finally, we briefly touched upon the question of whether replacing the search for an efficient solution to the economic organisation by the notion of growth maximisation is a meaningful thing to do. Notwithstanding the ability of measures like GDP per capita to capture the successes or failures of economic organisation, it became evident that in advanced economies the trend is for the annual growth rates to fall. They will, of course, not become zero (or not necessarily so) but they are going to be sufficiently low to make them a meaningless social and economic objective.

Appendix

In this Appendix, we shall offer a diagrammatic representation of the way in which the economy distributes the returns to factors, its possible relationship with income and the reasons why shares of returns to labour and capital change.

Consider an economy that uses labour (L) (which is an abstraction of all types of labour) and capital (K) (which too is an abstraction of all sorts of capital goods [for simplicity sake we ignore land as a special category]) to produce one good (x) (which, again, represents all the goods produced in the economy). We assume that the total output of the economy is a result of the use of two factors: labour and capital. This also implies, technically, that the output of the economy can be attributed to the contribution of these inputs.

This, of course, is a thorny and problematic issue which lies at the heart of great conflicts but which we shall not explore here. I will only say that the difficulty arises from two related questions. The first is whether it is indeed true that we can distinguish the contribution to output of non-human factors (capital) from human ones. The second related question is whether and how should the rewards for productive activities be distributed between the various contributors. Evidently, if one argues that it is not possible to distinguish between the contribution of labour and capital, this will raise a question with regard to the principle which should guide their returns. At one extreme case, we can find Marx's labour theory of value, according to which there is no aspect of the production process which is not based on human labour. The problem with capital or machinery, accordingly, is not whether they contribute to output but whether, being the product of past labour, they should be owned by anyone except the workers. Consequently, all returns to the production process belong to workers, though the distinction between current labour and past labour requires some epistemological clarifications. For rationalists, like Marx, the aggregate of workers (the working class) is the historical entity representing workers at all times. Such an argument, of course, will not be easily understood by empiricists. Nevertheless, the Marxian claim that workers contribute to the production process more labour than is needed for their social subsistence means that they have a claim of ownership over the value that has been produced by those hours in which they work beyond that which they need (also known as surplus value).

At the other extreme we have the view according to which we can easily distinguish between the contributions of each factor of production. Neither labour alone nor capital alone can produce the output; therefore, each factor contributes something. But while there is no dispute that both factors contribute to output,[73] the question of how to measure this contribution remains unclear. Adam Smith, for instance, sensibly argued that the value of all that is produced must be comprised of what the various participating elements take out of it. Accordingly, it is always made up of what workers are being paid (wages), what the people who forward capital are being paid (profits) and what landlords are being paid (rent).[74] In the ideal state of affairs, these components are based on what those who are involved in the production process need for their social subsistence but this is not explicitly connected to what they contribute to the production process.

Modern economics—being impressed by the mathematical properties of continuous twice-differentiable real-number functions—declared eureka. The way to distinguish between that which the two factors contribute is according to the contribution of the last unit used, or, to use another term, the 'marginal product of that factor'. Thus, if we have a

---

[73] Marx does not deny the role of capital in the production process but believes that capital is just past labour that has been unduly possessed by capitalists who are not directly involved in the production process.

[74] Smith's world was dominated by agriculture. In our story, there is only capital and the distinction between rent and profits is really the distinction between what we call normal profits (when capital receives the market rate of return, or what capital owners lend to the production process) and profits above normal, which is usually accrued to those who own the production process.

field in which workers are employed in the production of, say, wheat, every additional worker will contribute diminishing increases in output. This, of course, stands to reason as if one has a single plot of land, it is easy to see that adding people will not increase output at the same rate. Had this been the case, it would have meant that we could introduce infinite number of workers on one plot of land to get infinite output.

But the question that arises is this: suppose that with five workers we produced 1500 kg of wheat on one plot of land. Suppose too that the contribution of the workers diminished such that the first worker gave us 500, the second 400, third 300, fourth 200 and fifth 100. Without them, the lot would yield nothing. What can we conclude from this about the contribution of labour? According to modern theory, the contribution of the last worker (his marginal product) was 100. Therefore, the total contribution of labour is $100 \times 5 = 500$. As the total amount of output is 1500, this means that 500 is the contribution of labour and 1000 is the contribution of the plot of land (and, therefore, the rewards of its owner). Now, for many, the idea of rewarding labour (or anything else) according to their contribution (i.e. equating wages to the marginal product) sounds reasonable and just. But one cannot overlook the fact that there is something peculiar here. Suppose that we begin with one worker only, his contribution to output will be 500 and this will also be the total amount of output. By the modern rule, the worker should be compensated by the full output even though it is clear to us that he or she could not have produced any wheat at all had it not been for the plot of land. Equally, when we now add the second worker who contributes 400, we will have 900 altogether. Each worker, however, will now receive 400. Does this mean that the first worker has not contributed 500?? This is clearly not right. But it is equally not right to say that the plot of land (or capital, more broadly conceived) contributed nothing when the first worker was there alone.

Nevertheless, this is how the convention works at the moment and it is important to bear in mind that there is nothing about it which is either obvious or straightforward. But we shall continue now to explain how the distribution of shares develops in modern economic, how it related to income distribution and what can change these shares.

Recall that we have an economy which is producing one aggregate good (x) using two aggregate inputs: capital (K) and labour (L). Suppose that the level of capital (K) is given (K_0) and that the economy must now decide on how much labour to allocate (this is the problem of allocation).[75] The marginal product of labour, or the contribution of the last unit employed, is the line in both the diagrams below which depicts what we call the marginal product of labour. We assume that the contribution of each additional unit of labour is falling when capital is fixed.

Allocation and distribution mechanism

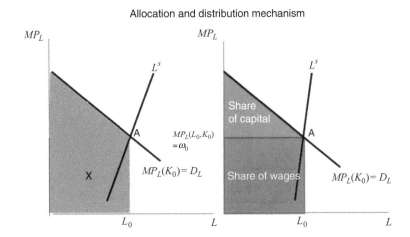

As one can imagine, and as we discussed above, the area under the marginal product line (the shaded area in the left-hand diagram—which is a summation of the contribution of each unit of labour) captures the total product (x). The marginal product line is also the demand for labour as employers—who seek to hire labour—would never wish to pay an hour of labour more than what it contributes to the total produce as this will have to come from their share in what has been produced. Alternatively, at any given wage level—and in competitive environment agents are price-takers—one would wish to employ workers as long as their contribution is greater or equal to what one has to pay them.

On the horizontal axis, we measure the amount of labour employed, while on the vertical axis we measure both marginal produce of labour and the real wages paid to workers ($\omega = \dfrac{w}{p}$).[76] The supply of labour is

---

[75] Naturally, in a full analysis we would need to allocate both labour and capital, but by analysing how to allocate labour for a given level of capital, we will uncover the basic principle which governs the allocation and distribution process.

[76] In this story where there is only one good, wage is in units of this product. In general, neither workers nor employers care about the money wage as they do about its real value which is measured

rising with real wages and reflects the amount of labour individuals wish to offer at any level of real wages given that leisure is also a desired economic good (i.e. rational choice). In a competitive market, there is only one price, which means that the wages paid to all workers is the one which is equal to the contribution of the last unit of labour. Now, the problem of allocation here is to choose the amount of labour the economy should use so that there will be an outcome which is both productive and allocative efficient. The allocation which would achieve this is the one where the real wage (ω_0) is equal to the contribution of the last worker and where the hours, which people would like to work, is equal to the hours, which employers would like to hire. This is depicted in the right-hand diagram and corresponds to point A.

The equilibrium level of wages is what led individuals to choose the amount of labour (L_0) that is the efficient allocation (which, in this case, would mean the one which maximises output). Had the wage level been higher, the demand for labour will be smaller and, therefore, less will be produced. However, the excess supply of labour will lead to what we call involuntary unemployment and unfulfilled rational plans (therefore, it will not be allocative efficient). If the level of wages were below the equilibrium one, the supply of labour will fall short of demand, and as fewer people are available for work, output will also be smaller. Hence, only at A, output will be maximised.

As this is a competitive market where everyone is paid the same, we also see from this the distribution of returns that will simultaneously ensue. The red area is the share of wages (it is the wage level multiplied by the number of hours worked). The blue area depicts what we will call in general the share of capital. This is comprised of the market return to capital—what the people who lend their capital to the firm will earn—plus the rent which is the earning above that level which is given to the owners of capital.

Is this also the distribution of income which will result from market interactions? The answer depends on whether individuals' access to income is associated with their economic function. Namely, if people have only

---

in units of goods. One of the problems of the labour markets that the goods by which workers evaluate their wages are not the same as those by which the employers do. This is a source of difficulty which we will not explore here.

one source of income, through either labour or capital, then the distribution of income in the economy would be exactly the same as the distribution of returns. Indeed, as is discussed further down the chapter, classical economists worked on the presumption that this is the case. Subsequently, the tension between returns to capital as the source of income of one group and returns to labour as a source of income for another, became an important part of the economic and public discourse. However, if we suppose, as does modern economics, that all individuals can access income through either wages or returns to capital, then such a tension would not exist and the distribution of the shares (the relative size of the blue and the red areas) would bear no relations to the distribution of income.

For this to happen, we must assume that all people in the economy own assets which are used in the production process. This means that all agents derive their income from both shares: they derive a wage from the work and a fraction of the returns to capital according to their share of ownership. But if it is the case, as is demonstrated in this chapter, that the vast majority of individuals have access only to wages, then the distribution of returns becomes a proxy for the distribution of income.

In the above right-hand diagram, it all looks reasonable as the shares of labour and capital are more or less the same. But it is easy to imagine that an outcome may happen where the share of wages is particularly low:

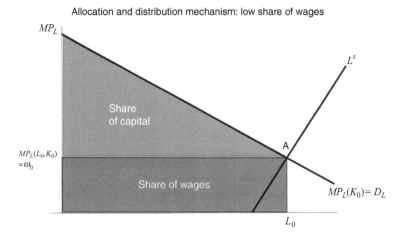

Allocation and distribution mechanism: low share of wages

If most people derive their income from labour alone and only a few from ownership of assets, it is clear that such a distribution where the share of wages is considerably smaller than that of capital will raise concerns in society. The way which the second welfare theorem comes into effect is discussed later in the chapter, so we will not repeat it here. What we will do is demonstrate diagrammatically how the share of wages may end up being so low.

The easiest explanation can be derived by comparing the above diagram with the previous one (the right-hand diagram). If technology and capital remain unchanged, the only way in which the share of wages will decline will be through the increase in the supply of labour. As is explained in the chapter, this is usually a reference to what we call Labour Force Participation. So, we are not thinking here about the increase in population but rather a possible increase in the labour force:

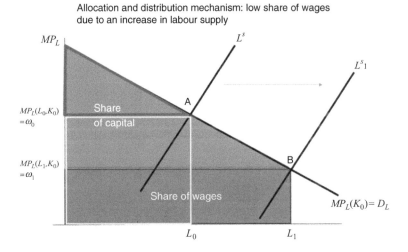

Allocation and distribution mechanism: low share of wages due to an increase in labour supply

In the above diagram, we can see the effects of an increase in the supply of labour. Markets will now take us from an equilibrium at point A to an equilibrium at point B where wages (in real terms) are lower, more people are employed and output increased. It is evident by comparing the share of wages at A (the yellow-lined rectangular) with its share in B that the share of wages has gone down. But notice that when there is an increase in the supply of labour, there is also an increase in output. So, while the share of labour has gone down, it is now a smaller share of a bigger pie. This, of course, can mean either a fall, an increase or no change in the total amount of income available for the increased number of people who depend on it. In the cases of fall or no change in the amount of income available for an increasing number of people, it clearly means that they will be worse off. Only when there is an increase in income is when we cannot be sure. But even if their income goes up, it will clearly go up by much less than the income of those who derive it from the returns on capital.

If there is a simultaneous change in both labour supply and the stock of capital (or technology), we have a more complex situation to consider:

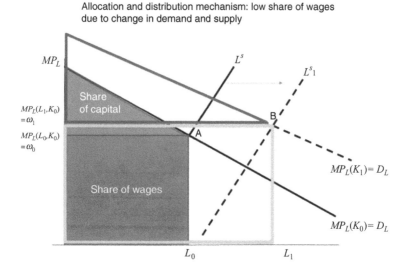

Allocation and distribution mechanism: low share of wages due to change in demand and supply

If we start at A and now both labour force and capital increase (which is, probably, what must have happened in reality), we may end up anywhere to the right of point A. If we end up at point B, we can see that the new share of wages is the heavy green rectangular and the new share of capital is the heavy purple triangle. Whether or not the share of wages has gone up is not obvious from this diagram as it depends on the overall increase in output which is now measured by the area under the new demand schedule. At point B the real wage has gone up but this can be associated with both increase and decrease of labour share. It is true that the greater is the increase in wages, the higher will be the probability that the share of wages (the green rectangular) is now greater than it was before.

However, for the share of wages to have a greater potential of increasing as we move from A to B, real wages should rise. This means that the productivity of labour as measured by the marginal product should increase too. If the labour market is not working, it is possible to face a situation where productivity increased but real wages fell:

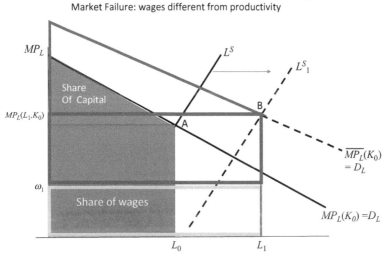

Allocation and Distribution mechanism: low share of wages
Market Failure: wages different from productivity

As we can see, now the shift upwards of the demand for labour is due entirely to an increase in labour productivity (the stock of capital is unchanged). This means that had the market worked, we would be in equilibrium at B where we cannot say what would happen to the share of labour. However, the wage level which workers are paid is now ω. So, as the level of real wages is lower than the productivity of workers, the share of wages will clearly be lower (the green rectangular) while the share of capital will be much greater. In this case, it is almost evident that the amount of income available for those who rely on wages alone will be considerably smaller.

Bibliography

Acemoglou, D., & Restrepo, P. (2016). *The Race Between Machine and Man: Implications of Technology for Growth, Factor Shares and Employment.* MIT Discussion Paper.

Acemoglou, D., & Robinson, J. (2012). *Why Nations Fail: The Origin of Power, Prosperity and Poverty.* London: Profile Books.

Afonso, A., & Jalles, J. T. (2011). *Economic Performance and Government Size.* Working Paper. European Central Bank.

Algan, Y., & Cahuc, P. (2006). *Civic Attitudes and the Design of Labour Market Institutions: Which Countries Can Implement the Danish Flexicurity Model?* IZA DP No. 1928.

Autor, D. H., & Dorn, D. (2013). The Growth of Low-Skill Service Jobs and the Polarization of the U.S. Labor Market. *American Economic Review, 103*(5), 1553–1597.

Clark, G. (2005). The Condition of the Working Class in England, 1209–2004. *Journal of Political Economy, 113*(6), 1307–1340.

Colander, D. (2000). New Millennium Economics: How Did It Get This Way, and What Way Is It? *Journal of Economic Perspectives, 14*(1), 121–132.

Colander, D. (2010). Models, Pedagogy and Crisis. In A. Arnon, J. Weinblatt, & W. Young (Eds.), *Perspectives on Keynes.* Springer.

Cullis, J. G., & Jones, P. P. (1987). *Microeconomics and the Public Economy: A Defence of the Leviathan.* Oxford: Basil Blackwell.

Daly, H. E., & Cobb, J. B. (1989). *For the Common Good: Redirecting the Economy Toward Community, the Environment, and a Sustainable Future.* Boston, MA: Beacon Press.

Easterlin, R. A. (2000). The Worldwide Standard of Living Since 1800. *Journal of Economic Perspectives, 14*(1), 7–26.

Eurostat. (2016). Retrieved from https://ec.europa.eu/eurostat/data/database.

Frey, C. B., & Osborne, M. A. (2013). *The Future of Employment: How Susceptible Are Jobs to Computerisation?* Oxford Martin School.

Goos, M., Manning, A., & Salomons, A. (2014). Explaining Job Polarization: Routine-Biased Technological Change and Offshoring. *American Economic Review, 104*(8), 2509–2526.

Green, F., & Zhu, Y. (2007). *Overqualification, Job Dissatisfaction, and Increasing Dispersion in the Returns to Graduate Education,* Centre of Economic Performance, LSE MHRLdp005.

Heritage Foundation. (n.d.). Retrieved from https://www.heritage.org/index/explore.

Jones, C., & Klenow, P. J. (2016). Beyond GDP? Welfare Across Countries and Time. *American Economic Review, 106*(9), 2426–2457.

Kornai, J. (2000). What the Change of System from Socialism to Capitalism Does and Does Not Mean. *Journal of Economic Perspectives, 14*(1), 27–42.

Loizidis, J., & Vamvoukas, G. (2005). Government Expenditure and Economic Growth: Evidence from Trivariate Causality Testing. *Journal of Applied Economics, 8*(1), 125–152.

Lucas, R. E. (2000). Some Macroeconomics for the 21st Century. *Journal of Economic Perspectives, 14*(1), 159–168.

Nussbaum, M. (1988). Nature, Functioning and Capability: Aristotle on Political Distribution. *Oxford Studies in Ancient Philosophy (Supplementary Volume), 6*, 145–184.

Nussbaum, M. C. (1992). Human Functioning and Social Justice: In Defense of Aristotelian Essentialism. *Political Theory, 20*(2), 202–246.

OECD. (2012). *Labour Losing to Capital.* Supporting Material for Chapter 3 of the 2012 OECD, Employment Outlook. Paris: OECD Publishing.

Office of National Statistics. (2018). Retrieved from https://www.ons.gov.uk/.

Organisation for Economic Co-operation and Development. (2017). Retrieved from https://data.oecd.org/.

Piketty, T. (2014). *Capital in the 21st Century.* Cambridge, MA: Harvard University Press.

Ram, R. (1986). Government Size and Economic Growth: A New Framework and Some Evidence from Cross Section and Time Series Data. *American Economic Review, 76*, 191–203.

Ram, R. (1987). Wagner's Hypothesis in Time Series and Cross Section Perspectives: Evidence from 'Real Data' from 115 Countries. *Review of Economics and Statistics, 69*, 184–204.

Rodrick, D. (2013). *Premature Deindustrialization.* NBER Working Papers 20935, National Bureau of Economic Research, Inc.

Rodrick, D. (2015). Unconditional Convergence in Manufacturing. *Quarterly Journal of Economics, 128*(1), 165–204.

Saez, E., & Zucman, G. (2016). Wealth Inequality in the United States Since 1913: Evidence from Capitalised Income Tax Data. *Quarterly Journal of Economics, 131*(2), 519–578.

Sen, A. (1985). *Commodities and Capabilities.* Amsterdam: North Holland.

Sen, A. (1992). *Inequality Reexamined.* Oxford: Clarendon Press.

Sen, A. (1999). *Development as Freedom.* New York: Anchor Books.

Slonimczyk, F. (2011). Earnings Inequality and Skill Mismatch in the U.S: 1973–2002, MPRA Paper No. 35449.

Solow, R. M. (2000). Toward a Macroeconomics of the Medium Run. *Journal of Economic Perspectives, 14*(1), 151–158.

Solow, R. M. (2009). Does Growth Have a Future? Does Growth Theory Have a Future? Are These Questions Related? *History of Political Economy, 41*(5), 27–34. Supplement.

Survey of Consumer Finance. (2016). Retrieved from https://www.federalreserve.gov/econres/scfindex.htm.

Talberth, D. J., Cobb, C., et al. (2007). *The Genuine Progress Indicator 2006: A Tool for Sustainable Development*. Oakland, CA: Redefining Progress.

Thaler, R. H. (2000). From Homo Economicus to Homo Sapiens. *Journal of Economic Perspectives, 14*(1), 133–141.

US Census. (2014). Retrieved from https://www.census.gov/programs-surveys/acs/news/data-releases/2014.html.

Wagner, A. (1893). *Grundlegung der Politische Oekonomie*. Leipzig: C. F. Winter.

Witztum, A. (2008). Social Attitudes and Re-distributive Policies. *Journal of Socio-Economics, 37*(4), 1597–1623.

Witztum, A. (2011). Ethics and the Science of Economics: Robbins's Enduring Fallacy. *Journal of the History of Economic Thought, 33*(4), 467–486.

Witztum, A. (2013). Keynes's Misguided Revolution. *Œconomia, 3*(2), 287–318.

World Development Indicators. (2017). Retrieved from https://datacatalog.worldbank.org/dataset/world-development-indicators.

World Value Survey. (2005–2009). Retrieved from http://www.worldvaluessurvey.org/WVSDocumentationWV5.jsp.

World Value Survey. (2014). Retrieved from http://www.worldvaluessurvey.org/WVSDocumentationWV6.jsp.

Zeira, J. (1998). Workers, Machines and Economic Growth. *Quarterly Journal of Economics, 113*, 1091–1113.

4

On Freedom and Justice: A Note Pertaining to Economics' Liberal Connections

Synopsis: *If the promise of economics' paradigmatic core is neither logically true nor relevant, could there be another reason why we may still wish to promote and defend the proliferation of the idea of competitive decentralisation (i.e. markets)? There could be. If markets do not really solve the economic problem and are not ethically neutral but they do provide people with, say, freedom and justice, then pursuing this form of economic organisation could still be justified. Moreover, if this were the case, the important association of competitive decentralisation with the basic expression of modern liberalism in the form of civic society can also be maintained.*

Both freedom and justice are complex and broad concepts, the examination of which goes well beyond the scope of this book. Nevertheless, we propose to focus on two relatively simple, though fundamental, expressions of them. In the first instance, we examine the association of markets with freedom. Specifically, we focus on a widely received association of markets with freedom of choice. We argue that freedom of choice involves the ability of agents to both freely choose from a given set, and have an unrestricted set from which to choose. We combine the two in what we term as 'sovereignty'. As economics assumes a conception of rationality which, by definition, reflects the former part of freedom, we focus our examination on the second (i.e. restrictions on the set of

© The Author(s) 2019
A. Witztum, *The Betrayal of Liberal Economics*,
https://doi.org/10.1007/978-3-030-10668-3_4

options available). We argue that by entering a market arrangement, individuals forgo sovereignty in two different ways. Firstly, they become constraint by the actions of other people who—not necessarily by individual intention as by collective action—create man-made constraint on their choice- set. Secondly, their ability to influence their own circumstances—that which J. S. Mill termed as 'real free-will'—is restricted in the sense that they are unable to choose not to participate in the game if the outcomes are no longer in their favour. To an extent, one can argue that entering an arrangement for a purpose may justify the loss of some liberties. In the case of Hobbes, for instance, individuals forgo all their liberties in return for security. However, even in Hobbes, people have not forgone their right to rebel if the promise for which they gave up their rights is violated. In our story, one can always argue that people enter market arrangement voluntarily, which means that they must know that they forgo the right to be free from the constraints created by individuals' collective actions. However, like in Hobbes, when the promised benefits are not provided, surely people must have a right to rebel. We show that the promise of benefits embedded in markets require that people adjust their specialisation—that which they will spend most of their time doing—according to the terms of trade. When these change, individuals are expected to change specialisation in order to benefit from the system. But if the cost of such a change is greater than the promised benefits, the individual has no option but to opt out of the game or invoke his, or her, right to rebel. The loss of sovereignty and command over one's own fate means that the freedom associated with idea of competitive decentralisation, or markets, is just an illusion.

On the question of justice, we argue that while the subject is broad and complex, there seems to be a thread which goes through both the breadth of its interpretations and its history. This is the idea of some sort of desert. We will try to demonstrate that the idea of **contribution-based desert** *is sufficiently widespread in public opinion. We also show that in spite of difficulties associated with the concept, it has a presence, in one form or another, in most approaches to the question of justice and, in particular, with reference to economic justice. Moreover, notwithstanding the debates about the role of desert in theories of justice, as the focus of our attention is the market mechanism itself, questions pertaining to initial allocations or final distributions— which have been a focus of considerable amount of attention—are not our concern. Instead, we concentrate on interactions between any two people and* *ask what a just interaction would look like. In this context, contribution-based desert is, perhaps, the only relevant application of justice. Therefore, we find the complete disappearance of any form of desert from modern discussions of* **economic justice** *intriguing. We identify a possible reason for this in the way in which modern economics captures the idea of interdependence in economic life. The reason why such developments should affect desert is mainly due to the possible erosion of clear causal explanations. If as a result of interdependence that which I get cannot be attributed to my action, I may not have a moral claim to it. Nevertheless, the fact that the reasons why people act may be complex and interwoven with other people's motivation does not alter the fact that as observers we can still examine whether in the end those who contributed more get a reward which is proportional to their contribution. Therefore, we look at three simple cases. In the first one, we look at the hypothetical origin of economic organisation which is the decision agents make to specialise and trade. We identify an orthogonality between those allocations which are consistent with the principle of contribution-based desert and those which are consistent with market solution (i.e. efficient). However, in this analysis, contribution-based desert was reflected in the price rather than through a direct association between the actual contribution and the actual outcome. In the second example, we looked more directly at the actual correspondence between the contribution and the outcome without examining the property of the price itself. Here too we discovered an orthogonality between those allocations which conformed with justice and those which were proposed by competitive interaction. Finally, in the third case, we brought all of it together and we looked at the actual general equilibrium model where all decisions pertaining to the relationship between contribution and reward are determined simultaneously. We notice here something far more decisive than that which we found in the earlier examples. Market prices are* **inherently inverse** *to the idea of contribution-based desert. This, of course, must lead to the conclusion that notwithstanding what one's opinion may be about initial or final distributions, one can rest assured that market mechanism and justice are orthogonal ideas.*

* * *

We have endeavoured to establish in the last two chapters that while it is true that competitive decentralisation constitutes an order in the sense that it leads to a co-ordinated outcome (synchronic order), this outcome cannot seriously be viewed as a natural order. For an order to be natural, it has to be sustainable (diachronic), and for an economic order to become such, it has to be sure not to offend moral, or social, sensitivities. Modern economics proposed to achieve this status by both claiming to solve the economic problem and declaring itself ethically neutral. However, as we have shown, this project has failed on both accounts. Moreover, the failure of the competitive paradigm to solve the problem or to remain ethically neutral has been both a theoretical failure and an empirical one.[1] The former is a logical flaw, and the latter, a relevance failure.

We also noted that these conclusions should not come as a surprise to anyone familiar with the developments of economic analysis yet most of the academic and public discourse surrounding economic (and social) organisation have not abandoned the claim that there are economic and social merits in the spread of competitive decentralisation.[2] Some of it may be associated with the conflation of the growth in material wellbeing—or just productive efficiency—with that which solves the economic problem. But there is another reason for the staying power of the paradigmatic core and it is the implicit association of markets with freedom and justice. Namely, while it may be the case that competitive decentralisation is not ethically neutral, the ethics with which it ends up being implicated is one that *should* be universally accepted as the foundation of any ethics. After all, which ethical system will not have freedom and justice at its heart? Moreover, if a system provides freedom and respects the most basic principle of justice—the original meaning of which is due share—there may still be scope for diversity in the conception of what is morally good and, hence, for diversity in cultures and societies. In other words,

---

[1] To remind the reader, we are referring here to the fact that governments are large because the public wants them so and a large number of people cannot access national income through markets. Those who can, face a diminishing share of it. Moreover, with the conditioning of efficiency (only productive) on particular distributions of property rights, the ability to associate the outcome with all possible distributions of income—which is required for the consequentialist ethical neutrality—is no longer possible.

[2] Notably, this is manifested in the continued use of efficiency as the criterion of economic performance and opportunity cost as the notion of price. Globalisation is another expression of this view.

freedom and justice as the foundation of ethics are near enough (or, per-haps, noble enough) to claim neutrality.

Leaving aside the question concerning the grounds upon which some-one may claim that their own views on freedom, justice and morality are universal, there is a question of whether, in its own terms, there is merit in this claim. We will, of course, not get into the question of whether freedom and due share are universally shared ethical principles—they certainly have a prominent presence in European thought—or whether they are understood in the same manner across epistemological and cul-tural divides, but we would like to examine the question of whether these attributed principles, as they are perceived from an economic perspective, indeed reside in some shape or form in the modern paradigm. One can easily imagine that even if competitive decentralisation fails to deliver a full solution to the economic problem or maintain ethical neutrality, the claim that it upholds freedom and justice is a powerful argument in its favour. To some, it may even be a sufficient reason for adopting these institutional arrangements knowing full well that they will not solve the economic problem as it is understood in modern economics.[3]

It may be of interest to note that a position like this chimes well with the intricate relationship which has been established in recent years between liberal economics (competitive decentralisation) and the idea of civic society.[4] If competitive decentralisation, or a system of laissez-faire, is based on freedom and upholds basic justice, it sounds reasonable to argue that the role of society is merely to keep the peace and uphold the law.[5] Individuals will then be able—in a decentralised fashion—to *freely*

---

[3] I must hasten and say that for those who would consider ethical claims as sufficient for the adop-tion of competitive decentralisation, the definition of the economic problem is very likely to be different indeed. Hence, if, in a somewhat Aristotelian manner, the objective of the economic sys-tem is to support the institutions of the just, or good, society, and if competitive decentralisation achieves just that, it stands to reason that one would wish these institutions to be established, proliferated and guarded. More recently, such a difference may constitute the dividing line between the Austrian school and the neoclassical paradigm.

[4] We will expand on this in Chap. 6 but what we mean by civic society—which is quite a dominant expression of what is today understood as liberalism—is an individualistic construction of society where the role of society is merely to facilitate voluntary human interactions.

[5] This is, in essence, what is behind the two welfare theorems. We would not have supposed that markets are consistent with whichever distribution society may wish if we also believed that mar-kets violate individual freedom or subvert justice. Equally, even critics in the spirit of Keynes do not

care for themselves without the fear that such interaction would lead to an outcome that might offend their natural sense of justice.[6] Upon such solid foundations, all forms of social, cultural and ethical differences may flourish on a *voluntary* basis.

Therefore, the question of whether economics' paradigmatic core can be crowned as the home of freedom and basic justice is of great significance. Nevertheless, we will not be able, in this short chapter and without a distraction from our main objectives, to even begin doing justice to the vast literature and history which is involved in addressing alternative theories of freedom and justice. We will also not be able to examine the complex relationship that exists between these two concepts which are not always necessarily compatible, a problem that has dogged the way liberalism is understood. Instead, what we propose to do in this chapter is to focus mainly on two very limited expressions of the two concepts and to examine them in the context of markets alone. What we mean by this is that we will not be asking questions about initial allocations or final distributions which are often seen as the building blocks of theories about economic justice, but rather concentrate on whether markets—the ultimate expression of competitive decentralisation and the intermediation mechanism between initial and final allocations—are consistent with some basic expressions of these two ideas.

The two forms of the ideas of freedom and justice to which we are referring are the notion of freedom of choice and the principle of proportional remuneration. The former notion suggests that as markets provide people with the ability to choose that which is best for themselves without restrictions, they epitomise the idea of liberty. Notwithstanding the important question of the initial conditions from which individuals enter the markets, the fact that market themselves do not add restrictions on their choices suggests that they preserve whatever freedom with which people came into the market. Thus, if society ensures that initial conditions are commensurate with whatever one believes to be the necessary conditions for freedom—which is, of course, a question of justice rather than freedom per se—competitive decentralisation (i.e. markets) will uphold those values because it is in itself an expression of freedom.

---

deny this property of markets but believe that the economy needs help in getting to where it wants to be (with markets).

[6] If indeed such a thing exists.

The second principle, the principle of proportional remuneration (or, due share), is an element of justice which seemed to have disappeared from more recent discussions on the meaning of economic justice. Instead, a great deal of attention has been given to either the initial allocation or the final distribution as the main object of such debates. Nevertheless, as we shall show, the idea of due share is very much prevalent in the public mind and has been quite dominant throughout history in human thinking about justice. The specific question with which we will be concerned is whether markets uphold the idea of due share in the way it transmits society between an initial allocation and a final distribution irrespective of the intrinsic nature of these distributions.

Naturally, if we reach the conclusion that markets are an expression of freedom and that they embody a process where individuals are rewarded proportionally to their contribution, it would mean that the association of markets with liberty and justice is justified. This means that there may be a good reason to uphold the idea of markets—competitive decentralisation—even if they fail to solve the economic problem and assuming that all agree that freedom of choice and due share are common to all conceptions of freedom and justice. But if, as indeed will be the case, we discover that markets and freedom of choice are by no stretch of imagination synonymous, and that the mechanism of competitive interactions violates the most basic principle of justice (due share), then the inevitable conclusion will have to be that there are no grounds whatsoever to either associate markets with liberty or uphold the competitive system because of the universality of its ethical significance rather than its ethical neutrality.

4.1 Freedom, Liberty and Sovereignty: A Note

Famously, von Mises, one of the founders of the Austrian school and a great supporter of the idea of spontaneous order,[7] contended: 'There is no kind of freedom and liberty other than the kind which the market econ-

---

[7] Though it is worth noting that von Mises, and the Austrian school in general, had a different conception of this order from the one adopted by modern neoclassical economics which was generated, among others, from the Lausanne school (notably, Walras) and the idea of spontaneous general equilibrium. Nevertheless, it seems that in terms of the freedom values of the market, there is a considerable amount of harmony between the schools.

omy brings about' (von Mises, *Human Action* Ch 15.6). More explicitly, he argued: 'A man is free in so far as he is permitted to *choose* ends and the means to be used for the attainment of those ends. A man's freedom is most rigidly restricted by the laws of nature as well as by the laws of praxeology' (ibid., my italics). And he continues: 'In the market economy, the laissez-faire type of social organization, there is a sphere within which the individual is free to *choose* between various modes of acting without being restrained by the threat of being punished' (ibid.). A similar line of reasoning continued down the path of the twentieth century with Hayek's *The Road to Serfdom* (1944) and Friedman's *Capitalism and Freedom* (1962) as, perhaps, the most familiar advocates.

Such a description of the economic system may well suit the Austrian perspective, which is more evolutionary in nature and is entirely focused on markets, but from neoclassical's point of view, things are a bit more complex. Here, as we said before, the markets—where decentralised competitive interactions take place—are effectively a transmission mechanism which transports the economy from some initial allocations of wealth, abilities and taste, to a final distribution of economic goods which will affect the stock of wealth as well as reward (or not) abilities. Therefore, caveats about such freedoms have certainly been raised but mainly with regard to the position of the agents when they come to interact freely through markets and much less so with regard to the freedoms which the markets themselves grant.[8] On both sides of the divide between libertarianism and egalitarianism, much of the focus has been on the initial condition from which decentralisation is unleashed. In this context both Nozick (1974) and Rawls (1973) emphasise the notion of equal opportunity. Nussbaum (1988, 1992) and Sen (1992, 1985) have expanded this to what came to be known as the capabilities approach, which is, in essence, about the freedom to achieve wellbeing which is based on one's capabilities (the real opportunity to be and do that which they have reason to value). This may indeed require interventions in the outcomes of market interactions—which could alter the initial condi-

---

[8] Namely, if there is a great inequality between two individuals in terms of their initial endowments (assets and abilities) one may think that they are not equally free irrespective of whether the mechanism of the market represents freedom of actions and interactions (and choice).

tions—but none of this is an explicit critique of the freedom which markets provide in terms of allowing people to freely choose their ends and the means by which they wish to achieve them. Instead, it is essentially about the allocation of some initial means which, if provided, will allow the freedom granted by markets to be consistent with what may appear to be also just.

More broadly put, the various ethical objections to the competitive system have most of the time been concentrated on the two ends of the process. They were concerned with either the initial allocation of resources which is the base upon which people make their initial choices or the final distribution which is less of an issue of freedom and more a question of justice or social conceptions of the good. But the mechanism of voluntary exchange by agents who are free to choose the ends and the means has not seriously been questioned. To put the question differently, could competitive decentralisation be synonymous with freedom if all agents were identical in all but taste when they enter the markets?

To a great extent, when people come to discuss markets, it very much sounds as if this is all about the freedom to choose. In terms of economics' paradigmatic core, the applicability of the argument seems quite straightforward. In a world where all individuals are powerless in terms of their ability to influence—by themselves—the decision parameters of others (the perfectly competitive environment),[9] and where they can make their own fully informed choices about ends and means given these parameters (which are equally exogenous for everyone), there is freedom and liberty. Though there is nothing explicit here about the extent of one's options, one often hears about the need to develop competitive environments as they *expand* individuals' choice and by implication increase the level of freedom.

But *freedom* is not a simple concept and its relationship to choice is even more complex. At the very least freedom must be about the ability to make a choice. This means that there must be at least two options; and that one should be able to become fully informed about the nature of each option and remain free from any influence or restrictions which are

---

[9] Recall that in a competitive environment economic decisions are based on prices which are determined in markets where no one individual has any influence on their values.

not dictated by the nature of things. By limiting the domain of discussion to those restrictions which are man-made (i.e. not natural), we are somewhat able to circumvent the important question of free-will. J. S. Mill, for instance, who was troubled by this question and who believed in the centrality of *ethology*—the theory of character formation—claimed that because most of what people do is very much a direct consequence of who they are and what their circumstances are, their free-will is not really expressed in terms of the choices they make but, rather, in terms of their ability to change these circumstances. This, in turn, is a question of what he calls individual development (*ethology*), which, in his view, consists mainly of their cognitive or intellectual progress.[10]

Though there is clearly a role for economics in providing the means for individual development and, subsequently, the means for changing one's circumstances (which, according to Mill, is real freedom), this will not be the focus of our discussion here.[11] Instead, we would like to focus on the freedom associated with the market even in an ideal set-up where initial conditions are such that we cannot see in them as an impediment to freedom or self-fulfilment. Consequently, we can put aside this important question of free-will and concentrate on choice itself.

We must distinguish between two types of restrictions that may interfere with the freedom of choice. The first is a restriction on the way in which one chooses; this includes both the process of choosing as well as the way in which one becomes informed about one's options. The second is the extent of those options from which one can make a choice. The two are, of course, related as restrictions on information, may include restriction on information about options that have been left out and not just about the nature of the available options. Nevertheless, to act as one wants—which is the dictionary definition of freedom—may be true of someone who faces a small set of options as well as someone who faces a large set of options. The question is, of course, what is it that defines the limit of one's wants[12] and how does this affect his or her freedom?

---

[10] Mill discusses these issues in *On Liberty* and his *Logic*. Ryan (1970) provides a discussion of Mill's position on free-will (Chap. 7). A treatment of the issue can also be found in Witztum (2005).

[11] For more on this, see Witztum (2005).

[12] This corresponds to what the capabilities approach presumes as the 'reason to value'. We should note that a similar issue arose in classical economics where authors like Smith deliberate the notion of effective demand.

When the set of options contained in what one can want is large, but agents cannot acquire information about the true nature of those options as well as face sanctions if they choose some of them, they will not be making genuinely free choices even though they can, as it were, choose what they want. But whether or not people face no such restrictions in a market economy is not altogether obvious. For one, even though economic theory assumes as standard that agents are well informed, most people, as a matter of fact, are usually quite poorly informed about most of their choices, and even when such information is available, there is considerable scope for it to be managed and manipulated by other agents in society. It is enough to mention advertising and the manipulation of search engines on the internet to persuade anyone that even though there are many options available to individuals, the choice they make cannot really be crowned as either well informed or free of influence. Unlike oppressive regimes, there are clearly no overt restrictions on acquiring information about one's options and no declared sanctions on others, but there may be other forms of tempering with the process of choosing that will undermine its apparent freedom. To some extent, it is much more disturbing not to be aware of interferences than to be fully aware of them. In the former case, there will be appearances of freedom, though reality may be very different indeed. In the latter, we may be sure to be less free but when we know the nature of the restrictions, we may be able to find ways to undermine them.

From a theoretical perspective, however, modern economics offers a conception (and the prospect) of an individual who is *by definition free*. The rational utility maximiser is an agent who can choose aims as well as means (recall that the utility function is ordinal and therefore a mere representation of preferences) and, in theory, he or she is always fully informed and is not influenced by any other individual member of society as they are all price-takers.[13] However, in economic analysis this is a *premise*, an assumption, rather than a conclusion that can be attributed to the nature of the system. In other words, economic theory assumes agents to

---

[13] We are, of course, referring to the logical limit and not to the large literature on asymmetric information, which is treated as a form of market failure for which there can be remedies in the form of mechanism designs.

be free in the sense that they will have all the information they need about their options and can make a choice, free from restrictions or interference. This, of course, suggests that competitive decentralisation, or the system of laissez-faire, is by definition free. Hence, to associate freedom with markets is somewhat a tautology. I will be surprised, however, if this is what people mean when they attribute freedom to competitive decentralisation. Therefore, if we assume that the *process* of making a choice is by definition completely free, the only aspect of freedom which is left open to the influence of the system is the extent of this choice or the restrictions which may or may not exist with regard to the options available to the agent. Put differently, if we want to argue that competitive decentralisation provides people with freedom when we assume people to have no restrictions on the way in which they *form their choice*, we must also show that it imposes no restrictions on the set of available options.

From a linguistic perspective, one could have used the distinction between *freedom* and *liberty* in order to distinguish between the two types of restrictions, but in the end they are the two sides of the same coin. One cannot really be free without liberty and one cannot have liberty and not be free. Nevertheless, liberty is more (though not exclusively) about being free from restrictions on the ***domain of choice*** (what one can and what one cannot do), while freedom is more about the ability to freely choose between alternatives (ends and means in most general terms) that *are available*. But if, as we said, we accept the conception of the individual in economics as being by definition free—in the way they make their decision (i.e. freedom)—then liberty, the determinant of the domain of choice, remains the only meaningful parameter to assess the economic system. However, to avoid awkward situations where we have to attribute freedom to fully informed agents who choose freely from a restricted domain (diminished liberty), I propose to use another word which is, to a great extent, an amalgamation of freedom and liberty: ***sovereignty***. A sovereign person is someone who is not only free to make choices from an available set but is also at liberty to influence the extent of the set (limited only by nature) or determine its boundaries. This will bring to the fore the question which we posed about that which determines the boundaries of want and how it connects to freedom (or sovereignty); and it could also be associated with Mill's idea that freedom is not really about choice as it is about changing the circumstances (being sovereign).

Suppose that a typical choice of an agent in an economic environment can be represented by a vector of two elements: (L_e, x), where L_e is leisure (which is an inverse measure of the work which the agent does) and x is the consumption he can have. Moreover, we know that there are some ***exogenous rules*** (what Mill would have called circumstances and von Mises the restrictions by nature) which connect the input of work the agent provides with the amount of consumption available to him or her. These rules consist of everything which may mediate between the act of work and the available reward. It could simply be the ability of the individual (which would be a natural constraint and, therefore, not a liberty or freedom issue); it could be the wage he or she earns which is a market-mediated return (that is already not natural but may not be traceable to any other individual action); or it could be other things which may affect that which is available to him or her like, for instance, wealth or assets (this, again, is not a natural constraint and the question will be whether there is anyone in particular, with power over another and, thus, a liberty issue).

So, let us begin with the most simplified situation. We have two individuals, I and II, who differ in their productivity either because of difference in abilities or because of attitudes to work and who are producing good x, which is produced on land. At the moment, there is no connection between them:

Choice sets of leisure and consumption: equal liberty

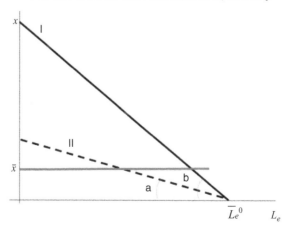

Each of the agents can choose any combination of leisure and consumption within the constraint (the heavy black line for I and the broken black line for II). Notice that in each case that which determines the size of their choice set is a combination of their natural abilities and their attitude towards work.[14] Therefore, the difference between them may not reflect any difference in their innate characteristics (i.e. abilities per se) but rather a difference in the level of effort they tend to put in their work. Also, recall that there is no connection between the individuals.[15] It is evident that the set of options available to agent I is greater than the one available to agent II. One can think of this as being simply the total number of available bundles or, as they both acquire a bundle made up of two economic goods only (leisure and x), the fact that agent I has more choice is denoted by the fact that the set of leisure available to both of them is the same but the set of x available to I is clearly greater than the set available for agent II.

They are both equally rational and well informed about the properties of each option. Does this mean that agent I—who has more options—is freer, or more sovereign, than agent II? Recall that there is no connection between the two individuals so the answer must be negative. As they both face the same kind of constraint, which is determined by nature, there are

[14] This means that for every hour of work agent I provides (i.e. one hour less of leisure) he can obtains b units of x. Individual II will get a units of x for each hour worked. The values of a and b represent what we call the marginal product of labour. While we normally assume it to be diminishing the more we use the resources (in this case, labour), it is simpler to consider it to be constant here. Note too that the differences in output per hour may not necessarily reflect differences in ability as it may be a reflection of dexterity or the attitude towards this particular work.

[15] The restriction imposed on the available set, here, is not really a liberty issue or a limitation of their freedom. Freedom does not really mean the ability to have what you want but, rather, the ability to have what you can want. Clearly, the main issue is that which determines what you 'can' want, but in our example here there is no connection between the individuals, so it is not the case that individual I could, should or would have liked to transfer some of what is available to him to the other. In addition, note that while the agent can choose any bundle inside the constraint, given the goal of the agent, the real set of choices would be all the bundles along the line (as he or she would want to have more of both). Von Mises makes this point very clearly: 'A man's freedom is most rigidly restricted by the laws of nature as well as by the laws of praxeology' (ibid.). In other words, restrictions which emanate from nature or what he calls the law of praxeology (i.e. logical consistency of actions, or choices) cannot be deemed as limitation on freedom as the latter must be defined within them.

no real (or man-made) limitations on their liberty. Therefore, they must be equally free even though the number of options available to each one of them is very different. Moreover, if we add to our story another natural constraint—such that there is a minimal level of consumption (denoted by the red line) which they must acquire in order to survive—we will see that individual I needs to work less (thus, can have more leisure) in order to survive than individual II. This, of course, is due to the differences in either their natural ability or natural disposition towards work. Nevertheless, they are still equally free as both the restrictions they face— separate from one another—are natural. Though one may feel intuitively that there is a significant difference between the worlds the two individuals face, this is not an issue of freedom per se as it could be a question of equity if the differences between their productivities were based on differences in their innate abilities. What we can already see here is the potential tension between freedom and justice. If we accept that in pure terms both are equally free, then pursuing equality (which is a form of justice— but not the only one) would necessarily mean a man-made restriction on the freedom of one of the agents.

Are they also equally sovereign? Again, in separation from each other, the answer must be in the affirmative as all constraints here are natural. The fact that one of them must work harder to survive so that he or she can be free to choose from the available set, does not mean that his or her sovereignty is different from the one who can afford to work less. On the other hand, had the red line in the above diagrams been a *man-made constraint*, then one could wonder whether the fact that one agent has to work harder to be able to have the same freedom to choose as the other is not a greater restriction on his or her sovereignty. While it is clear that in such a case, both face a similar level of freedom (both face the exact same restrictions even though one of them is man-made), the fact that one agent has greater command of the extent of the natural set available to him than the other means that they do not enjoy the same level of sovereignty. Diagrammatically, we can see this in the following way:

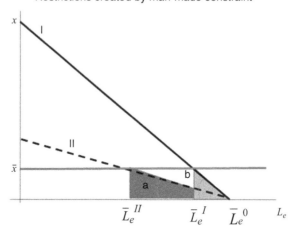

The man-made restriction has created the shaded triangles which are part of their natural set but is no longer accessible to them. As the relative size of this triangle for agent I is distinctly smaller than it is for agent II, agent I should be deemed more sovereign in the sense that he has greater command over his natural set. If one wishes to give the man-made red-line constraint an interpretation, this could be seen as a standard of living dictated by social norms. Hence, for all agents to participate in society, they must have enough income to support such activities but if this means a greater restriction on their choices, the poorer members of society are less sovereign than their richer counterparts.

However, until now we assumed that the individuals are separated from one another in the sense that they were not aware of the other's circumstances (and, hence, the red-line constraint is natural too). But if they become aware of the other, some things may begin to change. While it is evident that they are still equally free in the sense that the only restrictions on their set of choices are natural, agent II may see that with different abilities (or dexterity), one could have had a larger set of options. If the case was that of difference in abilities, then as such, this would not make a difference. If we resort back to a combination of Adam Smith's notion of effective demand (we cannot desire or want that which is beyond our reach) and the idea of the freedom to be that which one has reason to value, embedded in capabilities approach, it would not be a legitimate claim for agent II to desire elements in the set of I which are not feasible for him. He has, as it were, no reason to value such outcomes. He may be envious and, in this sense, his wellbeing reduced but it will be difficult to argue that his freedom or sovereignty has been affected. If, however, they were of equal ability but the difference between them was dexterity, then, clearly, agent II could have changed his own circumstances and reach all the options available to I. Either way, their awareness of the other would not really change either their freedom or sovereignty.

But all of this will change if they become members of one community. Suppose now that the two individuals are part of a competitively decentralised economic system where they acquire their consumption good x by working as employees in its production. We suppose too that the land on which they work now belongs to someone else who does not produce x but has such expertise in improving the land so that their productivity has now increased to a^* and b^* respectively. It is important to emphasise that we are not describing here a choice which the agents make when they decide to come together and work in a competitive decentralised system. Rather, we assume that they were born into such a system and the institutional arrangements—man-made—are in place. We will discuss the fundamental presumption behind the benefits of coming together in a competitive arrangement and its significance to freedom further below.

In the competitive decentralises system into which they have been born, they will receive in return for their labour that which is determined by a competitive market. Given that the equilibrium wage (in real terms) will be a productivity measure of the last hour worked and assuming that both of them are employed, it means that the wage level will be set at the productivity level of agent II (i.e. $\omega = a^*$).[16] Therefore, both agents will now face the same choice set corresponding to II's newly defined set in the diagram below.

---

[16] Note that there is one labour market for x and that the difference in the agents' productivity may reflect their personal dispositions towards work rather than expertise, or abilities, in producing the good (i.e. one of them may be keener on work than the other). Therefore, there will not be separate markets for the different types of 'abilities' as they do not reflect different skills.

To avoid questions about whether the markets would have been adopted in the first place, we begin with the case (left-hand diagram) where it is clear why the agents would have wanted to be in a market arrangement:

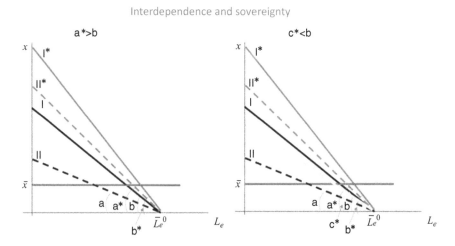

Interdependence and sovereignty

In the left-hand diagram, $a^* > b > a$, which means that the material benefits from moving into competitive decentralisation where a land-owner has the skills to improve the quality of land, is shared by both of them. Their new set of options from which they are now expected to choose freely is greater than the one they would have had without the man-made institutions erected by the idea of the market.[17] That which agent I produced above that which he receives ($b^* - a^*$ per unit of labour) is now the return earned by the owner of land whose work increased their productivity. While this clearly means that they will both benefit materially from this man-made organisation, we are not concerned with this as we are with the question of their freedom and sovereignty. Clearly, however, they are both as free and sovereign as they were in the previous, natural, setting. Namely, if their original set of options (the ones defined by a and b respectively) were the ones representing only natural restric-

---

[17] They both will have the same choice set delineated by the broken blue line in the left-hand diagram which is clearly greater than the original set of agent I (denoted by the heavy black line) and the original set of agent II (denoted by the broken black line).

tions, then the man-made institutions have *not* restricted any of these further, which means that they remain at least as free and sovereign as they were in the original natural state. So has the expansion of the set of choices for each one of them meant that they are now either freer or more sovereign?

In the same manner that agent I was not freer than agent II in the natural state just because he had a larger set of options, neither of them should be considered freer just because their set of options increased. The only possible change in their position with regard to freedom and liberty would be in terms of the second—subsistence, or red line—constraint. Now, both of them can work less before they can enjoy their freedom. In this respect, the survival constraint is much less restrictive than it was in the natural state and, in this respect, they may have more sovereignty in the sense that those parts of the set which were in principle available to them but about which they had no choice will be relatively smaller.[18] So, it is this, rather than the mere expansion of choice (though the two may be related) which could potentially be the reason why people may associate markets with greater sovereignty (rather than freedom). But even in this sense, the jubilation may be premature.

Recall that the two agents we examined have not themselves been those who made the institutional change; they were born into it. Now, suppose too that over the years, as population increases, there will be many more individuals with whichever natural abilities. This means that as labour supply expands wages will, at some stage, fall to the level of, say, $c^* < b$. This is the picture in the right-hand diagram.

Clearly, agent I will now face a set of options which is smaller than the one he could have had under the original natural arrangement. Alternatively, the natural set could also have been his set within the competitive system had he *owned* the land he was working on. In such a case, as he has no skills to improve the land, his productivity would fall back to b and the overall output of the economy will be smaller. Agent II, on

---

[18] When we say 'were in principle available to them', we mean that all the points in the shaded areas in the previous diagram were potentially possible in the sense that individuals could have chosen to be there. However, this would mean that they may not survive. Therefore, they cannot choose it. However, this is very different from simply wanting something which one does not have the means to have (like the options agent I has and are not available to agent II).

the other hand, faces a set of options which is still distinctly greater than the one he faced in the original situation or the one he would face had he also owned the land. Are these two individuals still equally free as they were before?

Assuming that agent I has no option of going it alone (i.e. return to a state of nature or, in other words, to opt out of the social arrangement), then both agents seem to face similar circumstances. They both have to choose between leisure and consumption; they both must acquire it through the labour market and they both get the same wages. Therefore, they appear to face the same restrictions and the same choice set which seems to suggest that they seem to enjoy the same level of freedom and sovereignty as one another. But this, of course, is not true. Firstly, given that the natural set for agent I is available to him even within the social arrangement (by making him the owner of the land on which he was working), the fact that this is not happening (probably due to the loss of collective output) suggests that he faces man-made restrictions over his natural set. Therefore, he is clearly less free than agent II for whom the man-made restriction has not further restricted what he would have had in a natural setting. Secondly, if we refer back to the social subsistence constraint, agent I has now a greater part of his natural set about which he has no choice while agent II has still a smaller part of this natural set about which he has no choice. Therefore, agent I is also less sovereign than agent II.

There is another way in which the decline in agent II's sovereignty can be expressed. As the natural set—which he clearly prefers—could be available under alternative social arrangement, then the lack of ability to change his circumstances when he wants to do so is an expression of lack of sovereignty or, that which Mill would have called, real free-will.

But before anyone interprets this as suggesting that in markets, the poor, or less able people benefit at the expense of the more able one, I hasten to say that the same fate which befell agent I will eventually befall agent II as well. As the labour force expands, wages will fall further until it is below the level of a—the productivity level of agent II in the natural state. This means that agent II will be in the exact same position as agent I in terms of reduced sovereignty in the market arrangement. The only agent who will definitely gain from this market arrangement is the one who now owns the land and has the skill of improving it so that agents I and II can experience greater productivity (a^* and b^* respectively). If such an agent has no skills or ability to produce x but only to make the soil more fertile, his natural set will be very small indeed which means that his sovereignty limited as most of his time will be spent on working in order to survive. Now, in the social arrangement, as the wages go down and agents I and II face further restrictions on their original set and reduced sovereignty, this agent's sovereignty will be significantly enhanced.

Going back to our original story and focusing on agent I, we should take note of what causes his predicament (and eventually, it would also cause agent II to be in the same situation). There are two reasons to why the choice set of agent I is trimmed: firstly, the fact that some of individual I's output has been institutionally channelled elsewhere, and, secondly, the fact that other individuals seek work too through the same labour market (thus reducing wages). So, the reason why agent I's available set was trimmed to the level below the one he could have had in the original arrangement is because of the **actions of other agents** (those who seek work and those who use their property rights to channel some of what would have been available to him in a natural state to another [$(b - c^*)$ per unit of labour]). In other words, agent I faced a restriction on his set of available choices emanating not from natural circumstances but from the actions of other members of society plus the rules of how the institutions of the markets are governed.

As we suggested before, the limitation on the sovereignty of agent I is more pronounced in our story as it is not only that the part of his choice set on which he has full command has relatively shrunk but also because there is really nothing he can do to change the circumstances (Mill's notion of real free-will). The only possible way, within a market system, to have changed the circumstances would have been to change ownership structures or redistribute property rights. If the ownership of the land were given to either agent I alone or both of them in the sense that each one owns the land on which he is working, the outcome for each agent will be the same as in the original state. As they lose the input of the landowner who had the ability to improve the land, their productivities will return to the original level of a and b respectively. They will now face the original sets (whether agent I owns both lands and they seek labour through market or each one of them owns his own plot which is more akin to the original state of affairs) where they will be equally sovereign as they only face natural constraints.

Either through redistribution of property rights or through a return to the original natural arrangement, the collective set of options will shrink.[19] Yet, as we argued, they will become equally free and sovereign. This means, above else, that freedom and sovereignty are not an attribute of the material success of the economy. It is when the distribution of returns associated with the generation of plenty reaches a certain point where something akin to an outside option—the original state—appears better for some individuals, that some agents would experience greater restrictions than are naturally necessary and will therefore become less free. Their corresponding lack of sovereignty will manifest itself by the increased share of options on which they have no command (they must work or else) and their inability to change the situation.

Put differently, while competitive decentralisation generates material wellbeing, it is not this—the expanded set of options—which allows it to be associated with ultimate freedom and sovereignty. Instead, it is the distribution of the produce of the economy which is detrimental to freedom. At some levels (in our case, when wages are high), the distribution of returns may be consistent with freedom and greater sovereignty but as the number of people dependent on the system increases and wages decline, this association breaks down. To some extent, some individuals are, in effect, prisoners of the others. It is, of course, not that the others intentionally wish to bring about restrictions on the freedom of others, but it is the way competitive decentralisation is organised which leads to this outcome. Equally, this means that the abandonment of allocative efficiency—the distributional characteristics of the outcome—in favour of productive efficiency and growth—the material dimension of the solution—also means abandoning the potential association between freedom, sovereignty and markets.

---

[19] Though this is not a case of missing market in uncertainty, it is a matter of specialisation. If the returns earned by the landowner who is a land specialist is distributed, he may either abandon his work and become a labourer or it will reduce his effectiveness and this will lower the productivity gains.

Naturally, for some individuals the freedom and sovereignty promised by competitive decentralisation will be provided but when there is disparity in freedom, one cannot really deem an organisation as the beacon of freedom. After all, even in oppressive regimes there are some people who are free and sovereign while others are not. No one would consider these organisations as an expression of freedom and individual sovereignty. One could say that this may be a question of proportion (how many are free relative to those restricted) but we will need to develop a convincing metrics to achieve a proper measure which takes into consideration the distribution of restrictions.

But there is a darker side to this problem of sovereignty in competitive decentralisation. In our previous example, it manifested itself with man-made restrictions on a set of options made up of bundles of economic goods comprised of leisure and consumption. The fact that individuals cannot acquire a bundle of leisure and goods may appear somewhat exaggerated as a statement about the loss of sovereignty. But it is not. If one considers the meaning of it, one must conclude that it is really about the option to opt out from organisations created by humans. This must be one of the most fundamental acts of sovereignty. If agent I, in our story, could say that he leaves the economic organisation, he would have been equally sovereign as those who wish to stay. What is not coming through in our example is the severity of this limitation. We would like to demonstrate this through another example which is associated with the most fundamental building block of competitive decentralisation and is the origin of the plenty—or the extension of the choice set—which is promised by the markets. We are referring to the issue of specialisation and trade.

Consider the following simple story. Suppose that there are two individuals, agent 1 and agent 2, in society who at first live an autarkic life. In a sense, this is a pre-social state which explains the economic raison d'être of society.[20] There are only two goods in the world (x and y) and the two individuals (or households, if you prefer) have different abilities. Thus, agent 1 can use labour to produce either 6 units of y or 3 units of x or any combination of the two. Individual 2 can use labour to produce

---

[20] But whether or not this is a good or meaningful story will be explored in the following chapters and, in particular, in Chap. 7.

either 3 units of y and 6 units of x or any combination of the two. Initially, household 1 produces efficiently the combination of 1.5 units of x and 3 units of y (which is the bundle (1.5,3)) and household 2 produces efficiently the combination of 3 units of x and 1.5 units of y (3,1.5):

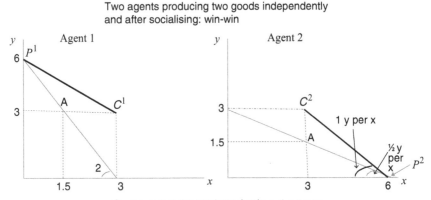

Two agents producing two goods independently
and after socialising: win-win

Suppose that the market price is p=1 y per x

The households are efficient as they are producing at a point (A) where they cannot have more of one good without forgoing another. It is clear that the opportunity cost (the price) of a unit of x in household 1 is 2 units of y per x (if the labour is directed from y to x, we lose 6 y and gain 3 x, so on average—as all is linear—the cost of 1 x is 2 y). By implication, the opportunity cost of y is ½ a unit of x in household 1. In household 2, the opportunity cost of x is ½ a unit of y and the opportunity cost of y is 2 units of x. Clearly, agent 1 has comparative advantage in producing y (as the cost of one 1 unit (1/2 an x) is less than it is in household 2 (2 units of y per x)).[21] For similar reasons, agent 2 has comparative advantage in x.

Notice that before anything else happens, at the outset, the two individuals are *fully sovereign* and *equally free*. They are in complete command over their destiny (so to speak) and the only constraints they experience are those imposed by nature. Now, given that they are both

---

[21] In the exposition of the economic paradigm in Chap. 2, Sect. 1 (2.1), you will find reference to this in points (f)–(h).

rational and perceive the economic problem in the same manner (i.e. they want to reconcile wants with scarcity), it stands to reason that they will choose to specialise and trade. In so doing they become dependent on each other (form society), but as their choice is rational and as they can always choose to go back to the initial arrangement, neither their sovereignty nor their freedom have been affected by such a move.

What specialisation and trade would mean, in this particular case, is that agent 1 will fully specialise in producing y, which he or she will trade for x in the market. Agent 2 will specialise in x and trade it for y in the market. In the above diagram, it means that agent 1 will move to produce at point P^1, where the household produces only the good in which they have comparative advantage (6 units of it), and agent 2 will move to produce at point P^2, where the household will produce the good in which they have comparative advantage (6 units of x). Notice that already we see an improvement when we look at the two of them together (i.e. the whole of society). Before they specialised and traded, the total amount of the goods produced by both of them would have been exactly 4.5 units of x and 4.5 units of y. We see that in terms of productive efficiency the move has certainly paid off and is a step in the right direction when we consider the solution to the economic problem.

But not only will this arrangement be collectively good, each of the agents involved will also improve their position in terms of solving their individual problem. As we can see, agent 1 for whom a unit of x would have cost 2 units of y if he or she produced it by themselves would be happy to exchange y for x at any price which is less than 2 units of y. Equally, agent 2 who would have gained ½ a unit of y if he or she produced one less unit of x, would be happy to exchange the x for anything greater than ½ a unit of y. The way that the price will be determined is in a competitive market where both agents will be price-takers in the sense that they cannot individually influence the price. Thus, sovereignty is maintained when we move to the market.

Suppose that in the market an equilibrium will be reached at the price of $\bar{p}_x = 1\,y\,\text{per}\,x$. Suppose too that each agent would like to continue consuming 3 units of the good they produce. The equilibrium in the market will appear like this:

	Agent 1	Agent 2
Demand for x	3	3
Supply of x	0	6
Demand for y	3	3
Supply of y	6	0

As the price of a unit of x is 1 y and vice versa, agent 1 will supply the market with 3 units of y, which they can exchange for 3 units of x. A similar story will hold for the other agent and we thus have an equilibrium.

Looking at the diagrams above, this equilibrium is depicted at point C^1 and point C^2 respectively. Clearly, each agent is consuming well beyond that which was feasible for them before the change. The change has benefitted everyone. There is no one who became worse off. Therefore, comparing the arrangement which led each one of them to A and the current arrangement, it is evident that point C is allocative efficient while A is not if C is possible.

Some would say that the expansion of the set of options which has become available to the individuals through specialisation and trade means that they have become freer than they were before. We, however, disagree and will be content to say that their sovereignty and freedom remained intact as they move into the market-based economic arrangement.

Suppose now that a third household joins the economy and that this is not optional. Namely, they cannot decide not to allow this agent to join. Suppose too that this household, when alone and in an autarkic state, can produce either 10 units of y or 4 units of x or any linear combination of the two:

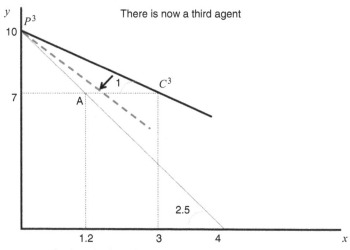

As the price is 1, the agent would want to specialise in y

Before joining, the agent produced and consumed at point A. The market price of x in the economy he now joins is 1 unit of y per x. This means that he can get more cheaply in the market (at the rate of 1 unit of y per x) instead of the cost he would pay if he produced it by himself (2.5 unit of y per x). Therefore, relative to the market, he has comparative advantage in producing y. So, he will move to produce at point P, where he is only producing y and given the market price (which he assumes is given) he will want to consume at point C 3 units of x and 7 units of y. What will happen when he enters the market?

	Agent 1	Agent 2	Agent 3
Demand for x	3	3	3
Supply of x	0	6	0
Demand for y	3	3	7
Supply of y	6	0	10

We can see that there is now a total demand for 9 units of x but only 6 units are produced, while there is a total demand for y of 13 units when 16 units of y are produced. This means that there is excess supply of y and excess demand for x. Therefore, the equilibrium price of x should rise and, by the same token, the price of y should fall. Suppose now that the equilibrium price of x increases to, say, 2.6 units of y per x. This means that agent 3 will still have comparative advantage in producing y and will stay at point P, although his consumption set will now be determined by the broken line. Therefore, he is still better off than he would have been had he not entered the social arrangement. Agent 2 too, who specialised in x, will carry on doing so as what he will get for x in the market (2.6 y) is still greater than what it costs him to produce (1/2 a unit of y). Agent 1, however, is a different story:

Agent 1's dilemma

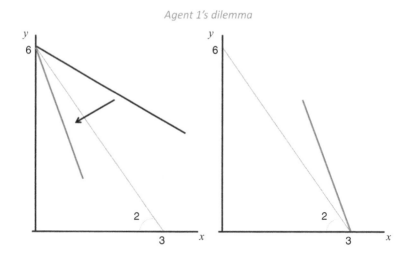

As the price of x rises above 2 y per x (which is what it costs him to produce), we move to the red line. On the left-hand side, we see the case when the agent chooses not to change specialisation. In such a case, he will clearly be worse off if he stayed in the market. Now, what economics assumes that will happen is that he will find himself switching specialisation (right-hand diagram) as he can now get more for a unit of x in the market than it costs him to produce. If indeed, the agent switches specialisation, then everyone still benefits from the move into the market economy.

There has been no change in what we said about the sovereignty and freedom of agents 2 and 3. But can we say the same about agent 1? Before agent 3 joined it was clear that agent 1 benefitted from the move to the market arrangement which left his sovereignty and freedom intact. Of all three agents, for agent 1 to continue to benefit from the market arrangement once agent 3 joins, he must go through a major adjustment. To benefit from the market, he must respond to the change in price of x by switching his specialisation.

If what an agent specialises in has no intrinsic value to him and if there are no costs to switching, then the move to the market will indeed maintain the full sovereignty of the agents. But if the specialisation chosen by agent 1 was something close to his heart and something which he loves to do, then switching is by no stretch of imagination costless.[22] If agent 1 insists on not switching his specialisation, he will find himself in the left-hand diagram where taking part in the market will make him worse off (he will be moving along the red line which is less than what he would have had, had he stayed in an autarkic state). Naturally, if agent 1 is fully sovereign, he can decide to opt out of the market arrangement and return to the autarkic state where he will work in producing both goods but not abandon his beloved occupation altogether. He will clearly be better off at point A in the original diagram than at any point on the red line in the above left-hand diagram.

Specialisation and trade is something we all do in modern economics. We try to establish that which we are good at (i.e. have a lower opportunity cost), hoping that it is also the thing we really like to do and we embark on specialisation and trade. Then prices change and we discover that we must change career. This, more or less, is the story I have been telling. The only difference between the reality of market economy and the above story is that most agents cannot choose to opt out of the market arrangement. We cannot say that given the change in relative prices which forces us to change career, we choose to leave the market and retire to our little farm where we can conduct a happy autarkic life continuing to do that which we think we are good at while doing other things too.

---

[22] This is not just a matter of intrinsic value; there will be cost to switching if there are skills involved in any specialisation.

This is simply not possible. Therefore, agent 1, in our story, will not really be able to return to his farm and will therefore be, so to speak, forced to enjoy the market benefit at a great personal cost. Can we maintain the argument that agent 1 has remained as sovereign as he was before he entered the market arrangement in the first place? I would content that this is not the case. The individual has lost the command which he used to have over that which he does with most of his time (in terms of work), and though one cannot point the finger at anyone who caused this to him—and therefore, this is not an obvious, or conspicuous, breach of his liberty—he is clearly less free than he was before even though the set of choices in terms of consumption has clearly increased.

From economics' perspective, this is not really an issue. As agents are rational in a way which allows them to substitute one thing for another, the idea of intrinsic value is an anathema.[23] Therefore, there is no breach of freedom in the demand that agent adjust their occupation according to market needs. Work, in these set-ups, is just a means to an end and what it is that one does is of no consequences as long as it generates a larger set of consumption possibilities. But one cannot seriously argue that what one does at work is of no consequences. Yes, he or she may be compensated for a lousy job with high income and may be willing to do a job he likes for less pay but there will always be some price at which the individuals will have to switch. In other words, one's occupation is a matter for the markets to decide. As such, it is one less domain over which a person remains fully sovereign.

There is something about this story which is reminiscent of the social contract theories about social organisation. From Hobbes through Locke to Rousseau, the moment people enter into a social contract they must forgo some of the freedom they enjoyed in the natural state. Similarly, when people become economically dependent on each other and when they enter the market arrangement, they have to forgo some of the freedoms they had before the economic state. In this respect, forgoing the right to fully command one's occupation means that everyone may indeed be less sovereign but as everyone is in the same position, one can evaluate this cost against the benefits to which it gives rise. It is not inconceivable

---

[23] We shall return to this point and the question of rationality in economic analysis in Chap. 7.

that people will say that they would rather lose the right to control what they do in return for material wellbeing. Such a conclusion, however, must be predicated on work being solely a means to an end. As we discussed in the previous chapter, this view is not universally shared and, which is even more important, some of it is the result of the way in which people are educated or, rather, indoctrinated. Put differently, when people enter a social contract they forgo at least one freedom and this is the freedom to hurt the other.[24] It is difficult to compare the 'freedom to hurt the other' with the 'freedom to engage with what one likes'. We can easily understand the former but we'll find it more difficult to defend the latter. The former is a reciprocity rule—we refrain from hurting the other so that they do not hurt us—but there is no reciprocity in the latter. The only reason I am willing to give up the freedom to do that which I would like to do is the promise of something completely different: material wellbeing. It is therefore much less evident that one would want to forgo the freedom to become, or do, that which one wants to be (which is, of course, reminiscent of the capabilities approach) or that forgoing this freedom is indeed a necessity.

Either way, the conclusion according to which people lose some of their sovereignty when they enter the market-based economic arrangement must be recognised. Whether or not this is what von Mises would call a 'natural' restriction depends on whether one views social contract as a natural development. This is, of course, most unlikely and almost a contradiction in terms. Consequently, one cannot really accept the association of markets with freedom or sovereignty. This is a misleading attempt to argue that the fact that people are free to choose from a given set should not be qualified by the nature of the restrictions on this set. Markets, to some extent, are a prison. One cannot choose to opt out of the game unless someone is very wealthy and one is constantly at the mercy of faceless collective of other people. The idea of having an intrinsic purpose in life and pursuing one's dream has been replaced with expediency of the pursuit of that which markets—and, hence, other people—dictate.[25]

---

[24] Clearly what this means depends on the social contract.

[25] One cannot but recall, in this context, Jean-Paul Sartre's famous saying from 'Huis Clos' (1943) that 'hell is other people'.

What is implied by this is that for markets to be associated with any form of freedom there has to be a way in which individuals have an option to reject that which the market offers. But for this to happen, they must have means for economic survival which are independent of their actions. This may be provided either by a distribution of ownership such that individuals can derive enough income from their share in assets so that they can choose to do in life that which they feel they should, or by providing them with some form of a universal income. Both of these methods suggest a non-market mechanism of allocation and distribution. In such a case, what would be the purpose of the market in the first place?

4.2   Markets, Justice and the Idea of Due Share

The fact that markets are not really synonymous with freedom may be a disappointment but it is not enough to completely undermine the ethical support for it. Yes, in the face of the failures of markets to deliver a solution to the economic problem in a manner which is ethically neutral, it would be nice if we could promote markets for their ethical qualities. But freedom alone is not the complete story and it would have been very difficult to construct an ethical support for markets on this basis alone. As we have seen in our discussion, freedom is a complex and, to some extent, elusive concept. Some may even argue that the limitations we have enumerated in the previous section are not enough to discredit the association of freedom with market as any other form of economic organisation is bound to introduce an even greater number of man-made constraints which would have meant much less freedom, or sovereignty, than the ones provided by the markets.[26]

But even if it were true that we could say that markets can be associated with a considerable degree of freedom, this would still not be enough to make the moral case for markets. While freedom is clearly an important element of any ethical theory, so is justice. Freedom is about our ability to act and be what we want, while ethics is primarily about the

---

[26] One of the best expressions of this position can be found in Hayek (1944).

evaluation of what we are and what we do. Surely an ethical theory which sets out the criteria for freedom must also provide the criteria for its evaluation: namely, what is good and what is right (the latter, clearly, is the domain of justice).

As we suggested earlier, the relationship between freedom and justice are complex; the former is about the licence to be and do things and the latter is about their restrictions. But this does not mean that the two are contradictory. Indeed, if we look at the two extreme expressions of the concepts across the epistemological divide, we will find, on the one hand, the libertarian approach (say, Nozick)—which is based on extreme methodological individualism—according to which freedom is justice, and, on the other hand, at the metaphysical collective extreme (say, Hegel) justice is freedom.[27] In between these two extremes, things are bound to be more balanced as well as complex. In terms of the economic discourse such problems may arise when one argues, for instance, about redistribution. Is taxation a restriction on individuals' freedom which is explained by the need to uphold justice (say, equality)? The answers to such a question very much depend on the kind of ethics one is employing. For a libertarian, there can be no justice in taxation, while for a follower of Marx there can be no justice in the freedom of capital owners to command the surplus value created by the workers. Capabilities approach too is a case in point. Capabilities is about the freedom to be or do that which one has *reason to value*, but to achieve such freedom there would be a need to provide individuals with the means to achieve this (and that, in turn, will depend on what one means by: that which people have *reason to value*).[28]

Therefore, it is evident that simply saying that markets uphold a degree of freedom cannot be perceived as sufficiently broad an ethical justification for it. Yes, if one is a libertarian, this may be enough as justice will be

---

[27] Dyde (1894) writes about Hegel's conception of freedom and correctly points out the need to distinguish between psychological and moral freedom. Accordingly, Hegel's conception is very much within the domain of being morally free: 'Indeed, complete moral freedom implies that within the reach of his volition must be not only a general good, but the ultimate good, however that may be defined' (p. 656). In simple terms this means that doing the right thing (that which is just) is the ultimate expression of individual's moral freedom.

[28] This, of course, is reminiscent of J. S. Mill's approach towards human development and individuality which we mentioned earlier.

entailed in freedom. But even on the side of methodological individualism this is not the only form of justice theory. It is enough to reflect on Rawls (1973) and the difference principle to contemplate the possibility that justice and freedom may not necessarily be the same thing. Consequently, one must endeavour to provide a broader ethical defence of market and this could be done by showing that it is an institution that upholds some basic and common notions of justice.

4.2.1 Justice as Due Share (Desert)

Justice, like freedom, is an incredibly complex concept about which there is monumental literature and competing ways of thinking. Nevertheless, like freedom, and in particular in the economic context, there are simpler, well-defined and quite widespread conceptions of it. People will always have an opinion, or an intuitive way of thinking, about what justice may mean, and even though a conception of justice should be a more sophisticated expression of human intellect and examination, it stands to reason that there should be some correspondence between the loftier way of thinking about it and the more prevalent way in which the public views the concept.

I do not think that it would be farfetched to claim that one of the most immediate and common conception of justice is the idea of desert, or due share.[29] We always expect people to get that which they deserve. Naturally,

---

[29] The ancient Greek word for justice is 'Δίκη' (dike), which originally meant 'due share' (see Spengler 1980, p. 79 for further elaboration). 'Due share', referred to by Δίκη, meant first of all the distribution of fate (Μοῖραι-Moirae), which, in other words, is strongly related to people's character (what they are) within the framework of some kind of a godly design. Later, this Homeric notion was transferred to the 'city state'. Both Plato and Aristotle saw the concept of justice as arising from a similar notion of 'due share' even though it was now confined to the framework of the 'city state' and its general governing laws. But while this notion of due share is based on what people are, in Aristotle there is already a distinction between due share emanating from personal virtues and that which is due to human action. In his case, this distinction was mostly felt in the distinction which he draws between distributive and rectificatory (or corrective) justice (Nic. Eth. V, 1131b14 1132a2). The former is based on one's qualities as a member of society, while the latter is focused on the outcome of voluntary (and non-voluntary) actions like exchange. Johnston (2011) claims that even at the distributive justice level the position was that of contribution-based desert rather than virtue-based desert: 'Aristotle's theory of distributive justice appears to be underpinned by a version of what later came to be called the contribution principle, which states

what it means to be deserving and what it is that one should get are much less obvious notions but it is still the case that most people would consider some form of reciprocity as a key to the idea of justice; they would consider a world where people systematically do not get that which they appear to deserve as an unjust world. Already in the Old Testament, the complaint about the unjust reality of the world is expressed in precisely these terms: the righteous suffers; the wicked prospers. In other words, the fundamental injustice we observer in the world is that where people do not get what they deserve.

But while some notions of desert or reciprocity may lie at the heart of the conception of justice, the idea itself may go well beyond this. There have indeed been many competing manifestations of the idea of justice, although in some sense there is an element of due share, or desert, in all of them. We already mentioned a libertarian position according to which justice is embedded in liberty. In such a case, if we all have similar initial conditions and everything we do from that point onwards is voluntary, then there is no justice other than the freedom to choose how to act. Whatever outcome such a system generates, it is consistent with justice even if, under some arithmetic, people do not get what they may consider to be their due share in the end. But even here, the expectation that there should be some equity (or rather, equality) in the initial state is already an idea of due share as the presumption is that given an equitable start, whatever we end up with, is entirely due to our own behaviour (hence, our due reward). It is, in a sense, the idea that whenever you act freely, you always reap that which you deserve.

At the other extreme there is egalitarianism which is more concerned with equality between people than with that which makes them different. However, here too, one must quickly qualify this statement as whether due share and equality are related conception of justice depends on what we mean by equality. If all people are deemed to be the same and if it is what they are which is the object of being deserving, then equality of outcome means exactly the same thing as due share. In other words, egalitarian principles—whether with regard to initial allocations or final dis-

---

(roughly) that it is just for people to reap rewards from a common enterprise that are proportional in value to the contributions they have made to that enterprise' (p. 71).

tribution—always entail a notion of due share which is based on what people are rather than on what they do. This continues to be the case even if we move further along the path from the extreme of freedom as justice to the extreme of justice as freedom. At the economic expression of this end, which may be demonstrated through the communist manifesto, we find ideals where everyone contributes according to their abilities and receives according to their needs. While this appears to completely disassociate desert from the conception of justice, this is not entirely so. It is evident that there should be no connection here between what people do and what they get, but the fact that they should receive things according to their need suggests a principle of due share, though this is not based on who they are or what they do but, rather, on what they need.

Indeed, when we talk about desert, in the broadest manner possible, we mean something along the line that 'A deserves x', where A is an object of morality (i.e. humans) and x can either be an action or a good. Hence, to derive the explicit theory of justice one would first need to explore the question of what makes A deserving; is it the fact that A is a human being? Is it because A has certain individual, moral or social qualities? Is it because A has certain collectively determined needs? Or is it because A has done something? Secondly, there is the question of why is x that which A deserves? What relationship might there be between x and the reason why A deserves it[30]? If someone steals bread, should x be a prison sentence? Should the person work in the bakery without any remuneration? Alternatively, if A acted in a way that produced x, can we be sure that A is responsible for x or were other factors involved too? Thirdly, and related to the second issue, is the question of how x stands in relation to A. In other words, if we discuss the case of stealing and prison, how long a sentence should someone get for stealing[31]? It is therefore not at all surprising that given this broad framework it is very difficult to escape from the principle of desert when we talk about justice and that the differences in the conceptions of justice are really differences in interpreting this kind of a statement.

---

[30] This is sometime referred to as the problem of responsibility.

[31] There are, of course, many more issues associated with understanding desert as an ethical concept. Not least is the question of whether desert—even as an ethical concept—is a concept of justice. Olsaretti (2003) provides a good anthology of the various aspects of this debate.

However, from our perspective—the point of view of markets and justice (or economic justice)—we are interested in something far less general and much better defined. We ask the question of whether within markets: 'A, who participated in causing x through his, or her, action, deserves a share of x' (where A is an economic actor and x is an economic good). In other words, we are interested in the question of whether competitive decentralisation respects some form of the principle of desert when it is applied to **actions** (i.e. what people do) rather than to **what people are**.[32] After all, what the market does is that for a given initial allocation of assets, abilities and taste, it produces a final distribution of economic goods through human interactions. Therefore, the question about whether markets themselves uphold the principle of justice must be confined to this process alone, the process where people act (based on their initial conditions) and receive something at the end of the process. It is therefore clear in this formulation who the desert- base is and why x is the subject of desert, though it may not be clear how much of x is due to A's action and whether or not this is a question of justice which needs to be enforced.

In as much as x may be due to the action of A, we must also bear in mind that though the economic system is that of human interactions, some inputs to the process which produces x may come from other means of production (like capital or land). This means that the question of the desert base may not be as straightforward as one would suppose. The share which, for instance, A's labour may have in producing x will, in part, depend on the nature of the claim which capital and land can make over the outcome of their collective endeavours. But as neither capital nor land are in themselves an object of morality, the question of legitimacy of ownership may impose some restrictions on the level of x due to A's labour. Nevertheless, even if the arguments legitimising ownership of land and capital are based on different principles from desert, this does not alter the role of desert in the examination of how markets allocate the product of human actions. The question of ownership may alter the initial condition and affect the proportionality of one's direct contribution

---

[32] By focusing on desert which is based on actions rather than individual character, we circumvent a great deal of the criticism which was levied against 'desert-based' conceptions of justice. When people are deserving because of the morality of their character, we run into immense difficulties of (a) identifying such characters and (b) arguing that they have a particular claim to things.

to the production of x, but this will still leave the question open about whether the individual who contributed to the production of x receives at the end of the process the share in this output which could be identified as proportional to his or her contribution.

Therefore, as markets are the arenas of human actions, we suggest that the concept of economic justice against which one should examine whether markets uphold the basic principle of justice is the concept of desert where the reason for deserving is what people do rather than who, or what, they are. In this respect, we propose here that the criterion of equality is not relevant to our investigation but not because we do not consider the question of equality as important to economic justice. It is because equality is, in a sense, a desert theory which is based on what people are, or what they may universally need as human beings and, therefore, is confined to the questions of initial or final distributions. Namely, whatever views we may have about the nature of the initial or the final distribution, this will be something for society to achieve through some forms of reallocation or redistribution. However, the question we are interested in is whether the process which leads from any initial allocation to a final distribution—a process which is characterised by actions of individuals who only differ in what they do rather than in who they are—fulfils a criterion of economic justice which should be relevant to the analysis of actions and interactions.

Evidently, what people are, may have an influence on the effects of what they do. Namely, if two individuals put the same amount of effort at work but one is naturally more capable than the other, the effects of their effort could be different. Indeed, Knight (1921) was extremely critical of the use of desert in the ethical evaluation of competitive systems because of this very reason (pp. 114–115). But we are asking a far more basic question as we are only interested in what people do irrespective of what they are: if all individuals were the same, would the differences in their contributions (say, level of effort whichever way we measure it) be reflected in their rewards. In other words, if the only thing which distinguishes one individual from another is the amount of effort they put, the idea of contribution-based desert will be the only concept of justice which is relevant. If markets satisfy this principle, we argue, one could uphold

the idea of competitive decentralisation for its compliance with basic justice. Naturally, whether or not society wishes to deal with natural differences in what people are as part of the pursuit of justice, this will have to
be a matter for either initial or final distributions. Markets, in such a case,
will not be an obstacle for justice. However, if we find that even when all
people are the same in their natural abilities but offer differential contributions and the market rewards them inversely to their contribution,
whatever we think of the natural differences between individuals, market
will become an obstacle of justice rather than a facilitator.

There is indeed a wealth of evidence to suggest that the idea of justice
as desert, in the sense of rewarding that which people do rather than that
which they are, is far more dominant in human thought and intuition.
Miller (1992, 1996) provides a summary of empirical evidence regarding
what people conceive the concept of justice to be. In line of what we said
earlier, he looks at the competing categories of 'need', 'desert' and 'equality'. It is true that they are all forms of desert according to the general
theory but in this case, 'desert' is the category referring to rewarding
actions rather than what people are, which is what lies at the heart of
equality and need. What is interesting is that he finds that desert (according to what people do) is, perhaps, the notion of justice most people
identify with more easily.

In confronting desert with equality, 78% of respondents to a survey
agree that '[u]nder a fair economic system, people with more ability
would earn higher salaries' (McClosky and Zaller 1984, p. 84). Also,
71% agreed that it is fairer to pay people according to how hard they
worked. With the help of other surveys Miller reaches the conclusion that
'we can say that when faced with a relatively simple choice between
equally and unequal distribution of income in society, the great majority
of people—70 percent or more—opt for the in-egalitarian position …
[t]he reasons given appear to amalgamate desert, incentives, and beliefs
about human nature' (Miller 1992, p. 565).

Some may see in these results a justification for the inequality which is
generated by market systems and an argument against redistribution.
However, this would be a misinterpretation of these results. To begin
with, there is a difference between asking a specific question about

whether one should be rewarded for greater effort and asking a more general question about society. One may wish for effort to be rewarded but this does not preclude that one may wish to see the needs of all members of society being dealt with as well. The two principles do not contradict each other but they will have an inevitable effect on the share in output that desert claims may command.

Secondly, there is the question of whether actual distributions really correspond to one's idea of desert. Namely, while people may think that effort and education should be rewarded, the economic system may produce inequalities which are inconsistent with this principle. Hence, the view according to which the public believes desert to be a principle of economic justice should not be confused with a defence of existing unequal distributions. Indeed, in one of the surveys, 76% of responders claimed that the 'differences in pay between the highly paid and the lowly paid are too great' (Miller 1992, p. 568). In another, 57% thought that 'effort to make everyone as equal as possible should be increased' (ibid.).

In confronting 'need' with 'desert', surveys produce an interesting picture. When asked to choose between basing income on skills and training or on family needs, 81% opted for the former (Kluegel and Smith 1986). At the same time, however, 'people believe … that a society's public arrangements should ensure that needs are met, and there is reasonable agreement about what we can count as need' (Miller 1992, p. 574).

To some degree, the apparent confusion between desert (according to actions) and principles like equality or fulfilment of needs is based on the fact that the surveys do not make a distinction between the various components of the system. One can desire to see an initial allocation of resources so that all agents are capable of fulfilling their needs (and if they are all the same, this will also mean equality); this is a statement about the stock (or wealth). At the same time, one could equally be concerned to see people—who have been ethically equated at the initial allocations—rewarded in proportion to their actual contribution while being in the system. In a world where the distribution of wealth is more or less equal, it is unlikely that some income inequality which may be due to differences in abilities or contribution to output will lead to a large number of people finding themselves unable to fulfil their needs.

There is more evidence in support of the centrality of desert, which is based on what people do rather than what they are in Marshall, G., A. Swift, D. Routh and C. Burgoyne (1999). More recently one can find evidence in experimental economics. Rustichini, Aldo and Alexander Vostroknutov (2014) conduct an experiment where individuals are invited to subtract income from another agent's return in different set-ups where in one case the differences in return are luck based and, in another, effort based. They conclude: 'First, when individuals evaluate differences in outcomes they take into account the origin of the inequality, what caused it or affected it, and adjust their evaluation accordingly. A difference in earnings entirely due to luck is regarded in a completely different way from one due to a combination of skill and effort. Individuals attach merit to an outcome when it is due to skill, and do not when it is due to luck. Thus, the concepts of moral desert and justice are deeply connected, and one needs the other for a proper definition.' Also, Kristjánsson (2017) makes the argument for the centrality of contribution-based desert theories as the key concept of justice in the mind of individuals.

Interestingly, in a study by Alesina et al. (2001) they find similar evidence, which is not based on experimentation, according to which there seems to be a positive correlation between the belief about income distribution being determined by luck and the desire to see more public spending (i.e. redistribution); namely, people would support redistribution if they think that the reason why there are income differentials are not based on merit. They find, for instance, that in countries like Denmark, the Netherlands or Germany, where social spending is relatively high (as percentage of GDP), the belief that luck determines income is also high. Whereas in countries like the USA or Canada such beliefs are low and, therefore, the level of social spending as percentage of GDP is also relatively low.[33]

---

[33] The data in the study is based on average of public spending as a percentage of GDP between 1960 and 1998 and the question of luck is based on the WVS with data between 1981 and 1997.

The causality here is not very clear but there is something about this evidence which suggests that people support redistributive policies—or the correction of income distributions—when they believe that the outcome of economic activities is a matter of luck. Luck, most definitely, seems to mean that the reward which individuals receive bears no relationship to what they do.

One can also learn something by looking at more recent evidence from the World Value Surveys (WVS). Individuals were given a situation where two secretaries are doing the same task but one of them puts more effort and is, therefore, paid more. They were asked whether they thought this to be fair. The worldwide respond suggests that an overwhelming majority considers this to be a fair situation, which means that the conception of contribution-based desert is widely perceived—across cultures—as an intuitive conception of justice:

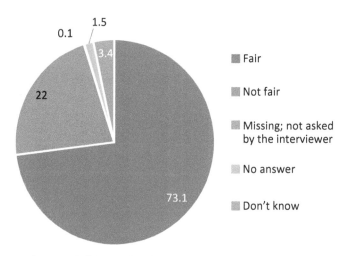

Paying more for greater effort: worldwide

Source: WVS (2005–2009)

Even though there are some anomalies (like Argentina and India), the percentage of those considering such an act to be fair is always greater than those who consider it to be unfair. Nevertheless, it is important to emphasise here that what is clearly implied about contribution-based desert in this survey is a desert which is based only on what people do assuming all other things being equal.

As we hinted before, we must accept that conception of justice, though based on strong intuition, is also influenced by the intellectual environment within which individuals live. Therefore, one would expect that in Anglo-Saxon countries, which tend to be more individualistic, the support for such a principle of justice would be greater than in Continental European economies where collective ideas have had a greater influence on public discourse:

Source: WVS (2005–2009)

Going back to the complete data base and by way of consistency and corroboration one can see that the same individuals are distinctly less keen on equality as a key concept which should determine the distribution of income:

Views on income distribution

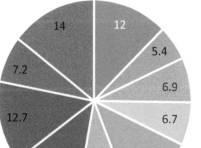

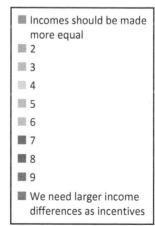

Source: WVS (2005–2009)

The scale goes from 1 (income should be made more equal) to 10 (we need large inequality as incentives), which means that between 1 and 4 we have those committed to equality and between 6 and 10 those committed to inequality. It is easy to see that those committed to equality form only 31% of the respondents while those committed to inequality form more than 50% of respondents.

There are a few observations one must make in this connection. Firstly, the wording of incentives in point 10 would have influenced respondents in the sense that it is now less evident that they support inequality because of the principle of desert or because of expediency. Secondly, while it is true that less support for equality may mean that in the mind of the public, contribution-based desert is a far more dominant principle of justice, this does not mean that they believe that the market produces an inequality which is consistent with this principle. After all, inequalities may arise because of differences in contribution but may also arise for other reasons which could be orthogonal to the idea of just desert.[34] Moreover, as we said before, support for contribution-based desert does not preclude the care for the others and the desire for income distribution to reflect some inequality but within a certain reasonable interval.

There are two pieces of evidence which strengthen this point of view. If we look at the 2010–2014 WVS cycle, we will find that the views about equality have somewhat changed. Of course, we must note that between the 2005–2009 wave and the 2010–2014 wave the world has gone through the 2008 financial crisis and its pronounced distributional aftermath. Had the support of contribution-based desert been independent of any other factor, we should have seen a similar distribution of responded to the question about income inequality. But this is not what we get:

---

[34] Namely, that differential reward is morally desirable only when people are of equal natural abilities (or their equivalence) but differ in their efforts contribution.

Views on income distribution (2014)

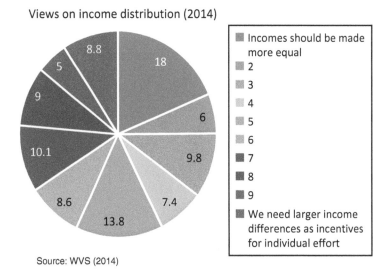

Source: WVS (2014)

Those who think that there should be greater equality now form 41.2% (as opposed to 31% in 2005–2009), while those who lean towards greater inequality stand on 41.5% (as opposed to over 50% in 2005–2009). I do not think that this suggests a change of heart with regard to the centrality of contribution-based desert (the secretary test was not conducted in this wave). Instead, it may be a reflection of the lack of confidence which people have developed with regard to the ability of markets to produce an income distribution where inequalities will reflect just deserts. Instead, they have noticed a world where those responsible for the crisis were unaffected by it, while those who had nothing to do with it were seriously affected. The fact that the swing was not greater is, perhaps, an indication of the strength of the belief in the contribution-based desert as a principle of justice.

The second piece of information may be seen as evidence of the mistrust that the public has towards the ability of the market to provide the right inequalities. When people were asked whether they think that in a democracy governments should tax the rich and subsidise the poor, the following answers were obtained:

Tax the rich and subsidise the poor

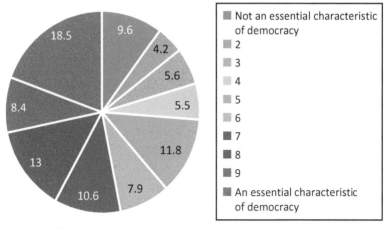

Source: WVS (2014)

Those who are definitely against taxing the rich and subsidising the poor (1–4) form only 24.9% of respondents and well above 58.4% are supportive of this (choosing 6–10). Under no circumstances should this be seen as a rejection of the contribution-based desert as a principle of justice. It is more likely to be a cry against the nature of the inequality which markets develop rather than a statement about how it should be. In other words, this piece of evidence, together with the previous ones, suggests that what it is that people consider to be a contribution-based desert is the one to which we have been referring to all along: a differential reward for people who only differ in their actions. By demanding a transfer of income from rich to the poor, the public desires for the population to be more equal in its initial conditions. If this happens, one can be more confident that the contribution-based desert will not be affected by criticism that the difference in contribution is the result of the differences between what people are rather than what they do.

Indeed, one further piece of evidence which should persuade us that the principle of contribution-based desert has not been abandoned even during the time of discontent with the way the economic system operates is the attitude which the public has towards receiving income without any contribution. In both waves, individuals were asked whether they thought it justifiable (and, hence, a moral issue) to claim benefits from the government. The results were as follows:

Claiming benefits from the government
(2005–2009)

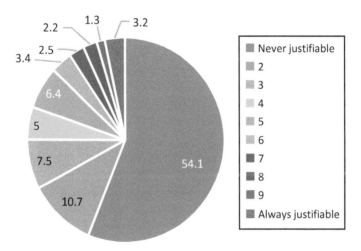

Claiming benefits from the government
(2010–2014)

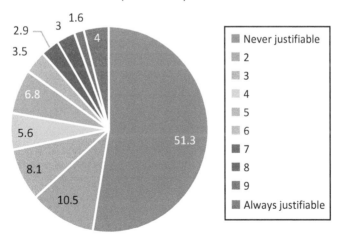

In 2005–2009, the wave in which individual clearly declared their belief in the contribution-based desert (the case of the secretary), those who leaned towards the never justifiable (1–4) made up 77.3%. It is enough to look at the percentage of those who were categorically opposed to this (never justifiable) (54.1%) to feel that the conclusion about the centrality of contribution-based desert is the right one. Now, in the wake of the crisis and the shaking of beliefs in the market, we see that in spite of a desire for greater equality and the wish to tax the rich and subsidise the poor, the public still thinks that it is wrong to receive income not in return for work. In the 2010–2014 cycle those who were adamant against the idea of unearned income fell from 54.1% to 51.3%. Those who leaned towards the 'never justifiable' (1–4) made up 75.5% (a fall from 77.3%).

In summary, there seems to be considerable evidence that the principle of contribution-based desert—based purely on what people do rather than what they are—is an intuitive conception of justice. We can learn this from the case of the secretary and the overall rejection of the idea of unearned income. However, this does not mean that (a) they may not be other considerations which the public may deem important and which may influence their views on income distribution (namely, they believe in contribution-based desert but within some reasonable levels of inequality); and (b) they consider the market as the mechanism which does produce the outcome one would expect according to the principle of contribution-based desert.

But not only in the mind of the public is *contribution-based desert* an important principle of justice, its place in the history of ethics—and in particular in that which may be relevant to economics—is quite prominent too. From Aristotle in Antiquity through St Thomas of Aquinas in the Middle Ages, Leibnitz, Locke, Hume and Smith during the Enlightenment to Spencer and J. S. Mill in the nineteenth century, the idea that justice is closely associated with some notion of a desert which is proportional to contribution has been quite prominent.[35]

---

[35] To properly survey this literature would require a separate volume. Here I am merely making the point that what seems to be the public intuition today has probably been around for a long time as it influenced (and has probably been influenced by) the more philosophical deliberations. The only point which I would like to make here is that while desert-based justice appeared in all these schol-

With the rise of the distinctly teleological Utilitarianism during the nineteenth century (which is also the origin of the Welfarist approach to values in economics), attention has shifted away from contribution-based desert, which is in essence more deontological in nature. However, we must emphasise that the criticism of desert theories of justice from the utilitarian perspective (in particular, Sidgwick (1907)[36]), as well as the egalitarian one (in particular, Rawls (1973)) has been mainly aimed at desert theories which assume people to be deserving for the virtues of their character (i.e. what they are) rather than because of what they do.

It is true that Rawls—taking his cue from Knight (1935)—appears also to argue explicitly against contribution-based desert when he explains his critique of desert which is based on moral virtue but his argument, I fear, is rather flawed. Rawls claims that if a person is deserving because of his or her moral virtue, then that which they deserve should be invariant of other considerations. This, of course, is quite straightforward. He then goes on to demonstrate this point by claiming that a competitive economy distributes income according to the principle of contribution (i.e. marginal product). However, the marginal product of, say, a worker, depends on how many people of similar quality take part in the market

---

ars, it has not always been about contribution-based desert. In Aristotle, as we mentioned in a previous footnote, both notions of moral virtue-based desert and action-based desert appear within his distinction between distributive and corrective justice. St Thomas of Aquinas, who tended more towards the virtue-based desert, still recognised the contribution-based desert through his commentary on Aristotle's analysis of exchange. He says there: 'In order to have just exchange, as many sandals must be exchanges for one house ... as the builder ... exceeds the shoemaker in his labour and cost' (CNE V ix, p. 426). This very basic form of a labour theory of value (which is also repeated in Adam Smith) implicitly supposes that the only difference between the individuals is the labour input rather than anything about their natural abilities or moral virtue. Leibnitz was definitely about contribution-based desert but as the contribution was broadly conceived, it would be something which is difficult to measure and, therefore, lends itself more easily to virtue. He says in his *Ultimate Origin of Things* (1697): 'There couldn't be a better standard in this matter than the *law of justice*, which lays down that everyone is to participate in the perfection of the universe, and to have personal happiness, in proportion to his own virtue and to the extent that his will will have contributed to the common good' (p. 353). But from Locke onwards, the role of a well-defined contribution as the base for desert and justice has been better established. In Locke and Hume, a lot has to do with property rights, and in Hume the reason is not even deontological but rather the usefulness of the idea. But in Smith, Spencer and Mill, the idea seems more akin to contemporary public opinion where desert is clearly a contribution-based idea.

[36] Though one must hasten to say that he would not have objected to this had contribution-based desert been a question of expediency (Sidgwick 1907, p. 280). This, of course, is similar to Hume's position, though I would argue against reading him as a utilitarian.

(supply) and the level of demand. Therefore, he concludes, the worth of the worker (measured in his contribution) varies as demand and supply change, which contradicts the presumption that they are deserving because of their invariant moral value (Rawls 1973, pp. 310–311). In other words, his claim seems to be that desert based on moral virtues is not a good theory because contribution is not really related to what people are.

However, the fallacy in this argument rests on the presumption that marginal product is indeed a measure of contribution and that the reason why people may be deserving is their moral virtue. If the reason why people are deserving is only their contribution rather than their intrinsic moral value, it stands to reason that what they deserve, or the value of their contribution, should not be invariant to circumstances. A writer who writes with pen and paper may have a different contribution—in an hour's work—if he used a computer. If the market rewards him by the value of his contribution, then his rewards will be different in the two different circumstances. But this is what it should be in a contribution-based desert theory and it does not make the claim that he should always receive the value of his contribution, logically inconsistent.

Rawls is probably right when he criticises the idea that a competitive economy which distributes income according to the principle of marginal product is generating an income distribution which is consistent with the principle of desert-based justice. He is certainly right if by desert-based justice he refers to desert which is based on moral virtue. But he would not have been right if by desert-based justice he refers to contribution-based desert unless he accepts that marginal product is not really a measure of contribution. In such a case, the problem will be the way in which we measure contribution and not the principle of contribution-based desert.

As we said earlier, Knight (1921, 1935) had a much more effective criticism in claiming that the problem of contribution-based desert is that it ignores initial conditions which may affect the value of the contribution and, in this respect, conflate that which people are with the outcome of that which they do. However, in saying this he too is ignoring the fact that in contribution-based desert analysis it may be possible to disentangle that which people are from that which they do. Exactly as in criminal law the verdict of guilty or not is independent of what people are but the punishment will take their character and initial conditions into account; in social justice we should also be able to distinguish between the desire to reward people by their contribution and the desire to ensure that they all have equivalent initial conditions.

Indeed, recently, there has been a renewed interest in contribution-based desert either directly (see, for instance, Feinberg (1970) and Olsaretti (2003)) or indirectly through developments, among egalitarians, in the discussion of responsibility as a criterion for redistribution or inequality (see, for instance, Arneson (1989, 1990), Cohen (1989, 1993) and Fleurbaey (2008)). This latter approach is effectively attempting to deal with the problem of disentangling that which is due to people's actions and that which is due to their initial conditions.

In any case, having established that in spite of its complexities and pitfalls desert-based justice is a widely held and recognised opinion, it is important to remind the reader that our concern in this chapter is a much more limited and well-defined problem. It is the question of whether markets—as a process of allocation and distribution—constitute a system which can be described as just so that one could advocate it even if it does not provide the desired solution to the economic problem or the promised ethical neutrality. We are therefore not interested here in the question of whether it is possible to correct markets' outcomes so that they would be consistent with some broader ethical principles about the nature of the final distribution. Instead, we are asking whether, given some initial just conditions (say, that all individuals have the same initial conditions), the market system would uphold the widely held view that people should be rewarded for their actions.

Therefore, in the context of markets we are only interested in the interactions and outcomes between people who are, in all other respects, considered as equal. Both contemporary public opinion and the history of ethics suggest that if it were possible to draw a clear causal relationship between a person's action and the outcome, and assuming that all individuals are motivated by the same reason, it would be just for people to reap the fruits of their actions. Indeed, in the market place of modern economics, all individuals are equally driven by the desire to better their conditions and there is nothing in their characters which allows us to distinguish between them. Therefore, the question of reward is entirely independent of the virtues, or lack of them, of the participants.

4.2.2 Desert and Markets in Modern Economics

Perhaps the first thing one must observe is that in spite of the appeal and dominance of the idea of contribution-based desert, it seemed to have played no role at all in the ethical and social debates surrounding modern economics. In part, of course, this was due to the deeply entrenched belief in economics' paradigmatic core which promised, among other things, ethical neutrality. But this would have explained the limited interest which people had in the moral significance of modern economics and not the absence of a particular aspect of moral analysis.

Indeed, most of the time, from the social or the moral perspective, the issues at hand were either the outcomes or the initial conditions but hardly ever the process through which the economy transits from one to the other which is, in fact, the real business of economics. Already Walras, who lays the foundation for the modern conception of how market operates in his theory of general equilibrium, draws a distinction between the working of the economy and the application of moral or social values to it.[37] He provides an exclusive study of economic interactions in his *Elements of Pure Economics* but proposes a separate and external study of the moral or social dimension of economic analysis in his much less known *Etude d'Economie Sociale*. What is interesting about this offering is that it is, in many respects, non-interventionist in the sense that it offers to deal with moral and social issues without commenting on the morality or social value of the way the economy operates. Hence, in the *Etude d'Economie Sociale* Walras proposes, among other things, public ownership of land which would provide society with redistributive powers without interfering or commenting on the way in which the economy generates the outcomes.[38]

---

[37] See his discussion in lesson 2 of the *Elements of Pure Economics*.

[38] This position whereby one addresses the problem of social justice without opposing private property which is a key component of the decentralised system, by making everyone own property

Later, throughout the twentieth century, social and moral perspectives on economic analysis have been confined to what became to be known as *Welfare Economics*.[39] Like Walras, the main concern was the correction of distributions which arise from economic interactions but unlike him there was a willingness to interfere in the system (through taxes and subsidies) even at some efficiency cost. However, here too, no questions have been asked about whether the process of economic interactions itself is violating any social or ethical principles.

The obsession with correcting the consequences of economics interaction was probably the result of the influence which Utilitarianism—a consequentialist ethical theory—had had on economic analysis. The search for alternative methods of moral evaluation has, almost naturally, led to increased interest in economic justice.[40] However, while the move from the teleological to the more deontological idea of justice has somewhat led to a broadening of interest in the desire to correct not only final distributions but also initial allocations, it has not really increased the interest in the actual process of economic interactions. It is as if it became obvious that if we correct either the initial allocation or the final distribution, then there can be nothing morally wrong with the working of markets.

To some extent, one may argue that if markets depict a natural phenomenon which we can continuously repair to fit our moral and social expectations, then there cannot be anything wrong with it. But while the shift from initial allocation to final distributions through the analysis of markets is a useful way of thinking about the world, the reality is that

---

(collective ownership of land) has also been promoted by Henry George in the USA (see a discussion of this influence in Cirillo (1984)).

[39] Welfare economics, as was stated before, in most general terms, can be defined as the theory which aims at *correcting* the outcomes of economic interaction without questioning its nature. Originally, in Pigou's *The Economics of Welfare* (1920), the need to correct the outcomes arose from the apparent inefficiency of the competition in the presence of externalities. Then, in the wake of the first and second welfare theorems it was all about correcting the system according to social values determined through the most elusive of concepts: the social welfare function. Sen (1970) was perhaps the only example of an attempt to question something more fundamental (the relationship between the idea of Pareto-efficiency and ethical ideas like liberalism) but this did not seem to have gained any grounds.

[40] Rawls (1973) was quite instrumental in generating these changes. In his two principles he addresses both the initial allocation (equal opportunity) and the final distribution (the difference principle).

people are always in the process and never really at either ends of the economic process. Therefore, if we knew that in the process of exchange there are some individuals who are always humiliated but we continuously compensate them for their humiliation, would we have to review the question of whether or not they are actually humiliated?

By way of contrast, ethical evaluations of economic systems prior to the modern and neoclassical era have been almost entirely confined to the process of economic interaction. The basic idea—since at least Aristotle—had been that an economic system is where people who are **dependent on each other** interact. The fact that they are dependent on each other means that one cannot really look at it as a purely voluntary exchange as, on many occasions, people have no choice but to engage in such interactions.[41]

When two self-sufficient individuals meet and discover that the other has something which they may want but could do without it, their interaction cannot really be the object of moral scrutiny as each one of them is sufficiently sovereign to make his own calculations about whether it is in his, or her, interest to go ahead with the exchange at any given conditions. They cannot really be described as interdependent. However, when individuals find themselves in a position where they have to specialise in producing one good only but are nevertheless in need of the other, they are, in a sense, completely dependent on the other. By choosing to specialise they are giving up some of their sovereignty. This is particularly so if they have no option of withdrawing and taking care of their own needs by themselves. In such an event, the interaction between the two individuals is not entirely voluntary and, therefore, as it means that the two agents may not be entirely equivalent in their trading position (one may be in slightly more desperate a need than the other), the potential for taking advantage of one another becomes an issue.[42] Therefore, the terms in which they make the exchange (which is the economic process) is the object of moral examination irrespective of anything else including the final distribution of goods which will emerge between the two individuals. The fact that trading and markets may be considered as a natural

---

[41] This corresponds to our discussion about the reduced sovereignty which individuals who choose to specialise face when they have no option of withdrawing from the game.

[42] Just, to Aristotle, means lawful and fair (Nic. Eth. Book V, 1129a21 b6), and fairness means not to take advantage of another, which, in other words, means not taking more than one's share.

phenomenon is not a reason not to contain, or limit, it if proven to be morally unacceptable.

Thus, all the way from Aristotle through St Thomas of Aquinas to the classical era, key scholars who wrote about economics were concerned with the ethical values of such an exchange. In other words, an important aspect of their moral examination seemed to have been the notion of a just exchange (expressed in terms of a 'just price') even if there were other aspects of justice to be considered. Almost invariably, the notion of the just price seemed to correspond to a notion of exchange which reflects the relative difficulties of making (or obtaining) the goods regardless of whether the people involved have differences in initial wealth or the distributional consequences of these prices.[43] In this respect, it is clearly an expression of the principle of contribution-based desert.

However, the proportionality of the price to the relative difficulty of producing goods does not necessarily tell us much about whose difficulty is involved, which could, in principle, raise problems for the question of contribution-based desert. In early days when labour was almost exclusively the means of production, the connection could not have been more obvious. But when the circumstances of production expand, the problem becomes more complex. Indeed, a good example of how a transition takes place from the basic concept of a just price reflecting immediate and direct relative difficulties to a more subtle relationship between price and due share can be found in the writings of Adam Smith. In his famous example of the hunt for deer and beaver, Smith clearly suggests that the ethical exchange between a deer and a beaver should reflect the hours it takes to hunt the two. Hence, if it takes two hours to hunt a deer and four hours to hunt a beaver, they should exchange two deer per beaver.[44] It

---

[43] There is a question here with regard to why prices which reflect relative difficulty of attainment correspond to the idea of contribution-based desert. If we consider the exchange of one unit of two goods, then if the contribution of hours in the production of one is greater than the other, the product of the greater contribution should command more of the product of a smaller contribution. Namely, we are not looking at how much an hour produces but we are looking at it from the point of view of the level of contribution per unit of the good. We shall say more about it further below.

[44] See Young (1986). We will return to the question of ethical pricing in our longer discussion of the classical perspective in Chap. 8.

means that the goods should exchange according to the relative contribution of those who bring them to market.

However, Adam Smith moved well beyond such a labour theory of value as he recognised that when there is more than one means of production involved in the process of producing a good, the question of just, or ethical, price reflecting the principle of desert is less tractable. Nevertheless, he did form a more general conception of the just price which reflects a broader conception of the principle of contribution-based desert. One expression of Smith's exasperation with the way market operates appears when he complains that those who do all the work (the labourers) get the lowest share of the product. Consequently, his notion of the just price, encapsulated in his conception of the natural price, is aimed at dealing with correcting this injustice and giving workers a greater share of the produce, commensurate with their contribution. The natural price, accordingly, is the price in which the greatest part possible, of the surplus created in one period, is directed towards the wage fund and, hence, would lead to an increase in wages.[45] In a way, this is almost an expression of Rawls's idea of the difference principle.

What is important to bear in mind is that none of these scholars thought that markets, or competitive interaction, will *necessarily* lead to the just exchange which reflects the contribution-based principle of desert. In their discussion of the just, or ethical, price, they were not *describing* the system but, rather, they were setting an ethical *reference point* against which to evaluate the morality of the economic system. It is for this reason that in Aristotle this is part of his discussion of corrective justice, which means that it was society's role to interfere in the natural

---

[45] I am aware of the fact that many interpret Smith's idea of the natural price as simply the 'cost of production' price, which in modern economics is the long-run equilibrium when prices equal the minimum average cost. I will provide a fuller explanation to why this is wrong in Chap. 8, where we discuss the classical perspective. It could be useful to note that in Cantillon's *Essai* (I.x) the concepts used are those of market price and intrinsic price, which is also described as the focus of market price fluctuations. At this stage, however, I will only make this brief comment to say that in Smith's natural price, all participants in the production process receive what can be understood as the value of a socially constructed consumption basket. In modern economics, in the long run, the price equals the cost of production but these costs may be well above that which is needed to perform socially. After all the normal rate of profit is determined in the market for present consumption and not according to any socially constructed measure.

course of things and to correct the prices which may be formed in a world without such intervention.

Smith too, thought that it is possible, in principle, for the competitive system to converge towards the natural, or just, price but by no way did he consider it to be a necessity or an intrinsic characteristic of the system. In other words, Smith realised that there are natural forces at work which may keep the system away from its ethical benchmark for a very long period of time. In fact, he was quite pessimistic about the ability of the system to reach its moral benchmark which could explain his repeated scepticism about the goodness of competitive decentralisation. Marx, on the other hand, went all the way and was clearly convinced that the market system would never lead the economy to its ethical benchmark. He used his labour theory of value to argue that whenever there is money involved in the process of exchange, some of the value created (that which he called surplus value and is the work labourers contribute above that which they need for their own reproduction) would be expropriated by someone who, according to Marx, could never have a legitimate claim to it.

The point I am making here is that until we reached the Walrasian era, there has always been an ethical concern with regard to the process of economic interaction because people are dependent on each other. Naturally, when the question is how one commodity—produced by one agent—exchanges with another—produced by the other—it is very much a question of contribution-based desert, which is entirely based on the actions of the individuals and not the moral values of their character. While it is true that some recognised that in a more sophisticated technological environment the relationship between individuals' effort and contribution and the price may not be as straightforward, they have not given up on the attempt to understand how the system rewards contributions.

So why has there been such a major change in the approach towards the ethics of economic systems and was it justified? Recall that if the only object of ethical evaluation is the initial allocation or final distribution and they are justified, then the support for market economics for ethical reasons even when it does not solve the economic problem could also be justified. It would almost be the same as saying that markets are ethically neutral.

That aspect of Walras's contribution which, we believe, is perhaps one of the main reasons for the disappearance of discussions of contribution-based desert as a criterion of justice, is the idea that inter-dependence—the foundation of economic life—implies contempora-neous simultaneity, or static general equilibrium.[46] As it still dominates economics' paradigmatic core, it has the potential of explaining why such a disappearance has been sustained for so long. The main reason why a static conception of general equilibrium, based on rational utility maximisers, as an ideal of interdependence and co-ordination can have such an effect on the use of contribution-based desert is that it raises serious difficulties in tracing meaningful *causal relationships* between agents' decisions/actions and outcomes. Without such a relationship *responsibility* will not be assignable and, consequently, a theory of des-ert will lose its meaning.[47]

Recall that desert theories, in general, require that a person should be rewarded according to the effects of his, or her, decisions (or actions). It means that we have to be able to identify the person who is deserving as well as that for which he, or she, may be responsible and, therefore, deserving. In a system of static general equilibrium, captured by the tool of simultaneous equations, it is more difficult to establish—in a mean-ingful way—what part of an effect of an individual action can be exclu-

---

[46] See discussions in Hicks (1983, pp. 85–93) and Schumpeter (1954, pp. 951–1052) and in par-ticular pp. 998–1025. It is true, however, that some scholars argue that there is more than that in Walras's model (see Morishima 1977; Witteloostuijn and Maks 1990) but as far as we are con-cerned this will make little difference. It is perhaps worth noting that there is nothing extraordinary by the choice of contemporaneous simultaneity as a way of testing whether competitive decentrali-sation leads to a co-ordinated outcome. Naturally, Walras did not think that the reality is that at any point in time, the economy is in equilibrium. But if one thinks that markets solve the eco-nomic problem or provides a co-ordination mechanism, it stands to reason that one has to demon-strate that the different individuals will indeed succeed in reaching a co-ordinated outcome. What better system can one contemplate other than contemporaneous simultaneity. If we are in a con-stant state of disequilibrium and there is never a co-ordinated outcome, it becomes more difficult to justify competitive decentralisation on these grounds. Indeed, for the Austrians who have not adopted the epistemological approach of Walras, it is less the co-ordination power and more the freedom associated with markets which is the great promise of market economies.

[47] The issue of responsibility has been a source of some debate in philosophy. Cupit (1996), Feldman (1996), Smilansky (1996) and Scheffler (1992) are a few examples. We have also mentioned the parallel increase in interest in responsibility in the egalitarian literature (Arneson 1989, 1990; Cohen 1989, 1993; Fleurbaey 2008).

sively attributed to this particular action (or effort).[48] If desert means, for instance, that a person should be rewarded in some proportion to his effort, we would need to look at the relationship between the decision to work and the individual's share in the final product. The latter, however, would involve an examination of not only the wages of the labourer (in relation to his effort), which is the equivalent of his or her income, but also the whole range of relative prices through which his share in output translates into a real return.

In the Walrasian system we know that the values of all these endogenous variables (wages as well as prices) are 'explained' (determined) by the exogenous ones. This means that all the parameters which will influence the distribution of the outcome are determined by taste parameters (as well as an initial distribution of assets). Therefore, individuals always choose to consume a vector of goods (including leisure) for any given set of prices. To achieve their desired outcome, they will need to contribute a certain number of hours of work. As we are in the realm of certainty, they already know that the return to their labour contribution will be the vector of goods which they have planned to consume. In other words, it is not as if they work first and then expect a return to their contribution; instead, their choice of labour is from the beginning designed to achieve the outcome which, in equilibrium, they will achieve. The return on their action is what they have expected it to be. In such a case, what other possible meaning can there be to the question of desert?

But while this may explain why desert has ceased to be a focus of interest, it also exposes the fallacy in this approach. In the Walrasian

---

[48] Following Elster (1983), I would like to make the distinction between 'causal relations' and 'causal explanation'. The former is a logical statement, describing a regular conjunction of kinds of events. 'Explanation', on the other hand, relates to the actual occurrence of specific events. In other words, two endogenous variables may have some kind of 'causal relationship' but the actual values of each of them are *explained* by the exogenous variables. When, in such a system, we study the relationship between the decision of an agent and the outcome of it, we can do so by using comparative statics. This, however, will only tell us about the 'causal relationships' in the model but will not offer a 'causal explanation'. Comparative statics is a professed hypothetical exercise that reveals at best the direction of change but no more than that (see, for instance, Klant 1984, Chap. 4, and in particular, pp. 146–149). In a system of simultaneous equation, only the exogenous variables are the 'explanada'. The idea of exogenous variables being the only 'causal explanada' in a simultaneous system has been discussed by many scholars (see, for instance, Popper (1959), Mackie (1974), Hicks (1979), Elster (1983) and Itkonen (1983)).

system agents know how it operates in the sense that they recognise the rules of the market. This does not mean that they approve of them or think them to be morally right. When they make their choices, these choices are subject to the rules under which the system produces outcomes. So yes, a person may realise that he needs to work, say, nine hours a day to generate the wages that will allow him to consume the basket he is planning to consume at these prices but one can still ask the question of whether the system, that is, the rules of the market, is such that the relationship between his choice of input and the outcome he can expect is one that will be consistent with contribution-based desert. Is there someone else in the system who was following the same logic—that is, deciding to work the number of hours that will give him the expected basket—worked less and managed to extract a greater basked of goods? If so, why?

To put it differently, most scholars who addressed economic issues in the past were aware of the way in which people interact in their economic lives. However, in addition to the attempt at explaining why this is so, they have also engaged with the question whether that which people do, that produces the economic system, is also something they would have accepted as morally good (the question of diachronic order). As we mentioned in the case of Smith, he was very much aware of the workings of demand and supply and therefore did not think that the deer and the beaver will *necessarily* exchange at their labour values. He was simply suggesting that only if they do will the system comply with what the people themselves consider to be just. Even when he added land and capital, and where he admitted that labour values may no longer represent the just exchange, he was still looking for the principle of contribution-based desert. It was not as if he thought that people make actual decisions based on whether they expect the return to be just. He was just judging the system, on their behalf, as an impartial observer.

In modern economics, it is the latter part which has been receding. The claim that competitive decentralisation can produce an order was not a novelty when Walras wrote his *Elements*. It is the way in which he demonstrated it which was novel. In particular, the use of formal logic gave greater impetus to the perception that economics is a science (like all other natural sciences) and, therefore, ethical evaluations are somewhat immaterial. By the time we get to the desire to correct the outcomes, the belief in the realism of contemporaneous simultaneity has taken root to the effect that ethics has been confined to the two extremes of the system (i.e. initial allocation or final distribution).

However, none of this suggests that we cannot ask the question of whether the market system generates an acceptable relationship between contribution and outcomes regardless of the reason why people contribute in the first place. What we will do now is examine a few examples that will expose the potential antagonism between the principle of contribution-based desert and the way in which markets operate. If this is indeed the case, the support for markets, which is not based on its ability to solve the economic problem through ethical neutrality, will have to be abandoned. If markets themselves restrict freedom and violates basic conceptions of justice, they should not be advocated when they also fail to solve the economic problem.

Let us begin our examination of whether in modern economics competitive decentralisation is consistent with the basic principles of contribution-based desert by looking at a very simple story which is similar to the one we examined in the previous section when the two individuals chose to specialise, become dependent on one another and trade through competitive markets. This is a simple case because there is complete symmetry between the two agents and their decision to enter the economic arrangements reflects complete sovereignty. Will the markets uphold the basic concept of contribution-based desert?

We begin by looking at a case where the difference in contribution (i.e. labour input) into the production of the goods to be traded is part of the initial conditions. Suppose that initially we have two individuals (or types of individuals) who, when alone, face the following economic problem:

Before becoming interdependent

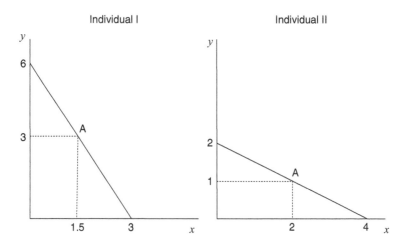

This means that individual I who can, with 1 unit of labour, either produce 6 units of *y* or 3 units of *x* or any linear combination of the two has comparative advantage in producing *y* (his opportunity cost of a unit of *y* is ½ an *x*). Individual II, on the other hand, who can produce either 2 units of *y* or 4 units of *x* or a linear combination of the two, has a comparative advantage in producing *x* (his opportunity cost of a unit of *x* is ½ a unit of *y*). So, it is in the interest of both individuals to enter into a social arrangement where they will trade the produce of their labour. Individual I will specialise in *y* and produce 6 units of it, and individual II will specialise in *x* and produce 4 units of it. They have 1 unit of labour each and they will now come to the market to exchange the fruits of their labour in a competitive environment.

To see how this works, we can put the two above diagrams one on top of the other so that in the lower-left corner we will have the origin of the left-hand diagram while in the top-right corner we will have the origin of the right-hand diagram:

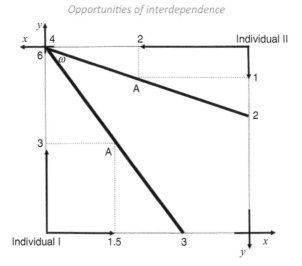

Opportunities of interdependence

This is a somewhat complex diagram but I will attempt to explain it. The heavy black lines from the top-left corner leading to the numbers 3 and 2 represent the original constraint which the individuals faced before they chose to specialise. This is what we have in the original diagrams above. The area in between these two heavy lines captures the gains from trade available to both individuals. These are bundles of the goods x and y which neither of them could have had if they did not enter the economic arrangement.

Once they choose to specialise, they find themselves with an endowments (ω) depicted in the left-hand top corner. It denotes the fact that once they specialise, individual I will have 6 units of y and no units of x at all while individual II will have 4 units of x and no units of y at all. Notice that the initial endowment (which is the initial condition for trade) suggests that as agent I invested his whole labour unit in the production of y, the amount of labour which went into each unit of y is 1/6 of a labour unit. Similarly, individual II invested his whole unit of labour in the production of x, which means that each unit of x required ¼ of his labour unit. One can clearly see that a principle of contribution-based desert suggests that the person who sells x, which contains 1.5 the amount of labour which went into a unit of y, should be able to command 1.5 units of x with 1 unit of y. Namely, the price of x which will reflect the relative contribution of both agents would be 1.5 y per x:

$$\frac{p_x}{p_y} = \frac{1/4}{1/6} = 1.5 \, ys \, \text{per} \, x$$

Contribution-based desert and trade

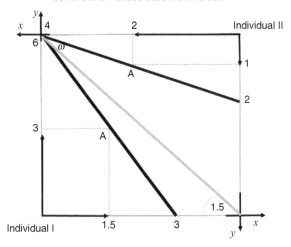

The heavy green line between their endowment and the other end of the box represents this very price which from Aristotle to Smith (in an equivalent set-up) has the role of the just price. It is, in the same manner as it is in the case of the hunters of deer and beavers, proportional to the contribution of labour which went into the production of a unit of the good. Recall that in terms of overall contribution, both agents invested all their labour in the production of the two goods. We assume the quality of their labour to be the same, which means that the fact that one of them produces 6 units of the good and the other just 4 has more to do with the nature of the production process than with the nature of the contribution. Therefore, the only way the idea of contribution-based desert can be expressed here is through the differences in the contribution of labour required in the production of each unit of the good.[49]

---

[49] If we changed the way we see contribution from the difficulty of attainment of a particular commodity to the productivity of labour, we would refer directly to the two individuals (rather than the goods) and say that individual I is more productive than individual II as his unit of labour produced 6 units of y while the same labour by individual I contributed only 4 units of x. However,

However, our two agents are rational and have subjective preferences over the two goods. These preferences, as we explained in Chap. 2, are represented by a utility function. This means that if we move along the green line we see that for individual I this implies more x at the expense of y. If we start from the endowment point where the individual has only y and no x, the utility of 1 unit of y is much smaller than that of 1 unit of x, of which he has not got any. Therefore, when we move along the green line, the utility of agent 1 will be increasing. A similar logic will be applied to individual II. When the utility of both agents increases, they will not stop exchanging x for y (and y for x) until at some point, when they have bought enough x that the loss of utility from y (of which they now have much fewer units) will be small enough to be offset by the increase in utility of x (of which he now has plenty). At this point, when it happens to both of them, they will agree to trade and it has the properties of an equilibrium as it is efficient in the sense that no individual can be made better off without the other one becoming worse off:

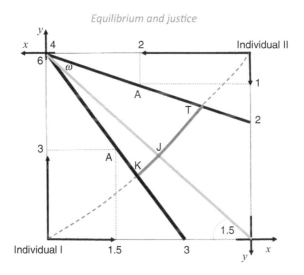

one can immediately see how this point of view would be wrong as it is not really true to say that individual I is more productive than individual II. Such a claim would have been meaningful if they both produced the same good. Therefore, it stands to reason that the difference between the contributions of the two individual is manifested in the difference in the difficulty of producing that which they own at the beginning of trade.

The red line going from the bottom left to the top right of the diagram is known as the contract curve. It is a collection of points where individuals can no longer increase their utility without making someone else worse off. They are all, therefore, allocative efficient. In terms of our description of the shift along the green line, point J represents that point where exchanging more *x* for *y* (and *y* for *x*) will make agent I (agent II) worse off. Indeed, point J is a potential equilibrium which is efficient on the contract curve (the red line).

As we know that the agents will choose something which was not available to them before, it means that competitive equilibrium will have to be a point on the heavy part of the red line between the heavy black lines (from K to T). What we see from here is the following: the set of allocations or equilibria, where the principle of contribution-based desert is satisfied is arranged along the green line. The set of allocations which are efficient and may constitute an outcome of market equilibrium are arranged along the red line. One is arranged from top left to bottom right, and the other is orthogonal, from bottom left to top right. This may suggest that contribution-based desert and competitive outcomes are, indeed, orthogonal.

Efficiency and justice

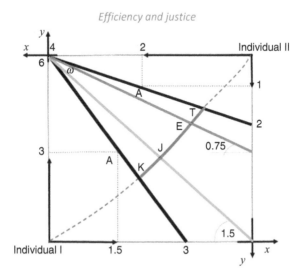

Of course, for any given initial conditions (which produced the endowment point) together with the taste parameters of the individuals, there will be only one competitive equilibrium. It could be point J but it could as easily be such that will take us to point E. The equilibrium price at point E is the blue line with the slope of 0.75 units of y per x. This means that competitive equilibrium produced a price where the agent who owns the commodity in which he had to invest 1.5 more labour than in 1 unit of the other good, will only receive 0.75 of the other good. The rate in which y and x exchange in the market is half the value of the good in terms of their relative labour contributions.[50]

It is true that J is also a possible outcome but this will only happen for a very specific set of taste parameters. Most of the time, the outcome will not be J and there is nothing in the mechanism of the market which allows the difference in relative initial contributions to have any significance in the determination of the final outcome except through the determination of the endowment point. This means that if we changed the initial conditions by giving individual II some of the y produced by individual I, the initial endowment will be at a different point where for the given set of taste parameters point J would have been the equilibrium. This, in essence, is the meaning of the second welfare theorem. The problem is, of course, on what grounds would society demand that agent I surrender some of the produce of his labour in favour of agent II. Either way, from our perspective, what matters in this little story is the orthogonal position of those outcomes which are consistent with competitive decentralisation and those which are consistent with respecting the principle of proportional remuneration or contribution-based ethics.

However, some may argue that the reason why in our story the outcomes of markets' interactions are orthogonal to those consistent with basic conception of justice is that we have left the decision about how

---

[50] It is easy to see that even if we treated the differences in contributions as the difference in productivity (where individual I is more productive than individual II as his unit of labour produced 6 units of y, while the same labour by individual I contributed only 4 units of x), the idea of justice would still be orthogonal to market outcomes. Evidently, all exchanges consistent with a contribution-based desert would have been organised along the blue line in the above diagram. They too will be orthogonal to the market distributions arranged along the red line.

much labour to invest and in what, outside the market analysis. Namely, in our story both agents invested the same overall amount of labour and, therefore, they are, in principle, equally deserving. As they were not given an option in what to invest their labour, one cannot expect that markets should correct the origin of the potential difference in their deservedness which emanated from the natural difference in their abilities that, subsequently, led to one specialising in y and the other in x. But such an argument will be somewhat disingenuous. After all, it was the lure of the market which instructed the agents to make the choices about their specialisation in such a way that in the end, the command of one's own labour over the labour of another stood in no particular relationship to the relative difficulty of attainment which was manifested in the difference in labour required to produce each unit of the two types of goods.

Nevertheless, it is, in fact, true that if we allowed all decisions to go through the market, the outcome will be indeed the price which is captured by the green line but it will no longer be the just price.

In our story, people specialise in some kind of a pre-market stage, and then entered market to exchange their goods so that they can both benefit from their specialisation and trade. The main components of the story are, therefore, that only labour is a means of production and that both individuals and workers own the entire product of their endeavour. To move to a world where all decisions go through the markets, we have to assume that the two agents seek work in a perfectly competitive labour market and the production of both goods is conducted in separate industries. In such a case, we will end up with market prices which will have the appearance of consistency with the just price.

In equilibrium with production and with as many other factors of production one may wish to add, the relative price of any two goods will be:

$$\frac{p^0_{\,x}}{p^0_{\,y}} = \frac{MC(x)}{MC(y)} = \frac{\dfrac{w^x}{MP^x_{\,L}}}{\dfrac{w^y}{MP^y_{\,L}}} = \frac{w^x}{w^y} \cdot \frac{MP^y_{\,L}}{MP^x_{\,L}} = \frac{MP^y_{\,L}}{MP^x_{\,L}} \; ys \text{ per } x$$

This is so if all markets are perfectly competitive, including the labour market where nominal wages are the same. In our case, this will correspond to what appears to be the just price (the green line) where the marginal products of labour in y were 6 and in x 4, but is it so?

To draw from this the conclusion that the market mechanism leads to the just price, we have to assume that labour is the sole means of production and that the workers earn the entire produce of their labour. But in such a case, there will be no labour market and there will be no distinction between 'wage' and total output. Therefore, the presumption that the outputs of y and x play any other role than being pre-trade endowments is not very plausible. In such a case, the determination of competitive prices will not be dependent on marginal product or any other measure of labour contribution. Secondly, as labour is the only input and its productivity is constant, the green line is both the just price and the market price. But if there are other factors of production (like land or capital), marginal product cannot be constant. As marginal product is changing, the inverse of the marginal product is no longer the labour input.[51]

In our example, the marginal product of labour in y was 6 because a unit of labour could do 6 units of y. It stands to reason that the labour input per 1 unit of y should be 1/6 which is also $\dfrac{1}{MP^y_{\,L}}$. But if the marginal product is falling (because there are other factors of production around), then the inverse of the marginal product is no longer a true measure of labour input. For instance, if we had the following table:

---

[51] This corresponds to the argument made by Knight and Rawls that marginal product—in the general case—is not a measure of labour contribution. In our example, with constant marginal product and no other factor, it does correspond to labour inputs.

y	L	MP^y_L	$\dfrac{1}{MP^y_L}$	Labour value (L/Y)
4	1	4	1/4 = 0.25	1/4 = 0.25
6	2	2	1/2 = 0.5	2/6 = 1/3 = 0.333
7	3	1	1	3/7 = 0.42

Clearly the inverse of the marginal product overstates the average labour input into each unit of the good. In such a case, while the green line will still be the market equilibrium, it will no longer be the just price as it will not correctly reflect the relative labour contribution which went into each unit of the good.

Therefore, our previous analysis was the one more relevant to our investigation and in it, contributions were made before people entered the market. In the set-up we had, with constant marginal product and complete ownership of the produce of one's own labour, the only thing relevant to the circumstances and competitive decentralisation, is expressed in the exchange which the individual can make between the two goods. This, as we saw, may indeed lead to the just price but there was nothing in the competitive process which necessitated it. The orthogonality between competitive equilibria and the just price remains.

To clarify this point further, let us make the question of contribution-based desert more explicit rather than trying to figure it out from the indirect deservedness embedded in produced goods—which is more dif-ficult to ascertain. Suppose then that at some original stage there is one plot of land and two individuals who are working it producing a good called x. The relationship between them is more complex. One of the individuals (say, individual 2) is the owner of the land and while he also participates in working it, he employs individual 1 as a worker. In the initial situation, there are no markets (one can think of it as a feudal stage with a landlord and a serf) and the agreement (assuming voluntary) between them is that the worker will contribute a certain number of hours (say, L^2_0) for which he will receive by way of wages: x^2_0. Individual I, the owner, is also committed to work a certain number of hours (say, L^1_0) and he will have the residual of what has been produced. Suppose, too, that both agents are equally productive so the total output is always $x = \alpha(L^1 + L^2)$.

Being rational agents, both individual would like to consume commodity x and leisure (the residual of which is the amount of labour they do).

Using the same method as before we will capture the two individuals in one diagram where the bottom-left end of the diagram represents individual 1 and the top right-hand diagram represents individual 2:

Precompetitive interaction state of affairs

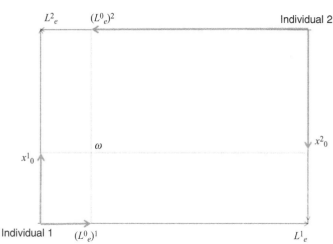

Point ω represents the initial endowment, or the situation between the individuals before we move into a market place of competitive decentralisation. They are each committed (by law) to provide the agreed amount of labour in return for the agreed amount of x. At point ω we can see that individual 1 (the owner), who committed to provide L^1_0 hours (and, therefore, is left with $L^0_e{}^1$ hours of leisure), will receive x^1_0 of the good produced. Similarly, for agent 2 from the top right-hand corner.

Now, in this context, the idea of what is contribution-based desert is fairly obvious. The more labour one contributed, the greater should be his share in the total produce. Naturally, as we have leisure on our axes, the more leisure one has (the less working hours he contributes), the less should be his share in output:

The loci of contribution-based desert

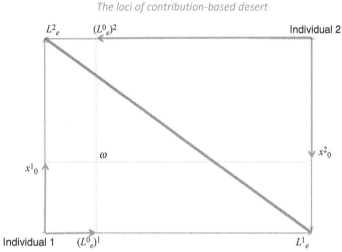

The heavy blue line from the top-left corner to the bottom-right corner depicts all allocations consistent with contribution-based desert. As we move down the line, the person who has more leisure (and, therefore, contributes less work) will receive a smaller part of the output.

Suppose now that they have moved into a competitive phase. Individual 1 is still the owner of the land and individual 2 still the worker and their initial commitments are still valid. However, the introduction of a competitive market means that they can now trade their obligations. In other words, a competitive market is created where the individuals can trade their assets which include their commitment to work and the promised reward. As in the previous story, both agents derive utility from consumption of the good and leisure and both are rational in the sense that they prefer more of both to less as well as are willing to replace one with the other according to the utility of each unit of the economic good:

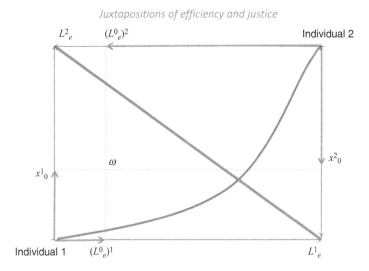

Juxtapositions of efficiency and justice

The red line, like before, depicts all the allocations which are allocative efficiency and, therefore, the competitive outcome of their trade will have to be a point on the red line (the contract curve). Again, we can see the orthogonal relationship between the collection of allocations which are consistent with the principle of contribution-based desert and those which are consistent with being a competitive outcome.

Using one further instrument—which have not been explicitly used before—we can find where the competitive equilibrium will be:

From inefficient injustice to efficient injustice

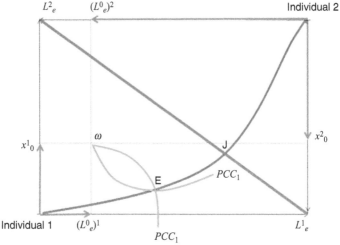

The green lines in the diagram describe what we call Price-Consumption-Curves (PCC), which denote the optimal choices of the two goods which the agent would choose at all possible prices. When they intersect at point E, it means that E is the competitive equilibrium as there will be complete compatibility between the choices of the two individuals in the sense that agent 1 (the worker) will be willing to trade some of his income in terms of x so that he can have more leisure and work less. This will be compatible with the amount of the good x the owner would wish to 'buy' in return for doing more work (to replace the labour of the worker). In this way, they are both better off in terms of their utilities than they were before they could have traded in their assets (which included their commitment to work and their share of output).

Clearly, point E is nowhere near point J, which would have been consistent with contribution-based desert. But what we can also see here is the fact that the position of E very much depends on the position of ω, which, in our story, contains two initial distributional parameters. On the one hand, it represents a notion of ownership structures which is encapsulated in the ability of the landlord to have dictated an initial contract where he worked very little and yet received the lion share of the produce of their collective output. On the other hand, it has the additional effect of ownership in its influence on the distribution of burden or the division of labour. At the initial point, the worker was not only receiving less but he was also doing more work (lower leisure).

However, even if we moved the initial allocation to the one consistent with contribution-based desert, it does not necessarily mean that the outcome of market exchange will preserve the justice of the initial position:

From initial (inefficient) justice to efficient injustice

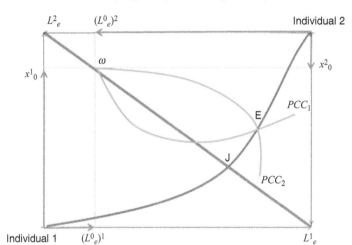

As we can see, at ω now there was justice in the original contract as the one doing most of the work also receives, proportionally, most of the produce of their combined work. Now, it is certainly possible that from this initial allocation trade will take us to point J. It is even very likely to be the case (mainly because we started with a just initial allocation). However, it is not necessarily so and a move towards a new point E, which will now violate the principle of contribution-based desert, is also possible. This means, again, that there is nothing inherent in the market mechanism which upholds the principle of contribution-based desert and, therefore, there is no inherent justice in the market mechanism.

So far, we have tried to demonstrate a certain orthogonality between the outcomes which are consistent with contribution-based desert and those which are proposed by competitive decentralisation. The significance of this orthogonality is in that it suggests that a competitive outcome which is consistent with basic justice is merely accidental and rare. This is not a particularly strong position to take when one wishes to advocate markets on the grounds of their compliance with justice.

But in the two cases we examined, there was one important absence and this is the choice of contribution. In the first case, contributions have been made before trade and were, therefore, exogenous to the market process. Nevertheless, we noted that given these conditions, markets will normally fail to uphold the basic principle of justice. In the second case, we moved one step forward when people could trade with their burden but they could only trade their allotted predetermined contribution (the given amount of labour input), which was given from the outset. Even here we saw that endogenising the distribution of burden would not necessarily lead to a just solution.

However, one may argue, as we suggested earlier, that the main feature of competitive decentralisation is that all decisions are made simultaneously and that causal explanations which will open the door for a clear deservedness are not really tractable. Namely, the decision which an agent makes about his input is the other side of the coin of his decision on consumption. In short, as agents adjust their inputs to that which they want to get as output, they cannot be considered to be deserving as their actions are almost entirely instrumental. While there may be some truth in the fact that such decisions are instrumental, this does not mean that we should not expect the system within which they seek to achieve their end to be consistent with basic justice. After all, justice is not confined to those who seek it explicitly. Therefore, we must still find a way to show that when the actual decision about the level of contribution (instrumental or otherwise) is endogenous, competitive decentralisation (i.e. markets) will ensure that those who contribute relatively more than the others should also command proportionately more than the others.

To examine this issue, there is no way of escaping some technical analysis which many readers my find too difficult to follow. Let me briefly say that what we are about to demonstrate is that competitive decentralisation consistently violates the basic conception of justice irrespective of initial conditions and, in particular, any initial distribution of ownership. This means that unlike our previous examples, we will show here that markets in their essence are orthogonal to the idea of contribution-based desert. As you can see, this is a serious charge and it is for this reason that we cannot escape the slight formal analysis. But if you are willing to accept my claim, you may move forward to the next section.

Consider, thus, an economy with two types of individuals, 1 and 2, and where there are two commodities, x and y. To examine the full correspondence between effort and reward, we choose to completely separate production and ownership. Individual 1 produces only x and his production function is $a \cdot L_1$. He also owns a given quantity of the other good y at the beginning of the process denoted by $\bar{y}$. Individual 2, on the other hand, produces only y, according to a similar production function $a \cdot L_2$, but he owns a given quantity of x at the beginning of the process denoted by $\bar{x}$. We have deliberately chosen the same productivity factor for the two agents so that effort and contribution could easily be interpreted in terms of labour units (hours).

Each individual has the same utility function in (x_i, y_i, l_i) but has a different aversion to labour:

$$u\left(x_i, y_i, l_i\right) = \alpha \ln x_i + \beta \ln y_i + \gamma_i \ln l_i$$

$$\alpha, \beta > 0 \quad \gamma_i < 0 \quad i = 1,2$$

where γ_i represents the disutility of work (and the utility of leisure).

We shall use y as a numeraire so that the only price in the system is $p = \dfrac{p_x}{p_y}$. This price represents that quantity of commodity y with which one can purchase 1 unit of commodity x. There will be two types of individuals who will derive an advantage from a high value of p: the person who initially owns x at the beginning (individual 2) and the agent who works to produce x (individual 1). Clearly, therefore, it is difficult to determine whether a particular value of the price of x (i.e. p) is consistent with contribution-based desert as the owner of x—who contributes no labour towards its production—also benefits from this price. Also, as all endogenous variables (including the price of x in units of y as well as the level of labour contribution) are determined by exogenous parameters which include taste parameters and an initial ownership structure, it is difficult to identify whether particular values represent a correspondence with a just price. Therefore, we should focus instead on comparative statics by asking the question of whether a decision to increase one's labour contribution will translate into an increase in one's command of other goods even though there will be other, unintended beneficiaries. Thus, a principle of proportional command of output relative to one's contribution is reduced in this context to mean that an increase in agent 1's labour contribution (to the production of x) should lead to an increase in the price of x, which will suggest that when the person who produces a good increases his effort (or contribution), competitive markets will reward him by providing him with greater command of other people's unchanged contribution.

The utility maximiser individual of type 1 would solve the following problem:

$$\max_{x_1, y_1, l_1} u\left(x_1, y_1, l_1\right) = \alpha \ln x_1 + \beta \ln y_1 + \gamma_1 \ln l_1$$

$$\text{s.t } y_1 + p\left(x_1 - al_1\right) = \overline{y}$$

Individual type 2 would solve the following one:

$$\max_{x_2, y_2, l_2} u\left(x_2, y_2, l_2\right) = \alpha \ln x_2 + \beta \ln y_2 + \gamma_2 \ln l_2$$

$$\text{s.t } y_2 + px_2 - al_2 = p\overline{x}$$

Deriving their demand for x, y and l will allow us to examine the equilibrium conditions. In particular, it would be useful to note that the optimal contribution of labour by agent 1 will be:

$$l^*_1 = \frac{-\gamma_1 \cdot \varphi \cdot \overline{y}}{1 + \gamma_1 \cdot \varphi \cdot p \cdot a}$$

where $\varphi = \dfrac{\beta}{\alpha \cdot \beta\left(\alpha + \beta\right)}$.

Therefore, $\dfrac{\partial l^*_1}{\partial \gamma_1} = \dfrac{-\varphi \cdot \overline{y}}{\left[1 + \gamma_1 \cdot \varphi \cdot p \cdot a\right]^2} < 0$ for any given price, which means that as the disutility of labour increases (a greater absolute value of γ_1 and a lower number) the individual will work more at any given price. The logic here is that as the disutility is greater, the agent would need more goods to compensate for it and increase his utility. This means that we can use the disutility of labour as a proxy for labour, or effort, contribution of the individuals.[52]

Solving the model will reveal the equilibrium price (and values of endogenous variable), which is determined entirely by exogenous ones:

$$p^* = \frac{\overline{y}\left(1 - \dfrac{\beta}{\alpha + \beta + \gamma_1}\right)}{\overline{x}\theta_2\left(1 + \dfrac{\gamma_2}{\beta a}\right)}$$

where $\theta_2 = \dfrac{1}{1 + \dfrac{\gamma_2}{\beta}} - \dfrac{\alpha}{\alpha + \beta + \gamma_2}$

Recall that $\gamma_i < 0$; hence, it is easy to see that as $\dfrac{\partial p^*}{\partial \gamma_1} > 0$ the price of x measured in units of y will rise as the disutility of labour for agent 1 diminishes. But agent 1 is the one who produces commodity x, and the higher is the price of x, the more is he rewarded for each unit of his effort in the production of x by being able to exchange the produce of his labour for more units of the other good. What we see here is that the greater is

___

[52] As a change in γ_1 will in the end also change the price, the additional condition for disutility of effort to be a proxy to labour input when taking this into account is that: $\gamma_1^2 \cdot \varphi \cdot a \cdot \dfrac{\partial p}{\partial \gamma_1} < 1$, which is quite likely to hold true as the values on the left-hand side of the equation are generally very small indeed and their product will be even smaller. In particular, with the exception of a, they are all likely to be smaller than 1 so their product will be much smaller so that even with a (which may be somewhat greater than 1 but not by much), the condition is likely to be satisfied. Moreover, while this is relevant to the final outcome in terms of the new price and the new level of labour contributed, the internal logic of the story always suggests that at first the response of the individual to increased disutility of labour would be the increase in labour contribution. See more in the following footnote.

his dislike of labour, the less will he command of the other good. If the conditions for disutility to be a proxy for labour supply hold (which is very likely), it also means that a greater actual contribution of labour will yield diminishing rewards.[53] Therefore, whether a response to difficulty of contribution alone (as expressed in the disutility of labour) or through a clear increase in contribution, the market's response would be to under-mine the position of the person who seems to carry the heavier burden. At the same time, the more of commodity *y* he owns at the outset, the better will be his position in the market.

To summarise, in this model of general equilibrium no causal explana-tion can be attributed to the actual effort of the two agents. Their choice of labour input, like that of all other endogenous variables is determined by the exogenous ones. Nevertheless, if we are willing to allow the taste parameter to become a proxy for effort, we can reveal that contemporane-ous general equilibrium will generate an inverse-desert principle. If we accept that greater disutility of labour means greater effort (every unit of labour invested by this individual required greater mental exertion), then we established that general equilibrium implies that interdependence cannot accommodate any form of desert theories.

However, to make the analysis more explicit in terms of labour contri-bution rather than just the disutility of labour as a proxy which, though may be true most of the time, will not necessarily be always true, we can slightly alter the story to make the labour decisions exogenous too. This, perhaps, is more similar to our original example except that now we have a more precise way to analyse both the way in which price may reflect

---

[53] It is important to emphasise that while the conditions from the last footnote which will allow us to be confident about the use of disutility as a proxy for labour contribution, the argument holds in general. While in terms of causal explanation, the actions of the agents are determined by the same thing which determines the price, in terms of causal relationship, the story is more complex. If we begin at an equilibrium and now, there is an increase in disutility of labour, and the immedi-ate response of the agent (the one producing *x* in this case) would be to increase his supply of labour so that he can produce more *x* and sell it (at the given price) to offset the loss of utility. Therefore, the agent will always first of all increase contribution when disutility of labour increases. The result of such an action would be to increase the supply of *x* and, therefore, reduce its price. The fall in price may have a secondary effect which may, in principle, make the agent withdraw some of the labour because he is no longer capable of offsetting it only through an increase in consumption through the trading of the *x* he produces for *y*.

relative contributions as well as how a change in contribution will affect the reward in terms of a change in price.

We are now looking at the two agents who bring with them to the market the produce of their labour. Labour, therefore, is no longer a choice variable but an exogenous one. In such a case, we will end up with the following equilibrium price:

$$p^* = \left[\frac{\overline{y} + al_2}{\overline{x} + al_1} \right] \left[\frac{\alpha + \beta}{\beta} - 1 \right]$$

Unlike our first example, where we could only say that market prices may, on some occasions, reflect the relative difference in contribution (the green line in the original diagrams), here we have taken into consideration all taste parameters and the way equilibrium is determined. What we see, therefore, is that as a rule the greater is the contribution of the person who produces x the lower will be its price in units of y. Again, as in the previous more general case, it is still true that ownership works in one's favour. Individual 1's position in the market is improved the more he owns of the other good. Note too that if none of them possessed any goods before trade (i.e. $\overline{x} = \overline{y} = 0$), the market price will become:

$$p^* = \left[\frac{l_2}{l_1} \right] \left[\frac{\alpha + \beta}{\beta} - 1 \right]$$

Where it never reflects the relative labour contribution and is, in fact, inversely related. This means that in terms of our original case, with more or less standard representation of taste parameters, competitive equilibrium will **never** meet the just price at point J.

Therefore, one must conclude that there is something inherent in the market mechanism which tends to respond to changes in burden expressed either in terms of disutility (as a measure of difficulty) or in terms of actual labour hours, by reducing the ability of those who carry greater burden to take advantage of their greater contribution.[54] On the other hand, market mechanisms seem to consistently favour those who trade assets. In our case, the assets needed to trade for x is a quantity of y and the assets needed to trade for y is a quantity of x. The higher is the stock of assets one owns, the better will be his, or her, marker position.

4.3   Conclusion

We have asked the question of whether there may be other, ethical, reasons why one may wish to promote and support the proliferation of markets in the world. If there were such reasons, the difficulties which markets have in solving the economic problem or in preserving ethical neutrality will cease to be an impediment. This is particularly so when we consider the connections which competitive decentralisation has had with some basic ideas of liberalism as expressed in the notion of the civic society.

The breadth of ethics is such that it was not possible, in this volume, to cover all things pertaining to the ethical implications of markets. Instead, we chose to focus on two concepts which seemed to us sufficiently fundamental to any conception of ethics so that if markets satisfy them, it would be a source of confidence in the ability to promote them for such reasons. The two concepts we focused on were those of freedom and justice. In general, our conclusion is that there is no obvious reason to associate markets with either freedom or the basic conception of justice. Given the failing we listed in the two previous chapters, the only way

---

[54] What we are saying here, in more general terms, is that markets tend to reward less, things which are in greater abundance. Therefore, the more effort of labour one offers, the less will be one's reward. Now, some may argue that in standard labour market analysis, increase in effort (i.e. marginal product) will lead to higher wages and, hence, greater reward. However, for this to be true we must assume that marginal product is indeed a measure of contribution. Here, I concur with both Knight and Rawls, who contest this proposition. Indeed, if a person works a certain number of hours at a given level of effort, his wage (which equals his marginal product) will be so and so. If there is no change in the person's contribution but another person joins the labour force, the marginal product of the first individual will go down even though he is doing the same as before. Surely, one cannot agree that the contribution of this person has gone down. Moreover, even when marginal product increases, the change is distributed between the worker, other factors and the owners whose claims on the additional output we must further clarify. It is for this reason that we adopted the more general approach embedded in general equilibrium where contributions can clearly be identified and where workers are the sole owners of the produce of their labour.

to see markets, is as a natural phenomenon which needs to be contained rather than promoted. In terms of our discussion in Chap. 1, the implication of all this is that competitive decentralisation is not really a natural order. It does not solve the economic problem, it is irrelevant, it is not ethically neutral and, in fact, it violates basic principles of freedom and justice. It is really neither a synchronic nor a diachronic order.

We saw that as far as freedom is concerned, the association of markets with freedom of choice is actually meaningless. It is not the option count which makes an individual free but rather the absence of man-made restrictions on their choice set, assuming as we did, that the rational utility maximiser is indeed an agent who is free to make his choices from a given set. To prevent confusion between the ability to have a process where one can freely choose and the set from which one is making a choice, we employed the concept of sovereignty. We argued that by entering a market arrangement individuals forgo sovereignty in two different ways. Firstly, they become constrained by the actions of other people who—not by individual intention as by collective action—create man-made constraints on their choice set. Secondly, their ability to influence their own circumstances—that which J. S. Mill termed as 'real free-will'—is restricted in the sense that they are unable to choose not to participate in the game if the outcomes are not in their favour.

To an extent, one can point to the fact that entering an arrangement for a purpose may justify the loss of some liberties. In the case of Hobbes, for instance, individuals forgo all their liberties in return for security. However, even in Hobbes, people have not forgone their right to rebel if the promise for which they gave up their rights is violated. In our story, one can always argue that people enter market arrangement voluntarily, which means that they must know that they forgo the right to be free from the constraints created by individuals' collective actions. However, like in Hobbes, when the promised benefits are not provided, surely people must have a right to rebel. We noticed that when the terms of trade change, individuals may be forced to change specialisation in order to benefit from the system. But if the cost of such a change is greater than the promised benefits, the individual has no option to opt out of the game or invoke his, or her, right to rebel. The loss of sovereignty and command over one's own fate means that freedom cannot really be associated with the idea of competitive decentralisation, or markets.

On the question of justice, we argued that while the subject is broad and complex, there seems to be a thread which goes through both breadth of interpretations and history. This is the idea of desert. We first of all demonstrated that the idea of contribution-based desert is widespread in public opinion. We then saw the complexity of the concept of desert and its association with different approaches to the conception of justice. In spite of many difficulties associated with the determination of who is the subject of desert and what is it that makes them deserving, we concluded that if all other things are equal, it is difficult to argue against the universality of the idea of contribution-based desert.

Notwithstanding the debate about the role of desert in theories of justice, we found intriguing the disappearance of the concept from discussions of modern conceptions of *economic justice*. A possible reason for the apparent demise of desert theories could have been the way in which modern economics captures the idea of interdependence in economic life. The reason why such development should affect desert is mainly due to the possible erosion of clear causal explanations. If as a result of interdependence that which I get cannot be attributed to my action, I may not have a moral claim on it.

Nevertheless, the fact that the reasons why people act may be complex and interwoven with other people's motivation does not alter the fact that as observers we can still examine whether in the end those who contributed more get a reward which is proportional to their contribution. Therefore, we looked at three simple cases. In the first one, we looked at the hypothetical origin of economic organisation which is the decision agents make to specialise and trade. We identify an orthogonality between those allocations which are consistent with the principle of contribution-based desert and those which are consistent with market solution (i.e. efficient). However, in this analysis, contribution-based desert was reflected in the price rather than through a direct association between the actual contribution and the actual outcome. Namely, we were only looking at the price—the mediator between initial and final allocation—and whether it conforms to the principle of desert.

In the second example, we looked more directly at the actual correspondence between the contribution and the outcome without examining the property of the price itself. Here too we discovered an orthogonality between those allocations which conformed with justice and those which were proposed by competitive interaction. Finally, in the third case, we brought all of it together and we looked at the actual general equilibrium model where all decisions pertaining to the relationship between contribution and reward are determined simultaneously. We noticed here something far more decisive than that which we found in the earlier examples. Market prices are inherently inverse to the idea of contribution-based desert. This, of course, must lead to the conclusion that notwithstanding what one's opinion may be about initial or final distribution, one can rest assured that market mechanisms and justice are orthogonal ideas.

Bibliography

Alesina, A., Glaeser, E., & Sacerdote, B. (2001). Why Doesn't the U.S. Have a European-Style Welfare System? *Brookings Papers on Economic Activity, 2,* 187–254.

Arneson, R. J. (1989). Equality and Equal Opportunity for Welfare. *Philosophical Studies, 56,* 77–93.

Arneson, R. J. (1990). Liberalism, Distributive Subjectivism, and Equal Opportunity for Welfare. *Philosophy and Public Affairs, 19,* 158–194.

Cirillo, R. (1984). Léon Walras and Social Justice. *American Journal of Economics and Sociology, 43*(1), 53–60.

Cohen, G. A. (1989). On the Currency of Egalitarian Justice. *Ethics, 99,* 906–944.

Cohen, G. A. (1993). Equality of What? On Welfare, Goods, and Capabilities. In M. Nussbaum & A. Sen (Eds.), *The Quality of Life* (pp. 9–29). Oxford: Clarendon.

Cupit, G. (1996). Desert and Responsibility. *Canadian Journal of Philosophy, 26,* 83–100.

Dyde, S. W. (1894). Hegel's Conception of Freedom. *Philosophical Review, 3*(6), 655–671.

Elster, J. (1983). *Explaining Technical Change.* Cambridge University Press.

Feinberg, J. (1970). Justice and Personal Desert. In *Doing and Deserving* (pp. 55–94). Princeton, NJ: Princeton University Press.

Feldman, F. (1996). Responsibility as a Condition for Desert. *Mind, 105,* 165–168.

Fleurbaey, M. (2008). *Fairness, Responsibility and Welfare*. New York: Oxford University Press.

Hayek, F. A. (1944). *Road to Serfdom*. London: Routledge Press.

Hicks, J. R. (1979). *Causality in Economics*. Oxford: Basil Blackwell.

Hicks, J. R. (1983). *Classics and Moderns*. Oxford: Basil Blackwell.

Itkonen, I. (1983). *Causality and Linguistic Theory*. Indiana University Press.

Johnston, D. (2011). *A Brief History of Justice*. Malden, MA: Wiley-Blackwell.

Klant, J. (1984). *The Rules of the Game*. Cambridge University Press.

Kluegel, J. R., & Smith, E. R. (1986). Social Institutions and Social Change. Beliefs About Inequality: Americans' Views of What Is and What Ought to Be. In *Hawthorne*. New York: Aldine de Gruyter.

Knight, F. H. (1921). *Risk, Uncertainty and Profits*. Boston, MA: Hart, Schaffner & Marx; Houghton Mifflin Co.

Knight, F. H. (1935). *The Ethics of Competition and Other Essays*. New York: Harper and Brothers.

Kristjánsson, H. (2017). *Justice and Desert-Based Emotions*. London: Routledge.

Mackie, J. L. (1974). *The Cement of the Universe*. Oxford: Clarendon Press.

Marshall, G., Swift, A., Routh, D., & Burgoyne, C. (1999). What Is and What Ought to Be: Popular Beliefs About Distributive Justice in Thirteen Countries. *European Sociological Review, 15*(4), 349–367.

McClosky, H., & Zaller, J. (1984). *The American Ethos: Public Attitudes Toward Capitalism and Democracy*. Cambridge, MA: Harvard University Press.

Miller, D. (1992). Distributive Justice: What the People Think. *Ethics, 102,* 555–593.

Miller, D. (1996). Two Cheers for Meritocracy. *The Journal of Political Philosophy, 4*(4), 277–301.

Morishima, M. (1977). *Walras' Economics*. Cambridge: Cambridge University Press.

Nozick, R. (1974). *Anarchy, State, and Utopia*. New York: Basic Books.

Nussbaum, M. (1988). Nature, Functioning and Capability: Aristotle on Political Distribution. *Oxford Studies in Ancient Philosophy (Supplementary Volume), 6,* 145–184.

Nussbaum, M. C. (1992). Human Functioning and Social Justice: In Defense of Aristotelian Essentialism. *Political Theory, 20*(2), 202–246.

Olsaretti, S. (2003). *Desert and Justice*. Oxford: Clarendon Press.

Popper, K. (1959). *The Logic of Scientific Discovery*. London: Hutchinson.

Rawls, J. (1973). *A Theory of Justice*. Oxford: Oxford University Press.

Rustichini, A., & Vostroknutov, A. (2014). Merit and Justice: An Experimental Analysis of Attitude to Inequality. *PLOS ONE, 10*(2), e0117646.

Ryan, A. (1970). *The Philosophy of J S Mill*. London: Macmillan.

Scheffler, S. (1992). Responsibility, Reactive Attitudes, and Liberalism in Philosophy and Politics. *Philosophy and Public Affairs, 21*, 299–323.

Schumpeter, J. A. (1954). *History of Economic Analysis*. London: Allen & Unwin.

Sen, A. (1970). The Impossibility of a Paretian Liberal. *Journal of Political Economy, 78*(1), 152–157.

Sen, A. (1985). *Commodities and capabilities*. Amsterdam: North Holland.

Sen, A. (1992). *Inequality Reexamined*. Oxford: Clarendon Press.

Sidgwick, H. (1907). *The Method of Ethics*. New York: The Macmillan Company.

Smilansky, S. (1996). Responsibility and Desert: Defending the Connection. *Mind, 105*, 157–163.

Spengler, J. J. (1980). *Origins of Economic Thought and Justice*. Carbondale, IL: Southern Illinois University Press.

van Witteloostuijn, A., & Maks, J. A. H. (1990). Walras on Temporary Equilibrium and Dynamics. *History of Political Economy, 22*(2), 223–237.

Witztum, A. (2005). Economic Sociology: The Recursive Economic System of J S Mill. *Journal of the History of Economic Thought, 27*(3), 251–282.

Young, J. (1986). The Impartial Spectator and Natural Jurisprudence: An Interpretation of Adam Smith's Theory of the Natural Price. *History of Political Economy, 18*(3), 365–382.

Bibliography

Acemoglou, D., & Restrepo, P. (2016). *The Race Between Machine and Man: Implications of Technology for Growth, Factor Shares and Employment*. MIT Discussion Paper.

Acemoglou, D., & Robinson, J. (2012). *Why Nations Fail: The Origin of Power, Prosperity and Poverty*. London: Profile Books.

Afonso, A., & Jalles, J. T. (2011). *Economic Performance and Government Size*. Working Paper. European Central Bank.

Aiello, L., & Dunbar, R. I. M. (1993). Neocortex Size, Group Size, and the Evolution of Language. *Current Anthropology, 34*, 184–193.

Akerlof, G. A., & Yellen, J. L. (1990). The Fair Wage-Effort Hypothesis and Unemployment. *Quarterly Journal of Economics, 105*, 255–283.

Alcock, J. (2005). *Animal Behaviour* (8th ed.). Sunderland, MA: Sinauer Associates.

Alesina, A., Glaeser, E., & Sacerdote, B. (2001). Why Doesn't the U.S. Have a European-Style Welfare System? *Brookings Papers on Economic Activity, 2*, 187–254.

Alfonso, A., & Turrini, A. (2008). *Government Expenditure and Economic Growth in the EU: Long-Run Tendencies and Short-Term Adjustment*. European Commission.

© The Author(s) 2019
A. Witztum, *The Betrayal of Liberal Economics*,
https://doi.org/10.1007/978-3-030-10668-3

Algan, Y., & Cahuc, P. (2006). *Civic Attitudes and the Design of Labour Market Institutions: Which Countries Can Implement the Danish Flexicurity Model?* IZA DP No. 1928.

Amit, V. (Ed.). (2015). *Thinking Through Sociality: An Anthropological Interrogation of Key Concepts.* Oxford: Berghahn Books.

Anemiya, T. (2007). *Economy and Economics of Ancient Greece.* London: Routledge.

Arensburg, B., Schepartz, L. A., Tillier, A. M., Vandermeersch, B., & Rak, Y. (1990). A Reappraisal of the Anatomical Basis for Speech in Middle Palaeolithic Hominids. *American Journal of Physical Anthropology, 83,* 137–146.

Aristotle. (1951). *The Politics.* Sinclair's translation. Penguin.

Aristotle. (1953). *Ethics (The Nicomachean Ethics).* Thomson's translation. Allen & Unwin.

Arneson, R. J. (1989). Equality and Equal Opportunity for Welfare. *Philosophical Studies, 56,* 77–93.

Arneson, R. J. (1990). Liberalism, Distributive Subjectivism, and Equal Opportunity for Welfare. *Philosophy and Public Affairs, 19,* 158–194.

Arrow, K. J. (1994). Methodological Individualism and Social Knowledge. *American Economic Review, 84*(2), 1–9.

Arrow, K. J., & Debreu, G. (1954). Existence of an Equilibrium for a Competitive Economy. *Econometrica, 22*(3), 265–290.

Arrow, K. J., & Hahn, F. H. (1971). *General Competitive Analysis.* San Francisco: Holden-Day.

Atkinson, A. B. (2015). *Inequality: What Can Be Done?* Cambridge, MA: Harvard University Press.

Autor, D. H., & Dorn, D. (2013). The Growth of Low-Skill Service Jobs and the Polarization of the U.S. Labor Market. *American Economic Review, 103*(5), 1553–1597.

Backhouse, R. E. (2006). The Keynesian Revolution. In R. E. Backhouse & B. W. Bateman (Eds.), *The Cambridge Companion to Keynes* (pp. 19–38). Cambridge: Cambridge University Press.

Barro, R. J., & Grossman, H. I. (1971). A General Equilibrium Model of Income and Employment. *American Economic Review, 61,* 82–93.

Becker, G. S. (1996). *Accounting for Taste.* Cambridge: Harvard University Press.

Benabou, R., & Tirole, J. (2006a). Belief in a Just World and Redistributive Politics. *Quarterly Journal of Economics, 121*(2), 699–746.

Benabou, R., & Tirole, J. (2006b). Incentives and Prosocial Behavior. *American Economic Review, 96*(5), 1652–1678.

Benassy, J.-P. (1986). *Macroeconomics: An Introduction to the Non-Walrasian Approach*. New York: Academic Press.

Bernheim, B. D. (1994). A Theory of Conformity. *Journal of Political Economy, 102*(5), 841–877.

Berns, L. (1994). Aristotle and Adam Smith on Justice: Cooperation Between Ancients and Moderns. *Review of Metaphysics, 48*(1), 71–90.

Binfield, K. (Ed.). (2004). *Writings of the Luddites*. Baltimore: Johns Hopkins University Press.

Binmore, K. (2005). *Natural Justice*. Oxford: Oxford University Press.

Binmore, K. (2006). Why Do People Cooperate. *Politics, Philosophy and Economics, 5*(1), 81–96.

Binmore, K. (2012). *Playing for Real*. Oxford: Oxford University Press.

Block, W. (1995). Ethics, Efficiency, Coasian Property Rights, and Psychic Income: A Reply to Demsetz. *Review of Austrian Economics, 8*(2), 61–125.

Bowles, S. (2004). *Microeconomics: Behaviour, Institutions, and Evolution*. Princeton, NJ: Princeton University Press.

Bowles, S., & Gintis, H. A. (2011). *A Cooperative Species: Human Reciprocity and Its Evolution*. Princeton, NJ: Princeton University Press.

Bridel, P. (2011). *General Equilibrium Analysis – A Century After Walras*. London: Routledge.

Buchanan, J. M. (1978). The Justice of Natural Liberty. In F. R. Glahe (Ed.), *Adam Smith and the Wealth of Nations: 1776–1976 Bicentennial Essays* (pp. 61–82). Boulder, CO: Colorado Associated University Press.

Burnham, T. C., & Johnson, D. P. (2005). The Biological and Evolutionary Logic of Human Cooperation. *Analyse & Kritik, 27*, 113–135.

Byrne, R. W., & Whiten, A. (Eds.). (1988). *Machiavellian Intelligence*. Oxford: Oxford University Press.

Camerer, C. F., Ho, T.-H., & Chong, J. K. (2004). Cognitive Hierarchy Models of Games. *Quarterly Journal of Economics, 119*, 861–898.

Campbell, T. D. (1971). *Adam Smith's Science of Morals*. London: Allen and Unwin.

Charness, G., & Rabin, M. (2002). Understanding Social Preferences with Simple Tests. *Quarterly Journal of Economics, 117*(3), 817–869.

Chaudhuri, A. (2011). Sustaining Cooperation in Laboratory Public Goods Experiments. A Selective Survey of the Literature. *Experimental Economics, 14*, 47–83.

Cirillo, R. (1984). Léon Walras and Social Justice. *American Journal of Economics and Sociology, 43*(1), 53–60.

Citrin, J. (2015). Are We All Now Multiculturalists, Assimilationists, Both or Neither? In C. Dustmann (Ed.), *Migration: Economic Change, Social Challenge* (pp. 138–160). Oxford University Press.

Clark, G. (2005). The Condition of the Working Class in England, 1209–2004. *Journal of Political Economy, 113*(6), 1307–1340.

Clower, R. W. (1965). The Keynesian Counterrevolution: A Theoretical Appraisal. In F. H. Hahn & F. P. R. Brechling (Eds.), *The Theory of Interest Rates* (pp. 103–125). London: Macmillan.

Coase, R. H. (1937). The Nature of the Firm. *Economica, 4*, 386–405.

Coase, R. H. (1960). The Problem of Social Cost. *Journal of Law and Economics, 3*, 1–44.

Cohen, G. A. (1989). On the Currency of Egalitarian Justice. *Ethics, 99*, 906–944.

Cohen, G. A. (1993). Equality of What? On Welfare, Goods, and Capabilities. In M. Nussbaum & A. Sen (Eds.), *The Quality of Life* (pp. 9–29). Oxford: Clarendon.

Colander, D. (2000a). New Millennium Economics: How Did It Get This Way, and What Way Is It? *Journal of Economic Perspectives, 14*(1), 121–132.

Colander, D. (2000b). The Death of Neoclassical Economics. *Journal of the History of Economic Thought, 22*(2), 127–143.

Colander, D. (2010). Models, Pedagogy and Crisis. In A. Arnon, J. Weinblatt, & W. Young (Eds.), *Perspectives on Keynes*. Springer.

Coles, J. L., & Hammond, P. J. (1986). *Walrasian Equilibrium Without Survival: Existence, Efficiency and Remedial Policy*. Technical Report no. 483. Stanford, CA: Institute for Mathematical Studies in the Social Sciences.

Crockett, S., Spear, S., & Sunder, S. (2008). Learning Competitive Equilibrium. *Journal of Mathematical Economics, 44*(7), 651–671.

Cullis, J. G., & Jones, P. P. (1987). *Microeconomics and the Public Economy: A Defence of the Leviathan*. Oxford: Basil Blackwell.

Cupit, G. (1996). Desert and Responsibility. *Canadian Journal of Philosophy, 26*, 83–100.

Daly, H. E., & Cobb, J. B. (1989). *For the Common Good: Redirecting the Economy Toward Community, the Environment, and a Sustainable Future*. Boston, MA: Beacon Press.

Davidson, P. (2007). *John Maynard Keynes*. New York: Palgrave Macmillan.

Davis, J. R. (1990). Adam Smith on the Providential Reconciliation of Individual and Social Interests: Is Man Led by an Invisible Hand or Misled by a Sleight of Hand? *History of Political Economy, 22*(2), 341–352.

Davis, J. B. (2003). *The Theory of the Individual in Economics: Identity and Value.* New York: Taylor & Francis.

Dawkins, R. (1976). *The Selfish Gene.* Oxford: Oxford University Press.

Deaton, A. (2013). *The Great Escape: Health, Wealth, and the Origins of Inequality.* Princeton, NJ: Princeton University Press.

Demsetz, H. (1979). Ethics and Efficiency in Property Rights Systems. In M. Rizzo (Ed.), *Times, Uncertainty, and Disequilibrium: Exploration of Austrian Themes.* Lexington, MA: D.C. Heath.

Dick, J. (1975). How to Justify a Distribution of Earnings. *Philosophy and Public Affairs, 4,* 248–272.

Dobb, M. (1973). *Theories of Value and Distribution Since Adam Smith: Ideology and Economic Theory.* New York: Cambridge University Press.

Dunbar, R. I. M. (1993). Co-evolution of Neocortical Size, Group Size and Language in Humans. *Behavioural and Brain Sciences, 16*(4), 681–735.

Dunbar, R. I. M. (1998). The Social Brain Hypothesis. *Evolutionary Anthropology, 6,* 178–190.

Dunbar, R. I. M. (2014). The Social Brain: Psychological Underpinnings and Implications for the Structure of Organizations. *Current Directions in Psychological Science, 24,* 109–114.

Durkheim, E. (1933 [1893]). *The Division of Labor in Society* (G. Simpson, Trans.). Glencoe, IL: The Free Press of Glencoe.

Dworkin, R. (2000). *Sovereign Virtue: The Theory and Practice of Equality.* Cambridge, MA: Harvard University Press.

Dyde, S. W. (1894). Hegel's Conception of Freedom. *Philosophical Review, 3*(6), 655–671.

Easterlin, R. A. (2000). The Worldwide Standard of Living Since 1800. *Journal of Economic Perspectives, 14*(1), 7–26.

Easterly, W., Alesina, A., & Baquir, R. (1999). Public Goods and Ethnic Divisions. *Quarterly Journal of Economics, 114*(4), 1243–1284.

Edgeworth, F. Y. (2003 [1881]). *Mathematical Psychics and Further Papers on Political Economy* (P. Newman, Ed.). Oxford: Oxford University Press.

Eller, J. D., & Coughlan, R. M. (1993). The Poverty of Primordialism: The Mystification of Ethnic Attachments. *Ethnic and Racial Studies, 16*(2), 183–201.

Elster, J. (1983). *Explaining Technical Change.* Cambridge University Press.

Elster, J. (1985a). *Solomonic Judgements: Studies in the Limitations of Rationality.* Cambridge University Press.

Elster, J. (1985b). *The Multiple Self.* Cambridge University Press.

Elul, R. (1995). Welfare Effects of Financial Innovation in Incomplete Markets Economies with Several Consumption Goods. *Journal of Economic Theory, 65*(1), 43–78.

Engel, C. (2007). How Much Collusion? A Meta-analysis on Oligopoly Experiments. *Journal of Competition Law and Economics, 3,* 491–549.

Engel, C. (2010). The Behaviour of Corporate Actors. A Survey of the Empirical Literature. *Journal of Institutional Economics, 6,* 445–475.

Eurostat. (2016). Retrieved from https://ec.europa.eu/eurostat/data/database.

Evensky, J. (1992). Ethics and the Classical Liberal Tradition in Economic. *History of Political Economy, 24*(1), 61–77.

Evensky, J. (1993). Adam Smith on the Human Foundation of a Successful Liberal Society. *History of Political Economy, 25*(3), 395–412.

Fehr, E., & Schmidt, K. M. (1999). A Theory of Fairness, Competition, and Cooperation. *Quarterly Journal of Economics, 114,* 817–868.

Feinberg, J. (1970). Justice and Personal Desert. In *Doing and Deserving* (pp. 55–94). Princeton, NJ: Princeton University Press.

Feldman, F. (1996). Responsibility as a Condition for Desert. *Mind, 105,* 165–168.

Fisher, F. M. (2011). The Stability of General Equilibrium – What Do We Know and Why Is It Important? In P. Bridel (Ed.), *General Equilibrium Analysis – A Century After Walras* (pp. 34–45). London: Routledge.

Fleischacker, S. (1999). *A Third Concept of Liberty: Judgment and Freedom in Kant and Adam Smith.* Princeton, NJ: Princeton University Press.

Fleurbaey, M. (2002). Development, Capabilities and Freedom. *Studies in Comparative International Development, 37,* 71–77.

Fleurbaey, M. (2008). *Fairness, Responsibility and Welfare.* New York: Oxford University Press.

Fleurbaey, M. (2009). Beyond GDP: The Quest for a Measure of Social Welfare. *Journal of Economic Literature, 47*(4), 1029–1075.

Fleurbaey, M., & Blanchet, D. (2013). *Beyond GDP: Measuring Welfare and Assessing Sustainability.* OUP.

Force, P. (2003). *Self-Interest Before Adam Smith: A Genealogy of Economic Science.* Cambridge University Press.

Frey, C. B., & Osborne, M. A. (2013). *The Future of Employment: How Susceptible Are Jobs to Computerisation?* Oxford Martin School.

Friedman, M. (1953). *Essays in Positive Economics.* Chicago University Press.

Friedman, M. (1978). Adam Smith's Relevance for 1976. In R. G. Fred (Ed.), *Adam Smith and the Wealth of Nations: Bicentennial Essays 1776–1976.* Boulder, CO: Colorado Associated University Press.

Gardner, A., & Grafen, A. (2009). Capturing the Superorganism: A Formal Theory of Group Adaptation. *Journal of Evolutionary Biology, 22,* 659–671.

Geertz, C. (1963). The Integrative Revolution: Primordial Sentiments and Civil Politics in the New States. In C. Geertz (Ed.), *Old Societies and New States: The Quest for Modernity in Asia and Africa* (pp. 105–157). New York: Free Press.

Gibbons, A. (2006). *The First Human: The Race to Discover Our Earliest Ancestors.* New York: Doubleday.

Gibbons, A. (2007). Food for Thought: Did the First Cooked Meals Help Fuel the Dramatic Evolutionary Expansion of the Human Brain? *Science, 316*(5831), 1558–1560.

Gintis, H. (2009). *The Bounds of Reason: Game Theory and the Unification of the Behavioral Sciences.* Princeton, NJ: Princeton University Press.

Gintis, H., Bowles, S., Boyd, R., & Fehr, E. (2005). Moral Sentiments and Material Interests: Origins, Evidence, and Consequences. In H. Gintis (Ed.), *Moral Sentiments and Material Interests: The Foundations of Cooperation in Economic Life* (pp. 3–39). Cambridge, MA: MIT Press.

Giocoli, N. (2003). *Modelling Rational Agents: From Interwar Economics to Early Modern Game Theory.* Cheltenham: Elgar.

Goos, M., Manning, A., & Salomons, A. (2014). Explaining Job Polarization: Routine-Biased Technological Change and Offshoring. *American Economic Review, 104*(8), 2509–2526.

Gordon, B. J. (1964). Aristotle and the Development of Value Theory. *Quarterly Journal of Economics, 78*, 115–128.

Gordon, R. J. (2016). *The Rise and Fall of American Growth: US Standards of Living Since the Civil War.* Princeton, NJ: Princeton University Press.

Goto, R., Okamoto, T., Kiers, E. T., Kawakita, A., & Kato, M. (2010). Selective Flower Abortion Maintains Moth Cooperation in a Newly Discovered Pollination Mutualism. *Ecology Letters, 13*, 321–329.

Gourevitch, V. (2004). *Rousseau: The Social Contract and Other Later Political Writings.* Cambridge: Cambridge University Press.

Grandmont, J.-M. (1977). Temporary General Equilibrium. *Econometrica, 45*(3), 535–572.

Grandmont, J.-M. (1983). *Money and Value.* Cambridge University Press.

Gray, J. (1983). *Mill on Liberty: A Defence.* London: Routledge & Kegan Paul.

Green, F., & Zhu, Y. (2007). Overqualification, Job Dissatisfaction, and Increasing Dispersion in the Returns to Graduate Education, Centre of Economic Performance, LSE MHRLdp005.

Greenwood, J. D. (1997). *The Mark of the Social: Discovery of Invention?* Rowman & Littlefield Publishers.

Griswold, C. L. (1999). *Adam Smith and the Virtues if Enlightenment.* Cambridge University Press.

Groenewegen, P. (1995). Keynes and Marshall: Methodology, Society, and Politics. In A. F. Cottrell & M. S. Lawlor (Eds.), *New Perspectives on Keynes*. Durham, NC: Duke University Press.

Grosby, S. (1994). The Verdict of History: The Inexpungeable Tie of Primordiality – A Response to Eller and Coughlan. *Ethnic and Racial Studies, 17*, 164–171.

Grossman, S., & Hart, O. (1986). The Costs and Benefits of Ownership: A Theory of Lateral and Vertical Integration. *Journal of Political Economy, 94*, 691–719.

Guscina, A. (2006). *Effects of Globalisation on Labour's Share in National Income*. IMF Working Paper.

Gutmann, A. (1980). *Liberal Equality*. Cambridge University Press.

Hahn, F. (1962). A Stable Adjustment Process for a Competitive Economy. *Review of Economic Studies, 29*, 62–65.

Hahn, F. H. (1973). *On the Notion of Equilibrium in Economics: An Inaugural Lecture*. Cambridge: Cambridge University Press.

Hamilton, W. D. (1964). The Genetical Evolution of Social Behaviour, I & II. *Journal of Theoretical Biology, 7*, 1–52.

Hamilton, W. D. (1970). Selfish and Spiteful Behaviour in an Evolutionary Model. *Nature, 228*, 1218–1220.

Hamilton, W. D. (1971). Selection of Selfish and Altruistic Behaviour in Some Extreme Models. In J. F. Eisenberg & W. S. Dillon (Eds.), *Man and Beast: Comparative Social Behavior* (pp. 57–91). Washington, DC: Smithsonian Press.

Hamilton, W. D. (1972). Altruism and Related Phenomena, Mainly in Social Insects. *Annual Review of Ecological Systematics, 3*, 193–232.

Hamilton, W. D. (1975). Innate Social Aptitudes of Man: An Approach from Evolutionary Genetics. In R. Fox (Ed.), *ASA Studies 4: Biosocial Anthropology* (pp. 133–153). London: Malaby Press. Reprinted in Hamilton, W. D. *Narrow Roads of Gene Land: Volume 1: Evolution of Social Behaviour*. New York: W. H. Freeman and Spektrum, pp. 329–351.

Hamilton, W. D. (1996). *Narrow Roads of Gene Land: I Evolution of Social Behaviour*. Oxford: W. H. Freeman.

Hamouda, O. F., & Price, B. B. (1997). The Justice of the Just Price. *European Journal of the History of Economic Thought, 4*(2), 191–216.

Hart, O. (1995). *Firms, Contracts and Financial Structure*. Oxford: Clarendon Press.

Hart, O., & Moore, J. (1990). Property Rights and the Nature of the Firm. *Journal of Political Economy, 98*, 1119–1158.

Hausman, D. M. (1992). *The Inexact and Separate Science of Economics*. Cambridge University Press.

Hayek, F. A. (1944). *Road to Serfdom*. London: Routledge Press.

Hayek, F. A. (1948). *Individualism and Economic Order*. London: Routledge Press.

Hayek, F. A. (1960). *The Constitution of Liberty*. Chicago: Chicago University Press.

Heinrich, J., Boyd, R., Bowles, S., Camerer, C., Fehr, E., & Gintins, H. (2004). *Foundation of Human Sociality*. London: Oxford University Press.

Heritage Foundation. (n.d.). Retrieved from https://www.heritage.org/index/explore.

Hicks, J. R. (1939). *Value and Capital*. Oxford University Press.

Hicks, J. R. (1977). *Economic Perspectives: Further Essays on Money and Growth*. Oxford: Clarendon Press.

Hicks, J. R. (1979). *Causality in Economics*. Oxford: Basil Blackwell.

Hicks, J. R. (1983). *Classics and Moderns*. Oxford: Basil Blackwell.

Hildebrand, W., & Kirman, A. P. (1988). *Equilibrium Analysis. Variations on Themes by Edgeworth and Walras*. New York and Amsterdam: North Holland.

Hobbes, T. (1651). *Leviathan*. London: Thomas Hobbes of Malmesbury.

Hodgson, G. (2007). Meanings of Methodological Individualism. *Journal of Economics Methodology, 14*(2), 211–226.

Hollander, S. (1965). On the Interpretation of the Just Price. *Kyklos, 18*, 615–634.

Hollander, S. (1987). *Classical Economics*. University of Toronto.

Hollis, M. (1987). *The Cunning of Reason*. Cambridge: Cambridge University Press.

Holloway, R. L. (1966). Cranial Capacity and Neural Reorganizations – A Search for Suitable Parameters. *American Anthropology, 68*, 103–121.

Holloway, R. L., Broadfield, D. C., & Yuan, M. S. (2005). Methods and Materials of Endocast Analysis. In *The Human Fossil Record: Brain Endocasts – The Paleoneurological Evidence* (Vol. 3). Hoboken, NJ: John Wiley & Sons, Inc.

Holmstrom, B., & Roberts, J. (1998). The Boundaries of the Firms Revisited. *Journal of Economic Perspectives, 12*(4), 73–94.

Hoover, K. D. (1995). Relative Wages, Rationality, and Involuntary Unemployment in Keynes's Labour Market. *History of Political Economy, 27*(4), 653–683.

Hume, D. (1975 [1777]). *Enquiries Concerning Human Understanding and Concerning the Principles of Morals*. Oxford: Oxford University Press.

Itkonen, I. (1983). *Causality and Linguistic Theory*. Indiana University Press.

Jaffe, W. (1977). A Centenarian on a Bicentenarian: Leon Walras's Elements on Adam Smith's Wealth of Nations. *Canadian Journal of Economics, 10*, 19–33.

Jevons, W. S. (1888 [1871]). *The Theory of Political Economy*. London: Macmillan and Co.

Johnston, D. (2011). *A Brief History of Justice*. Malden, MA: Wiley-Blackwell.

Jones, C., & Klenow, P. J. (2016). Beyond GDP? Welfare Across Countries and Time. *American Economic Review, 106*(9), 2426–2457.

Kaldor, N. (1972). The Irrelevance of Equilibrium Economics. *Economic Journal, 82*, 1237–1255.

Kant, I. (1964 [1785]). *Groundwork of the Metaphysic of Morals*. Harper and Row.

Kay, J. (2003). *The Truth About Markets*. London: Allen Lane the Penguin Press.

Keynes, J. M. (1921). *The Collected Works of John Maynard Keynes: Treaties on Probability* (Vol. 8, A. Robinson & D. Moggridge, Eds.). London: Macmillan.

Keynes, J. M. (1933). *The Collected Works of John Maynard Keynes: Essays in Biography* (Vol. 10, A. Robinson & D. Moggridge, Eds.). London: Macmillan.

Keynes, J. M. (1963 [1926]). The End of Laissez-Faire. In *Essays in Persuasion*. London: W.W. Norton & Company.

Keynes, J. M. (2007 [1936]). *The General Theory of Employment, Interest and Money*. London: Palgrave.

Khalinraj, S., & Khilnani, S. (2001). *Civil Society, History and Possibilities*. Cambridge University Press.

Kirzner, I. M. (2000). Human Nature and the Character of Economic Science: The Historical Background of the Misesian Perspective. *Harvard Review of Philosophy, 8*, 14–23.

Klant, J. (1984). *The Rules of the Game*. Cambridge University Press.

Kluegel, J. R., & Smith, E. R. (1986). Social Institutions and Social Change. Beliefs About Inequality: Americans' Views of What Is and What Ought to Be. In *Hawthorne*. New York: Aldine de Gruyter.

Knight, F. H. (1921). *Risk, Uncertainty and Profits*. Boston, MA: Hart, Schaffner & Marx; Houghton Mifflin Co.

Knight, F. H. (1928). Historical and Theoretical Issues in the Problem of Modern Capitalism. *Journal of Economic and Business History, 1*, 119–136. Reprinted in *On the History & Method of Economics*. Review article on *Der Moderne Kapitalismus: Historisch-systematische Darstellung des gesamteuropäischen Wirtschaftslebens von seinen Anfängen bis zur Gegenwart*, vol. III: *Das Wirtschaftsleben im Zeitalter des Hochkapitalismus*, by Werner Sombart.

Knight, F. H. (1935). *The Ethics of Competition and Other Essays*. New York: Harper and Brothers.

Kornai, J. (2000). What the Change of System from Socialism to Capitalism Does and Does Not Mean. *Journal of Economic Perspectives, 14*(1), 27–42.

Krebs, J. R., & Davies, N. B. (1993). *An Introduction to Behavioural Ecology* (3rd ed.). Oxford: Blackwell Scientific Publications.

Kristjánsson, H. (2017). *Justice and Desert-Based Emotions*. London: Routledge.

Krueger, J. I. (2008). Methodological Individualism in Experimental Games: Not So Easy to Dismiss. *Acta Psychologica, 128*(2), 398–401.

Krugman, P. (2009a). How Did Economist Get It So Wrong. *New York Times Magazine.*

Krugman, P. (2009b). *The Conscience of a Liberal*. New York: W.W. Norton.

Kuhn, T. S. (1970). *The Structure of Scientific Revolution*. Chicago: University of Chicago Press.

Kuznets, S. (1934). *National Income 1929–1932. A Report to the U.S. Senate, 73rd Congress, 2nd Session*. Washington, DC: US Government Printing Office.

Laidler, D. E. W. (1999). *Fabricating the Keynesian Revolution*. Cambridge University Press.

Laidler, D. E. W. (2006). Keynes and the Birth of Modern Macroeconomics. In R. E. Backhouse & B. W. Bateman (Eds.), *The Cambridge Companion to Keynes*. Cambridge: Cambridge University Press.

Lange, O. (1935). Marxian Economics and Modern Economic Theory. *Review of Economics Studies, 2*(3), 189–201.

Lange, O., & Taylor, F. M. (1938). *On the Economic Theory of Socialism*. Minneapolis: Minnesota University Press.

Langholm, O. (1998). *The Legacy of Scholasticism in Economic Thought: Antecedents of Choice and Power*. New York: Cambridge University Press.

Laozi (Lao Tzi). (2002). *The Daodejing* (P. J. Ivanhoe, Trans.). New York: Seven Bridges Press.

Lapidus, A. (1994). Norm, Virtue and Information: The Just Price and Individual Behavior in Thomas Aquinas' Summa Theologiae. *The European Journal of the History of Economic Thought, 1*, 435–473.

Leibnitz, G. W. (1951 [1697]). *On the Ultimate Origin of Things* (P. P. Wiener, Ed.). New York: Charles Scribner's Sons.

Leibnitz, G. W. (1996 [1704]). *New Essays on Human Understanding* (P. Remnant & J. Bennett, Eds.). Cambridge: Cambridge University Press.

Leijonhufvud, A. (1968). *On Keynesian Economics and the Economics of Keynes*. Oxford: Oxford University Press.

Leslie, T. E. C. (1969 [1870]). On the Philosophical Method of Political Economy. In *Essays in Political Economy*. New York: Augustus M. Kelley Publishers.

Levi, I. (1982). Liberty and Welfare. In A. Sen & B. Williams (Eds.), *Utilitarianism and Beyond*. London: Cambridge University Press.

Levinson, S. C., & Enfield, N. J. (2006). *Roots of Human Sociality: Culture, Cognition and Interaction*. Berg Publishers.

Lipkes, J. (1999). *Politics, Religion and Classical Political Economy in Britain: J S Mill and His Followers*. Macmillan Press.

Locke, J. (1689). *Two Treaties of Government*. London: Awnsham Churchill.

Locke, J. (1894 [1690]). *An Essay Concerning Human Understanding* (2 vols., A. C. Fraser, Ed.). Oxford: Clarendon Press.

Locke, J. (1958 [1695]). *The Reasonableness of Christianity: With a Discourse of Miracles, and Part of a Third Letter Concerning Toleration* (I. T. Ramsey, Ed.). Stanford, CA: Stanford University Press.

Loizidis, J., & Vamvoukas, G. (2005). Government Expenditure and Economic Growth: Evidence from Trivariate Causality Testing. *Journal of Applied Economics, 8*(1), 125–152.

Lucas, R. E. (2000). Some Macroeconomics for the 21st Century. *Journal of Economic Perspectives, 14*(1), 159–168.

Lynne, G. D. (2006). Towards a Dual Motive Metaeconomic Theory. *Journal of Socio-Economics, 35*, 634–651.

Mackie, J. L. (1974). *The Cement of the Universe*. Oxford: Clarendon Press.

Maine, H. (1897). *Lectures on the Early History of Institutions*. London: John Murray.

Maine, H. S. (1920 [1861]). *Ancient Law: Its Connection with the Early History of Societies and Its Relation to Modern Ideas*. London: John Murray.

Mandel, A., & Gintis, H. (2014). Stochastic Stability in the Scarf Economy. *Mathematical Social Sciences, 67*(C), 44–49.

Mandeville, B. (1988 [1732]). *The Fable Also Wrote an Enquiry into the Origins of Moral Virtues*. Liberty Press.

Manea, M. (2015). Models of Bilateral Trade in Networks. In Y. Bramoulle, A. Galeotti, & B. Rogers (Eds.), *The Oxford Handbook on the Economics of Networks*. Oxford University Press.

Manski, C. F. (2000). Economic Analysis of Social Interactions. *Journal of Economic Perspectives, 14*(3), 115–136.

Marglin, S. (2010). *The Dismal Science: How Thinking Like an Economist Undermines Community*. Harvard University Press.

Marshall, A. (1952). *Principles of Economics* (8th ed.). New York: Macmillan.

Marshall, G., Swift, A., Routh, D., & Burgoyne, C. (1999). What Is and What Ought to Be: Popular Beliefs About Distributive Justice in Thirteen Countries. *European Sociological Review, 15*(4), 349–367.

Marx, K. (1906–1909). *Capital: A Critique of Political Economy* (3 vols.). Chicago: Charles H. Kerr.

Maryanski, A., & Turner, J. H. (1992). *The Social Cage: Human Nature and the Evolution of Society*. Stanford, CA: Stanford University Press.

Mas-Colell, A., Whinston, M. D., & Green, R. J. (1995). *Microeconomic Theory*. New York: Oxford University Press.

Maslin, M. A., & Christensen, B. (2007). Special Issue: African Paleoclimate and Human Evolution. *Journal of Human Evolution, 53*, 443–634.

McClosky, H., & Zaller, J. (1984). *The American Ethos: Public Attitudes Toward Capitalism and Democracy*. Cambridge, MA: Harvard University Press.

Meek, R. (1977). Mr. Sraffa's Rehabilitation of Classical Economics. In *Smith, Marx and After* (pp. 119–136). London: Chapman & Hall.

Meier, S. (2006). *The Economics of Non-selfish Behaviour; Decisions to Contribute Money to Public Goods*. London: Edward Elgar Publishing.

Menger, C. (1981 [1871]). *Principles of Economics* (J. Dingwall & B. F. Hoselitz, Trans., with an Introduction by Friedrich A. Hayek). New York: New York University Press.

Mill, J. S. (1874). *A System of Logic, Ratiocinative and Inductive* (8th ed.). New York: Harper & Brothers Publishers.

Mill, J. S. (1909 [1848]). *Principles of Political Economy* (W. Ashley, Ed.). London: Augustus M. Kelley Publishers.

Mill, J. S. (1967). Essays on Economics and Society. In J. M. Robson (Ed.), *Collected Works* (Vols. 4–5). Toronto and London: Toronto University Press and Routledge & Kegan Paul.

Mill, J. S. (1969a [1861]). Utilitarianism. In J. M. Robson (Ed.), *Collected Works: Essays on Ethics, Religion and Society* (Vol. 10). Toronto and London: Toronto University Press and Routledge & Kegan Paul.

Mill, J. S. (1969b). Essays on Ethics, Religion and Society. In J. M. Robson (Ed.), *Collected Works* (Vol. 10). Toronto and London: Toronto University Press and Routledge & Kegan Paul.

Mill, J. S. (1975). *J S Mill: Three Essays*. Oxford: Oxford University Press.

Miller, D. (1992). Distributive Justice: What the People Think. *Ethics, 102*, 555–593.

Miller, D. (1996). Two Cheers for Meritocracy. *The Journal of Political Philosophy, 4*(4), 277–301.

von Mises, L. (1966). *Human Action: A Treatise on Economics*. Chicago: H. Regnery.

Mokyr, J. (2014). Culture, Institutions and Modern Growth. In S. Galiani & I. Sened (Eds.), *Institutions, Property Rights, and Economic Growth* (pp. 151–191). London: Cambridge University Press.

Montesquieu, C. (1989 [1748]). *The Spirit of the Laws*. New York: Cambridge University Press.

Moore, G. C. (1995). The Role of Cliffe Leslie in the Early Stages of the English *Methodenstreit. Journal of the History of Economic Thought, 17*, 57–77.

Moore, G. C. (1999). John Kells Ingram, the Comtean Movement, and the English *Methodenstreit. History of Political Economy, 31*(1), 53–78.

Morishima, M. (1977). *Walras' Economics*. Cambridge: Cambridge University Press.

Munro, H. (1975). *The Ambivalence of Bernard Mandeville*. Oxford: Clarendon Press.

Negishi, T. (1985). *Economic Theories in a Non-Walrasian Tradition*. Cambridge University Press.

Noonan, J. T., Jr. (1957). *The Scholastic Analysis of Usury*. Harvard University Press.

Nozick, R. (1974). *Anarchy, State, and Utopia*. New York: Basic Books.

Nussbaum, M. (1988). Nature, Functioning and Capability: Aristotle on Political Distribution. *Oxford Studies in Ancient Philosophy (Supplementary Volume), 6*, 145–184.

Nussbaum, M. C. (1992). Human Functioning and Social Justice: In Defense of Aristotelian Essentialism. *Political Theory, 20*(2), 202–246.

Nussbaum, M. C. (2000). *Women and Human Development: The Capabilities Approach*. New York: Cambridge University Press.

Nussbaum, M. C. (2011). *Creating Capabilities*. Cambridge, MA: Harvard University Press.

O'Donnell, R. M. (1992). The Unwritten Books and Papers by Keynes. *History of Political Economy, 24*(4), 767–817.

OECD. (2012). *Labour Losing to Capital*. Supporting Material for Chapter 3 of the 2012 OECD, Employment Outlook. Paris: OECD Publishing.

Office of National Statistics. (2018). Retrieved from https://www.ons.gov.uk/.

Olsaretti, S. (2003). *Desert and Justice*. Oxford: Clarendon Press.

Oostebeek, H., Sloof, R., & Van de Kuilen, G. (2004). Cultural Differences in Ultimatum Game Experiments: Evidence from a Meta-analysis. *Experimental Economics, 7*, 171–188.

Organisation for Economic Co-operation and Development. (2017). Retrieved from https://data.oecd.org/.

Osborne, M. J., & Rubinstein, A. (1990). *Bargaining and Markets*. Academic Press.

Pack, S. J. (1991). *Capitalism as a Moral System: Adam Smith's Critique of the Free Market Economy*. London: Edward Elgar.

Pareto, V. (1972 [1909]). *Manual of Political Economy* (A. Schwier & A. N. Page, Trans.). London: Macmillan.

van Parijs, P. (1995). *Real Freedom for All: What (If Anything) Can Justify Capitalism.* Oxford: Oxford University Press.

Passingham, R. E. (1982). *The Human Primate.* San Francisco: Freeman.

Patinkin, D. (1965). *Money Interest and Prices* (2nd ed.). New York: Harper and Row.

Peffer, R. G. (1990). *Marxism, Morality, and Social Justice.* Princeton, NJ: Princeton University Press.

Phelps, E. (2013). *Mass Flourishing: How Grassroots Innovation Created Jobs, Challenge, and Change.* Princeton, NJ: Princeton University Press.

Pigou, A. C. (1920). *The Economics of Welfare.* London: Macmillan.

Piketty, T. (2014). *Capital in the 21st Century.* Cambridge, MA: Harvard University Press.

Piketty, T., & Zucman, G. (2014). Capital Is Back: Wealth-Income Ratios in Rich Countries 1700–2014. *Quarterly Journal of Economics, 129*(3), 1255–1310.

Pinker, S. (2002). *The Blank Slate: The Modern Denial of Human Nature.* New York: Viking.

Plato. (1974). *The Republic* (D. Lee, Trans.). Penguin.

Plato. (1994). *Gorgias* (R. Waterfield, Trans.). Oxford: Oxford University Press.

Polanyi, K. (1944). *The Great Transformation: The Political and Economic Origins of Our Time.* Boston: Beacon Press.

Popper, K. (1959). *The Logic of Scientific Discovery.* London: Hutchinson.

Portes, A., & Vickstrom, E. (2015). Diversity, Social Capital and Cohesion. In C. Dustmann (Ed.), *Migration: Economic Change, Social Challenge* (pp. 161–186). Oxford University Press.

Pullen, J. (2010). *The Marginal Productivity Theory of Distribution: A Critical History.* London: Routledge.

Ram, R. (1986). Government Size and Economic Growth: A New Framework and Some Evidence from Cross Section and Time Series Data. *American Economic Review, 76*, 191–203.

Ram, R. (1987). Wagner's Hypothesis in Time Series and Cross Section Perspectives: Evidence from 'Real Data' from 115 Countries. *Review of Economics and Statistics, 69*, 184–204.

Rawls, J. (1973). *A Theory of Justice.* Oxford: Oxford University Press.

Reader, S. M., & Laland, K. M. (2002). Social Intelligence, Innovation, and Enhanced Brain Size in Primates. *Proceeding of the National Academy of Science in the United States of America, 99*(7), 4436–4441.

Reinert, E. S. (2007). *How Rich Countries Got Rich and Why Poor Countries Stay Poor.* London: Constable.

Ricardo, D. (1951 [1817]). *On the Principles of Political Economy and Taxation* (P. Sraffa, Ed.). Cambridge University Press

Robbins, L. (1935). *Essay on the Nature and Significance of Economic Science.* London: Macmillan.

Robinson, J. (1974). History versus Equilibrium. *Indian Economic Journal, 21*(3), 202–213.

Rodrick, D. (2013). *Premature Deindustrialization.* NBER Working Papers 20935, National Bureau of Economic Research, Inc.

Rodrick, D. (2015). Unconditional Convergence in Manufacturing. *Quarterly Journal of Economics, 128*(1), 165–204.

Roemer, J. E. (1981). *Analytical Foundations of Marxian Economic Theory.* Cambridge University Press.

Rose, A. K. (2012). *Protectionism Isn't Countercyclic (Anymore).* CEPR Discussion Paper 8937.

Rosenberg, N. (1979). Adam Smith and Laissez-Faire Revisited. In G. P. O'discroll Jr. (Ed.), *Adam Smith and Modern Political Economy.* Iowa State University Press.

Rosenberg, N. (1990). Adam Smith and the Stock of Moral Capital. *History of Political Economy, 22*(1), 1–18.

Roth, G., & Dicke, U. (2005). Evolutions of Brain Size and Intelligence. *Trends on Cognitive Science, 9*(5), 250–257.

Rothbard, M. (1990). Concept of the Role of Intellectuals in Social Change Towards Laissez-Faire. *Journal of Libertarian Studies, 9*(2), 43–67.

Rousseau, J.-J. (1992 [1755]). *A Discourse on the Origin of Inequality* (D. A. Cress, Trans.). Indianapolis: Hackett.

Rousseau, J.-J. (1998 [1762]). *The Social Contract.* London: Wordsworth Edition.

Rubinstein, A. (2007). Instinctive and Cognitive Reasoning: A Study of Response Times. *The Economic Journal, 117*, 1243–1259.

Rustichini, A., & Vostroknutov, A. (2014). Merit and Justice: An Experimental Analysis of Attitude to Inequality. *PLOS ONE, 10*(2), e0117646.

Ryan, A. (1970). *The Philosophy of J S Mill.* London: Macmillan.

Sachs, J. L., Mueller, U. G., Wilcox, T. P., & Bull, J. J. (2004). The Evolution of Cooperation. *Quarterly Review of Biology, 79*, 135–160.

Saez, E., & Zucman, G. (2016). Wealth Inequality in the United States Since 1913: Evidence from Capitalised Income Tax Data. *Quarterly Journal of Economics, 131*(2), 519–578.

Samuelson, P. (1977). A Modern Theorist's Vindication of Adam Smith. *American Economic Review, 67*, 42–49.

Samuelson, P. (1978). The Canonical Classical Model of Political Economy. *Journal of Economic Literature, 16*, 1415–1434.

Sangheon, L., McCann, D., & Messenger, J. C. (2007). *Working Time Around the World: Trends in Working Hours, Laws and Policies in a Global Comparative Perspective*. New York: Routledge.

Scarf, H. (1960). Some Examples of Global Instability of Competitive Equilibrium. *International Economic Review, 1*, 157–172.

Scheffler, S. (1992). Responsibility, Reactive Attitudes, and Liberalism in Philosophy and Politics. *Philosophy and Public Affairs, 21*, 299–323.

Scheparts, L. A. (1993). Language and Modern Human Origins. *Yearbook of Physical Anthropology, 36*, 91–126.

Schmitt, P. M. (2004). On Perceptions of Fairness: The Role of Valuations, Outside Options, and Information in Ultimatum Bargaining Games. *Experimental Economics, 7*(1), 49–73.

Schumpeter, J. A. (1954). *History of Economic Analysis*. London: Allen & Unwin.

Scitovsky, T. (1992). *The Joyless Economy*. Oxford: Oxford University Press.

Seligman, A. B. (2000). Civil Society as Idea and Ideal. In S. Chambers & W. Kymlicka (Eds.), *Alternative Conceptions of Civil Society* (pp. 13–33). Princeton University Press.

Sen, A. (1970). The Impossibility of a Paretian Liberal. *Journal of Political Economy, 78*(1), 152–157.

Sen, A. (1985). *Commodities and Capabilities*. Amsterdam: North Holland.

Sen, A. (1987). *Ethics and Economics*. London: Basil Blackwell.

Sen, A. (1992). *Inequality Reexamined*. Oxford: Clarendon Press.

Sen, A. (1999). *Development as Freedom*. New York: Anchor Books.

Sen, A. (2002). *Rationality and Freedom*. Cambridge, MA: Harvard University Press.

Sen, A. (2009). *The Idea of Justice*. London: Allen Lane.

Shackle, G. L. S. (1967). *The Years of High Theory: Invention and Tradition in Economic Thought 1926–1939*. Cambridge: Cambridge University Press.

Shackle, G. L. S. (1973). *Epistemics and Economics*. Cambridge: Cambridge University Press.

Sherman, P. W. (1977). Nepotism and the Evolution of Alarm Calls. *Science, 197*, 1246–1253.

Sidgwick, H. (1907). *The Method of Ethics*. New York: The Macmillan Company.

Skidelsky, R. (1992). *John Maynard Keynes, Volume II: The Economist as Saviour, 1920–1937*. London: Macmillan.

Slonimczyk, F. (2011). Earnings Inequality and Skill Mismatch in the U.S: 1973–2002, MPRA Paper No. 35449.

Smilansky, S. (1996). Responsibility and Desert: Defending the Connection. *Mind, 105*, 157–163.

Smith, A. (1976a [1759]). *The Theory of Moral Sentiments* (D. D. Raphael & A. L. Macfie, Ed.). Oxford: Clarendon Press.

Smith, A. (1976b [1776]). *An Inquiry into the Nature and Causes of the Wealth of Nations* (2 vols., R. H. Campbell & A. S. Skinner, Eds.). Oxford: Clarendon Press.

Smith, A. (1978). *Lectures on Jurisprudence* (R. L. Meek, D. D. Raphael, & P. G. Stein, Eds.). Indianapolis, IN and Oxford: Liberty Classics and Oxford University Press.

Smith, A. (1980). *Essays on Philosophical Subjects* (W. P. D. Wightman & J. C. Bryce (Eds.), with a General Introduction by D. D. Raphael & A. Skinner). Indianapolis, IN and Oxford: Liberty Classics and Oxford University Press.

Smith, J. M. (1982). *Evolution and the Theory of Games*. Cambridge: Cambridge University Press.

Smith, A. (1983). *Lectures on Rhetoric and Belles Lettres* (J. C. Bryce, Ed.). Indianapolis, IN and Oxford: Liberty Classics and Oxford University Press.

Smith, V. L. (1998). The Two Faces of Adam Smith. *Southern Economic Journal, 65*, 1–19.

Solow, R. M. (2000). Toward a Macroeconomics of the Medium Run. *Journal of Economic Perspectives, 14*(1), 151–158.

Solow, R. M. (2009). Does Growth Have a Future? Does Growth Theory Have a Future? Are These Questions Related? *History of Political Economy, 41*(5), 27–34. Supplement.

Solow, R., & Stiglitz, J. (1968). Output, Employment, and Wages in the Short Run. *The Quarterly Journal of Economics, 82*(4), 537–560.

Spencer, H. (1897 [1874–1875]). *The Principles of Sociology*. New York: Appleton.

Spengler, J. J. (1955). Aristotle on Economic Imputation and Related Matters. *Southern Economic Journal, 21*(4), 371–389.

Spengler, J. J. (1980). *Origins of Economic Thought and Justice*. Carbondale, IL: Southern Illinois University Press.

Sraffa, P. (1960). *The Production of Commodities by Means of Other Commodities*. Cambridge University Press.

St Augustine. (1998). *The City of God Against the Pagans* (R. W. Dyson, Trans.). New York: Cambridge University Press.

St Thomas of Aquinas. (1914 [1265–1274]). *The Summa Theologica* (Parts I–II). London: Burns Oates & Washbourne Ltd.

St Thomas of Aquinas. (1938 [1265]). *On the Governance of Rulers: (De regimine principum)* (G. B. Phelan, Trans.). New York: Sheed & Ward.

Steedman, I. (1977). *Marx After Sraffa.* London: Verso Press.

Stephan, H., Frahm, H., & Baron, G. (1981). New and Revised Data on Volumes of Brain Structures in Insectivores and Primates. *Folia Primatol, 35,* 1–29.

Stiglitz, J. (2012). *The Price of Inequality.* New York: W.W. Norton.

Stiglitz, J. E., Sen, A., & Fitoussi, J.-P. (2009). *Report by the Commission on the Measurement of Economic Performance and Social Progress.*

Stout, D. (2011). Stone Toolmaking and the Evolution of Human Culture and Cognition. *Philosophical Transactions of the Royal Society B, 366,* 1050–1059.

Sugden, R. (1989). Spontaneous Order. *Journal of Economic Perspectives, 3*(4), 85–97.

Sugden, R. (2009). Neither Self-Interest Nor Self Sacrifice: The Fraternal Morality of Market Relationship. In S. A. Levin (Ed.), *Games, Groups, and Global Good* (pp. 259–283). Dordrecht: Springer.

Survey of Consumer Finance. (2016). Retrieved from https://www.federalreserve.gov/econres/scfindex.htm.

Talberth, D. J., Cobb, C., et al. (2007). *The Genuine Progress Indicator 2006: A Tool for Sustainable Development.* Oakland, CA: Redefining Progress.

Tattersall, I. (2000). Once We Were Not Alone. *Scientific American, 282*(1), 56–62.

Thaler, R. H. (2000). From Homo Economicus to Homo Sapiens. *Journal of Economic Perspectives, 14*(1), 133–141.

Tomasello, M. (1999). *The Cultural Origins of Human Cognition.* Cambridge, MA: Harvard University Press.

Townshend, H. (1937). Liquidity-Premium and the Theory of Value. *Economic Journal, 47,* 157–169.

Tuomela, R. (2000). *Cooperation.* London: Kluwer Academic Publishers.

US Census. (2014). Retrieved from https://www.census.gov/programs-surveys/acs/news/data-releases/2014.html.

Uzawa, H. (1959). Walras' Tatonnement in the Theory of Exchange. *Review of Economic Studies, 27,* 182–194.

Verbeek, B. (2002). *Instrumental Rationality and Moral Philosophy.* London: Kluwer Academic Publishers.

Viner, J. (1927). Adam Smith and Laissez-Faire. *Journal of Political Economy, 35*(2), 198–232.

Vinicius, D. L., Goulart, R., & Young, R. J. (2013). Selfish Behaviour and an Antipredator Response in Schooling Fish? *Animal Behaviour, 86*(2), 443–450.

Vivenza, G. (2001). *Adam Smith and the Classics: The Classical Heritage in Adam Smith's Thought*. Oxford: Oxford University Press.

Wagner, A. (1893). *Grundlegung der Politische Oekonomie*. Leipzig: C. F. Winter.

Walker, D. A. (1996). *Walras' Market Models*. Cambridge: Cambridge University Press.

Walras, L. (1860). *L'économie politique et la justice: Examen critique et réfutation des doctrines économiques de M. P.-J. Proudhon précédes d'une introduction à l'étude de la question sociale*. Paris: Guillaumin.

Walras, L. (1896). *Etudes D'Economie Sociale*. Lausanne: F. Rouge.

Walras, L. (1954 [1874]). *Elements of Pure Economics* (W. Jaffe, Trans.). London: George Allen & Unwin Ltd.

Walsh, V., & Gram, H. (1980). *Classical and Neo-classical Theories of General Equilibrium: Historical Origin and Mathematical Structure*. Oxford: Oxford University Press.

Weber, M. (1922). *Economy and Society* (G. Roth & C. Wittich, Ed.). Berkeley: University of California Press.

Weber, M. (1947). *The Theory of Social and Economic Organisation*. New York: Free Press.

Weingart, P., Mitchell, S., Richardson, P., & Maasen, S. (1997). *Human by Nature: Between Biology and the Social Sciences*. Mahwah, NJ: Erlbaum.

West, E. G. (1996). Adam Smith on the Cultural Effects of Specialisation: Splenetics versus Economics. *History of Political Economy, 28*(1), 83–105.

West, S. A., Griffin, A. S., & Gardner, A. (2007). Social Semantics: Altruism, Cooperation, Mutualism, Strong Reciprocity and Group Selection. *Journal of Evolutionary Biology, 20*, 415–432.

West, S. A., Mouden, C. E., & Gardner, A. (2011). Sixteen Common Misconceptions About the Evolution of Cooperation in Humans. *Evolution and Human Behavior, 32*, 231–262.

Westneat, D. F., & Fox, C. W. (2010). *Evolutionary Behavioral Ecology*. Oxford: Oxford University Press.

Wicksteed, P. H. (1933 [1910]). *The Common Sense of Political Economy*. London: George Routledge & Sons Ltd.

von Wieser, F. (1967 [1927]). *Social Economics* (A. Ford Hinrichs, Trans.). New York: Augustus M. Kelley Publishers.

Williamson, O. (1975). *Markets and Hierarchies: Analysis and Antitrust Implications*. New York: Free Press.

Williamson, O. (1985). *The Economic Institutions of Capitalism*. New York: Free Press.

van Witteloostuijn, A., & Maks, J. A. H. (1990). Walras on Temporary Equilibrium and Dynamics. *History of Political Economy, 22*(2), 223–237.

Witztum, A. (1997). Distributional Consideration in Smith's Concept of Economic Justice. *Economics and Philosophy, 13*, 242–259.

Witztum, A. (1998). A Study into Smith Conception of the Human Character: Das Adam Smith Problem Revisited. *History of Political Economy, 30*(3), 489–513.

Witztum, A. (2005a). Economic Sociology: The Recursive Economic System of J S Mill. *Journal of the History of Economic Thought, 27*(3), 251–282.

Witztum, A. (2005b). Property Rights and the Rights of the Property Less: A Note on Adam Smith's Jurisprudence. *Economics and Philosophy, 21*(2), 279–289.

Witztum, A. (2008). Social Attitudes and Re-distributive Policies. *Journal of Socio-Economics, 37*(4), 1597–1623.

Witztum, A. (2011). Ethics and the Science of Economics: Robbins's Enduring Fallacy. *Journal of the History of Economic Thought, 33*(4), 467–486.

Witztum, A. (2012). The Firm, Property Rights and Methodological Individualism. *Journal of Economic Methodology, 19*(4), 339–355.

Witztum, A. (2013). Keynes's Misguided Revolution. *Œconomia, 3*(2), 287–318.

Witztum, A. (2016). Experimental Economics, Game Theory and Das Adam Smith Problem. *Eastern Econ Journal, 42*(4), 528–556.

World Development Indicators. (2017). Retrieved from https://datacatalog. worldbank.org/dataset/world-development-indicators.

World Value Survey. (2005–2009). Retrieved from http://www.worldvaluessur-vey.org/WVSDocumentationWV5.jsp.

World Value Survey. (2014). Retrieved from http://www.worldvaluessurvey.org/ WVSDocumentationWV6.jsp.

Young, J. (1986). The Impartial Spectator and Natural Jurisprudence: An Interpretation of Adam Smith's Theory of the Natural Price. *History of Political Economy, 18*(3), 365–382.

Zeira, J. (1998). Workers, Machines and Economic Growth. *Quarterly Journal of Economics, 113*, 1091–1113.

Index[1]

---

[1] Note: Page numbers followed by 'n' refer to notes.

© The Author(s) 2019   **327**
A. Witztum, *The Betrayal of Liberal Economics*,
https://doi.org/10.1007/978-3-030-10668-3